Maximum Likelihood for Social Science

This volume provides a practical introduction to the method of maximum likelihood as used in social science research. Michael D. Ward and John S. Ahlquist focus on applied computation in $\mathcal{R}$ and use real social science data from actual, published research. Unique among books at this level, it develops simulation-based tools for model evaluation and selection alongside statistical inference. The book covers standard models for categorical data, as well as counts, duration data, and strategies for dealing with data missingness. By working through examples, math, and code the authors build an understanding about the contexts in which maximum likelihood methods are useful and develop skills in translating mathematical statements into executable computer code. Readers will not only be taught to use likelihood-based tools and generate meaningful interpretations, but they will also acquire a solid foundation for continued study of more advanced statistical techniques.

MICHAEL D. WARD is Professor Emeritus at Duke University. He has taught at Northwestern University, the University of Colorado, and the University of Washington. He worked as a principal research scientist at the WZB Berlin Social Science Center and held a municipal chair at the University of Pierre Mendès France (Grenoble II). His work began with a study of the links between global and national inequalities, continued with seminal articles on the conflict processes in the Cold War, and more recently turned to analyses of networks of conflict and cooperation in the contemporary era. At Duke, he established an innovative research lab of graduate and undergraduate students focusing on conflict prediction. One of the first political scientists to focus on the role of prediction in scholarly and policy work, he continues these efforts in his company, Predictive Heuristics, a data analytics firm that provides risk analysis for commercial and institutional clients.

JOHN S. AHLQUIST is Associate Professor of Political Economy at UC San Diego's School of Global Policy and Strategy and a 2017–18 Fellow at Stanford's Center for Advanced Study in the Behavioral Sciences. He previously held faculty positions at the University of Wisconsin, Madison, and Florida State University. His work has focused on the political structure and actions of labor unions, as well as the politics of redistribution and social insurance in a globalized economy. His methodological interests have spanned statistical models for network data, machine learning and cluster analysis, and the analysis of survey list experiments. He is author of more than twenty journal articles appearing in a variety of outlets, including the *American Journal of Political Science, American Political Science Review, Journal of Politics*, and *Political Analysis*. His most recent book (with Margaret Levi; 2013) is *In the Interest of Others*. He is a past winner of a variety of prizes, including the Mancur Olson Award, the Michael Wallerstein Award, and the APSA Labor Project Best Book Award. Ahlquist holds a PhD from the University of Washington and B.A. from UC Berkeley.

Analytical Methods for Social Research

Analytical Methods for Social Research presents texts on empirical and formal methods for the social sciences. Volumes in the series address both the theoretical underpinnings of analytical techniques as well as their application in social research. Some series volumes are broad in scope, cutting across a number of disciplines. Others focus mainly on methodological applications within specific fields such as political science, sociology, demography, and public health. The series serves a mix of students and researchers in the social sciences and statistics.

Series Editors

R. Michael Alvarez, *California Institute of Technology*
Nathaniel L. Beck, *New York University*
Lawrence L. Wu, *New York University*

Other Titles in the Series

Maximum Likelihood for Social Science

Strategies for Analysis

MICHAEL D. WARD
Duke University

JOHN S. AHLQUIST
University of California, San Diego

CAMBRIDGE
UNIVERSITY PRESS

CAMBRIDGE
UNIVERSITY PRESS

University Printing House, Cambridge CB2 8BS, United Kingdom

One Liberty Plaza, 20th Floor, New York, NY 10006, USA

477 Williamstown Road, Port Melbourne, VIC 3207, Australia

314–321, 3rd Floor, Plot 3, Splendor Forum, Jasola District Centre, New Delhi – 110025, India

79 Anson Road, #06–04/06, Singapore 079906

Cambridge University Press is part of the University of Cambridge.

It furthers the University's mission by disseminating knowledge in the pursuit of
education, learning, and research at the highest international levels of excellence.

www.cambridge.org
Information on this title: www.cambridge.org/9781107185821
DOI: 10.1017/9781316888544

First published 2018

Printed in the United States of America by Sheridan Books, Inc.

A catalogue record for this publication is available from the British Library.

Library of Congress Cataloging-in-Publication Data
Names: Ward, Michael Don, 1948– author. | Ahlquist, John S., author.
Title: Maximum likelihood for social science : strategies for analysis/
   Michael D. Ward, John S. Ahlquist.
Description: 1 Edition. | New York : Cambridge University Press, 2018. |
Series: Analytical methods for social research
Identifiers: LCCN 2018010101 | ISBN 9781107185821 (hardback) |
   ISBN 9781316636824 (paperback)
Subjects: LCSH: Social sciences–Research. | BISAC: POLITICAL SCIENCE / General.
Classification: LCC H62 .W277 2018 | DDC 300.72–dc23
LC record available at https://lccn.loc.gov/2018010101

ISBN 978-1-107-18582-1 Hardback
ISBN 978-1-316-63682-4 Paperback

Contents

Figures

Tables

Preface

This project began many years ago at the University of Washington's Center for Statistics and the Social Sciences (CSSS). There two ambitious graduate students, John S. Ahlquist and Christian Breunig (now at the University of Konstanz), asked Michael D. Ward if he would supervise their training in maximum likelihood methods so that they could be better prepared for taking more advanced CSSS courses as well as those in the statistics and biostatistics departments. Ward gave them a stack of materials and asked them to start by preparing a lecture on ordinal regression models. Ward subsequently developed a class on maximum likelihood methods, which he has taught at the University of Washington (where it is still taught by Christopher Adolph) and, more recently, at Duke University. Ahlquist has gone on to teach a similar course at Florida State, the University of Wisconsin, and UC San Diego.

The point of the course was singular, and this book has a simple goal: to introduce social scientists to the maximum likelihood principle in a practical way. This praxis includes (a) being able to recognize where maximum likelihood methods are useful, (b) being able to interpret results from such analyses, and (c) being able to implement these methods both in terms of creating the likelihood and in terms of specifying it in a computational language that permits empirical analysis to be undertaken using the developed model.

The text is aimed at advanced PhD students in the social sciences, especially political science and sociology. We assume familiarity with basic probability concepts, the application of multivariate calculus to optimization problems, and the basics of matrix algebra.

OUR APPROACH

We take a resolutely applied perspective here, emphasizing core concepts, computation, and model evaluation and interpretation. While we include a chapter that introduces some of the important theoretical results and their derivations, we spend relatively little space discussing formal statistical properties. We made this decision for three reasons. First, there are several ways to motivate the likelihood framework. We find that a focus on a method's "desirable properties" in a frequentist setting to be a less persuasive reason to study maximum likelihood estimators (MLE). Instead we prefer to emphasize the powerful conceptual jump that likelihood-based reasoning represents in the study of statistics, one that enables us to move to a Bayesian setting relatively easily. Second, the statistical theory underlying the likelihood framework is well understood; it has been for decades. The requisite theorems and proofs are already collected in other excellent volumes, so we allocate only a single chapter to recapitulating them here. Rather, we seek to provide something that is missing: an applied text emphasizing modern applications of maximum likelihood in the social sciences. Third, and perhaps most important, we find that students learn more and have a more rewarding experience when the acquisition of new technical tools is directly bound to the substantive applications motivating their study.

Many books and even whole graduate training programs start with so-called Ordinary Least Squares (OLS). There is a certain logic to that. OLS is easy to teach, implement, and utilize while introducing a variety of important statistical concepts. OLS was particularly attractive in a world before powerful modern computers fit in our pockets. But OLS can be viewed as a special case of a more general class of models. Practically speaking, a limited range of social science data fit into this special case. Data in the social sciences tend to be lumpier, often categorical. Nominal, truncated, and bounded variables emerge not just from observational datasets but in researcher-controlled experiments as well (e.g., treatment selection and survival times). Indeed, the vast majority of social science data comes in forms that are profitably analyzed without resort to the special case of OLS. While OLS is a pedagogical benchmark, you will have to look hard for recent, state-of-the-art empirical articles that analyze observational data based on this approach. After reading this book and working through the examples, student should be able to fit, choose, and interpret many of the statistical models that appear in published research. These models are designed for binary, categorical, ordered, and count data that are neither continuous nor distributed normally.

WHAT FOLLOWS

We have pruned this book down from versions that appeared earlier online. We wanted the main text to focus entirely on the method and application of maximum likelihood principles. The text is divided into four parts.

Part I (Chapters 1–4) introduces the concept of likelihood and how it fits with both classical and Bayesian statistics. We discuss OLS only in passing, highlighting how, under certain assumptions, it can be thought of as a maximum likelihood estimator. We identify and derive the major theoretical results and then show how to apply them in the context of binary response variables. Chapter 4 provides a discussion of how MLE is implemented computationally, with a particular emphasis on the $\mathcal{R}$ computational environment.

Part II (Chapters 5 and 6) is the core of this volume. Its two chapters cover model selection and interpretation. Unique among texts at this level, we emphasize that model selection must occur prior to any inference about estimated parameters or other quantities. We argue explicitly for a wide application of an out-of-sample predictive heuristic in this area, something that is seeing increased attention with the machine learning revolution. In Chapter 6, we discuss how we might use the models we fit, and we focus on the power of modern computation to present nuanced and detailed interpretation of our statistical findings. We de-emphasize mechanical hypothesis testing against arbitrary null values, instead focusing on estimating meaningful quantities of interest and discussing our uncertainty around these estimates. In both chapters we include reflections on the mechanics and aesthetics of constructing tables and displays for effective communication, as well as thoughts on improving research transparency and credibility. While the material covered in this section is in no way unique to the study of maximum likelihood, we view this section as critical to continued progress in studying both maximum likelihood and more advanced statistical and computational topics.

Part III (Chapters 7–10) covers the Generalized Linear Model (GLM). Chapter 7 is short, introducing the basic structure of the GLM and some terminology and concepts. Chapters 8–10 present models for categorical variables, both ordered and nominal, as well as integer counts. Unlike some other texts for categorical data, these chapters are designed to be approached in a particular order and all rely on concepts and computational tools developed in Parts I and II.

In Part IV (Chapters 11 and 12) of the book we introduce more advanced topics. In Chapter 11 we begin the process of relaxing the standard assumption of conditional independence by presenting an introduction to duration models. This chapter is somewhat idiosyncratic, glossing over many of the details and complications one might expect in a full-fledged treatment of survival analysis, not to mention time series. Instead, we focus on how we can develop models for data that are inherently connected in time using likelihood tools and principles. Chapter 12 takes on the ubiquitous problem of missing data. We view this subject as woefully understudied in graduate training, while also presenting the pedagogical opportunity to discuss model construction and computation from a different perspective. We have also found that many of the most successful student replication projects came from critical interrogation of the earlier scholars' treatments of missing data.

Covering all the material in this book in a 15-week semester with beginning graduate students is certainly a challenge; doing so in a 10-week academic quarter is even more demanding. In a quarter-length course or with first-year students we have found that Chapters 2, 4, and 7 are better left as reference, instead emphasizing intuition, computation, and examples. When the temporal budget constraint binds, we typically allow student interest to determine whether we focus on duration models or missing data.

SPECIAL FEATURES

This volume contains several special features and sections that deserve further elaboration.

Real Examples from Published Research

Each chapter contains at least one example drawn from actual published social science research. These examples use real data drawn from scholars' data repositories to illustrate the models, highlight the modeling assumptions involved, and present detailed interpretations. All these datasets are archived in the online repository accompanying this volume.

$\mathcal{R}$ Code

This is an applied, computational text. We are particularly interested in helping students transform mathematical statements into executable computer code. $\mathcal{R}$ has become the dominant language in statistical computing because it is object-oriented, based on vectors; still has the best statistical graphics; and is open-source, meaning it is free to students and has a large network of contributors submitting new libraries almost daily. The newest statistical tools generally appear in $\mathcal{R}$ first.

We include code directly in the text in offset and clearly marked boxes. We include our own comments in the code chunks so students can see annotation clarifying computational steps. We also include $\mathcal{R}$ output and warnings in various places to aid in interpreting actual $\mathcal{R}$ output as well as trouble-shooting. All analysis and graphics are generated in $\mathcal{R}$. The online repository contains the $\mathcal{R}$ code needed to reproduce all tables and graphics.

"In case you were wondering ..."

Throughout the text there are special boxes labeled "In case you were wondering ...." The purpose of the boxes is to provide basic information about important mathematical tools and statistical distributions. These are things not easily defined in the main text and likely already familiar to some readers while appearing de novo to others. Our goal is to provide this information at the point of need while setting it off from the main text and marking it as "supplemental."

We do not refer to the boxes directly in the main text, unlike equations, tables, figures, and code chunks. The title of the boxes reflects their function and status; they present supplemental information for the curious.

"Further Reading"

Each chapter ends with a "further reading" section. These sections all follow a similar format, with subheadings for "applications," "past work," "advanced study," and "software notes," depending on the context these have for different topics.

The "applications" section highlights two to four studies using the tools discussed in that chapter and published in major social science journals in the last four years. These studies are meant to be examples of the types of papers students might consider when choosing replication projects.

The "past work" section is designed to provide pointers to the major contributors to the development and popularization of these tools in the social sciences. The "advanced study" section collects references to more advanced texts and articles where interested students can look for more detail on the math or computational algorithms. We consulted many of these texts in writing this book.

In the "software notes" sections we collect references to the major $\mathcal{R}$ libraries that we found useful in preparing the book or in conducting analysis ourselves. Since $\mathcal{R}$ is open-source, these references will surely become stale. We nevertheless thought it beneficial to collect references to $\mathcal{R}$ packages in a single place in each chapter.

NOTATION GLOSSARY

In our experience students often find mathematical notation a particularly frustrating barrier. To mitigate that problem we have included a notation "glossary" at the beginning of the book

ONLINE RESOURCES

The online repository, maxlikebook.com, accompanying this volume contains

- all datatsets used in this volume,
- $\mathcal{R}$ code for producing all tables and graphics,
- suggested problem sets and partial solutions, and
- some of our teaching slides.

We expect that repository content will evolve as we continue to teach this material and receive feedback from other instructors and students.

Acknowledgments

We would like to thank colleagues and former students worldwide, including Kathryn Alexander, Andrew Ballard, Sanuel Bagg, Jeanette Birnbaum, Anders Bjorn, Sarah Bouchat, Xun Cao, Chris Carrington, Mariana Carvalho Barbosa, Hannah Chapman, Cindy Cheng, Hsiao Chi, Andrew Cockrell, Amelia Cronan, Chris de Sante, Yao-yao Dai, Jared Daugherty, Matt Dickenson, Nhat-Dang Do, Zhang Dong, Cassy Dorff, Michael Duda, Mark Dudley, Josh Eastin, Idil Edes, Brian Engelsma, Brad Epperly, Amy Finnegan, Laura Frankel, Marcela García-Castañon, Asaph Glosser, Brian Greenhill, Ana Guzman, Andrew Heiss, John Holbein, Molly Hogan, Hsiao-Chi Hsu, Ashley Jochim, Arzu Kibris, Jin-Young Kim, Dimitrii Kofanov, Tobias Konitzer, Sabino Kornrich, Sophie Lee, Tae-dong Lee, Rosanna Shuk-Yin Lee, Brian Ho-Yin Lee, Ning Leng, Josh Lerner, Yuting Li, Nimah Mazaheri, Shahryar Minhas, Zoe Nemerever, Alexandra Oprea, Mathias Orlowski, Victoria Paniagua, Francisco Pedraza, Ryan Powers, Barry Pump, Ben Radford, Carlisle Rainey, Eric Schmidt, Kristan Seibel, Jeffry Smith, David Sparks, Won Steinbach, Tanja Srebotnjak, Rebecca Szper, Aaron Tsang, Ashley Thirkill, Jason Thomas, Linda Tran, Peter Vining, Samantha Vortherms, Austin Wang, Zach Warner, Simon Weschle, Undes Wen, Michelle Wolfe, Xinyan Xuan, McKenzie Young, Steve Zech, and countless others for β-testing this material in an unusual format. They were old-school: reading text, asking questions, finding mistakes, asking questions, doing homework, asking questions, etc.

Several colleagues gave us valuable feedback on the manuscript and the content of the courses on which it was based. We would like to thank Christian Breunig, Seth Hill, Susan Holmes, Will Moore, Molly Roberts, Alex Tahk, and Yiquing Xu. We are grateful to Michael Alvarez and Neal Beck for their advice, diligence, and high standards. Ethan J. Davis provided superb feedback as well.

In very different ways both authors received institutional support from the Center for Statistics and the Social Sciences (CSSS) at the University of

Washington, under the leadership of Adrian Raftery and subsequently by Thomas Richardson. This book would not have happened with the intellectual environment CSSS provided. Ahlquist benefited from the institutional support of the University of Wisconsin–Madison and from the School of Global Policy and Strategy as well as the department of political science at UC San Diego. Final editing of the book ocurred while Ahlquist was a fellow at the Center for Advanced Studies in the Behavioral Sciences at Stanford University. Joshua Penney was extremely helpful in the production process. We are grateful for his patience and skill in navigating the final process.

Notes on Notation

We generally follow notational standards common in applied statistics. But to a student, notation can often prove a barrier. This notation "glossary" is meant to ease the transition to reading notation-heavy material and provide a place to look up unfamiliar symbols. The underlying assumption is that students have already been introduced to basic probability, calculus, and linear algebra concepts.

Random variables and sets are denoted using script capitals. Thus, for example, $X = \{\ldots, -2, 0, 2, \ldots\}$ denotes the set of even integers. $Y \sim f_N(0, 1)$ states that Y is random variable that is distributed according to a Gaussian normal distribution with mean of 0 and variance of 1. We will denote the set of admissible values for X (its support) as $\mathcal{X}$.

Both upper- and lowercase letters can represent functions. When both upper- and lowercase versions of the same letter are used, the uppercase function typically represents the integral of the lowercase function, e.g., $G(x) = \int_{-\infty}^{x} g(u)du$.

To conserve notation we will use $f_s(\cdot; \theta)$ to represent the probability distribution and mass functions commonly used in building Generalized Linear Models. θ denotes generic parameters, possibly vector-valued. The subscript will denote the specific distribution:

- f_B is the Bernoulli distribution
- f_b is the binomial distribution
- f_β is the Beta distribution
- f_c is the categorical distribution
- f_e is the exponential distribution
- f_{EV_1} is the type-I extreme value distribution
- f_Γ is the Gamma distribution
- f_{GEV} is the generalized extreme value distribution
- f_L is the logistic distribution

- f_{lL} is the log-logistic distribution
- f_m is the multinomial distribution
- $f_{\mathcal{N}}$ is the Gaussian (Normal) distribution
- f_{Nb} is the negative binomial
- f_P is the Poisson distribution
- F_W is the Weibull distribution

To conform with conventional terminology and notation in $\mathcal{R}$, we refer to one-dimensional vectors as *scalars*. Scalars and observed realizations of random variables are denoted using lowercase math script. $\Pr(Y_i \leq y_i)$ denotes the probability that some random variable, Y_i, takes a value no greater than some realized level, y_i.

Matrices are denoted using bolded capital letters; $\mathbf{X}_{n \times k}$ is the matrix with n rows and k columns. The symbol T denotes matrix or vector transposition, as in $\mathbf{X}^{\mathsf{T}}$. Vectors are represented with bolded lowercase letters, e.g., $\mathbf{x}_i$. In our notation we implicitly treat all vectors as *column* vectors unless otherwise stated. For example, $\mathbf{x}_i$ is a column vector even though it may represent a row in the $\mathbf{X}_{n \times k}$ matrix. "Barred" items denote the sample mean e.g., $\bar{\mathbf{y}}$.

Lowercase Greek letters are typically reserved for parameters of models and statistical distributions. These parameters could be either scalars or vectors. Vectors will be expressed in bold font. Where more specificity is needed we will subscript.

"Hatted" objects denote fitted or estimated quantities; when used in the context of an MLE then hatted objects are the MLE. For example, β might be a regression parameter and $\hat{\beta}$ is the estimated value of that parameter.

Common functions, operators, and objects:

- $\propto$ means "is proportional to"
- $\overset{\cdot}{\sim}$ means "approximately distributed as"
- $\overset{d}{\to}$ means "convergence in distribution."
- $\overset{p}{\to}$ means "convergence in probability," what some texts denote plim.
- $\mathbb{1}(\cdot)$ is the indicator function that returns a 1 if true and a 0 otherwise.
- $\mathrm{cov}(\cdot, \cdot)$ is the covariance function
- $\det(\cdot)$ is the determinant of a square matrix
- $E[\cdot]$ is the expectation operator
- $\exp(\cdot)$ is the exponential function
- $\Gamma(\cdot)$ is the Gamma function
- $\mathbf{I}_n$ is the $n \times n$ identity matrix
- $\mathcal{I}(\cdot)$ is the expected Fisher information
- $I(\cdot)$ is the observed Fisher information
- *iid* means "independently and identically distributed."
- $\Lambda(\cdot)$ is the logistic cumulative distribution function
- log is the logarithm. If no base is given, then it denotes the natural logarithm (base e)

- ∇ is the gradient vector of some function.
- $\Phi(\cdot)$ is the standard Normal cumulative distribution function
- $\phi(\cdot)$ is the standard Normal density function
- $\Pr(\cdot)$ denotes probability
- $\mathrm{var}(\cdot)$ is the variance function

## PART I

CONCEPTS, THEORY, AND IMPLEMENTATION

1

Introduction to Maximum Likelihood

1.1 INTRODUCTION TO MAXIMUM LIKELIHOOD

The method of maximum likelihood is more than a collection of statistical models or even an estimation procedure. It is a unified way of thinking about model construction, estimation, and evaluation. The study of maximum likelihood represents a transition in methodological training for social scientists. It marks the point at which we possess the conceptual, mathematical, and computational foundations for writing down our own statistical estimators that can be custom-designed for our own research questions. A solid understanding of the principles and properties of maximum likelihood is fundamental to more advanced study, whether self-directed or formally course-based.

To begin our introduction to the maximum likelihood approach we present a toy example involving the most hackneyed of statistics contrivances: coin flips. We undertake this example to illustrate the mechanics of the likelihood with maximal simplicity. We then move on to a more realistic problem: describing the degree of association between two continuous variables. Least squares regression – the portal through which nearly every researcher enters the realm of applied statistics – is a common tool for describing such a relationship. Our goal is to introduce the broader likelihood framework for statistical inference, showing that the familiar least squares estimator is, in fact, a special type of maximum likelihood estimator. We then provide a more general outline of the likelihood approach to model building, something we revisit in more mathematical and computational detail in the next three chapters.

1.2 COIN FLIPS AND MAXIMUM LIKELIHOOD

Three friends are trying to decide between two restaurants, an Ethiopian restaurant and a brewpub. Each is indifferent, since none of them has previously

3

eaten at either restaurant. They each flip a single coin, deciding that a heads will indicate a vote for the brewpub. The result is two heads and one tails. The friends deposit the coin in the parking meter and go to the brewpub.

We might wonder whether the coin was, in fact, fair. As a data analysis problem, these coin flips were not obtained in a traditional sampling framework, nor are we interested in making inferences about the general class of restaurant coin flips. Rather, the three flips of a single coin are all the data that exist, and we just want to know how the decision was taken. This is a binary outcomes problem. The data are described by the following set in which 1 represents heads: $\{1, 1, 0\}$. Call the probability of a flip in favor of eating at the brewpub θ; the probability of a flip in favor of eating Ethiopian is thereby $1 - \theta$. In other words, we assume a Bernoulli distribution for a coin flip.

In case you were wondering ... 1.1 Bernoulli distribution

Let $Y \in \{0, 1\}$. Suppose $\Pr(Y = 1) = \theta$. We say that Y follows a Bernoulli distribution with parameter θ:

$$Y \sim f_B(y; \theta) = \begin{cases} \theta^y (1 - \theta)^{1-y} & \forall \quad y \in \{0, 1\}, \\ 0 & \text{otherwise} \end{cases}$$

with $E[Y] = \theta$ and $\text{var}(Y) = \theta(1 - \theta)$.

What value of the parameter, θ, best describes the observed data? Prior experience may lead us to believe that coin flips are equiprobable; $\hat{\theta} = 0.5$ seems a reasonable guess. Further, one might also reason that since there are three pieces of data, the probability of the joint outcome of three flips is $0.5^3 = 0.125$. This may be a reasonable summary of our prior expectations, but this calculation fails to take advantage of the actual data at hand to inform our estimate.

A simple tabulation reveals this insight more clearly. We know that in this example, θ is defined on the interval $[0, 1]$, i.e., $0 \leq \theta \leq 1$. We also know that unconditional probabilities compound themselves so that the probability of a head on the first coin toss times the probability of a head on the second times the probability of tails on the third produces the joint probability of the observed data: $\theta \times \theta \times (1 - \theta)$. Given this expression we can easily calculate the probability of getting the observed data for different values of θ. Computationally, the results are given by $\Pr(y_1 \mid \hat{\theta}) \times \Pr(y_2 \mid \hat{\theta}) \times \Pr(y_3 \mid \hat{\theta})$, where y_i is the value of each observation, $i \in \{1, 2, 3\}$ and $\mid \hat{\theta}$ is read, "given the proposed value of θ." Table 1.1 displays these calculations in increments of 0.1.

TABLE 1.1 *Choosing a restaurant with three flips of a fair coin?*

Observed Data			
y	$\hat{\theta}$	$\theta^{1s} \times (1 - \theta)^{0s}$	$f_B(y \mid \hat{\theta})$
{1, 1, 0}	0.00	$0.00^2 \times (1 - 0.00)^1$	0.000
{1, 1, 0}	0.10	$0.10^2 \times (1 - 0.10)^1$	0.009
{1, 1, 0}	0.20	$0.20^2 \times (1 - 0.20)^1$	0.032
{1, 1, 0}	0.30	$0.30^2 \times (1 - 0.30)^1$	0.063
{1, 1, 0}	0.40	$0.40^2 \times (1 - 0.40)^1$	0.096
{1, 1, 0}	0.50	$0.50^2 \times (1 - 0.50)^1$	0.125
{1, 1, 0}	0.60	$0.60^2 \times (1 - 0.60)^1$	0.144
{1, 1, 0}	0.67	$0.67^2 \times (1 - 0.67)^1$	0.148
{1, 1, 0}	0.70	$0.70^2 \times (1 - 0.70)^1$	0.147
{1, 1, 0}	0.80	$0.80^2 \times (1 - 0.80)^1$	0.128
{1, 1, 0}	0.90	$0.90^2 \times (1 - 0.90)^1$	0.081
{1, 1, 0}	1.00	$1.00^2 \times (1 - 0.00)^1$	0.000

The a priori guess of 0.5 turns out not to be the most likely to have generated these data. Rather, the value of $\frac{2}{3}$ is the most likely value for θ. It is not necessary to do all of this by guessing values of θ. This case can be solved analytically.

When we have data on each of the trials (flips), the Bernoulli probability model, f_B, is a natural place to start. We will call the expression that describes the joint probability of the observed data as function of the parameters the *likelihood function*, denoted $\mathcal{L}(y; \theta)$. We can use the tools of differential calculus to solve for the maximum; we take the logarithm of the likelihood for computational convenience:

$$\mathcal{L} = \theta^2 (1 - \theta)^1$$

$$\log \mathcal{L} = 2 \log \theta + 1 \log(1 - \theta)$$

$$\frac{\partial \log \mathcal{L}}{\partial \theta} = \frac{2}{\theta} - \frac{1}{(1 - \theta)} = 0$$

$$\hat{\theta} = \frac{2}{3}.$$

The value of θ that the maximizes the likelihood function is called the *maximum likelihood estimate*, or MLE.

It is clear that, in this case, it does not matter who gets heads and who gets tails. Only the number of heads out of three flips matters. When Bernoulli data are grouped in such a way, we can describe them equivalently with the closely related *binomial* distribution.

In case you were wondering ... 1.2 Binomial distribution

Let $Y \sim f_B(y; p)$ where $\Pr(Y = 1) = p$. Suppose we take n independent draws and let $X = \sum_{i=1}^{n} Y_i$. We say that X follows a binomial distribution with parameter $\theta = (n, p)$:

$$X \sim f_b(x; n, p)$$

$$\Pr(X = k) = \begin{cases} \binom{n}{k} p^k (1-p)^{n-k} & \forall \quad k \in \{0, \ldots, n\}, \\ 0 & \forall \quad k \notin \{0, \ldots, n\} \end{cases}$$

where $\binom{n}{k} = \frac{n!}{k!(n-k)!}$ and with $E[X] = np$ and $\text{var}(X) = np(1-p)$. The Bernoulli distribution is a binomial distribution with $n = 1$.

Jacob Bernoulli was a Swiss mathematician who derived the law of large numbers, discovered the mathematical constant e, and formulated the eponymous Bernoulli and binomial distributions.

Analytically and numerically the MLE is equivalent whether derived using the Bernoulli or binomial distribution with known n. Figure 1.1 illustrates the likelihood function for Bernoulli/binomial data consisting of two heads and one tail. The maximum occurs at $\hat{\theta} = 2/3$.

1.3 SAMPLES AND SAMPLING DISTRIBUTIONS

Trying to decide whether the coin used to choose a restaurant is fair is a problem of statistical inference. Many inferential approaches are plausible; most catholic among them is the classical model based on *asymptotic* results obtained by imagining repeated, independent samples drawn from a fixed population.[1] As a result, we often conceptualize statistics calculated from samples as providing information on a population parameter. For example, suppose $x_1, \ldots, x_n$ comprise a random sample from a population with a mean of μ and a variance of σ^2. It follows that the mean of this sample is a random variable with a mean of μ and variance that is equal to σ^2/n. Why? This is true, since the expected value of the mean of an independent sample is the mean of the population from which the sample is drawn. The variance of the sample is, similarly, equal to the variance of the population divided by the size of the sample.[2] This is demonstrated graphically in Figure 1.2.

---

[1] In statistics, asymptotic analysis refers to theoretical results describing the limiting behavior of a function as a value, typically the sample size, tends to infinity.

[2] This is the most basic statement of the Central Limit Theorem. We state the theorem more formally in Section 2.2.2.

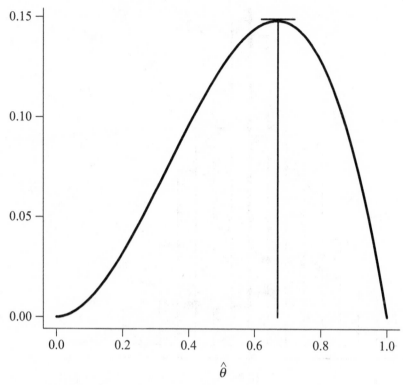

FIGURE 1.1 The likelihood/probability of getting two heads in three coin tosses, over various values of θ.

This basic result is often used to interpret output from statistical models as if the observed data are a sample from a population for which the mean and variance are *unknown*. We can use a random sample to calculate our best guesses as to what those population values are. If we have either a large enough random sample of the population or enough independent, random samples – as in the American National Election Study or the Eurobarometer surveys, for example – then we can retrieve good estimates of the population parameters of interest without having to actually conduct a census of the entire population. Indeed, most statistical procedures are based on the idea that they perform well in repeated samples, i.e., they have good sampling distribution properties.

Observed data in the social sciences frequently fail to conform to a "sample" in the classical sense. They instead consist of observations on a particular (nonrandom) selection of units, such as the 50 US states, all villages in Afghanistan safe for researchers to visit, all the terror events that newspapers choose to report, or, as in the example that follows, all the data available from the World Bank on GDP *and* CO_2 emissions from 2012. In such situations,

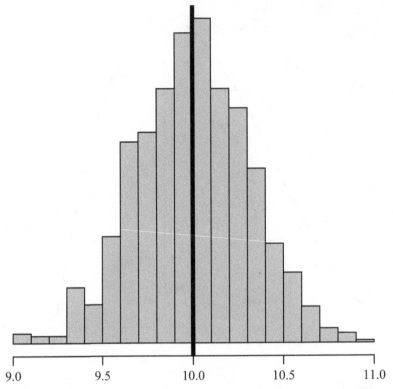

FIGURE 1.2 Illustrating the Central Limit Theorem with a histogram of the means of 1,000 random samples of size 10 drawn from a population with mean of 10 and variance of 1.

the basic sampling distribution result is more complicated to administer. To salvage the classical approach, some argue for a *conceptual* sampling perspective. This often takes the form of a hypothetical: you have data on all 234 countries in the world at present, but these are just a sample from all the *possible* worlds that might have existed. The implied conclusion is that you can treat this as a random sample and gain leverage from the basic results of sampling distributions and the asymptotic properties of the least squares estimators.

Part of the problem with this line of attack is that it sets up the expectation that we are using the observed data to learn about some larger, possibly hypothetical, population. Standard inference frequently relies on this conception, asking questions like "How likely are estimates at least as large as what we found if, in the larger population, the 'true value' is 0?" We speak of estimates as *(non)significant* by way of trying to demonstrate that they did not arise by chance and really do reflect accurately the unobserved, underlying population parameters. In the same way, we argue that the estimators we employ are good if they produce *unbiased* estimates of population parameters. Thus we conceptualize the problem as having estimates that are shifted around by estimators and sample sizes.

But there is a different way to think about all of this, a way that is not only completely different, but complementary at the same time.

In case you were wondering … 1.3 Bias and mean squared error

A statistical estimator is simply a formula or algorithm for calculating some unknown quantity using observed data. Let $T(X)$ be an estimator for θ. The bias of $T(X)$, denoted bias(θ), is

$$\text{bias}(\theta) = \text{E}[T(X)] - \theta.$$

The mean squared error, MSE(θ), is given as

$$MSE(\theta) = \text{E}[(T(X) - \theta)^2]$$
$$= \text{var}(T(X)) + \text{bias}(\theta)^2.$$

1.4 MAXIMUM LIKELIHOOD: AN OVERVIEW

The principle of maximum likelihood is based on the idea that the observed data (even if it is not a random sample) are more likely to have come about as a result of a particular set of parameters. Thus, we flip the problem on its head. *Rather than consider the data as random and the parameters as fixed, the principle of maximum likelihood treats the observed data as fixed and asks: "What parameter values are most likely to have generated the data?"* Thus, the parameters are random variables. More formally, in the likelihood framework we think of the joint probability of the data as a function of parameter values for a particular density or mass function. We call this particular conceptualization of the probability function the *likelihood*, since it is being maximized with respect to the parameters, not on the sample data. The MLEs are those that provide the density or mass function with the highest likelihood of generating the observed data.

1.4.1 Maximum Likelihood: Specific

The World Bank assembled data on gross domestic product and CO_2 emissions for many countries in 2012. These data are accessible directly from $\mathcal{R}$ via the library WDI (Arel-Bundock, 2013). If we believe that CO_2 pollution is a linear function of economic activity, then we might propose the simple model $Y =$

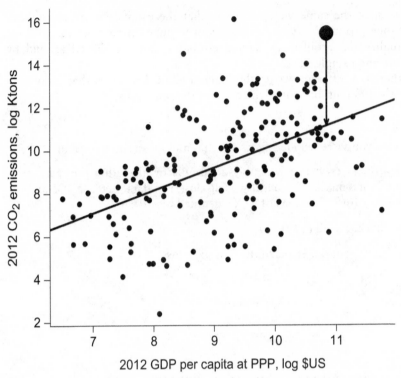

FIGURE 1.3 2012 GDP per capita and CO_2 emissions. The prediction equation is shown as a straight line, with intercept and slope as reported in Table 1.2. The large solid dot represents the United States and the length of the arrow is its residual value given the model.

$\beta_0 + \beta_1 X + \varepsilon$, where Y is the logged data on CO_2 emissions and X is the logged data on gross domestic product (GDP), both taken for 183 countries in the year 2012. The ε term represents the stochastic processes – sampling, measurement error, and other omitted factors – that cause a particular country's observed CO_2 emissions to deviate from the simple linear relationship.

A scatterplot of these data appear in Figure 1.3, with an estimate of the linear relationship included as a straight line. The United States is highlighted for its CO_2 emissions well in excess of what the linear relationship expects, given its per capita GDP. The vertical arrow highlights this positive *residual*.

How can we choose the parameters for the prediction line using maximum likelihood? The first step in constructing any likelihood is the specification of a probability distribution describing the outcome, Y_i. Here we will turn to the Gaussian distribution. If we assume that observations are independently and identically distributed (iid) – they follow the same distribution and contain no dependencies – then we write

$$Y_i \overset{iid}{\sim} \mathcal{N}(\mu_i, \sigma^2). \tag{1.1}$$

Equation 1.1 reads as "Y_i is distributed iid normal with mean μ_i and variance σ^2." When used as a part of a likelihood model, we will adopt the following notational convention:

$$Y_i \sim f_{\mathcal{N}}(y_i; \mu_i, \sigma^2).$$

In case you were wondering ... 1.4 Gaussian (normal) distribution

We say that the random variable $Y \in \mathbb{R}$ follows a Gaussian (or normal) distribution with parameter vector $\theta = (\mu, \sigma^2)$ if the probability distribution function can be written as

$$Y \sim f_{\mathcal{N}}(y; \theta) = \frac{1}{\sqrt{2\pi\sigma^2}} \exp\left[-\frac{(y-\mu)^2}{2\sigma^2} \right], \tag{1.2}$$

with $E[Y] = \mu$ and $var(Y) = \sigma^2$. The special case in which $\mu = 0$ and $\sigma = 1$ is called the standard normal distribution. The standard normal density and distribution functions are written as $\phi(\cdot)$ and $\Phi(\cdot)$, respectively.

The normal distribution was first derived by Karl Freidrich Gauss and published in his 1810 monograph on celestial mechanics. In the same volume, Gauss derived the least squares estimator and alluded to the principle of maximum likelihood. Gauss, a child prodigy, has long been lauded as the foremost mathematical mind since Newton. Gauss's image along with the formula and graph of the normal distribution appeared on the German 10 mark banknote from 1989 until the mark was superseded by the Euro.

The Marquis de Laplace first proved the Central Limit Theorem in which the mean of repeated random samples follows a Gaussian distribution, paving the way for the distribution's ubiquity in probability and statistics.

Next, we develop a model for the expected outcome – the mean – as a function of covariates. We assume a linear relationship between (log) per capita GDP and (log) CO_2 emissions: $Y_i = \beta_0 + \beta_1 x_i + \varepsilon_i$. This implies that $\varepsilon_i = y_i - \beta_0 - \beta_1 x_i$. As a result, assuming that Y_i is normal with $\mu = \beta_0 + \beta_1 x_i$ is equivalent to assuming that $\varepsilon_i \sim f_{\mathcal{N}}(\varepsilon_i; 0, \sigma^2)$. That is, assuming Y is iid normal is equivalent to assuming that the errors come from a normal distribution with mean zero and a fixed, constant variance.

Setting aside, for the moment, the connection between ε_i and the independent variable (log per capita GDP), we can further specify the probability distribution for the outcome variable from Equation 1.2:

$$f_{\mathcal{N}}(\varepsilon_i) = \frac{1}{\sigma\sqrt{2\pi}} \exp\left[\frac{-(\varepsilon_i)^2}{2\sigma^2}\right].$$

This yields:

$$f_{\mathcal{N}}(\varepsilon_i) = \frac{1}{\sigma\sqrt{2\pi}} \exp\left[\frac{-(y_i - \beta_0 - \beta_1 x_i)^2}{2\sigma^2}\right].$$

Crucially, we need to transform this density function for a single observation into a likelihood for the complete sample. The likelihood is simply a formula for the joint probability distribution of the sample data. The joint probability of independent events A and B, which could represent two outcomes in two separate cases, is simply $\Pr(A) \times \Pr(B)$. The probability of the entire set of observed data is the product of each observation's marginal probability – under this assumption of independence. Since we have assumed that the errors are all independent of one another, the joint probability is just a product of marginal probabilities. Similarly, the likelihood will be a product of the $f_{\mathcal{N}}(\varepsilon_i)$ for each observation, i, in the sample. Thus, the likelihood is

$$\mathcal{L}(\beta_0, \beta_1, \sigma \mid \{y_1, \ldots, y_n\}, \{x_1, \ldots, x_n\})$$

$$= (2\pi\sigma^2)^{-n/2} \prod_{i=1}^{n} \exp\left\{\frac{-1}{2\sigma^2}(y_i - \beta_0 - \beta_1 x_i)^2\right\}$$

$$= (2\pi\sigma^2)^{-n/2} \exp\left\{\sum_{i=1}^{n} \frac{-1}{2\sigma^2}(y_i - \beta_0 - \beta_1 x_i)^2\right\}.$$

The likelihood is a function of the parameters (here, β and σ) and all of the data on the dependent and independent variables, i.e., it is the formula for the joint probability distribution of the sample. With a likelihood function and the data we can now use the tools of optimization to find the set of parameter values that maximize the value of this likelihood function.

Before doing this, however, the likelihood function can be simplified quite a bit. First, because we are interested in maximizing the function, any monotonically increasing function of the likelihood can serve as the maximand. Since the logarithmic transformation is monotonic and sums are easier to manage than products, we take the natural log. Thus, the *log-likelihood* is:

$$\log \mathcal{L} = \log \left\{ (2\pi\sigma^2)^{-n/2} \exp \left[\frac{-1}{2\sigma^2} \sum_{i=1}^{n} (y_i - \beta_0 - \beta_1 x_i)^2 \right] \right\}$$

$$= -\frac{n}{2} \log(2\pi\sigma^2) - \frac{1}{2\sigma^2} \sum_{i=1}^{n} (y_i - \beta_0 - \beta_1 x_i)^2$$

$$= -\frac{1}{2} n \log(2\pi) - n \log\sigma - \frac{\sum_{i=1}^{n} (y_i - \beta_0 - \beta_1 x_i)^2}{2\sigma^2}.$$

Terms that are not functions of parameters to be estimated may be dropped, since these terms only scale the likelihood while leaving it proportional to the original. The maximizing arguments are unchanged. Dropping $\frac{1}{2} n \log(2\pi)$ we have,

$$\log \mathcal{L} = -n \log\sigma - \frac{\sum_{i=1}^{n} (y_i - \beta_0 - \beta_1 x_i)^2}{2\sigma^2}, \tag{1.3}$$

To further simplify matters and because many computer optimization programs default to minimization, we often use $-2 \log \mathcal{L}$,

$$-2 \log \mathcal{L} = n \log\sigma^2 + \frac{\sum_{i=1}^{n} (y_i - \beta_0 - \beta_1 x_i)^2}{\sigma^2},$$

and for a fixed or known σ this simplifies to a quantity proportional to the sum of squared errors:

$$-2 \log \mathcal{L} \propto \sum_{i=1}^{n} (y_i - \beta_0 - \beta_1 x_i)^2. \tag{1.4}$$

In practice, there are two ways to solve the likelihood maximization problem. First, if an analytic solution is apparent, then we can solve the likelihood for its extrema directly by taking partial derivatives with respect to each parameter and setting them to zero, as we did with the coin-flipping example. In many instances, however, the derivatives of the likelihood function do not have nice, closed-form solutions. Maximization occurs via numerical techniques described briefly later here and in more detail in Chapter 4.

In the linear-normal case we can find the MLE using analytical methods. Nevertheless, it can be useful to plot the likelihood as a function of parameter values. Figure 1.4 does just that, displaying the likelihood surface for β_1. We can see that the maximum occurs near 1.06.

Using R to Maximize the Likelihood
In this book we emphasize turning mathematical statements and principles into executable computer code in the $\mathcal{R}$ statistical computing environment. For the CO_2 emissions example we can assemble the data directly in $\mathcal{R}$.

Least Squares as MLE

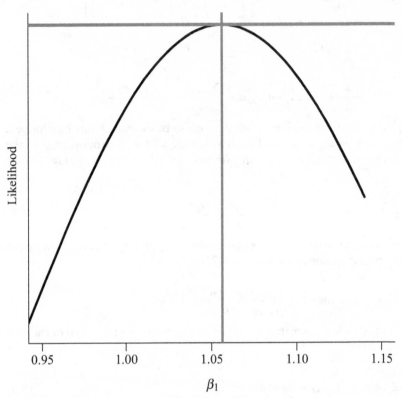

FIGURE 1.4 Likelihood as a function of possible values for β_1.

$\mathcal{R}$ Code Example 1.1 *Assembling the data*

```
library(WDI) #library for retrieving WDI data
wdi<-WDI(country = "all",
    indicator = c("EN.POP.DNST",              #pop density
      "EN.ATM.CO2E.KT",                        #CO2 emissions
      "NY.GDP.PCAP.PP.CD"),                     #GDPpcPPP
    start = 2012, end = 2012, extra = TRUE, cache = NULL)
wdi<-subset(wdi, region !="Aggregates") #removing country aggregates
wdi<-na.omit(wdi) # Omit cases with NA; See chapter on missing data
names(wdi)[4:7]<-c("pop.den", "co2.kt","gdp.pc.ppp","wb.code")
attach(wdi)
```

It is easy to estimate the linear-normal regression in $\mathcal{R}$ using a maximum likelihood. In subsequent chapters, we will explain the heuristics used to interpret the MLE results and use $\mathcal{R}$'s many built-in functions to maximize the likelihood. But here we demonstrate how we might program the likelihood function directly and then pass it to one of $\mathcal{R}$'s numerical optimization routines. This requires a few steps:

Step 1: Set up data matrices.

$\mathcal{R}$ Code Example 1.2 *Step 1: Set up data matrices*

```
x.mat  <-  cbind(1,log(gdp.pc.ppp))   #note the column of 1s
y.vec  <-  log(co2.kt)
```

Step 2: Define the log-likelihood function, which can have several different parameterizations. Here we use $\log \mathcal{L}$ as expressed in Equation 1.3.

$\mathcal{R}$ Code Example 1.3 *Step 2: Log-likelihood function*

```
loglik.my <- function(par,X,y) {
  y <- y.vec
  X <- x.mat
  k <- ncol(X); n <- nrow(X)
  xbeta <- X%*%par[1:k]                          # matrix notation
  sigma <- sqrt(1/(n-k)*sum((y-xbeta)^2))        # assumed known here
  sum(-log(sigma)-(1/(2*sigma^2))*(y-xbeta)^2)   # log-likelihood
}
```

Step 3: Pass the likelihood function to an optimizer, along with a vector of initial guesses for parameter values. Practically speaking, least squares estimates are often good starting guesses, but here we supply arbitrary initial values. For any iterative, numerical procedure it is a good idea to include a convergence check in your code, as shown. It is also important to store the Hessian matrix (see Chapter 2), if possible, for post regression analyses.

$\mathcal{R}$ Code Example 1.4 *Step 3: Call optimizer*

```
mle.fit <- optim(
  par=c(5,5),         # starting values
  fn=loglik.my,       # function to minimize
  method = "BFGS",    # algorithm choice
  control = list(
    trace=TRUE,       # trace optimization progress
    maxit=1000,       # max 1000 iterations
    fnscale = -1),    # changes minimizer to maximizer;
  hessian = TRUE)     # return Hessian matrix (see ch. 2).
if(mle.fit$convergence!=0)
  print("WARNING: Convergence Problems; Try again!")
```

Step 4: Now, we can calculate all the standard diagnostics. We provide code for making a table of regression estimates, including standard errors, z-scores, and p-values. To preview the theory introduced in Chapter 2, inverting[3] the Hessian matrix will provide the variance-covariance matrix, the square root of the diagonal of which contains the estimated standard errors for the parameters. The ratio $\hat{\beta}_i/\sigma_{\hat{\beta}_i}$ is the z-score (or asymptotic t-score).

$\mathcal{R}$ Code Example 1.5 *Step 4: Post-estimation analysis*

```
# Calculate standard BUTON output.
stderrors <- sqrt(-diag(solve(mle.fit$hessian)))
z <- mle.fit$par/stderrors
p.z <- 2 * (1 - pnorm(abs(z))) #p-values
out.table <- data.frame(Est=mle.fit$par,SE=stderrors,Z=z,pval=p.z)
round(out.table,2)
     Est    SE      Z  pval
1  -0.30  1.21  -0.25  0.80
2   1.06  0.13   8.08  0.00
```

These results imply that, in the set of countries examined, higher levels of GDP are associated with higher levels of CO_2 emissions. The estimated coefficient for GDP (β_1) is approximately 1.04 (with a standard error of 0.13, resulting in a t-ratio of 8). This means that for every order-of-magnitude increase in GDP per capita, there will be an order-of-magnitude increase in annual CO_2 emissions, on average.

1.4.2 The Least Squares Approach

Another way to choose values for β_0 and β_1 is the least squares approach; the "best" values are those that minimize the sum of squared deviations from the prediction line. As above, each error is $\varepsilon_i = y_i - (\beta_0 + \beta_1 x_i)$. We minimize the total squared error, also known as the sum of squared errors (SSE):

Definition 1.1 (Sum of squared errors (SSE)).

$$\text{SSE} = \sum_{i=1}^{n} [y_i - (\beta_0 + \beta_1 x_i)]^2.$$

Comparing this approach to Equation 1.4 yields an important result: under certain conditions, minimizing the SSE is equivalent to maximizing the log-likelihood. Specifically, if the model for the mean is linear in the parameters and the outcome is assumed to be distributed iid normal, then the least

---

[3] The $\mathcal{R}$ function solve() calculates the matrix inverse.

TABLE 1.2 *Standard output for the OLS regression of log CO_2 emissions on log per capita GDP. Data drawn from World Bank Data Repository, 15 January 2017.*

	$\hat{\beta}$	$\sigma_{\hat{\beta}}$	t-Ratio	p-Value
Constant	−0.30	1.22	−0.25	0.80
log per capita GDP	1.06	0.13	8.04	0.00
$n = 184$				
$R^2 = 0.26$				
$F_{1,182} = 64.6$				

squares estimator can be justified by the more general principle of maximum likelihood.

Minimizing the SSE (or maximizing the likelihood) is a standard mathematical procedure that involves taking the derivative of the SSE separately with respect to β_0 and β_1, setting both equal to 0, and solving the resultant set of equations. This analytically produces least square estimates of β_0 and β_1:

$$\hat{\beta}_0 = \bar{y} - \hat{\beta}_1 \bar{x},$$

$$\hat{\beta}_1 = \frac{\sum_{i=1}^{n}(y_i - \bar{y})(x_i - \bar{x})}{\sum_{i=1}^{n}(x_i - \bar{x})^2}.$$

Generalizing the model to include k predictor variables in an $n \times k$ *design matrix*, $\mathbf{X}$, we can write the least squares estimator in matrix form as

$$\hat{\beta}^{\text{OLS}} = (\mathbf{X}^{\mathsf{T}}\mathbf{X})^{-1}\mathbf{X}^{\mathsf{T}}\mathbf{y}.$$

Regressing log CO_2 on log per capita GDP using OLS in $\mathcal{R}$ produces the quantities displayed Table 1.2. The OLS estimates are identical to the MLE results calculated above. This table reports the standard $\mathcal{R}$ summary output for a linear regression, including t- and F-statistics, and p-values. These quantities will be absent from virtually all of the tables you see in the remainder of the book. We will go into details about why in subsequent chapters.

1.5 MAXIMUM LIKELIHOOD: GENERAL

Having seen two examples, we can restate the process of applying the likelihood principle in more general terms. In the likelihood framework, modeling begins with two statements. The *stochastic* statement describes our assumptions about the probability distribution (or distributions, in the case of a mixture) that govern our data-generating process. The *systematic* statement describes our model for the parameters of the assumed probability distribution. For example, in the case with one independent variable and assuming a linear relationship between the independent variables and the mean parameter, we get:

stochastic component : $Y_i \sim f(\theta_i)$

systematic component : $\theta_i = \beta_0 + \beta_1 x_i$.

Here, f is some probability distribution or mass function. We might choose the Gaussian, but it could be a variety of others such as the binomial, Poisson, or Weibull that we explore in this book.

Once we specify the systematic and stochastic components, we can construct a likelihood for the data at hand.

Step 1: Express the joint probability of the data. For the case of independent data and distribution or mass function f with parameter(s) $\boldsymbol{\theta}$, we have:

$$\Pr(y_1 \mid \theta_1) = f(y_1; \theta_1)$$
$$\Pr(y_1, y_2 \mid \theta_1, \theta_2) = f(y_1; \theta_1) \times f(y_2; \theta_2)$$
$$\vdots$$
$$\Pr(y_1, \ldots, y_n \mid \theta_1, \ldots, \theta_n) = \prod_{i=1}^{n} f(y_i; \theta_i)$$

Step 2: Convert the joint probability into a likelihood. Note the constant, $h(\mathbf{y})$, which reinforces the fact that the likelihood does not have a direct interpretation as a probability. A likelihood is defined only up to a multiplicative constant:

$$\mathcal{L}(\boldsymbol{\theta} \mid \mathbf{y}) = h(\mathbf{y}) \times \Pr(\mathbf{y} \mid \boldsymbol{\theta})$$
$$\propto \Pr(\mathbf{y} \mid \boldsymbol{\theta}) = \prod_{i=1}^{n} f(y_i \mid \theta_i)$$

Step 3: Use the chosen stochastic and systematic components to specify a probability model and functional form. For a simple linear regression model, let f be the Gaussian (normal) distribution, and we have:

$$\mathcal{L}(\boldsymbol{\theta} \mid \mathbf{y}) = h(\mathbf{y}) \times \prod_{i=1}^{n} f_{\mathcal{N}}(y_i \mid \theta_i)$$
$$\theta_i = (\mu_i, \sigma^2)$$
$$\mu_i = \beta_0 + \beta_1 x_i$$
$$\mathcal{L}(\mu, \sigma^2 \mid \mathbf{y}) = \prod_{i=1}^{n} (2\pi\sigma^2)^{-1/2} \exp\left[\frac{-(y_i - \mu_i)^2}{2\sigma^2} \right]$$

Step 4: Simplify the expression by first taking the log and then eliminating terms that do not depend on unknown parameters.

$$\log \mathcal{L}(\mu, \sigma^2 \mid \mathbf{y}) = \sum_{i=1}^{n} \log \left\{ (2\pi\sigma^2)^{-1/2} \exp \left[\frac{-(y_i - \mu_i)^2}{2\sigma^2} \right] \right\}$$

$$= \sum_{i=1}^{n} \left[-\frac{1}{2} \log(2\pi) - \frac{1}{2} \log(\sigma^2) \right.$$

$$\left. -\frac{1}{2\sigma^2} (y_i - (\beta_0 + \beta_1 x_i))^2 \right]$$

$$-2 \log \mathcal{L}(\mu, \sigma^2 \mid \mathbf{y}) = \sum_{i=1}^{n} \left[\log(2\pi) + \log(\sigma^2) + \frac{1}{\sigma^2} (y_i - (\beta_0 + \beta_1 x_i))^2 \right]$$

The first term, $\log(2\pi)$, is simply a constant, unrelated to any of the parameters to be estimated, and can be dropped.

$$-2 \log \mathcal{L}(\mu, \sigma^2 \mid \mathbf{y}) = \sum_{i=1}^{n} \left[\log(\sigma^2) + \frac{1}{\sigma^2} (y_i - (\beta_0 + \beta_1 x_i))^2 \right]$$

Step 5: Find the extrema of this expression either analytically or by writing a program that uses numerical tools to identify maxima and minima.

1.6 CONCLUSION

This chapter presented the core ideas for the likelihood approach to statistical modeling that we explore through the rest of the book. The key innovation in the likelihood framework is treating the observed data as fixed and asking what combination of probability model and parameter values are the most likely to have generated these specific data. We showed that the OLS estimator can be recast as a maximum likelihood estimator and introduced two examples, including one example of a likelihood programmed directly into the statistical package $\mathcal{R}$.

What are the advantages of the MLE approach in the case of ordinary least squares? None; they are equivalent, and the OLS estimator can be derived under weaker assumptions. But the OLS approach assumes a linear model and unbounded, continuous outcome. The linear model is a good one, but the world around can be both nonlinear and bounded. Indeed, we had to take logarithms of CO_2 and per capita GDP in order to make the example work, forcing linearity on our analysis that is not apparent in the untransformed data. It is a testament to "marketing" that the OLS model is called the ordinary model, because in many ways it is a restricted, special case. The maximum likelihood approach permits us to specify nonlinear models quite easily if warranted by either our theory or data. The flexibility to model categorical and bounded variables is a benefit of the maximum likelihood approach. In the rest of this book, we introduce such models.

1.7 FURTHER READING

Applications

A great strength of the likelihood approach is its flexibility. Researchers can derive and program their own likelihood functions that reflect the specific research problem at hand. Mebane and Sekhon (2002) and Carrubba and Clark (2012) are two examples of likelihoods customized or designed for specific empirical applications. Other custom applications in political science come from Curtis Signorino (1999; 2002).

Past Work

Several other texts describing likelihood principles applied to the social sciences have appeared in the past quarter-century. These include King (1989a), Fox (1997), and Long (1997).

Software Notes

For gentle introductions to the $\mathcal{R}$ language and regression, we recommend Faraway (2004) and more recently Fox and Weisberg (2011) and James E. Monogan, III (2015). Venables and Ripley (2002) is a canonical $\mathcal{R}$ reference accompanying the MASS library.

2

Theory and Properties of Maximum Likelihood Estimators

Maximum likelihood is a unified framework for model building and statistical inference. Others approach maximum likelihood as simply a technique for model estimation that happens to have desirable statistical properties. For Bayesians, the process of specifying a likelihood is core to the statistical enterprise. In this chapter we examine the likelihood function in greater detail, exploring features and assumptions commonly invoked in estimation of likelihood-based models. We identify and derive statistical properties of the maximum likelihood estimator critical for justifying the computational strategies subsequently developed in this book. The key result in this regard is the MLE's asymptotic normality. This chapter is the most technically dense in this volume, focusing on "just the math." We defer computational examples for more extensive treatment in subsequent chapters.

2.1 THE LIKELIHOOD FUNCTION: A DEEPER DIVE

The results of statistical analysis often appear in published work as a Big Ugly Table of Numbers (BUTON). BUTONs display select quantities as reported by a particular procedure applied to specific, observed data. But most statistical models both entail assumptions and engender much more output than what typically appears in a BUTON. In building a likelihood-based model we posit a joint probability distribution for the observed data. In estimating the specified model we construct a generative analogue of the processes at work. Formally,

> **Definition 2.1** (Likelihood and MLE). Suppose we observe data, x, assumed to have been generated under the probability model $f(x; \theta^*)$, where the "true" parameter θ^* is unknown. The *likelihood* of θ given x is

$$\mathcal{L}(\theta \mid x) = h(x)f(x;\theta)$$
$$\propto f(x;\theta),$$

for some function h. The *Maximum Likelihood Estimator (MLE) for θ^**, denoted $\hat{\theta}$, is

$$\hat{\theta} \equiv \arg\max_{\theta} \mathcal{L}(\theta \mid x).$$

Note the presence of $h(x)$, an *unknown* scaling factor that is a function of the data but not the parameter. This factor reflects the likelihood principle.

Definition 2.2 (Likelihood Principle). The *likelihood principle* says that, after data have been collected, all the information relevant for inference about θ is contained in the likelihood function for the observed data under the assumed probability model. Moreover, two likelihood functions that are proportional to one another contain the same information about θ.

Thus, the likelihood has no scale nor any direct interpretation as a probability. Rather, we interpret likelihoods relative to one another. In what follows we suppress the term $h(x)$, as it only adds to notational complexity, and it cannot be estimated in any case.

Information about θ^* comes from *both* the observed data and our assumptions about the data-generating process (DGP), as embodied in the probability model $f(x;\theta)$. The likelihood function does more than generate values for tables. It provides a mathematical structure in which to incorporate new data or make probabilistic claims about yet-to-be-observed events.

As we saw in Chapter 1, likelihoods from independent samples sharing a DGP are easily combined. If x_1 and x_2 are independent events governed by the same $f(x;\theta^*)$, then $\mathcal{L}(\theta \mid x_1,x_2) = f(x_1;\theta)f(x_2;\theta)$, and the log-likelihood is $\log \mathcal{L}(\theta \mid x_1,x_2) = \log f(x_1;\theta) + \log f(x_2;\theta)$.

2.1.1 Likelihood and Bayesian Statistics

R. A. Fisher came to believe that likelihood is a self-contained framework for statistical modeling and inference. But the likelihood also plays a fundamental role in Bayesian statistics.

Bayesian thinking builds on Thomas Bayes's Rule, which provides a principled way in which to combine our prior knowledge and beliefs with newly acquired data to generate an updated set of beliefs. Formally, if we are concerned with the value of $\boldsymbol{\theta}$, we might describe our current beliefs about that value with the prior probability distribution $\Pr(\boldsymbol{\theta})$. We then observe new data, $\mathbf{x} = (x_1, \ldots, x_n)$, and seek to describe our updated or "posterior" beliefs, $\Pr(\boldsymbol{\theta} \mid \mathbf{x})$. Bayes's Rule states

Theorem 2.1 (Bayes's Rule).

$$\Pr(\theta \mid \mathbf{x}) = \frac{\Pr(\mathbf{x} \mid \theta)\Pr(\theta)}{\Pr(\mathbf{x})}$$
$$\propto \Pr(\mathbf{x} \mid \theta)\Pr(\theta)$$
$$\propto \mathcal{L}(\theta)\Pr(\theta).$$

Proof The result follows directly from the fact that $\Pr(\theta, \mathbf{x}) = \Pr(\theta \mid \mathbf{x})$ $\Pr(\mathbf{x}) = \Pr(\mathbf{x} \mid \theta)\Pr(\theta)$. □

From Bayes's Rule we see that the posterior distribution of θ is the prior times the likelihood, scaled by the marginal probability of the data, $\mathbf{x}$. As the volume of observed data increases, the information in the data dominate our prior beliefs and the Bayesian posterior distribution comes to resemble the likelihood function. If we assume that $\Pr(\theta)$ follows a uniform distribution with support that includes $\hat{\theta}$, then the mode of the posterior distribution will be the MLE. Under somewhat more general conditions, the posterior distribution for θ approximates the asymptotic distribution for the MLE discussed in Section 2.2.2. Although Bayesian thinking and the analysis of fully Bayesian models is much more involved, the likelihood framework and the logic of Bayesian statistics are closely linked. In many situations, a parametric Bayesian approach and the likelihood framework will yield similar results, even if the interpretation of these estimates differs.

2.1.2 Regularity

The method of maximum likelihood summarizes the information in the data and likelihood function with $\hat{\theta}$. To find this maximum we might simply try many values of θ and pick the one yielding the largest value for $\mathcal{L}(\theta)$. This is tedious and carries no guarantee that the biggest value we found is the biggest that could be obtained. Calculus lets us find the extrema of functions more quickly and with greater certainty. The conditions under which we can apply all the machinery of differential calculus in the likelihood framework are referred to as "regularity conditions."

These regularity conditions can be stated in several ways. Some are quite technical. Figures 1.4 and 1.1 provide some intuition. For a likelihood to be "regular," we would like it to be smooth without any kinks or holes (i.e., continuous), at least in the neighborhood of $\hat{\theta}$. In regular problems, we also require that the MLE not fall on some edge or boundary of the parameter space, nor does the support of the distribution or mass function for X depend on the value of θ. Likelihoods with a single maximum, rather than many small, local hills or plateaus, are easier to work with.

With regularity concerns satisfied, the log-likelihood will be at least twice differentiable around the MLE. Each of these derivatives of the log-likelihood is important enough to have a name, so we address each in turn.

2.1.3 Score

The vector of first partial derivatives of a multivariate function is called the *gradient*, denoted ∇. The score function is the gradient of the log-likelihood. Evaluated at a particular point θ, the score function will describe the steepness of the log-likelihood. If the function is continuous, then at the maximum or minimum, this vector of first partial derivatives equals the zero vector, 0.

> **Definition 2.3** (Score function). Given log-likelihood, $\log \mathcal{L}(\theta)$, and observed data x, the *score function*, $S(\theta)$, is
>
> $$S(\theta) \equiv \nabla_\theta \log \mathcal{L}(\theta) = \frac{\partial}{\partial \theta} \log \mathcal{L}(\theta),$$
>
> and the MLE $\hat{\theta}$ solves the score equation: $S(\hat{\theta}) = 0$.

If we imagine that the data we observe are but one realization of all observable possible data sets given the assumed probability model, $f(x; \theta)$, then we can consider the score function as a random variable. As a matter of vocabulary, we refer to the *score statistic* when the score is considered as a random variable (with θ fixed at the "true" value for the DGP). In Theorem 2.2 we derive the expected value of the score statistic.

> **Theorem 2.2.** *If the likelihood function $\mathcal{L}(\theta)$ satisfies appropriate regularity conditions, then $E[S(\theta)] = 0$, where the expectation is taken over possible data X with support $\mathcal{X}$.*

Proof

$$
\begin{aligned}
E[S(\theta)] &= \int_{\mathcal{X}} f(x; \theta \mid \theta) \frac{\partial}{\partial \theta} \log \mathcal{L}(\theta) dx \quad \text{(score def., expectation)} \\
&= \int_{\mathcal{X}} \frac{\frac{\partial}{\partial \theta} \mathcal{L}(\theta)}{\mathcal{L}(\theta)} f(x; \theta \mid \theta) dx \quad \text{(Chain Rule, derivative of ln)} \\
&= \int_{\mathcal{X}} \frac{\frac{\partial}{\partial \theta} \mathcal{L}(\theta)}{f(x; \theta \mid \theta)} f(x; \theta \mid \theta) dx \quad \text{(likelihood def.)} \\
&= \int_{\mathcal{X}} \frac{\partial}{\partial \theta} \mathcal{L}(\theta) dx \quad \text{(algebra)} \\
&= \frac{\partial}{\partial \theta} \int_{\mathcal{X}} \mathcal{L}(\theta) dx \quad \text{(regularity conditions)} \\
&= \frac{\partial}{\partial \theta} \int_{\mathcal{X}} f(x; \theta \mid \theta) dx \quad \text{(likelihood def.)} \\
&= \frac{\partial}{\partial \theta} 1 = 0 \quad \text{(pdf def., derivative of a constant).}
\end{aligned}
$$

$\square$

2.1.4 Fisher Information

Recall the likelihood surface displayed in Figure 1.1. The peak of this curve represents the most likely value of the parameter to have generated the observed data, whereas points near the peak are less likely. A likelihood function steeply curved around the MLE is one in which values of θ close to $\hat{\theta}$ are much less likely than $\hat{\theta}$. The data, in the context of the likelihood function, provide a lot of information about θ. It is precisely estimated. Conversely, a likelihood function that is nearly flat around the MLE is one in which finding the maximum is hard since values near the maximum are nearly as likely as the MLE. In the limiting case of a flat likelihood, a single MLE does not exist since several values are equally consistent with the observed data.

The second derivative is closely related to the notion of curvature of a function. It is no surprise that the second derivative of the log-likelihood is critical in both estimating the MLE and describing our uncertainty. Intuitively the bigger the absolute value of the second derivative the more "curved" the function. Since the second derivative is negative at any local maximum we know that the second derivative of the likelihood will be negative at $\hat{\theta}$ (assuming appropriate regularity conditions). Taking the negative of the second derivative gives us an index of how much information about θ we have at the MLE. This quantity is called *Fisher information*.

Definition 2.4 (Observed Fisher Information). Assuming appropriate regularity conditions for $f(x; \theta)$, the *observed Fisher Information*, $I(\theta)$, is given as

$$I(\hat{\theta}) \equiv -\frac{\partial}{\partial \theta} S(\theta)|_{\hat{\theta}}.$$

Note that observed Fisher information is a quantity, not a function. It is calculated by evaluating the second derivative of the log-likelihood at the MLE, itself calculated using the observed data.

Just as we did with the score function and score statistic we might think of the observed Fisher information as resulting from only one of many possible data sets we could observe from the DGP described by $f(x; \theta)$. If we imagine θ as fixed and then average over possible data sets, we have *expected* Fisher information, i.e., how much information about θ can we expect from the random variable X. We will define expected Fisher information a bit differently from observed information and then show how we can get from expected information to our expression for observed information.

Definition 2.5 (Expected Fisher Information). Assuming appropriate regularity conditions for $f(x; \theta)$, the *expected Fisher Information*, $\mathcal{I}(\theta)$, is given as

$$\mathcal{I}(\boldsymbol{\theta}) \equiv \mathrm{E}[S(\boldsymbol{\theta})S(\boldsymbol{\theta})^\mathsf{T}],$$

where the expectation is taken over possible data X with support $\mathcal{X}$.

There are several equivalent ways of writing the expected information, including as the negative expected derivative of the score:

Theorem 2.3. *Assuming appropriate regularity conditions for $f(x;\theta)$,*

$$\mathcal{I}(\boldsymbol{\theta}) = \mathrm{var}[S(\boldsymbol{\theta})] \tag{2.1}$$

$$= -\mathrm{E}\left[\frac{\partial}{\partial\boldsymbol{\theta}}S(\boldsymbol{\theta})\right], \tag{2.2}$$

where the expectation is taken over possible data X with support $\mathcal{X}$.

Proof We state the proof for the case where θ is single-valued (scalar), but it readily generalizes to the case where $\boldsymbol{\theta}$ is a vector. Noting that $\mathrm{var}(Y) = \mathrm{E}[Y^2] - \mathrm{E}[Y]^2$, and by applying Theorem 2.2, we obtain Equation (2.1).

To prove Equation (2.2), note that $S(\theta) = \frac{\partial}{\partial\theta}\log f(x;\theta) = \frac{f'(x;\theta)}{f(x;\theta)}$. Then by the quotient rule,

$$\frac{\partial}{\partial\theta}S(\theta) = \frac{f''(x;\theta)f(x;\theta) - f'(x;\theta)^2}{f(x;\theta)^2}$$

$$= \frac{f''(x;\theta)}{f(x;\theta)} - \left(\frac{f'(x;\theta)}{f(x;\theta)}\right)^2$$

$$= \frac{f''(x;\theta)}{f(x;\theta)} - S(\theta)^2.$$

It follows that

$$\mathrm{E}\left[\frac{\partial}{\partial\theta}S(\theta)\right] = \int_{\mathcal{X}}\left(\frac{f''(x;\theta)}{f(x;\theta)} - S(\theta)^2\right)f(x;\theta)dx$$

$$= \int_{\mathcal{X}}f''(x;\theta)dx - \int_{\mathcal{X}}S(\theta)^2 f(x;\theta)dx$$

$$= \int_{\mathcal{X}}f''(x;\theta)dx - \mathcal{I}(\theta).$$

The assumed regularity conditions let us reverse the order of differentiation and integration, implying that the first term of the last expression is $\frac{\partial^2}{\partial\theta^2}\int_{\mathcal{X}}f(x;\theta)dx = 0$, since $f(x;\theta)$ is a probability density function. □

When $\boldsymbol{\theta}$ is a k-dimensional vector, we use $H(\boldsymbol{\theta})$ to refer to its matrix of second partial derivatives, also known as the *Hessian* matrix.[1]

---

[1] The name Hessian refers to the mathematician Ludwig Otto Hesse, not the German mercenaries contracted by the British Empire.

Definition 2.6 (Hessian matrix). Given a twice-differentiable function such as a regular log-likelihood $\log \mathcal{L}(\boldsymbol{\theta})$ with k-dimensional parameter $\boldsymbol{\theta}$, the $k \times k$ *Hessian matrix* $H(\boldsymbol{\theta})$ is given as

$$H(\boldsymbol{\theta}) = \frac{\partial}{\partial \boldsymbol{\theta}} S(\boldsymbol{\theta})$$

$$= \frac{\partial^2 \log \mathcal{L}(\boldsymbol{\theta})}{\partial \boldsymbol{\theta} \partial \boldsymbol{\theta}^\mathsf{T}}$$

$$= \begin{bmatrix} \dfrac{\partial^2 \log \mathcal{L}(\boldsymbol{\theta})}{\partial \theta_1^2} & \cdots & \dfrac{\partial^2 \log \mathcal{L}(\boldsymbol{\theta})}{\partial \theta_1 \partial \theta_k} \\ \vdots & \ddots & \vdots \\ \dfrac{\partial^2 \log \mathcal{L}(\boldsymbol{\theta})}{\partial \theta_k \partial \theta_1} & \cdots & \dfrac{\partial^2 \log \mathcal{L}(\boldsymbol{\theta})}{\partial \theta_k^2} \end{bmatrix}.$$

Expected Fisher information, written in terms of the Hessian matrix, is therefore

$$\mathcal{I}(\boldsymbol{\theta}) \equiv \mathrm{E}\left[S(\boldsymbol{\theta})S(\boldsymbol{\theta})^\mathsf{T}\right] = -\mathrm{E}[H(\boldsymbol{\theta})].$$

In any particular application, the observed Fisher information is now a $k \times k$ matrix of numbers.

The distinction between expected and observed Fisher information is somewhat subtle. Observed information is closest to the actual data in any particular application. Statistical programs like $\mathcal{R}$ use and report quantities based on the observed Fisher information. In many routine applications using models from the exponential family, the observed and expected Fisher information are equivalent at the MLE. Expected information is a theoretical idea used mainly to derive some of the MLE's properties that are utilized in frequentist statistics. While these properties may be interesting, the idea of averaging across hypothetical data sets generated by a fixed parameter sits uneasily with the basic likelihood principle of treating observed data as fixed and parameters as unknown quantities.

Fisher Information from Independent Samples

Just as we can combine likelihoods from independent events or samples governed by the same DGP, we can also combine Fisher information. If we observe n independent samples from $f(x; \boldsymbol{\theta})$ then we can construct the log-likelihood as

$$\log \mathcal{L}(\boldsymbol{\theta} \mid \mathbf{x}) = \sum_{i=1}^{n} \log \mathcal{L}(x_i; \boldsymbol{\theta}).$$

It follows that $H(\boldsymbol{\theta} \mid \mathbf{x}) = \sum_{i=1}^{n} H(\boldsymbol{\theta} \mid x_i)$. So, from the definition of $\mathcal{I}(\boldsymbol{\theta})$, we get

$$\mathcal{I}(\theta) = -\sum_{i=1}^{n} \mathrm{E}\left[H(\theta \mid x_i)\right] = n\mathcal{I}(\theta \mid x_i).$$

In other words, the expected Fisher information from a random sample of size n is simply n times the expected information from a single observation.

2.2 PROPERTIES OF MAXIMUM LIKELIHOOD ESTIMATORS

With knowledge of the score, Hessian, and Fisher information in hand, we can derive some of the most useful statistical properties of the likelihood function and MLE.

2.2.1 Invariance

One frequently useful property of the MLE is that, for any sample size, the MLE is *functionally invariant*:

> **Theorem 2.4.** *Let* $g(\cdot)$ *be a function. If* $\hat{\theta}$ *is the MLE of* θ, *then* $g(\hat{\theta}) = \widehat{g(\theta)}$.

Proof We prove this result supposing that $g(\cdot)$ is injective (this is a simplifying, though not necessary, assumption). If $g(\cdot)$ is one-to-one, then $\mathcal{L}(g^{-1}(g(\theta))) = \mathcal{L}(\theta)$. Then, since $\hat{\theta}$ is the MLE, our previous statement implies that $\hat{\theta} = g^{-1}(\widehat{g(\theta)})$. Therefore applying $g(\cdot)$ to both sides, we see that $g(\hat{\theta}) = \widehat{g(\theta)}$. □

In words, a transformation of the MLE equals the MLE of that transformation. We can use the invariance property to easily re-parameterize our models for estimation and interpretation. For example, if we estimated a variance parameter, $\widehat{\sigma^2}$, we can easily calculate the MLE for the standard deviation ($\hat{\sigma} = \sqrt{\widehat{\sigma^2}}$) or precision ($\widehat{\sigma^{-2}} = 1/\widehat{\sigma^2}$).

2.2.2 Large-Sample Properties

Let $\hat{\theta}_n$ be the MLE for the parameters θ given sample size n and probability model $f(x; \theta)$. The other oft-cited properties of MLEs are asymptotic, i.e., they are derived as the limiting behavior of the MLE for a sequence of $\{\hat{\theta}_n\}$ as we let $n \to \infty$. The theoretical basis for these results relies on the Law of Large Numbers and the Central Limit Theorem. We state both here by way of review and without proofs, which can be quite technical.

> **Theorem 2.5** (Weak Law of Large Numbers). *Assume an infinite sequence of independent and identically distributed (i.i.d.) random*

variables, X_i, with finite expected value, μ. Let $\bar{X}_n = \frac{1}{n}\sum_{i=1}^{n} X_i$. Then $\bar{X}_n \xrightarrow{p} \mu$ as $n \to \infty$.

Theorem 2.6 (Central Limit Theorem). *Assume an infinite sequence of i.i.d. random variables, X_i, with finite expected value, μ, and finite variance, σ^2. Let $\bar{X}_n = \frac{1}{n}\sum_{i=1}^{n} X_i$. Then $\sqrt{n}(\bar{X}_n - \mu) \xrightarrow{d} \mathcal{N}(0,\sigma^2)$ as $n \to \infty$.*

In case you were wondering ... 2.1 ≈ Taylor Series

The Taylor series approximation to a function is a widely used tool in statistics, especially when relying on the Central Limit Theorem to derive asymptotic results. A Taylor series represents a differentiable function at a point by a polynomial approximation at that same point. In the theory of maximum likelihood we are most commonly interested in quadratic approximations.

Suppose we have a function $\log \mathcal{L}(\theta)$ and we are interested in its approximation around a point, $\hat{\theta}$. The second-order, or quadratic Taylor approximation around $\hat{\theta}$ is

$$\log \mathcal{L}(\theta) = \log \mathcal{L}(\hat{\theta}) + (\theta - \hat{\theta})\frac{\partial}{\partial \theta} \log \mathcal{L}(\hat{\theta})$$

$$+ \frac{1}{2}(\theta - \hat{\theta})\frac{\partial^2}{\partial\theta\partial\theta^{\mathsf{T}}} \log \mathcal{L}(\hat{\theta}) + R,$$

where R is the remainder. We typically work with a truncated Taylor series omitting the remainder, often described as an "approximation" ($\approx$).

Consistency of the MLE

Suppose that the data generating process for x is $f(x, \theta^*)$, so that θ^* is the "true" value of θ that generates the data. Then the MLE $\hat{\theta}$ is *consistent*; that is, given infinite data, the MLE collapses to the "true" parameter value θ^*. We present one statement of the theorem and give a sketch of the proof for scalar θ to provide the key intuition.

Theorem 2.7 (Consistency of the MLE). *Let θ^* be "true" value for θ. Assuming appropriate regularity conditions for $f(\mathbf{x}; \theta^*)$, and that $\mathbf{x} = (x_1, \ldots, x_n)$ forms an i.i.d. sample from $f(x; \theta^*)$, and further that $\mathcal{L}(\theta)$ is globally concave, then $\hat{\theta} \xrightarrow{p} \theta^*$ as $n \to \infty$.*

Proof   We sketch the proof for the case of scalar θ, but it readily generalizes to the multiparameter case. First note that the sample likelihood function converges to the expected log-likelihood by the Law of Large Numbers:

$$\frac{1}{n} \log \mathcal{L}(\theta \mid \mathbf{x}) = \frac{1}{n} \sum_{i=1}^{n} \log \mathcal{L}(\theta \mid x_i)$$

$$\overset{p}{\to} \mathrm{E}\left[\log \mathcal{L}(\theta \mid \mathbf{x})\right].$$

We then show that θ^* is the maximizer of the expected log-likelihood by showing that θ^* satisfies the first-order conditions (FOC) for a maximum. The FOC are

$$\frac{\partial}{\partial \theta} \mathrm{E}\left[\log \mathcal{L}(\theta^* \mid \mathbf{x})\right] = \int_{\mathcal{X}} \frac{f'(x; \theta)}{f(x; \theta)} f(x; \theta^*) dx = 0,$$

which follows from the regularity conditions and the definition of the log-likelihood. The FOC are satisfied when $\theta = \theta^*$ by Theorem 2.2.   □

Asymptotic Distribution of the MLE

The MLE is *asymptotically normally distributed*. This property justifies conventional hypothesis testing and z-scores for MLE results. As we will show shortly, the square root of the main diagonal of $-H(\hat{\theta})^{-1}$ gives us the standard errors so frequently seen in BUTON. But the likelihood approach contains much more than just point estimates and standard errors. The normality result allows us to use modern computing technology to combine the $\hat{\theta}$, the Hessian matrix, and the (multivariate) normal distribution to describe our models in much more interesting and informative ways. The normality result provides the framework for simulating nearly any quantity of interest from a likelihood-based model, including predictions of yet-to-be-observed data. The MLE's limiting distribution has a direct connection to the Bayesian approach of interpreting models via the posterior distribution.

We state Slutsky's Theorem without proof.

Theorem 2.8 (Slutsky's Theorem). *Let A_n, B_n, and X_n be sequences of random variables such that $A_n \overset{p}{\to} a$, $B_n \overset{p}{\to} b$, and $X_n \overset{d}{\to} X$ then $A_n + B_n X_n \overset{d}{\to} a + bX$.*

Theorem 2.9 (Distribution of the MLE). *Let $\mathbf{x} = (x_1, \dots, x_n)$ form an i.i.d. sample from $f(x; \theta^*)$ with corresponding likelihood $\mathcal{L}(\theta \mid \mathbf{x})$, which satisfies the regularity conditions for a consistent MLE. Then $\sqrt{n}(\hat{\theta}_n - \theta^*) \overset{d}{\to} \mathcal{N}(0, \mathcal{I}(\theta^*)^{-1})$.*

Proof The proof begins with a Taylor series expansion of the FOC around $\hat{\theta}_n$, where θ_0 is some point between $\hat{\theta}_n$ and θ^*:

$$0 = S(\hat{\theta}_n) \approx S(\theta^*) + H(\theta_0)(\hat{\theta}_n - \theta^*).$$

It follows that

$$(\hat{\theta}_n - \theta^*) = -H(\theta_0)^{-1} S(\theta^*)$$

$$\sqrt{n}(\hat{\theta}_n - \theta^*) = -\left(\frac{1}{n} H(\theta_0)\right)^{-1} \frac{1}{\sqrt{n}} S(\theta^*).$$

By the Law of Large Numbers we have

$$H(\theta_0) = \frac{1}{n} \sum_{i=1}^{n} H(\theta_0 \mid x_i) \overset{p}{\to} E\left[H(\theta^*)\right] = -\mathcal{I}(\theta^*)$$

and, by the Central Limit Theorem, we have

$$\frac{1}{\sqrt{n}} S(\theta^*) = \frac{1}{\sqrt{n}} \sum_{i=1}^{n} S(\theta^* \mid x_i) \overset{d}{\to} \mathcal{N}\left(0, \mathcal{I}(\theta^*)\right).$$

Therefore the result follows from Theorem 2.8. □

In actual applications we need to estimate the asymptotic variance of the MLE. Since the MLE is consistent, we can do this by substituting observed Fisher information, $I(\hat{\theta})^{-1}$, for the expected Fisher information, $\mathcal{I}(\theta^*)^{-1}$. This result implies that $\hat{\theta} \overset{.}{\sim} \mathcal{N}(\theta^*, I(\hat{\theta})^{-1})$, or, in words, the sampling distribution of the MLE is approximately normal with the mean centered at the true value of θ and covariance matrix given by the inverse of the Fisher information, reinforcing the intuition that more information should lead to more precise estimates.

Recalling that $I(\hat{\theta}) = -H(\hat{\theta})$, we can also see that the variance of the MLE is given by the negative inverse of the Hessian. The diagonal elements of this covariance matrix give the variance of each element of θ. If we take the square root of the diagonal elements, we obtain our estimates of the standard errors for $\hat{\theta}$.

Other Properties

We mention two other properties of the MLE only in passing. First, the asymptotic distribution of the MLE implies that the MLE is *efficient* in that it reaches the Cramér-Rao lower bound. The MLE achieves this *asymptotically*. In other words, the MLE attains the smallest possible variance among all consistent estimators. Equivalently, the MLE achieves (asymptotically) the smallest mean-squared error of all consistent estimators.

> **In case you were wondering ... 2.2 Cramér-Rao lower bound**
>
> The Cramér-Rao Lower Bound (CRLB) states that if $T(X)$ is an unbiased estimator for θ, then $\text{var}(T(X)) \geq \mathcal{I}(\theta)^{-1}$. Any unbiased estimator achieving the CRLB achieves the minimum possible variance and therefore attains maximal efficiency.

There is *no* guarantee that the MLE is unbiased. For example, the MLE for the normal variance is biased. In fact, the MLE is frequently biased in small samples. But bias is a second-order concern here for three reasons. First, bias disappears as n increases (Theorem 2.7). In most applications, we are well away from the point where small-sample bias will be material. Second, bias in the MLE can be estimated and accounted for, if needed, using the cross-validation methods discussed in Chapter 5. Third, even if $T(X)$ is unbiased, any nonlinear transformation of $T(X)$ will be biased; unbiasedness is not robust to re-parameterization.

2.3 DIAGNOSTICS FOR MAXIMUM LIKELIHOOD

How can we evaluate the results of a model estimated by maximum likelihood? Since we cannot recover the constant $h(x)$ the value of the (log) likelihood at the MLE is, by itself, not meaningful. What we can do, however, is compare likelihoods for different values of θ given the same underlying observed data and likelihood function. The value of the likelihood at the MLE enters into several of the most commonly discussed model diagnostic and comparison tools: the *likelihood ratio*, the *score* test, the *Wald* statistic, the the Akaike Information Criterion (AIC), and the Bayesian Information Criterion (BIC). The first three of these all have asymptotic distributions that underpin conventional frequentist hypothesis testing.

2.3.1 Likelihood Ratios

The most straightforward way to compare likelihoods is simply to divide one by the other, canceling out the unknown scaling factor, $h(\mathbf{x})$.

> **Definition 2.7** (Likelihood ratio). Given a probability model $f(x; \theta)$, observed data x, and two hypothesized values of θ, namely θ_R and θ_G, we define the likelihood ratio as
>
> $$\log\left(\frac{\mathcal{L}(\theta_R \mid x)}{\mathcal{L}(\theta_G \mid x)}\right) = \log \mathcal{L}(\theta_R \mid x) - \log \mathcal{L}(\theta_G \mid x).$$

Since the value of the log-likelihood for the sample is the sum of the likelihoods for each observation, the likelihood ratio must be calculated based on the *exact same* observed data for both. The only thing that differs between the likelihood functions in the numerator and denominator of the ratio is the candidate values of θ. With this likelihood ratio we can assess the relative strength of evidence in favor of particular θ values.

The likelihood ratio is used to compare "nested" models, i.e., two models in which one is a restricted or special case of the other. Recall the simple regression of CO_2 on per capita GDP from Section 1.4.1. In that example $\theta_R = (\beta_0, \beta_1, \sigma^2)$. Suppose we fit a second model, wherein we include population density as a covariate with associated regression coefficient β_2. In the second model, we have $\theta_G = (\beta_0, \beta_1, \beta_2, \sigma^2)$. In the first model, we implicitly constrained the β_2 coefficient to be 0. The first model is thus a special case of the more general second one. If the restriction is appropriate, i.e., θ^* lies in the more restricted parameter space, then the (log) likelihoods of the two models should be approximately equal at their respective MLEs. The likelihood ratio should be approximately one or, equivalently, the difference in the log-likelihoods should be about 0. For reasons that will be clear shortly, the conventional definition of the *likelihood ratio statistic* is

$$\mathrm{LR}(\theta_R, \theta_G \mid \mathbf{x}) = -2 \log \frac{\mathcal{L}(\theta_R \mid \mathbf{x})}{\mathcal{L}(\theta_G \mid \mathbf{x})}.$$

Some presentations reverse the numerator and denominator of the likelihood ratio, leading to a likelihood ratio statistic without the negative sign.

Distribution of the Likelihood Ratio Statistic

In the CO_2 emissions example, we obtain a log-likelihood of -395.2 for the restricted model, i.e., the model excluding population density, whereas we obtain -392.4 for the more general model. Our likelihood ratio is -2.8 and our likelihood ratio statistic is 5.7. Is this a lot? It turns out that under the assumption that the parameter space for the restricted model is correct (along with regularity conditions), the likelihood ratio follows a known asymptotic distribution.

> **In case you were wondering ... 2.3 χ^2 distribution**
>
> Suppose $X_1, \ldots, X_n$ are i.i.d. samples from $\mathcal{N}(0, 1)$. Let $Z = \sum_{i=1}^{n} X_i^2$. We say that
>
> $$Z \sim \chi_n^2.$$
>
> This distribution has n "degrees of freedom," with $\mathrm{E}[Z] = n$ and $\mathrm{var}(Z) = 2n$.

Theorem 2.10. *Let* $\mathbf{x} = (x_1, \ldots, x_n)$ *be an i.i.d. sample from some distribution* $f(x; \theta^*)$ *with corresponding likelihood* $\mathcal{L}(\theta \mid \mathbf{x})$ *satisfying* *standard regularity conditions. Let $r = dim(\boldsymbol{\theta}_R) \leq dim(\boldsymbol{\theta}_G) = g$; that is, the elements of $\boldsymbol{\theta}_R$ are a subset of those of $\boldsymbol{\theta}_G$. Under the hypothesis that $\boldsymbol{\theta}^* = \hat{\boldsymbol{\theta}}_R$,*

$$LR(\hat{\boldsymbol{\theta}}_R, \hat{\boldsymbol{\theta}}_G \mid \mathbf{x}) \overset{d}{\to} \chi^2_{g-r}.$$

Proof We sketch the proof for scalar θ. We suppress the subscript n on the MLEs.

Begin with a second-order Taylor expansion of the log-likelihood around the MLE:

$$\log \mathcal{L}(\theta_r) \approx \log \mathcal{L}(\hat{\theta}) + (\hat{\theta} - \theta_r)S(\hat{\theta}) - \frac{1}{2}I(\hat{\theta})(\hat{\theta} - \theta_r)^2$$

$$\approx \log \mathcal{L}(\hat{\theta}) - \frac{1}{2}I(\hat{\theta})(\hat{\theta} - \theta_r)^2 \quad \text{(by } S(\hat{\theta}) = 0\text{)}.$$

This implies that the likelihood ratio statistic is

$$LR \approx -2\left[\log \mathcal{L}(\hat{\theta}) - \frac{1}{2}I(\hat{\theta})(\hat{\theta} - \theta_r)^2 - \log \mathcal{L}(\hat{\theta})\right]$$

$$\approx I(\hat{\theta})(\hat{\theta} - \theta_r)^2$$

$$= I(\hat{\theta})(\hat{\theta} - \theta)^2.$$

From Theorem 2.9 we know that $\sqrt{n}(\hat{\theta} - \theta^*) \overset{d}{\to} \mathcal{N}\left(0, I(\theta^*)^{-1}\right)$, so $\sqrt{n}I(\hat{\theta})^{\frac{1}{2}}$ $(\hat{\theta} - \theta^*) \overset{d}{\to} \mathcal{N}(0, 1)$. Therefore $nI(\hat{\theta})(\hat{\theta} - \theta^*)^2 \overset{d}{\to} \chi^2_1$. $\qquad\square$

This theorem states that the likelihood ratio statistic for two nested models is distributed χ^2 under the "null" hypothesis, which states that the more restricted model is the "correct" model. The degrees of freedom of the null distribution equals the number of parameter restrictions imposed as we go from the general to restricted model. We can therefore calculate the probability of observing a likelihood ratio statistic at least as great as the one we observe for our data set and proposed models. In the CO_2 emissions example, we calculate this p-value as 0.02.

Statistical packages will often report a *model χ^2*. This refers to the χ^2 value for the likelihood ratio comparing the estimated model to the null model – a model with all coefficients except the intercept constrained to equal 0. This statistic answers the usually boring question: "Is the model you fit noticeably better than doing nothing at all?"

A related quantity is model deviance, which compares the model we built to a "perfect" or "saturated" model (i.e., a model with a parameter for every observation). Deviance is given by

$$D(\mathbf{x}) = -2\left[\log \mathcal{L}(\hat{\boldsymbol{\theta}}_b|\mathbf{x}) - \log \mathcal{L}(\hat{\boldsymbol{\theta}}_s|\mathbf{x})\right],$$

where $\hat{\boldsymbol{\theta}}_b$ is the MLE of $\boldsymbol{\theta}_b$, representing the model we built, and $\hat{\boldsymbol{\theta}}_s$ is the MLE of the saturated model. Since this is simply a likelihood ratio, it too follows a χ^2_{n-k} distribution, where n denotes the number of observations in our sample and k denotes the number of parameters in our model.

Statistical packages routinely report "null deviance" and "residual deviance." The former is the deviance of the null model, and the latter is the deviance of the built model. Letting $\log \mathcal{L}(\hat{\boldsymbol{\theta}}_0)$ be the maximized log-likelihood of the null model and noting that

$$\text{Residual deviance} - \text{null deviance} = -2 \left[\log \mathcal{L}(\hat{\boldsymbol{\theta}}_b | \mathbf{x}) - \log \mathcal{L}(\hat{\boldsymbol{\theta}}_s | \mathbf{x}) \right]$$
$$- \left(-2 \left[\log \mathcal{L}(\hat{\boldsymbol{\theta}}_0 | \mathbf{x}) - \log \mathcal{L}(\hat{\boldsymbol{\theta}}_s | \mathbf{x}) \right] \right)$$
$$= -2 \left[\log \mathcal{L}(\hat{\boldsymbol{\theta}}_b | \mathbf{x}) - \log \mathcal{L}(\hat{\boldsymbol{\theta}}_0 | \mathbf{x}) \right],$$

it is easy to see that the difference between null and residual deviances is simply another way of calculating the "model χ^2."

2.3.2 Score and Wald Tests

Score Tests
Score tests appear occasionally, also going under the names *Lagrange multiplier*, *Rao score test*, and the *locally most-powerful test*. The score test relies on the score function to consider the slope of the log-likelihood once we constrain a particular parameter to have some hypothesized value. If the constraint is appropriate, then the slope of the log-likelihood near the constraint should be about 0 since, at the maximum of the likelihood function, the derivative with respect to the parameters equals 0. More formally, the score test compares the slope of the log-likelihood at the hypothesized value, $\boldsymbol{\theta}_0$, against the curvature of the likelihood as described by Fisher information.

Definition 2.8 (Score test). Given a log-likelihood, $\log \mathcal{L}(\theta)$, and a hypothesized value, θ_h, the score test for scalar θ is given as

$$\frac{S(\theta_h)}{\sqrt{\mathcal{I}(\theta_h)}} \overset{\cdot}{\sim} \mathcal{N}(0,1) \qquad \text{if } \theta^* = \theta_h,$$

$$\frac{S(\theta_h)^2}{\mathcal{I}(\theta_h)} \overset{\cdot}{\sim} \chi^2_1 \qquad \text{if } \theta^* = \theta_h.$$

For k-dimensional parameter $\boldsymbol{\theta}$ in which $\boldsymbol{\theta}_h$ imposes $p \leq k$ constraints and holds the other $k-p$ at their MLE, e.g., $\boldsymbol{\theta}_h = (\theta_{1,0}, \ldots, \theta_{p,0}, \hat{\theta}_{p+1}, \ldots, \hat{\theta}_k)$, the score statistic is

$$S(\boldsymbol{\theta}_h)^\mathsf{T} \mathcal{I}(\boldsymbol{\theta}_h)^{-1} S(\boldsymbol{\theta}_h) \overset{\cdot}{\sim} \chi^2_p \qquad \text{if } \boldsymbol{\theta}^* = \boldsymbol{\theta}_h.$$

Wald Tests

We also have the Wald test, which is simply the squared difference of the estimated parameters from some constrained value (typically zero), weighted by the curvature of the log-likelihood.

> **Definition 2.9** (Wald test). Given a log-likelihood, $\log \mathcal{L}(\theta)$ and hypothesized θ_h, the Wald test for scalar θ is given as
>
> $$W = \frac{(\hat{\theta} - \theta_h)^2}{I(\hat{\theta})}.$$
>
> If $\theta^* = \theta_h$ then $W \overset{\cdot}{\sim} \chi_1^2$.
> For k-dimensional parameter $\boldsymbol{\theta}$, in which hypothesized $\boldsymbol{\theta}_h$ imposes $p \leq k$ constraints, the Wald statistic is
>
> $$W = (\hat{\boldsymbol{\theta}} - \boldsymbol{\theta}_h)^{\mathsf{T}} I(\hat{\boldsymbol{\theta}})^{-1} (\hat{\boldsymbol{\theta}} - \boldsymbol{\theta}_h).$$
>
> Under the maintained hypothesis, $W \overset{\cdot}{\sim} \chi_p^2$.

The Wald test is a generalized version of the standard t-test, which imposes only one restriction. For scalar θ, we have $\hat{\theta} \sim \mathcal{N}(\theta, I(\hat{\theta})^{-1})$, which implies a t-ratio of $\frac{\hat{\theta} - \theta_0}{I(\hat{\theta})^{1/2}}$. The t-ratio is asymptotically standard normal, so the square of this ratio, the Wald statistic, is asymptotically χ_1^2.

Comparing the Tests

Figure 2.1 displays a simplified geometric interpretation of the three test statistics. In this example θ_0 represents the hypothesized or restricted value, sometimes called the null. From here we can see that the likelihood ratio (LR) represents the difference in the value of the log-likelihood function evaluated at its unrestricted maximum and evaluated at θ_0. The Lagrange multiplier (LM) test is the slope of the log-likelihood evaluated at θ_0, while the Wald (W) statistic is the difference between $\hat{\theta}$ and θ_0.

The likelihood ratio, score, and Wald tests all seek to describe how the likelihood changes as we impose restrictions on a relatively narrow class of models. All rely on standard regularity assumptions in order to derive limiting distributions. All three tests are equivalent given a large enough sample.

The relative strengths and weaknesses of these three tools were more important when computing power was scarce and model estimation tedious and computationally expensive. For example, the likelihood ratio test enables the construction of likelihood-based confidence intervals. But the likelihood ratio requires fitting (at least) two different models, whereas the score test and Wald tests have the advantage of requiring the estimation of only one. Score tests are widely used in some time series estimation applications. But in an era of fast computing and cheap data storage, this advantage is not what it once was. Moreover, it is rare that we have one and only one model under consideration.

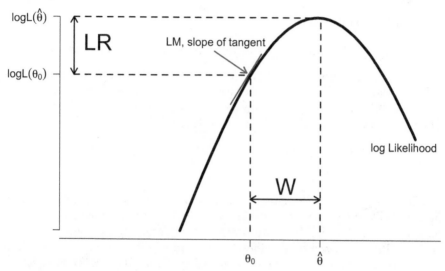

FIGURE 2.1 Geometrical interpretation of the likelihood ratio (LR), Lagrange mulitplier/score (LM), and the Wald (W) test statistics.

Typically we are interested in several working models that we must evaluate and choose among.

In small samples and particular situations, there can be other differences between the tests. The Wald test, in particular, calculates $I(\hat{\theta})$ using the actual, observed MLE rather than assuming that θ_0 represents the correct model. In other words, there are two approximations involved with the Wald test, one for the estimate of the MLE and a second for the approximation of the variance. This can lead to some strange results in small samples. A second drawback for the Wald test is that it can yield different answers under re-parameterizations of θ, something that should not affect the MLE.

All three of these diagnostic tools are firmly rooted in the null hypothesis testing framework in which the analyst proposes a specific value for θ and then considers the probability of witnessing a value at least as great as those if the null were correct. While this method of reasoning has its virtues it also has drawbacks, not least that the null hypothesis is arbitrary, overly specific, and becomes increasingly likely to be rejected as $n \to \infty$. In evaluating model fit and adequacy we have better tools, some of which also build on the likelihood function.

2.3.3 Akaike Information Criterion (AIC) and the Bayesian Information Criterion (BIC)

The maximized likelihood, $\hat{\mathcal{L}}$, serves as the basis for two more recently developed diagnostic quantities: AIC and BIC.

Definition 2.10 (AIC). The Akaike Information Criterion, AIC, is given as

$$\text{AIC} = -2\log\hat{\mathcal{L}} + 2k,$$

where k is the number of estimated parameters in the fitted model.

The Bayesian Information Criterion, known as BIC or, occasionally, the Schwarz Bayesian Criterion, is another model diagnostic. At the theoretical level, the BIC is an approximation to the Bayes factor – the posterior odds of two models, each conditional on the observed data.

Definition 2.11 (BIC). The BIC is defined as

$$\text{BIC} = -2\log\hat{\mathcal{L}} + k\log n.$$

For both of these information criteria, smaller values are "better." Just as in the likelihood values on which they are based, neither the AIC nor BIC have meaningful scale. They are useful in comparison only. Since both the AIC and BIC are based on likelihoods, they can be differenced across models *holding observed data constant*. Both the AIC and the BIC penalize models for greater complexity, unlike the LR and other such tests. Holding the maximized likelihood fixed, both criteria prefer simpler models with fewer parameters. Inspecting the two formulas, it is easy to see that that BIC imposes a higher penalty than the AIC so long as $n \geq 8$ or, in other words, almost all the time. Neither of these information criteria has a limiting distribution, so there is no need to specify particular null models or hypotheses. Rather, these criteria are better thought of in the context of selecting among a series of working models.

2.4 WHAT IF THE LIKELIHOOD IS WRONG?

Many of the MLE's desirable properties are predicated on the untestable assumption that our probability model correctly captured some objective, "true" DGP. If the model is wrong, then parameter estimates can be (but are not necessarily) biased and inconsistent. So what, then, is the MLE estimating?

Suppose we specify a probability model $f(x; \theta)$, but some other $g(x)$ describes the true DGP. The MLE is then $\hat{\theta} = \arg\max_{\theta} \text{E}_g[\mathcal{L}(\theta \mid \mathbf{x})]$, where the expectation is taken over the unknown distribution, $g(x)$. If the regularity conditions invoked for $f(x)$ also apply to $g(x)$, we have $\text{E}_g[S(\hat{\theta})] = 0$. In other words, the MLE is doing the best it can given the constraints of the probability model assumed.

How good is this approximation? Or, equivalently, how costly is a particular distributional assumption? This is not a question that can be answered in a vacuum, disconnected from plausible competing models and actual data. Rather, this challenge highlights how important it is that we state and critically evaluate modeling assumptions *in a specific application*. In the likelihood framework this is achieved by comparing models using the diagnostics just described, particularly AIC and BIC, which do not rely on formal null hypotheses. An alternative, complementary, and arguably more flexible strategy involves using working models to generate predicted values, the correctness of which can be used to adjudicate among competing sets of assumptions. We take up this strategy in detail in Chapter 5.

2.4.1 Robust Variance and Standard Errors

Under certain circumstances we can develop corrections for some misspecification problems. If $\hat{\theta}$ is still consistent for θ^* under the misspecified model, then we can arrive at the correct variance estimates (asymptotically). Such a variance estimate is said to be "robust" to this particular form of model misspecification. Formally:

> **Theorem 2.11.** *Let* $\mathbf{x} = (x_1,\ldots,x_n)$ *form an i.i.d. sample from unknown* $g(x)$. *Let* $\hat{\theta}$ *be a consistent estimator of* θ^* *under the assumed probability model,* $f(x;\theta^*)$. *Then*
>
> $$\sqrt{n}(\hat{\theta}_n - \theta^*) \xrightarrow{d} \mathcal{N}\left(0, \mathcal{I}(\theta^*)^{-1}\Omega\mathcal{I}(\theta^*)^{-1}\right).$$
>
> *where*
>
> $$\Omega = E_g\left[S(\theta)S(\theta)^\mathsf{T}\right]\big|_{\theta^*}$$
> $$\mathcal{I}(\theta^*) = -E_g\left[H(\theta)\right]\big|_{\theta^*}.$$

We say that $\hat{\theta}_n \overset{\cdot}{\sim} \mathcal{N}\left(\theta^*, \mathcal{I}(\theta^*)^{-1}\Omega\mathcal{I}(\theta^*)^{-1}\right)$.

Theorems 2.11 and 2.9 look nearly identical and their proofs proceed in similar fashions (i.e., Taylor expansion around the MLE). The key difference is that in Theorem 2.11 the expectation is taken with respect to all possible data, which is governed by unknown distribution or mass function $g(\mathbf{x})$; in Theorem 2.9 we assumed that we had the distributional assumptions correct. If our assumption about the DGP is correct and $g(\mathbf{x}) = f(\mathbf{x})$, then the term $\mathcal{I}(\theta^*)^{-1}\Omega\mathcal{I}(\theta^*)^{-1}$ collapses to the conventional inverse Fisher information, $\mathcal{I}(\theta^*)^{-1}$.

In actual estimation we replace the expectations by their corresponding sample analogues, i.e.,

$$\hat{\Omega} = \frac{1}{n}\sum_{i=1}^{n} S(\hat{\theta} \mid x_i)S(\hat{\theta} \mid x_i)^\mathsf{T}$$

$$I(\hat{\theta}) = -\frac{1}{n}\sum_{i=1}^{n} H_i(\hat{\theta}) = -\frac{1}{n}\sum_{i=1}^{n}\frac{\partial}{\partial\theta}S(\hat{\theta} \mid x_i)$$

The variance estimator $I(\hat{\theta})^{-1}\hat{\Omega}I(\hat{\theta})^{-1}$ is referred to as a *sandwich variance estimator*, since $\hat{\Omega}$ is sandwiched between the inverse information matrices. The sandwich estimator yields MLE variance estimates that are (asymptotically) correct, even when the specification for the likelihood is incorrect. This seems, at first glance, to be a powerful result (due to Huber (1967)). Indeed, many papers report robust standard errors of various types, relying, at least implicitly, on Huber's result. Social scientists seem justifiably worried that their data contain dependencies that might affect inference. But they also seem willing to believe that their models for the conditional mean are correct. As Freedman (2006) points out, if the model itself is misspecified, then the parameter estimates are likely biased and this problem will not go away with more data. If the model is correct, we have no need for variance corrections in the first place. Having more "correct" standard errors around a biased estimate may be of dubious value.

Robust Standard Errors: Specific

The variance of the OLS estimator is expressed as:

$$\text{var}(\hat{\boldsymbol{\beta}}^{\text{OLS}}) = (\mathbf{X}^{\mathsf{T}}\mathbf{X})^{-1}\mathbf{X}^{\mathsf{T}}\text{E}(\boldsymbol{\varepsilon}\boldsymbol{\varepsilon}^{\mathsf{T}})\mathbf{X}(\mathbf{X}^{\mathsf{T}}\mathbf{X})^{-1}.$$

By assuming homoskedasticity we can substitute $\sigma^2\mathbf{I}$ for $\text{E}(\boldsymbol{\varepsilon}\boldsymbol{\varepsilon}^{\mathsf{T}})$ and simplify this expression considerably. But what if that assumption is wrong? If the error variance is nonconstant but all our other assumptions are satisfied, then we will continue to have a consistent estimator for $\boldsymbol{\beta}$, but we will end up with incorrect standard errors and possibly erroneous inference. White (1980) proposed using the OLS residuals to estimate $\text{E}(\boldsymbol{\varepsilon}\boldsymbol{\varepsilon}^{\mathsf{T}})$, specifically by proposing $\mathbf{V}$ where $\text{diag}(\mathbf{V}) = \hat{\varepsilon}_i^2$. Thus the Huber-White heteroskedastic consistent covariance estimator is given by

$$\text{var}_{\text{hc}}(\hat{\boldsymbol{\beta}}^{\text{OLS}}) = (\mathbf{X}^{\mathsf{T}}\mathbf{X})^{-1}\mathbf{X}^{\mathsf{T}}\mathbf{V}\mathbf{X}(\mathbf{X}^{\mathsf{T}}\mathbf{X})^{-1}.$$

It is possible to motivate and derive robust standard errors for the linear regression model without appealing to likelihood theory. But, from a likelihood perspective, it is straightforward to verify that $\mathbf{X}^{\mathsf{T}}\mathbf{X}$ is the Fisher information for the homoskedastic linear-normal regression model. Heteroskedasticity-corrected standard errors are a form of robust sandwich estimators.

2.5 CONCLUSION

We derived the important features of MLEs that we will rely upon in subsequent chapters. First, we highlighted that parametric models require the assumption of a specific probability model. These distributional assumptions must be stated and evaluated. In the subsequent chapters we will present out-of-sample heuristics from which we can make pragmatic judgments about modeling assumptions. Once a model is specified, we showed how the MLE, under general conditions, is asymptotically consistent and normally distributed. The covariance of the asymptotic distribution is given by the negative inverse of the log-likelihood's Hessian matrix, evaluated at the MLE. We also discussed existing tools for evaluating and diagnosing in-sample model fit. These tools include the likelihood ratio, score, and Wald statistics that rely on asymptotic reasoning and null hypothesis testing. But we also have the AIC and BIC that are specifically geared to comparing competing working models without resorting to arbitrary null hypotheses.

The results presented in this chapter assume that the probability model satisfies basic regularity conditions. Although the models we discuss in the remainder of this volume are "regular" likelihoods, those sculpted for specific analysis problems may not be. Or if they are they may still present a challenging likelihood surface for numerical optimization programs. When using such tools we must be careful to establish that the likelihood function is "regular" near the MLE. Graphical tools are usually best here.

2.6 FURTHER READING

Past Work

Aldrich (1997) provides a history of Fisher's development and justifications of maximum likelihood. See Pawitan (2013, ch. 1) and Stigler (2007) for excellent intellectual histories of the development of the theory and method of maximum likelihood in the mid-20th century.

Hirotugu Akaike (1981) notes that "AIC is an acronym for 'an information criterion'," despite it often being denoted Akaike's Information Criterion (Akaike, 1976, 42).

Advanced Study

Edwards (1992) argues for a fully developed likelihood paradigm for all scientific inference, focussing on the complete likelihood function rather than just the MLE. LeCam (1990) collects and summarizes several examples of how the likelihood approach can go awry by way of establishing "Principle 0: Don't trust any principle." See Mayo (2014) with the associated discussion for a critical treatment of the likelihood principle. More general and rigorous proofs of several results in this chapter can be found in standard advanced texts such as Greene (2011) and Cox and Barndorff-Nielsen (1994). General and rigorous treatments of basic probability concepts, the Law of Large Numbers, the Central Limit Theorem, and other elementary topics can be found in Resnick (2014).

The sandwich variance estimator has been extended in numerous ways, particularly to data that are "clustered" in space or time. See, for example, Cameron et al. (2008); Cameron and Miller (2015). King and Roberts (2014) argue that the divergence between robust and conventional standard errors can be used as a diagnostic tool for model misspecification, but see also Aronow (2016).

Software Notes

Several $\mathcal{R}$ libraries implement various robust and clustered standard error estimators for a variety of different models and data structures. These include clusterSEs (Esarey, 2017), pcse (Bailey and Katz, 2011), plm (Croissant and Millo, 2008), rms (Harrell, Jr., 2017), and sandwich (Zeileis, 2004).

3

Maximum Likelihood for Binary Outcomes

3.1 BINARY RESPONSES

The normal distribution is the starting place for many analyses for a variety of good reasons: it arises naturally in repeated sampling situations; it is flexible; and it crops up frequently in nature. But many concepts in social science and public policy are inherently categorical or bounded. Voting is often a choice between two (frequently terrible) discrete alternatives. By and large, survey respondents are in or out of the labor force; individuals are married or not married. Countries experience a civil war or they do not. In some cases, there may be a plausibly continuous range of values that are interesting, such as the level of conflict between two countries, but we may only observe that quantity if it is sufficiently large to be recognizable as a militarized dispute or a war. In these examples, observations contain information about social phenomena measured at a binary level. Often, this is recorded as 0 for no/not/absent and 1 for yes/present, but these numbers are a convenience, not a necessary structure. Votes in the US Senate are recorded as *Yea* and *Nay*, for example, and, by convention, translated into 1*s* and 0*s*. But the translation could be to any two arbitrary digits or symbols because it is not the numerical characteristics we can use. The 1s are not one unit larger than the 0s. Rather, these two digits are used in a set theoretic fashion: cases are in the set of 1s or in the set of 0s, exclusively and exhaustively.

Binary data can be organized in a variety of ways, among which two are dominant. The social sciences traditionally use a case-based orientation, in which each row is an individual case and each column represents a variable on which each case is observed. It is common in other fields (e.g., medicine) to organize the data by the covariate class or stratum, with the binary variable reported as the number of "successes" among the total number of cases in each class. Table 3.1 illustrates these two data structures.

TABLE 3.1 *Alternative data structures for binary data.*

	Covariates		Response	Covariates	Class Size	Response
Case	$x_{i,1}$	$x_{i,2}$	y_i	$(x_1,x_2)_k$	m_k	y_k
i	Gender	Employed	Voted	(Gender, Employed)		Voted
1	M	yes	no	$(M,yes)_1$	2	1
2	M	no	yes	$(M,no)_2$	4	3
3	M	no	no	$(F,yes)_3$	1	0
4	F	yes	no	$(F,no)_4$	2	1
5	F	no	no			
6	F	no	yes			
7	M	no	yes			
8	M	no	yes			
9	M	yes	yes			

In the left panel of Table 3.1 we see the traditional case-based orientation. On the right, we display the same data using the grouped binary data orientation. Responses are reported in the form of the number of successes (y_k) in each of k covariate classes, out of m_k possible successes, such that $0 \leq y_k \leq m_k$.

Grouped versus ungrouped is an important distinction even though the underlying binary data may be identical. Ungrouped (case-based) data has a natural connection with the Bernoulli distribution, whereas grouped data are easily described using the closely related binomial distribution. With grouped data, the normal approximation is more readily useful; asymptotic assumptions can be based on imagining that m or n approach ∞, although grouped data become increasingly cumbersome as the number of covariates (and therefore combinations thereof) increase, especially when covariates are continuously valued.

This simple example holds another tiny point that will reemerge often in the analysis of nominal data: more often than not, the data are not actually recorded as numbers but as discrete categories of labels, often referred to as *factors*. Some software packages deal with this nuance automatically, but often the analyst must translate these words into integers. For the record, the integer 1 is almost always the code for the occurrence of the event in probability space.

3.2 BINARY DATA

As a running example, we consider the Mroz (1987) study of female labor force participation. Although the example is a bit dated, the data have several attributes that make them worth revisiting here. Mroz analyzed data taken from the Panel Study of Income Dynamics (PSID) on 753 women and their experience in the labor market in 1975. Mroz was interested in female labor

TABLE 3.2 *Select variables from Long's (1997) reexamination of Mroz's (1987) female labor force participation study.*

Variable Name	Description
LFP	1 if respondent is in paid labor force; else 0
young kids	Number of children younger than 6
school kids	Number of children ages 6 to 18
age	Age in years
college	1 if attended college; else 0
wage	Woman's expected after tax wage rate (logged)

force participation, i.e., the decision to seek employment in the formal paid labor market. For this example we use five of the variables described in Long (1997, p. 37), as shown in Table 3.2.

3.2.1 Odds, Odds Ratios, and Relative Risk

Odds are one way of expressing probabilities. If you flip a (fair) coin twice, what is the probability of getting two heads? The probability is $\frac{1}{2} \times \frac{1}{2} = 0.25$, but we might also say that the *odds* are one-to-three. In other words we should expect one pair of heads for every three "failures." Formally,

$$\omega_i \equiv \text{Odds}(y_i = 1) = \frac{\Pr(y_i = 1)}{1 - \Pr(y_i = 1)}.$$

Notice that probabilities and odds are both bounded by zero at the lower end. But odds are unbounded at the upper end, while probabilities are bounded by 1; this means that the odds are not symmetric, but skewed. As a result, the odds is frequently made even more odd by taking the natural logarithm:

$$\log \omega_i = \log \left[\frac{\Pr(y_i = 1)}{1 - \Pr(y_i = 1)} \right].$$

Another less commonly used but arguably more intuitive quantity is *relative risk*, also called the *risk ratio*. Relative risk is simply the probability of one event divided by the probability of another. In the coin example the probability of two heads is the same as the probability of two tails, so the relative risk is 1.

The Mroz data consists of 753 married white women between the ages of 30 and 60, 428 of whom were in the paid labor force at some time during 1975. The probability of a white American woman being in the labor force in 1975, p, is estimated by the proportion of women in the sample who participated in the labor force during that year, $\hat{p} = \frac{428}{753} = 0.568$. By extension, the probability that a woman is not employed would be estimated as $1 - \hat{p} = 0.432$. The ratio

TABLE 3.3 *Labor force participation and the number of young children.*

| | Young Children | | | |
In Labor Force?	0	1	2	3
No	231	72	19	3
Yes	375	46	7	0
Odds of LFP	1.62	0.64	0.37	0.00
Risk, relative to 0 young children	1.00	0.63	0.44	0.00

of these two numbers is the odds, ω. The odds of a woman being employed in these data is:

$$\hat{\omega} = \frac{\hat{p}}{1 - \hat{p}} = \frac{0.568}{1 - 0.568} = 1.3,$$

which means that it is about 30% more likely that a woman is employed than not.

Consider the following data from the Mroz study, given in Table 3.3. How does the probability that a woman has young children influence her odds of being a paid participant in the labor force? Compare the odds for being in the labor for women with no young children, to those with one young child. Such calculations are given as:

- The probability of labor force participation (LFP) for a woman with *zero* young children is $\hat{p}_0 = \frac{375}{(375+231)} = 0.619$, which implies the odds of $\hat{\omega}_0 = \frac{0.619}{1-0.619} = 1.62$.

- The probability of LFP for a woman with *one* young child is $\hat{p}_1 = \frac{46}{(46+72)} = 0.39$, which implies the odds of $\hat{\omega}_0 = \frac{0.39}{1-0.39} = 0.64$. Her risk of LFP relative to a woman with no young children is $\frac{0.39}{0.619} = 0.63$.

- The probability of LFP for a woman with *two* young children is $\hat{p}_2 = \frac{7}{(7+19)} = 0.27$, which implies the odds of $\hat{\omega}_0 = \frac{0.27}{1-0.27} = 0.37$. Her risk of LFP relative to a woman with no young children is $\frac{0.27}{0.619} = 0.44$.

- The probability of employment for a woman with *three* young children is $\hat{p}_3 = \frac{0}{(3)} = 0.0$, which implies the odds of $\hat{\omega}_0 = \frac{0}{1-0.0} = 0.0$. Her risk of LFP relative to a woman with no young children is $\frac{0}{0.619} = 0$.

This illustrates that the odds of being employed are about 1.6 (to 1) for women with no young children, whereas these odds fall to about 0.6 for those with just one child younger than six years of age, and further fall to approximately 0.4 if there are two young children. A woman with one young child has a 37% lower probability of being in the labor force than a woman with no young children.

In some fields, especially medicine, people are interested in the *odds-ratio*. For example, the odds-ratio for being employed given you have zero versus one young child is simply $\frac{1.62}{0.64} = 2.56$, which means that the odds a woman is employed if she has no young children is about two and one-half times the odds of her being employed if she has a single child under five. Similarly, a woman with one young child is not quite twice as likely to be employed as a woman with two young children ($\frac{0.64}{0.37} = 1.73$). But all these women are *enormously* more likely to be employed than a woman with three young children under five.

The odds are notoriously difficult to describe and interpret. There is extensive empirical work documenting how people's interpretation of risk assessments, including the odds and odds ratios, do not coincide with probability theory.

3.3 THE LINEAR PROBABILITY MODEL

The *linear probability model* fits a linear regression model to a binary response variable, often using OLS. Mroz (1987) is a famous application of the linear probability model. In this section we follow Long (1997), showing what can go wrong with pressing the OLS button when your dependent variable cannot be considered unbounded, much less normally distributed.

We fit a linear regression model with LFP as the dependent variable and the four other variables as predictors. While recognizing that the dependent variable is binary, the OLS estimates produce what is called a linear probability model, which is specified as

$$\Pr(Y_i = 1 \mid \mathbf{x}_i) = \mathbf{x}_i^{\mathsf{T}} \boldsymbol{\beta}$$

where $\mathbf{X} = (1, \text{young kids, school kids, age, college})$, i.e., a matrix with a row for each observation and a column for each of the four independent variables along with a vector of ones for the intercept. The term $\mathbf{x}_i$ is a vector of length 5 for observation i. The vector $\boldsymbol{\beta} = (\beta_0, \beta_1, \beta_2, \beta_3, \beta_4)$ contains the intercept and slope parameters to be estimated. Using OLS to fit the model produces the results presented in Table 3.4.

This table shows that families with more children under age five are less likely to have a female in the paid labor force, at least in 1975. The estimated coefficient for this relationship is -0.3. One might be tempted to state that each child under five will reduce by about 0.3 the probability that a woman will be in the paid labor force.

A negative relationship seems reasonable, but the model predicts that a mother of 3-year-old quintuplets will have a negative probability of being in the labor force. While holding a full-time paid job seems difficult in such a situation, can the probability be less than zero? In the observed data the

48 *Maximum Likelihood for Binary Outcomes*

TABLE 3.4 *Linear probability model of labor force participation (LFP) as a function of five independent variables plus an intercept.*

	$\hat{\beta}$	$\sigma_{\hat{\beta}}$	*t*-Ratio	*p*-Value
intercept	1.10	0.13	16.53	0.00
young kids	−0.30	0.04	−8.37	0.00
school kids	−0.02	0.01	−1.17	0.24
age	−0.01	0.00	−5.60	0.00
college	0.13	0.04	3.19	0.00
wage	0.12	0.03	3.82	0.00
n	753			
$\hat{\sigma}$	0.46			
$\overline{R}^2$	0.13			

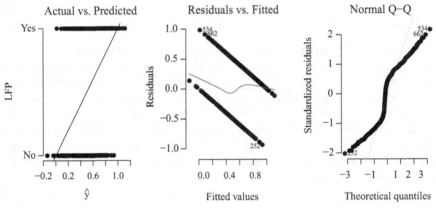

FIGURE 3.1 Diagnostic plots of the linear probability model described in Table 3.4.

model produces many predictions outside the [0,1] interval. Three predicted probabilities are below zero, with the largest at −0.14, indicating that one woman has a negative fourteen percent chance of being employed, clearly nonsensical. Similarly, there are five predictions that are greater than one, including the largest at 1.12.

It is clear that the linear probability model can and will produce results that are nonsensical and difficult to explain to the secretary of labor should she ask you how you arrived at a negative probability. Other problems arising with the LPM appear in the diagnostic plots in Figure 3.1. The left panel shows the dependent variable plotted against the predicted values of the dependent variable, along with the line representing the regression line. All the true values of the dependent variable are at the top and the bottom of this plot, but the prediction line takes on continuous, linear values both inside the range [0, 1] and outside. The middle panel shows two clusters of residuals, one representing the values when the predicted values are subtracted from 1, another when predicted values are subtracted from 0. These residuals clearly cannot be normally distributed, nor do several other conditions for the linear model remain credible. In particular, the variance of the residuals around the regression line is not constant but is rather grouped in two clumps that correspond to the 1s and 0s in the data. The model is heteroskedastic by construction since the calculated variance of the dependent variable as estimated depends not only on the values of the independent variables but also on the estimated values of the parameters $(\hat{\beta})$. The bottom line is that the model produces results that are nonsensical in the domain of prediction, even if the coefficients may remain unbiased.

In short, the LPM:

- runs the risk of making nonsensical predictions. If any of the predicted probabilities from the LPM are outside the $[0, 1]$ interval, then the OLS estimate of the LPM is biased and inconsistent (Horrace and Oaxaca, 2006). The more nonsensical predictions the model makes, the more biased the estimates are;
- assumes that the relationship between a covariate and the probability of a success is constant across all values of the covariate;
- will generate residuals with inherent heteroskedasticity that give biased confidence intervals for parameter estimates.

With these weaknesses, why do we still see the LPM employed, especially in some subfields of economics? There are several arguments, some more convincing than others:

- In the situation where we actually have a randomly assigned treatment and all we care about is the average treatment effect, then OLS and logit/probit will give effectively identical answers. Moreover, under binary randomized treatment, the functional form problems do not affect the ability to estimate treatment effects. So why bother with the complications? (Angrist and Pischke, 2009, p. 107)
- Recent emphasis on causal identification has led to a reliance on so-called fixed effects in short panels and a myopic focus on "marginal effects." These are arguably better implemented in an OLS framework. Similarly, *instrumental variables* strategies are currently easier to implement and have some desirable properties under a LPM. We do not discuss these topics in this volume.
- Heckman and Snyder, Jr. (1997) provide a rigorous justification for the LPM as an exact representation of a specific class of random-utility models which impose asymmetric random shocks on decision makers' utilities. In other words, the LPM is sometimes an attractive procedure for theoretical or aesthetic reasons.
- Some argue that the LPM is a simple approach that is feasible when there are too many observations to maximize a likelihood, even with modern

computing power. One colleague ran a logistic regression on a database with 50 million observations, using SAS. So if you have more than $50,000,000$ cases, maybe this is justifiable.

- The LPM will not necessarily give nonsensical predictions in all situations, so in cases where this does not happen it may be useful. But how can you know this unless you actually check the alternative?

- Standard errors can be "corrected" ex post for the heteroskedasticity (see Section 2.4.1), so the biased standard error problem goes away. However, you can transform virtually anything post-estimation.

- Some argue for the LPM because of the apparent arbitrariness of the distributional assumptions of logit and probit models, relying on the fact that classical OLS makes weaker distributional assumptions about Y and the error process.

- Some argue that LPM coefficients are "easy" to interpret, whereas regression coefficients for logit or probit are "hard" or require more effort to communicate to audiences.

Our position is that statistical models are fit for a variety of reasons, only some of which have causal identification as their objective. Ultimately any statistical model is a description of a DGP that combines data and a set of assumptions. As such, we favor evaluating statistical models using comparative, predictive heuristics as we discuss in detail in Chapter 5. This emphasis on model comparison and prediction generally leads us to prefer versions of logit and probit in most applied circumstances. Logit and probit models may have drawbacks in some situations, but, in our experience the LPM is virtually never a superior *predictive* model for binary data.

3.4 THE LOGIT MODEL, A.K.A. LOGISTIC REGRESSION

What if we made different assumptions about the process generating our (binary) data? The logit model is one way of doing so.

The introduction of logistic regression is typically attributed to David Cox (1958). Cox credits the introduction of the term to Joseph Berkson. The *logit* transformation relies on the odds, as developed above, to map a probability into the unbounded real line. A logit transformation of the variable $p \in [0, 1]$ is given as the log of the odds:

$$\text{logit}(p) = \log\left(\frac{p}{1-p}\right).$$

The logistic transformation, also known as the inverse logit, accomplishes the goal of mapping real-valued variable, x, into the $[0, 1]$ interval appropriate for probabilities:

$$\text{logit}^{-1}(x) = \frac{e^x}{1+e^x} = \frac{1}{1+e^{-x}}.$$

In the next section, this transformation is used to develop a standard, nonlinear approach to modeling binary dependent variables.

3.4.1 The Logit Model

Binary outcomes are modeled as Bernoulli trials. A Bernoulli random variable (e.g., a coin flip) is defined by a single parameter, θ, which describes the probability of a "success."

Using our standard setup, we can express such a Bernoulli model in terms of two components:

stochastic: $Y_i \sim f_B(y_i; \theta_i)$

or, alternatively,

$$\Pr(Y_i = y_i) = \theta_i^{y_i}(1 - \theta_i)^{1-y_i} = \begin{cases} \theta_i & \text{for} \quad y_i = 1 \\ 1 - \theta_i & \text{for} \quad y_i = 0 \end{cases}$$

and

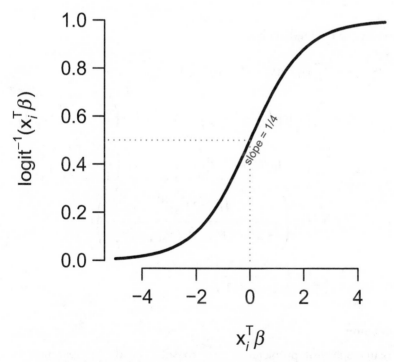

FIGURE 3.2 The logistic function is nonlinear with range bounded by 0 and 1. It is nearly linear in the midrange, but is highly nonlinear towards extrema.

systematic: $\theta_i \equiv \mathrm{logit}^{-1}\left(\mathbf{x}_i^{\mathsf{T}}\boldsymbol{\beta}\right) = \dfrac{1}{1 + e^{-\mathbf{x}_i^{\mathsf{T}}\boldsymbol{\beta}}},$

where for each observation i, Y_i is the binary dependent variable, $\mathbf{x}_i$ is the k-vector of $k - 1$ independent variables and a constant, and $\boldsymbol{\beta}$ is a vector of k regression parameters to be estimated, as always. Since the mean of a Bernoulli variable must be between 0 and 1, the inverse logit function is one way to link the systematic component to the outcome domain. For reference, some presentations will highlight the inverse logit, while others will present material in terms of the logit.

The inverse logit transformation is shown graphically in Figure 3.2. The x-axis represents the value of $\mathbf{x}_i^{\mathsf{T}}\boldsymbol{\beta}$, called the *linear predictor*, while the curve portrays the logistic mapping of these linear predictor values into the $[0, 1]$ probability interval on the y-axis. The midpoint of the line is at a probability of 0.5 on the y-axis. The logistic curve is nearly linear around this point with a slope of approximately $\frac{1}{4}$.

Given the systematic and stochastic components of this kind of model, the joint probability of the data is straightforward:

$$\mathrm{Pr}(\mathbf{y} \mid \boldsymbol{\theta}) = \prod_{i=1}^{n} \theta_i^{y_i}(1 - \theta_i)^{1-y_i}$$

which gives rise to the log-likelihood,

$$\begin{aligned}
\log \mathcal{L}(\boldsymbol{\theta} \mid \mathbf{y}) &= \sum_{i=1}^{n}\left[y_i \log \theta_i + (1 - y_i)\log(1 - \theta_i)\right] \\
&= \sum_{i=1}^{n}\left[y_i \log\left(\frac{1}{1 + e^{-\mathbf{x}_i^{\mathsf{T}}\boldsymbol{\beta}}}\right) + (1 - y_i)\log\left(1 - \frac{1}{1 + e^{-\mathbf{x}_i^{\mathsf{T}}\boldsymbol{\beta}}}\right)\right] \\
&= \sum_{i=1}^{n}\left[-y_i \log(1 + e^{-\mathbf{x}_i^{\mathsf{T}}\boldsymbol{\beta}}) + (1 - y_i)\log\left(\frac{e^{-\mathbf{x}_i^{\mathsf{T}}\boldsymbol{\beta}}}{1 + e^{-\mathbf{x}_i^{\mathsf{T}}\boldsymbol{\beta}}}\right)\right] \\
&= \sum_{i=1}^{n} \log\left(\frac{\left(e^{-\mathbf{x}_i^{\mathsf{T}}\boldsymbol{\beta}}\right)^{(1-y_i)}}{\left(1 + e^{-\mathbf{x}_i^{\mathsf{T}}\boldsymbol{\beta}}\right)^{(1-y_i)}\left(1 + e^{-\mathbf{x}_i^{\mathsf{T}}\boldsymbol{\beta}}\right)^{y_i}}\right) \\
&= \sum_{i=1}^{n} \log\left(\frac{e^{-\mathbf{x}_i^{\mathsf{T}}\boldsymbol{\beta}(1-y_i)}}{1 + e^{-\mathbf{x}_i^{\mathsf{T}}\boldsymbol{\beta}}}\right).
\end{aligned}$$

3.4.2 Estimation

This particular class of problems is easy to solve by the computation of numerical derivatives, but it may be helpful to know that the partial derivative of the log-likelihood with respect to a particular slope parameter, β_j, is given by

R Code Example 3.1 *MLE for Logit*

```
# getting data
colnames(lfp)<-c("LFP","young.kids","school.kids","age",
    "college.woman", "college.man", "wage", "income")
lfp$lfpbin<-rep(0,length(lfp$LFP))
lfp$lfpbin[lfp$LFP=="inLF"]<-1
attach(lfp)
x<-cbind(young.kids, school.kids, age,
    as.numeric(college.woman)-1, wage)
y<-lfpbin

# simple optimization of logit for Mroz data
binreg <- function(X,y){
    X <- cbind(1,X)                 #1s for intercept
    negLL <- function(b,X,y){       #the log-likelihood
        p<-as.vector(1/(1+exp(-X %*% b)))
        - sum(y*log(p) + (1-y)*log(1-p))
        }
    #pass the likelihood to the optimizer
    results <- optim(rep(0,ncol(X)), negLL, hessian=T, method="BFGS", X=X,y=y)
    list(coefficients=results$par,varcovariance=solve(results$hessian),
        deviance=2*results$value,
        converged=results$convergence==0) #output an convergence check.
}

mlebin.fit<-binreg(x,y)
# some results ...
round(mlebin.fit$coefficients,2)
>[1]   2.88  -1.45  -0.09  -0.07   0.61   0.56
```

$$\frac{\partial \log \mathcal{L}}{\partial \beta_j} = \sum_{i=1}^{n} (y_i - \theta_i)x_{ij}.$$

The gradient of the logit log-likelihood is then a vector of k such partial derivatives.

In Example 3.1 we present a simple $\mathcal{R}$ program that implements the logistic regression log-likelihood and finds the MLE. The matrix **X** contains the independent variables from the Mroz study and y holds the 0s and 1s reflecting whether or not each of the 753 women surveyed is an active participant in the wage labor force.

These results can also be obtained more readily via the `glm()` procedure in $\mathcal{R}$. We go in to more of the details of the $\mathcal{R}$ syntax for `glm` in Section 7.3.1 but we introduce it here because the function – and $\mathcal{R}$'s formula notation – is used in subsequent chapters. The `glm` function handles categorical or "factor" variables without forcing the user to translate them into numbers. Estimation and output appear in Example 3.2.

At the top of the $\mathcal{R}$ output in Example 3.2, we see some basic information on the model. "Call" simply reproduces the formula that was used to fit the model, for ease of reference. The next set of numerical results describes the residual

$\mathcal{R}$ Code Example 3.2 *Using* `glm` *to estimate logit*

```
fit.glm<-glm(lfpbin ~ young.kids + school.kids + age +
          college.woman + wage,
             family = binomial(link = "logit"), data = lfpdata)
summary(fit.glm)
#which results in the following output
Call:
glm(formula = lfpbin ~ young.kids + school.kids + age + college.woman +
    wage, family = binomial(link = "logit"), data = lfp)


Deviance Residuals:
    Min        1Q     Median        3Q        Max
-2.0970   -1.1148     0.6463    0.9821     2.2055


Coefficients:
                      Estimate  Std. Error  z value  Pr(>|z|)
(Intercept)            2.87807     0.62291    4.620  3.83e-06
young.kids            -1.44670     0.19363   -7.471  7.94e-14
school.kids           -0.08883     0.06676   -1.331  0.183336
age                   -0.06796     0.01246   -5.452  4.99e-08
college.womanCollege   0.61112     0.19372    3.155  0.001607
wage                   0.55867     0.14893    3.751  0.000176


(Dispersion parameter for binomial family taken to be 1)

Null deviance: 1029.75  on 752  degrees of freedom
Residual deviance:  925.31  on 747  degrees of freedom
AIC: 937.31

Number of Fisher Scoring iterations: 4
```

distribution. The default is for `glm` to return *deviance residuals*, which is each observation's contribution to the residual deviance as defined in Section 2.3. We can see here that the deviance residuals are not centered on 0 and do not appear to be symmetric.

The main output is the description of the regression coefficients and their estimated standard errors. Below that $\mathcal{R}$ tells us that it fit a canonical Generalized Linear Model with an assumed dispersion parameter; we take this up in Chapter 7. The bottom section of the output displays basic model fit information, including the AIC. Finally, the summary output tells us how many steps the optimizer needed to arrive at its answer. In this case, it was four; we go into details in the next chapter.

3.4.3 Output and Interpretation

The standard output from a logistic regression is the same as for most regression models, a BUTON, shown in Table 3.5 and reproducing (in a cleaned-up form) the information returned by $\mathcal{R}$'s `summary` command.

TABLE 3.5 *Logit estimation of female labor force participation (LFP).*

	$\hat{\beta}$	$\sigma_{\hat{\beta}}$	z-Ratio	p-Value
intercept	2.88	0.62	4.62	0.00
young kids	−1.45	0.19	−7.47	0.00
school kids	−0.09	0.07	−1.33	0.18
age	−0.07	0.01	−5.45	0.00
college	0.61	0.19	3.16	0.00
wage	0.56	0.15	3.75	0.00
n	753			
AIC	937			

While the signs and p-values of these estimates are similar to those found using the LPM, the estimates themselves are quite different. These estimates, as presented in the table, require more care in interpretation for two basic reasons. First, the underlying model is nonlinear, so, unlike OLS, the effect of a particular covariate on the response is not constant across all levels of the independent variable. To see this, we calculate the *marginal effect*, or the rate of change of the outcome variable with respect to a particular independent variable, x_k. We take the derivative of the systematic component with respect to the independent variable of interest:

$$\frac{\partial E[Y_i]}{\partial x_{ki}} = \frac{\partial \theta_i}{\partial x_{ki}} = \beta_k \frac{\exp(\mathbf{x}_i^T \boldsymbol{\beta})}{\left(1 + \exp(\mathbf{x}_i^T \boldsymbol{\beta})\right)^2}.$$

This equation shows that the change in the predicted outcome induced by a change in x_k is reflected not just in the regression coefficient β_k. The marginal effect also depends on the value of x_k *and the values of all the other covariates in the model*. In other words, a variable's marginal effect in a logit model is not constant; it depends on the covariate values at which it is evaluated.

As a first-order approximation, we can use the fact that the logistic curve is steepest in the middle. Since the slope of the inverse logit is 0.25 at that point, dividing $\hat{\beta}_k$ by 4 gives an estimate of the maximum difference a one-unit change in x_k can induce in the probability of a success (Gelman and Hill, 2007, p. 82). Thus, an additional young child reduces the probability of labor force participation by about 40%, i.e., $\frac{-1.45}{4} = -0.4$.

Second, the logit model is a linear regression on the log odds. As a result, the exponentiated regression coefficients are odds ratios; a coefficient greater than 1 represents an increase in the relative probability of obtaining a 1 in the dependent variable. An exponentiated coefficient less than 1 represents a decrease in the probability of, in this case, being employed.

This exponentiation trick can be useful for analysts, but if you want to confuse someone – say a student, client, or journalist – try describing your results in terms of either log odds or odds ratios. In some fields, such as medicine, these are routinely reported, and scholars in these fields seem to have a firm handle on their meaning, but in general it is better to interpret your results in terms of the original scales on which the data were measured. To this end, two different approaches have evolved for interpreting logistic regression results on the probability scale.

The Method of "First Differences"

The method of first differences estimates the "effect" of x_k on E[Y] by calculating the change in the predicted Y for different values of x_k. The method is generally useful if the analyst is interested in interpreting and evaluating the regression coefficients near the central tendencies of the independent variables. In calculating central tendencies we typically employ the median for ordered or continuous variables and the mode for categorical variables, although other choices are certainly possible. The central tendencies for all independent variables in the Mroz data are displayed in the first column of Table 3.6. The abbreviations in parentheses are used in some equations below.

Using these values in combination with the estimated coefficients facilitates calculation of a predicted probability for a "typical" respondent. That respondent is represented as a set of specific values for the covariates: a 42 and one-half year old woman, with no young children, but one child between 6 and 18. She has not attended college, and her log wage rate is 1.1. This vector of covariate values represents a specific *scenario* on which to calculate the model's implications.

In the Mroz example, we can evaluate the probability of being in the labor force depending on whether the woman attended college, holding all the other independent variables at their respective central tendencies. We let $\bar{x}_{-coll}$ represent the vector of central tendencies for all variables except college education. If we are interested in the implied consequence of having attended college, we difference the following two equations:

TABLE 3.6 *The central tendencies (medians and modes) for the variables included in the analysis of labor force participation in Table 3.5.*

Variable	Central Tendency (full)	No College	College
intercept	1.00	1.00	1.00
young kids (k5)	0.00	0.00	0.00
school kids (k618)	1.00	1.00	1.00
age	42.54	43.00	41.50
college (coll)	0.00	0.00	1.00
wage	1.10	0.98	1.40

$$\Pr\left(y = 1 \mid \text{coll} = 0, \overline{\mathbf{x}}_{\neg\text{coll}}\right)$$

$$= \frac{\exp(\hat{\beta}_0 + \hat{\beta}_1\overline{k5} + \hat{\beta}_2\overline{k618} + \hat{\beta}_3\overline{age} + \hat{\beta}_4 * 0 + \hat{\beta}_5\overline{wage})}{1 + \exp(\hat{\beta}_0 + \hat{\beta}_1\overline{k5} + \hat{\beta}_2\overline{k618} + \hat{\beta}_3\overline{age} + \hat{\beta}_4 * 0 + \hat{\beta}_5\overline{wage})}$$

$$\Pr\left(y = 1 \mid \text{coll} = 1, \overline{\mathbf{x}}_{\neg\text{coll}}\right)$$

$$= \frac{\exp(\hat{\beta}_0 + \hat{\beta}_1\overline{k5} + \hat{\beta}_2\overline{k618} + \hat{\beta}_3\overline{age} + \hat{\beta}_4 * 1 + \hat{\beta}_6\overline{wage})}{1 + \exp(\hat{\beta}_0 + \hat{\beta}_1\overline{k5} + \hat{\beta}_2\overline{k618} + \hat{\beta}_3\overline{age} + \hat{\beta}_4 * 1 + \hat{\beta}_6\overline{wage})},$$

which more simply (and generally) is

$$\Pr\left(y = 1 \mid \text{coll} = 0, \overline{\mathbf{x}}_{\neg\text{coll}}\right) = \left. \frac{\exp\left(\overline{\mathbf{x}}^{\mathsf{T}}_{\neg\text{coll}}\hat{\boldsymbol{\beta}}\right)}{1 + \exp\left(\overline{\mathbf{x}}^{\mathsf{T}}_{\neg\text{coll}}\hat{\boldsymbol{\beta}}\right)} \right|_{\text{coll}=0}$$

$$\Pr\left(y = 1 \mid \text{coll} = 1, \overline{\mathbf{x}}_{\neg\text{coll}}\right) = \left. \frac{\exp\left(\overline{\mathbf{x}}^{\mathsf{T}}_{\neg\text{coll}}\hat{\boldsymbol{\beta}}\right)}{1 + \exp\left(\overline{\mathbf{x}}^{\mathsf{T}}_{\neg\text{coll}}\hat{\boldsymbol{\beta}}\right)} \right|_{\text{coll}=1}.$$

Substituting these values into the linear predictor, $\mathbf{x}_i^{\mathsf{T}}\hat{\boldsymbol{\beta}}$, and then using the inverse logit transformation, we calculate $\hat{\theta}_i$ for this "typical" respondent as 0.63. A similar calculation in which the woman attended college produces 0.75. The difference between these two scenarios is 0.13; the model predicts that having attended college increases the probability of being in the labor force by 20%, holding all the other measured attributes of the woman at "typical" levels.

But suppose we want to take account of the fact that women in the sample who have attended college look different than those who did not on a variety of dimensions. For example, Table 3.6 shows that college-attending women have a median wage rate of 1.4, against a median of 0.98 for women who did not attend. To make a comparison in this case we construct two more scenarios. In the first the values of the covariates take on those for a "typical" woman who never attended college, as shown in the second column of Table 3.6. The model predicts that such a woman has a 0.60 probability of being in the labor force. The second scenario uses the typical covariate values for college-attending women, as displayed in the third column of the table. This woman is predicted to have a 0.79 probability of being in the labor force, for a difference of 0.19 between these scenarios. The typical women who attended college in 1973 was 24% more likely to be in the labor force than the typical woman who did not.

These examples illustrate how the interpretation of nonlinear models requires the analyst to decide what types of comparisons best illustrate the model's implications for the purpose at hand. The structure of the model reinforces a more general point: there is no single-number summary that communicates all the model's interesting insights.

The basic approach to first differences is accomplished in a small number of computationally tedious steps:

1. Construct two (or more) scenarios, each embodied in a different vector of values for the covariates. Let $\mathbf{x}_\alpha$ represent the vector of the independent values for the first scenario and $\mathbf{x}_\omega$ be the second scenario.
2. If the model function is defined as m, the first difference is
   $m\left(\mathbf{x}_\alpha \mid \hat{\boldsymbol{\beta}}\right) - m\left(\mathbf{x}_\omega \mid \hat{\boldsymbol{\beta}}\right)$. For a logistic regression this is simply
   $\frac{1}{1+e^{-\mathbf{x}_\alpha^T \hat{\boldsymbol{\beta}}}} - \frac{1}{1+e^{-\mathbf{x}_\omega^T \hat{\boldsymbol{\beta}}}}$.
3. A simple table can be arranged showing the first difference for each variable, under two different conditions.

The method of first differences is almost always a better way of presenting and interpreting logistic regression results than trying to calculate odds, odds ratios, or logged odds ratios. The method requires the construction of alternative scenarios, not just unit changes in independent variables. For example, compare a 30-year-old woman with three young children and no college education with a 50-year-old college-educated woman with no children. Who is more likely to be in the labor force? These kinds of policy scenarios are well suited to the difference method for interpretation of logistic regression.

The method of first differences has one large disadvantage: it returns single numbers – *point estimates* – for each comparison, with no accompanying estimate of our uncertainty around this estimate. Based on simple point estimates, the implications of a good model may play out the same as those from a bad one. For instance, what should we conclude if the standard errors in the example above were all 10? Should that not be reflected in our interpretation of the results?

3.4.4 Estimation Uncertainty around the MLE

In Chapter 2 we showed that the MLE is (asymptotically) consistent and normally distributed. As a practical matter this means that $\hat{\boldsymbol{\theta}} \sim \mathcal{N}\left(\hat{\boldsymbol{\theta}}, -H(\hat{\boldsymbol{\theta}})^{-1}\right)$, that is the covariance of the MLE is the negative of the inverse of the Hessian, evaluated at the MLE. The standard error is the square root of the diagonal of the covariance matrix. Importantly, the standard errors alone do not describe how the various parameters are correlated.

It is easy to extract, look at, and use the variance-covariance matrices. Table 3.7 reports just such a matrix for the logit model of labor force participation reported in Table 3.5. It is straight forward to confirm that the square root of the diagonal elements of this matrix are identical to the standard error estimates reported in Table 3.5.

TABLE 3.7 *The matrix* $cov(\hat{\beta})$ *from the Mroz estimation in Table 3.5.*

	Intercept	Young Kids	School Kids	Age	College	Wage
intercept	$\sigma^2_{\hat{\beta}_0}=0.388$	−0.061	−0.023	−0.007	0.001	−0.020
young kids	−0.061	$\sigma^2_{\hat{\beta}_1}=0.037$	0.002	0.001	−0.005	−0.001
school kids	−0.023	0.002	$\sigma^2_{\hat{\beta}_2}=0.004$	0.000	0.000	0.001
age	−0.007	0.001	0.000	$\sigma^2_{\hat{\beta}_3}=0.000$	−0.000	−0.000
college	0.001	−0.005	0.000	−0.000	$\sigma^2_{\hat{\beta}_4}=0.038$	−0.007
wage	−0.020	−0.001	0.001	−0.000	−0.007	$\sigma^2_{\hat{\beta}_5}=0.022$

3.4.5 Graphical Presentation of Effects in Logistic Regression

Rather than just having point predictions, we would like to interpret models in light of our uncertainty. Similarly, we would like to have an understanding of a good part of the response surface, not just at one or two values. The first differences approach can be informative, though it typically ignores information about the estimation uncertainty, generally contained in the variance-covariance matrix.

Fortunately, with modern computing power combined with likelihood theory we can directly simulate the quantities of interest, incorporating our uncertainty rather than just relying on standard errors of coefficients. Essentially, we simulate *expected values* and *predicted values* by drawing parameter vectors from their asymptotic distribution:

1. Estimate the model by maximizing the likelihood function, storing the coefficient point estimates and the variance-covariance matrix. Let the former be denoted $\hat{\boldsymbol{\beta}}$ and the latter $\text{cov}(\hat{\boldsymbol{\beta}})$.

2. Create a set of values for the independent variables that represents a scenario of analytic or substantive interest. For a single scenario, this might consist of a single value for each of the independent variables. Often, all but a single independent variable of interest are set to their central tendencies. The special variable is set to some specified value. Denote this vector of independent variables representing a scenario of interest $\mathbf{x}_\alpha$.

3. Draw a new vector of parameter values from the multivariate $\mathcal{N}\left(\hat{\boldsymbol{\beta}}, \text{cov}(\hat{\boldsymbol{\beta}})\right)$. Denote this vector of k elements $\tilde{\boldsymbol{\beta}}$. This draw uses the covariance (off-diagonal) of the different parameters, whereas conventional BUTON reporting only provides the (square root of) diagonal elements.

4. Given $\tilde{\boldsymbol{\beta}}$ and $\mathbf{x}_\alpha$, calculate $\tilde{\theta} = \text{logit}^{-1}\left(\mathbf{x}_\alpha^{\mathsf{T}} \tilde{\boldsymbol{\beta}}\right)$. We now have one draw of the *expected value* of the outcome variable under the scenario described in $\mathbf{x}_\alpha$, namely $\text{E}\left[Y \mid \mathbf{x}_\alpha, \tilde{\boldsymbol{\beta}}\right]$. This value incorporates one realization of the estimation uncertainty.

5. To calculate *predicted values*, use the expected values just calculated to simulate the outcome variable $\tilde{Y}$ by a random draw from the stochastic component of the model: $f_B(\tilde{\theta})$.

6. *Important:* Don't do these steps just once; do them hundreds of times. Suppose we draw c different coefficient vectors and construct several different scenarios, $\mathbf{x}_1, \mathbf{x}_2, \ldots, \mathbf{x}_s$. Let $\tilde{B}_{c \times k}$ be the matrix of c draws from $\mathcal{N}\left(\hat{\boldsymbol{\beta}}, \text{cov}(\hat{\boldsymbol{\beta}})\right)$, and let $\mathbf{X}_{k \times s}$ be the matrix containing the s scenarios. $\tilde{B}\mathbf{X}$ will be the $c \times s$ matrix, with each column representing c different draws of the linear predictor value for a particular scenario.

We can use these columns to summarize both the central tendency
(mean) and uncertainty (standard deviation or quantile interval)
surrounding the model's predictions.

Using this approach, we can construct and display many scenarios simultaneously, leading to dense and informative interpretations of the model. For
example, we may wish to look at the predicted "effect" of the wage rate on
the probability of being in the labor force, comparing women with no young
children to those with one young child over the range of observed wage rates.
Figure 3.3 illustrates exactly this comparison. We display the 95% confidence
bands around the predicted employment probability for each wage rate, holding
all other covariates at central tendencies and varying the number of young
children in the home. Code for generating this figure follows in Example 3.3.

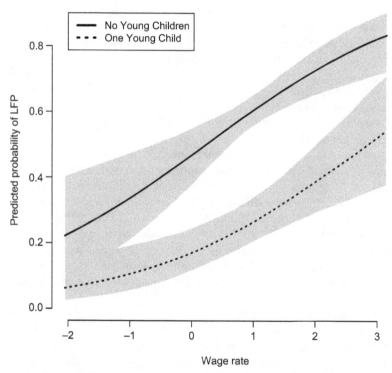

FIGURE 3.3 Plot displaying the 95% confidence bands for the predicted probability of
LFP across different wage rates for women with and without young children. The
estimated relationship between wages and employment probability differs between the
two groups of women.

3.5 AN EXAMPLE: US SENATE VOTING

In October 2009, Tom Coburn – a Republican US senator from Oklahoma – introduced an amendment to House Resolution 2847 that would strip all funding for political science research from the National Science Foundation (NSF) budget. The amendment was defeated in a roll call vote on November 2, 2009. Uscinski and Klofstad (2010) used this vote as a way of probing the impact of senators' individual, constituency, and institutional characteristics on their vote. They treated these Senate votes as independent binary data; their tool of choice was logistic regression.

Votes are not exactly binary, as some senators will abstain, but on the Coburn Amendment there were 98 recorded votes out of 100 senators. Thirty-six senators voted in favor of the amendment, while 64 voted against 2. As is typical, votes in favor are typically coded as a numeric 1 and votes against as 0. We fit two models. In the first we include only a single predictor: the senators' partisan affiliations (Democrat or not). In the second we include all of Uscinski and Klofstad's covariates. They grouped these variables into three categories: individual, constituency, and institutional. In terms of individual characteristics, two variables are pertinent: the gender of the senator and whether they majored in political science in college. Constituency effects basically focus on whether the senator's state has a large number of prominent doctoral programs in political science, gets substantial awards from the National Science Foundation, and has voters who have petitioned the subcommittee concerning the amendment. Finally, Uscinski and Klofstad measure how long until each senator's next election and whether the senator was a member of the Subcommittee on Labor, Health, and Human Services.

Maximum likelihood estimation of this model produces the standard BUTON, given as Table 3.8. The results indicate that partisanship was a strong predictor of senators' votes on the Coburn Amendment. Comparing the two models in terms of the differences in the log-likelihood, we see that including many more covariates does indeed improve the model fit (higher likelihood); the likelihood ratio is 24 with a χ^2 value of 0.01. But the AIC improvement for the full model relative to the simpler one is modest, reflecting the fact that the full model includes eleven more parameters. Using the BIC, with its heavier penalty for complexity, we see a preference for the simpler model.

An alternative form of presentation is the coefficient plot. Figure 3.4 displays such a plot for the second model and omitting the intercept. In this display it is easy to see which coefficients are near special values, such as zero. The points represent coefficient point estimates and the lines are the ± 2 standard error (approximate 95%) interval around the estimated coefficient. We find this a more satisfying way of displaying regression output than the standard BUTON with asterisks, but complications can ensue when variables are on wildly different scales.

R Code Example 3.3 *Post Estimation Analysis*

```
#scenarios: going from min to max of female wages
#comparing women with one young child to one with none.
#all other covariates at sample median/mode
library (MASS)
inv.logit<-function(x){
  1/(1+exp(-x))
}


#the wage values for the scenarios
lwg.range <- seq(from=min(lfp$wage), to=max(lfp$wage),by=.1)

#women w/o young kids
x.lo <- c(1, #intercept
          0, #young.kids
          median(lfp$school.kids),
          median(lfp$age),
          0, #college
          median(lfp$wage))
X.lo <- matrix(x.lo, nrow=length(x.lo), ncol=length(lwg.range))
X.lo[6,] <- lwg.range #replacing with different wage values

#women with young kid(s)
x.hi <- c(1, #intercept
          1, #young.kids
          median(lfp$school.kids),
          median(lfp$age),
          0, #college
          median(lfp$wage))
X.hi <- matrix(x.hi, nrow=length(x.hi), ncol=length(lwg.range))
X.hi[6,] <- lwg.range #replacing with different wage values

B.tilde <- mvrnorm(1000, coef(fit.glm), vcov(fit.glm)) #1000 draws of
     coefficient vectors
s.lo <- inv.logit(B.tilde %*% X.lo) #matrix of predicted probabilities
s.hi <- inv.logit(B.tilde %*% X.hi) #matrix of predicted probabilities
s.lo<-apply(s.lo, 2, quantile, c(0.025, 0.5, .975)) #95\% CI and median
s.hi<-apply(s.hi, 2, quantile, c(0.025, 0.5, .975)) #95\% CI and median


#plotting the results
plot(lwg.range, s.lo[2,], ylim=c(0,.9), xlab = "wage index",
     ylab = "Predicted Probability of LFP",
     main = "Wages, Children, and LFP", bty="n",
     col="white")
polygon(x=c(lwg.range, rev(lwg.range)), #confidence region
     y=c(s.lo[1,], rev(s.lo[3,])),
     col=grey(0.8), border=NA)
polygon(x=c(lwg.range, rev(lwg.range)), #confidence region
     y=c(s.hi[1,], rev(s.hi[3,])),
     col=grey(0.8), border=NA)
lines(lwg.range, s.hi[2,], lty=3, lwd=2)
lines(lwg.range, s.lo[2,], lwd=2)
legend(-2, 0.9, legend = c("No Young Children",
     "One Young Child "),lty = c(1,3),lwd=3)
```

TABLE 3.8 *Replication of Table 1 in Uscinski and Klofstand (2010).*

	Dependent Variable: Vote "Nay" on Coburn Amendment	
	(Simple Model)	(Full Model)
Democrat	3.120	3.300
	(0.575)	(0.853)
Gender (Female)		−0.408
		(0.977)
Political Science Major in College		1.160
		(0.907)
Number of Top 20 Political Science Programs		2.080
		(0.996)
Number of Top 50 Political Science Programs		1.020
		(0.770)
Total Number of Political Science Programs		−0.183
		(0.433)
Percentage with Advanced Degrees		2.350
		(1.250)
Number of Amendment Petitioners		−0.011
		(0.016)
Number of NSF Grants 2008		0.157
		(0.345)
Years to Next Election		0.486
		(0.229)
Member of Labor HHS Subcommittee		1.390
		(0.968)
Seniority		−0.0002
		(0.041)
Constant	−0.802	−3.780
	(0.334)	(1.600)
n	98	98
$\log \mathcal{L}$	−42.800	−30.600
AIC	89.700	87.300
BIC	94.800	121.000

3.5.1 Model Evaluation

Logistic regression assigns observations probabilistically to one of two classes. There are a variety of diagnostics which help to assess the performance of such classifiers beyond the standard log-likelihood based measures. We take the view that, in general, single number summaries are, individually, inadequate. But it is useful to understand them.

In weather prediction, where forecasts are generally based on probabilities (30% chance of rain tomorrow, for example), the *Brier score* is often employed.

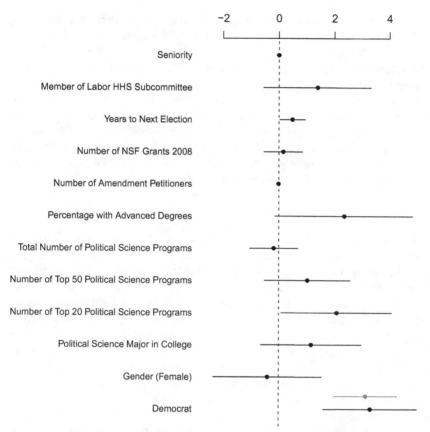

FIGURE 3.4 A coefficient plot of the logit regression of US Senate votes on the Coburn Amendment to eliminate NSF funding for political science. Horizontal bars are 95% confidence intervals. The lighter gray point and error bar represents estimates from the simple model.

Definition 3.1 (Brier Score). The Brier score (Brier, 1950) for a binary classifier such as logistic regression is defined as

$$B_b \equiv \frac{1}{n}\sum_{i=1}^{n}\left(\hat{\theta}_i - y_i\right)^2,$$

where the predicted probabilities are $\hat{\theta}_i$ and the observed binary outcomes are given as y_i.

Lower values reflect better predictions. The Brier score for the logit model containing only partisanship is 0.14 against 0.09 for the more complicated model.

Another approach is to generate a 2 × 2 table of predicted values against actual values, which will be distributed χ^2 with 1 degree of freedom. To do this, however, we must specify a specific threshold, t, that will map predicted probabilities into failures (0) and successes (1). Where $\hat{\theta}_i > t$ the model predicts 1s, otherwise the outcome is coded as a predicted 0. Often, and perhaps by default, analysts use $t = 0.5$ as a cutoff. Applying that same value to the predicted probabilities from the full model in the Coburn example, we recover the results in Table 3.9. There are 15 incorrect predictions; the χ^2 is 40, which is highly unlikely for a 2 × 2 table with 98 observations. But this also begs the question, "What is special about 0.5?," especially when the raw probability of voting "nay" is 0.65? Why focus on just one threshold?

ROC Curves

The *Receiver Operating Characteristic (ROC) Curve* (don't ask about the name) builds on the idea of comparing correct predictions against false positives. But rather than choosing one particular threshold, ROC curves display this comparison for all thresholds between 0 and 1. ROC curves are based on the idea that the relative costs of mis-predicting a failure (false negative) versus mis-predicting a success (false positive) can vary depending on the problem at had. More formally, let the cost of a false positive relative to the cost a false negative be denoted C. The optimal prediction for an event ($\hat{y} = 1$) that minimizes the total expected cost occurs when $t > 1/(1 + C)$; otherwise, $\hat{y} = 0$. Hence, if the false positives and false negatives are equally costly, then $C = 1$. If, however, the cost of mis-predicting an event is twice as costly as mis-predicting the absence of an event, then $C = 2$ and the cutoff would be at $t = 1/3$. The appropriate value for C in any particular application is, of course, a policy problem. The threshold should be established in terms of the human and physical costs of mis-predicting say, the absence of war, versus mis-predicting a war. The ROC curve is a way of summarizing the ratio of the rate of false positives to the rate of false negatives over the entire range of t.

ROC curves plot the true positive rate (percent of actual successes correctly predicted, for some fixed threshold) against the false positive rate (percent of

TABLE 3.9 *Predicted versus observed votes for the Coburn Amendment, with* $t = 0.5$ *for mapping probabilities into event space. Calculations are based on the second model in Table 3.8.*

	Observed 0	Observed 1
Predicted 0	27	8
Predicted 1	7	56

ROC Plots for Competing Models

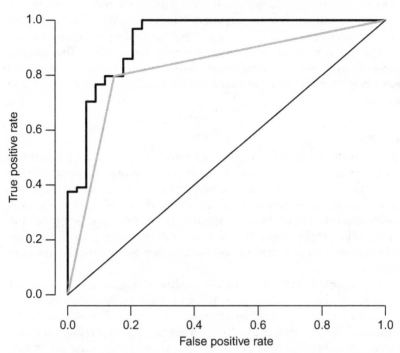

FIGURE 3.5 Receiver Operator Characteristics (ROC) curve for the logit models of the vote on the Coburn Amendment. The gray line is generated by the partisanship-only model (AUC= 0.83). The black line is generated by the full model (AUC= 0.93).

false positives out of actual failures).[1] The threshold values, t, that generates each particular point in the curve are not visible in the plot. Better models will have low false positive rates when they also have high true positive rates, whereas worse-performing models will have ROC curves that are close to the diagonal.

Figure 3.5 illustrates the ROC curves generated by both models in Table 3.8. The simpler model (the gray line) has one step, corresponding to the fact that the underlying model has only one (binary, categorical) predictor. ROC curves from competing models can be used heuristically to compare the fit of various model specifications, though this is a bit of an art. In this example the more complicated model, as reported in Uscinski and Klofstand's original paper, is better at predicting in-sample for all values of t.

---

[1] The false positive rate is also 1 − specificity, where specificity is the percent of failures correctly predicted as such.

Some prefer the "area under the ROC curve" (AUC) as a single-number summary of model performance as derived from the ROC; we report these values in the caption. These single number summaries are unfortunate since they lend a false sense of precision and certainty in comparing model performance while discarding the fact that model performance may differ across t. Two models could conceivably provide very different trade-offs between false positives and false negatives relevant to decision makers. This would be masked by simple comparison of AUCs.

Separation Plots

Many models in the social sciences will not have any predicted probabilities that are greater than 0.5. This is not necessarily a symptom of a poorly fitting model. Rather, it is driven, in part, by the underlying frequency of events. When the observed number of events is small relative to the number of trials, as is the case with international conflict, we should expect small absolute predicted probabilities. What really concerns us is the model's ability to distinguish more likely events from less likely ones, even if they all have small absolute probabilities.

To visually compare different models' abilities to usefully discriminate between cases, we can sort the observations by their predicted probabilities and then compare this sorting to actual, observed events. This is exactly the strategy followed by Greenhill et al. (2011) in developing their *separation plot*. In these plots, dark vertical bars are observed events, in this case nay votes. Light bars are nonevents. If the model perfectly discriminated between events and nonevents, then successes would cluster to the right of the plot and failures to the left; the plot would appear as two starkly defined color blocks. A model that performs poorly would appear as a set of randomly distributed vertical lines.

Figure 3.6 displays separation plots for each of the models in Table 3.8. The predicted probabilities are ranked from low to high (shown as a black line), a red bar indicates a vote against the amendment, and a cream colored bar is a vote in favor. Consistent with the results from the ROC plot, we see that the full model is better at discriminating nay votes from the other senators.

Model Interpretation

There is some evidence that the more complicated full model of Uscinski and Klofstand is better at predicting Senate votes on the Coburn Amendment. How can we interpret these findings? One way is to use the exponentiated logit coefficients, as presented in Table 3.10. These values represent the odds ratios for different values of the covariate. This makes some sense in the context of partisanship; the odds of a Democrat voting nay are 27 times greater than a Republican. But it is harder to interpret what these values say about continuous predictors. Odds ratios are a tough sell.

Party-Only Model

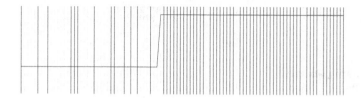

Full Model

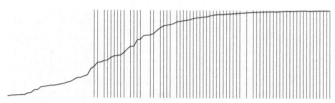

FIGURE 3.6 Separation plots for the partisan-only and full models of US Senate voting on the Coburn Amendment.

Using our strategy of constructing scenarios of interest and then simulating from the sampling distribution we can make more nuanced and easily expressed interpretations of the model. These interpretations have the added benefit of incorporating our uncertainty while reflecting the nonlinearity inherent in both the model and in categorical data. Here we are interested in how the predicted probability of nay vote changes as senators approach reelection for Democrats and non-Democrats.[2] To generate this scenario, we hold the other covariates at their mean or modal values and then vary the time-until-election from one to five years. We display these results in Figure 3.7.

US Congressional elections are only held in even-numbered years, so we only observe three values for the number of years-to-election: one, three, and five. This is reflected in the plot. The figure indicates three implications of the model. First, the gap in voting behavior is driven, unsurprisingly, by partisanship. Democrats are almost certain to vote "nay," regardless of their proximity to reelection. Their predicted probability is nearly at the top of the plot. Second, the gap between Democrats and non-Democrats narrows modestly as reelection is further in the future. Third, the uncertainty around the predicted probability for non-Democrats is considerable. The predicted probability at five years until reelection is about 0.9, well within the confidence bounds

---

[2] There were two independent senators at the time, Joe Lieberman of Connecticut and Bernie Sanders of Vermont, both of whom voted nay.

TABLE 3.10 *Odds Ratios for the replication of table 1 in Uscinski and Klofstand (2010).*

	OR	2.5 %	97.5 %
Democrat	27.00	6.08	190.48
Gender (Female)	0.66	0.10	4.89
Political Science Major in College	3.20	0.57	21.44
Number of Top 20 Political Science Programs	8.01	1.42	89.54
Number of Top 50 Political Science Programs	2.78	0.65	14.47
Total Number of Political Science Programs	0.83	0.34	1.92
Percentage with Advanced Degrees	10.53	1.21	181.70
Number of Amendment Petitioners	0.99	0.96	1.02
Number of NSF Grants, 2008	1.17	0.57	2.30
Years before Next Election	1.63	1.06	2.66
Member of Labor HHS Subcommittee	4.00	0.65	31.22
Seniority	1.00	0.92	1.08

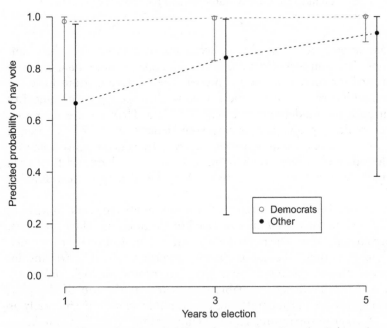

FIGURE 3.7 The predicted probability of voting "nay" on the Coburn Amendment as reelection approaches for Democrat and non-Democrat US senators. All other covariates are held at their central tendencies. The vertical bars are 95% confidence bands.

for both a Democrat in that year as well as for the "typical" non-Democrat who is facing an election within the year. In other words, the "effect" of proximity to an election appears weak and only visible among non-Democrats. This insight would not be discernible simply by examining BUTON or odds ratios.

3.6 SOME EXTENSIONS

3.6.1 Latent Variable Formulation for Binary Data

Imagine that the phenomenon we seek to observe is actually continuous but, unfortunately, we are only able to observe it imperfectly. We observe the underlying *latent* variable when it passes some threshold. And even then we do not observe actual value but only the fact that it crossed the observability point. While we do not need such a specification for deriving the logit model, it is conceptually useful and underpins several more complicated models, so it bears discussion here.

Consider a discrete, binary outcome Y_i which is based on an unobserved latent variable Z_i as:

$$Y_i = \begin{cases} 1 & \Longleftrightarrow & z_i > \tau \\ 0 & \Longleftrightarrow & z_i \leq \tau \end{cases}$$

$$Z_i = \mathbf{x}_i^\mathsf{T} \boldsymbol{\beta} + \varepsilon_i$$

$$\varepsilon_i \sim f,$$

where τ is a threshold above which we observe an event, and f is some probability distribution. Since this threshold is unobserved and, in some sense, arbitrary, we set $\tau = 0$.[3]

Making different assumptions about the distribution of the error term, f, yields different models. If we assume the errors are distributed via a logistic probability distribution with mean zero and scale parameter fixed at 1, we arrive back at the logit model we derived above. If we instead assume that $\varepsilon_i \sim \mathcal{N}(0, 1)$ and denoting $\Phi(\cdot)$ as the corresponding cumulative distribution function, we arrive at the *probit* model:

$$\begin{aligned} \Pr(Y_i = 1) &= \Pr(z_i > 0) \\ &= \Pr\left(\mathbf{x}_i^\mathsf{T} \boldsymbol{\beta} + \varepsilon_i > 0\right) \\ &= \Pr\left(\varepsilon_i > -\mathbf{x}_i^\mathsf{T} \boldsymbol{\beta}\right) \\ &= 1 - \Phi\left(-\mathbf{x}_i^\mathsf{T} \boldsymbol{\beta}\right) \\ &= \Phi\left(\mathbf{x}_i^\mathsf{T} \boldsymbol{\beta}\right), \end{aligned}$$

---

[3] We could set τ to any other value and then simply subtract that constant from the linear predictor to yield an equivalent model. In other words, τ is not identified.

where the last step follows from the symmetry of the normal distribution, i.e., $\Phi(x) = 1 - \Phi(-x)$. Predicted probabilities and statistical inference under a probit specification are nearly identical to those from a logit. The coefficient values will differ; it turns out that logit coefficients divided by 1.6 should give a close approximation to the estimated coefficients from a probit regression. Our approach for generating meaningful interpretations of model estimates and implications fits the probit case just as easily.

In case you were wondering ... 3.1 Logistic distribution

Let Y be a random variable with support along the entire real line. Suppose that the cumulative distribution function (CDF) for Y can be written as

$$\Pr\left(Y \leq y\right) = \Lambda(y; \mu, \sigma) = \frac{1}{1 + \exp\left(-\frac{y-\mu}{\sigma}\right)}. \tag{3.1}$$

We say that Y follows a *logistic distribution* with parameter vector $\theta = (\mu, \sigma)$. We write $Y \sim f_L(y; \mu, \sigma)$. $E[Y] = \mu$ and $\text{var}(Y) = \sigma^2 \pi^2 / 3$.

There is rarely, if ever, a statistical reason for preferring a logit model to a probit or vice versa. Some disciplines prefer the probit, others use the logit more frequently. Sometimes there are aesthetic reasons to prefer one to the other. For example, the *strategic probit* model (Signorino, 1999) emerges from an extensive form game where the stochastic components are normal distributions. Occasionally there are computational reasons to prefer one specification over another but, in general, the choice between logit and probit is inconsequential for the purposes of inference and prediction.

3.6.2 Heteroskedastic Probit

The standard probit model assumes that the error distribution has fixed, unit variance. But it may be the case that the error variance will depend on variables that are included in the model. For example, in survey data different subgroups might differ in the levels of information they have about a topic, so the variance around their group-specific average (latent) response may also differ. Davidson and MacKinnon (1984) developed an extension to the probit model that can account for this variance relationship. This model goes by the name *heteroskedastic probit*.

The heteroskedastic probit model relies on the fact that we can transform a $\mathcal{N}(0, \sigma^2)$ variable into a $\mathcal{N}(0, 1)$ variable by dividing the standard deviation, σ. So we can by rewrite the standard probit model as

$$\Pr(Y_i = 1) = \Pr\left(\frac{\varepsilon_i}{\sigma} > -\frac{\mathbf{x}_i^\mathsf{T}\boldsymbol{\beta}}{\sigma}\right)$$

$$= \Phi\left(\frac{\mathbf{x}_i^\mathsf{T}\boldsymbol{\beta}}{\sigma}\right).$$

To complete the model we must specify a relationship between covariates and σ_i. Since the standard deviation is nonnegative the exponential function is useful here:

$$\sigma_i = \exp(\mathbf{v}_i^\mathsf{T}\boldsymbol{\gamma}),$$

where $\mathbf{v}$ is the vector of covariates thought to be linked to the variance, and γ is a vector of the to-be-estimated parameters. Given $\mathbf{X}$ and $\mathbf{V}$ we can now state the log-likelihood:

$$\log \mathcal{L}(\boldsymbol{\beta}, \boldsymbol{\gamma} \mid \mathbf{X}, \mathbf{V}, \mathbf{y})$$

$$= \sum_{i=1}^{n}\left[y_i \log \Phi\left(\frac{\mathbf{x}_i^\mathsf{T}\boldsymbol{\beta}}{\exp(\mathbf{v}_i^\mathsf{T}\boldsymbol{\gamma})}\right) + (1 - y_i)\log\left[1 - \Phi\left(\frac{\mathbf{x}_i^\mathsf{T}\boldsymbol{\beta}}{\exp(\mathbf{v}_i^\mathsf{T}\boldsymbol{\gamma})}\right)\right]\right]$$

$$= \sum_{i=1}^{n}\left[y_i \log \Phi\left(\mathbf{x}_i^\mathsf{T}\boldsymbol{\beta}\exp(-\mathbf{v}_i^\mathsf{T}\boldsymbol{\gamma})\right) + (1 - y_i)\log \Phi\left(-\mathbf{x}_i^\mathsf{T}\boldsymbol{\beta}\exp(-\mathbf{v}_i^\mathsf{T}\boldsymbol{\gamma})\right)\right].$$

3.6.3 Complimentary Logistic Model, a.k.a. *cloglog*

Another complication arises when we consider the fact that both the logistic and normal distributions are symmetric. This symmetry carries over to the logit and probit transformations: $\text{logit}(\theta) = -\text{logit}(1 - \theta)$ and $\Phi^{-1}(\theta) = -\Phi^{-1}(1 - \theta)$. This implies that as a predictor, x, becomes large $\theta(x)$ approaches 1 at the same rate that it approaches 0 as x becomes small.

In some circumstances we might worry that the process we are examining is not symmetric in this way. This can occur, for example, when the probability of an event is extremely small or very large, even with good variation in the predictor variable. A different choice of function mapping $\mathbf{x}_i^\mathsf{T}\boldsymbol{\beta}$ into $[0, 1]$ can allow for asymmetry.

The complimentary logistic model, often called the *complementary log-log* or *cloglog*, is one possibility. The model is still based on Bernoulli trials but now $\log(-\log(1 - \theta_i)) = \mathbf{x}_i^\mathsf{T}\boldsymbol{\beta}$ or, equivalently, $\theta_i = 1 - \exp(-\exp(\mathbf{x}_i^\mathsf{T}\boldsymbol{\beta}))$. As displayed in Figure 3.8, we can see that the predicted probabilities approach 1 much faster than 0 under the cloglog specification.

An immediate difference between the cloglog model and logit/probit is that the model is not symmetric with respect to the coding of the outcome variable. In the Coburn Amendment example, swapping the coding of the dependent

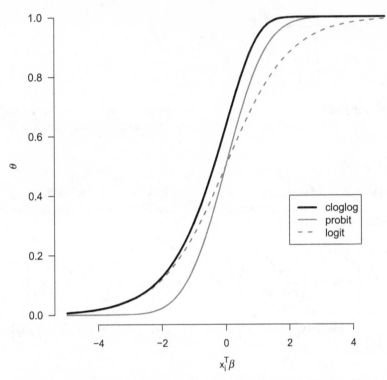

FIGURE 3.8 The (inverse) logit, probit, and complementary log-log functions, mapping the linear term into θ. Logit and probit are symmetric around $\theta = 0.5$, whereas the cloglog approaches 1 faster and 0 more slowly.

variable such that "nays" are 0 would have no effect on the estimates reported in Table 3.8 beyond flipping their signs. Nothing else, including model fit, would change. In a cloglog model, however, this symmetry does not hold.

3.6.4 An Example: Civil Conflict

In new democracies, prior autocratic leaders with military ties often retain a strong political presence in the new regime. Such legacies may have consequences for subsequent political stability. Cook and Savun (2016) examined how the structure of prior authoritarian government relates to a binary coding of civil conflict in new democracies, 1946–2009. Their primary analysis relied on logistic regression.

The Cook and Savun data contain a heterogeneous group of countries and a comparatively small number of conflicts (69) relative to the number of country-years, presenting an opportunity to apply the modeling extensions just described. Table 3.11 is the BUTON reflecting this exercise. In the first column

TABLE 3.11 *Replication and extension of table II in Cook and Savun (2016).*

	logit (1)	probit (2)	het. probit (3)	cloglog (4)	log-log (5)
	Dependent Variable: Civil Conflict Onset				
Military	0.96	0.45	0.17	0.87	−0.32
	(0.28)	(0.14)	(0.07)	(0.27)	(0.11)
Personal	0.15	0.09	0.07	0.14	−0.09
	(0.65)	(0.32)	(0.10)	(0.62)	(0.24)
Party	−0.45	−0.22	−0.05	−0.40	0.14
	(0.67)	(0.30)	(0.10)	(0.65)	(0.21)
GDP (lagged)	−0.30	−0.15	−0.04	−0.27	0.11
	(0.17)	(0.08)	(0.03)	(0.17)	(0.05)
Population (lagged)	0.53	0.24	0.13	0.51	−0.16
	(0.12)	(0.06)	(0.03)	(0.10)	(0.05)
Peace years	−0.45	−0.23	−0.06	−0.42	0.17
	(0.18)	(0.09)	(0.04)	(0.16)	(0.07)
n	2575	2575	2575	2575	2575
$\log \mathcal{L}$	−239	−240	−236	−238	−242
AIC	498	500	495	496	503
BIC	557	558	559	555	562

Note: Following Cook and Savun, standard errors are clustered by country and cubic splines estimated but omitted from the table. Lagged population is the only variance-term covariate for the heteroskedastic probit model.

we repeat their logit analysis, while the second column fits the same model as a probit. In the third column we fit a heteroskedastic probit using population as the only covariate in the model for σ. In the last two columns we fit two cloglog models. The first of these continues the coding, assigning conflict onset a 1 and nonconflict a 0, whereas in the "log-log" model we reverse the coding of the dependent variable.

Unsurprisingly, different distributional assumptions produce different numerical estimates for the regression parameters. But the raw values reported in the table turned out to yield very similar descriptions of the DGP, as indicated by the log-likelihood, AIC, and BIC values. This is further confirmed in Figure 3.9, which shows that model fit is virtually identical across these alternatives. The ratio of coefficient estimates to their standard errors are also similar across models. Note, however, that the parameter estimates for the cloglog and log-log models are not opposites, reflecting the asymmetry in the assumed distribution. In this example several model variations produce effectively the same answer.

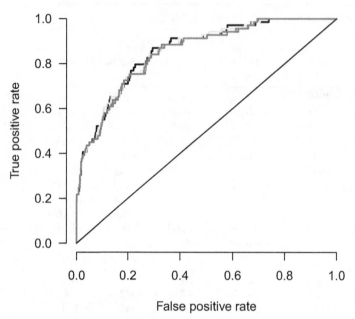

ROC curves for the five models reported in Table 3.11. The models all fit the data similarly.

3.7 SUMMARY OF GENERAL APPROACH TO BINARY VARIABLES

When outcomes are binary, analysis tools that assume a normally distributed response are often inappropriate. If we imagine that our outcome can be modeled as a Bernoulli trial, combined with a linear predictor term that can be mapped into the probability space, then we can derive a variety of models for binary data. Given a link function and a probability distribution, these models are easily estimated using maximum likelihood. Logit and probit are the most commonly used and can be considered interchangeable.

Interpretation of nonlinear models is more involved than for OLS since marginal effects (and the uncertainty around them) depend on the values of the covariates. Standard tables of coefficients and standard errors are not terribly informative about the model's implications. We advocate for a general procedure in which the analyst constructs substantively meaningful and defensible scenarios (i.e., vectors of covariate values) and then uses a large number of samples from the limiting distribution to generate many values of particular quantities of interest. In this way, the analyst can both make substantive interpretations at meaningful values while communicating her uncertainty around those values.

3.8 FURTHER READING

Applications

Logit and probit models are widely employed across the social sciences in both observational and experimental work. Among many recent examples, Einstein and Glick (2017) look at how a constituent's race affects whether and how public housing bureaucrats respond to information requests. Baturo (2017) examines the predictors of political leaders' activities after leaving office.

Past Work

Joseph Berkson was a statistician with the Mayo Clinic and most well-known for his pioneering studies of the link between tobacco smoking and lung cancer in the 1960s. Berkson's work on the logistic regression – as an explicit correction to using a normal distribution for studying probabilities – began in 1944 (Berkson, 1944). Subsequently, Berkson produced several important works relating to this topic (Berkson, 1946, 1953, 1955). However, work on using sigmoid curves (akin to logistic curves) dates back to the work of Bliss (1935), who worked with Fisher at the Galton Laboratory, University College, London; R. A. Fisher followed Karl Pearson as the Galton Professor at the UCL in 1934.

Glasgow and Alvarez (2008) provide a recent summary of likelihood-based models for discrete choice, along with their extensions. Alvarez and Brehm (1995, 2002) is an early derivation and application of the heteroskedastic probit in the study of American public opinion. Nagler (1994) proposes the *scobit* model that allows for a logistic distribution that is scaled so as to not require an assumption of symmetry around 0. A challenge with the scobit model is that there is often insufficient information in the covariates to cleanly estimate both the regression weights and the ancillary parameter governing symmetry of the distribution.

Software Notes

We used the arm library's coefplot command (Gelman and Su, 2016), but the coefplot (Lander, 2016) extends this functionality in a number of ways. The verification (NCAR – Research Applications Laboratory, 2015) and scoring (Merkle and Steyvers, 2013) libraries can be used to calculate the Brier score. The separationplot library (Greenhill et al., 2015) calculates and displays separation plots. glmx (Zeileis et al., 2015) provides a way to estimate probits (and other models) allowing for heteroskedasticity.

The $\mathcal{R}$ package Zelig package (Imai et al., 2008, 2009) and its progeny have implemented a general syntax for estimating several classes of models, including logit, probit, and many other types of models. It facilitates for nonprogrammers the calculation and display of quantities of interest and associated uncertainty under different scenarios.

4

Implementing MLE

In this chapter, we discuss the methods and challenges of actually implementing likelihood methods in modern computers. Understanding the likelihood surface is a good place to start. We outline the most commonly used numerical algorithms for finding the MLE. While these algorithms often work with no problem, there can be challenges. We provide suggestions for trouble-shooting computational problems. We discuss these initially as if they were purely computational problems, but often such problems are linked with substantive modeling issues like collinearity of predictors and perfect separation in categorical data.

4.1 THE LIKELIHOOD SURFACE

The likelihood surface is simply the likelihood (or, more commonly, the log-likelihood) displayed as a function of parameter values. Visualizing the likelihood surface is the most basic tool for understanding whether a particular likelihood function is regular and, if not, where problems might arise in finding the MLE.

We have already examined the regular likelihood surface for the Bernoulli model in Figure 1.1. To see how visualizing the likelihood surface can highlight problems or challenges in estimation, we consider two irregular likelihoods, each relying on the uniform distribution.

In case you were wondering ... 4.1 Uniform distribution

Suppose X is a sample from the closed interval $[a, b]$ where all values in this interval have equal probability of being drawn. We say that $X \sim \text{Unif}[a, b]$ where the distribution function, $f(x)$, is

$$f(x) = \begin{cases} \frac{1}{b-a} & x \in [a,b] \\ 0 & \text{otherwise} \end{cases},$$

with $E[X] = \frac{a+b}{2}$ and $\text{var}(X) = \frac{(b-a)^2}{12}$.

4.1.1 Examples

Irregular Likelihood Surface

Let $\mathbf{x} = (x_1, \ldots, x_n)$ be n independent draws from $\text{Unif}[-\theta, \theta]$. In this example the parameter, θ, determines the support for the probability model, something we recognized as a violation of regularity conditions. Nevertheless, we can construct a likelihood using our standard procedure:

$$\mathcal{L}(\theta \mid \mathbf{x}) = \prod_{i=1}^{n} \frac{1}{2\theta}$$
$$= (2\theta)^{-n}.$$

This likelihood assigns positive probability for any $\mathbf{x}$ such that $x_i \in [-\theta, \theta], i \in \{1, \ldots, n\}$ and 0 otherwise. Figure 4.1 plots the likelihood function for θ

Uniform Likelihood

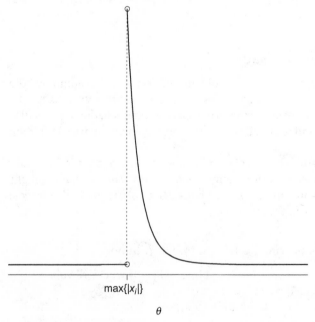

$\max\{|x_i|\}$

θ

FIGURE 4.1 The likelihood surface for $\mathcal{L}(\theta \mid \mathbf{x})$ where the probability model is $X \sim \text{Unif}(-\theta, \theta)$.

given fixed **x**. The likelihood surface is clearly irregular, displaying sharp discontinuities at the MLE.[1] Standard properties of the MLE will not hold in this case.

Flat Likelihood Surface

Suppose our data, **x**, are now hypothesized to be drawn from Unif$[\theta - 2, \theta + 2]$. The likelihood is now $\mathcal{L}(\theta \mid \mathbf{x}) = 4^{-n}$, i.e., the likelihood is a constant. Figure 4.2 plots this likelihood surface for fixed and observed data, **x**.

A flat likelihood implies that many values of θ are consistent with the observed data.[2] Obviously such cases are irregular, but, more problematically, flat likelihoods indicate a model where the parameter is *not identified*.

In this toy example we constructed a perfectly flat likelihood surface. But in some real-world applications, the curvature of the likelihood surface is sufficiently slight that the computer cannot tell the difference between the flat likelihood and a nearly flat one. This may happen when, for example, two covariates in a regression model are almost perfectly collinear. Most statistical programs generate an error when this happens, but some will still present

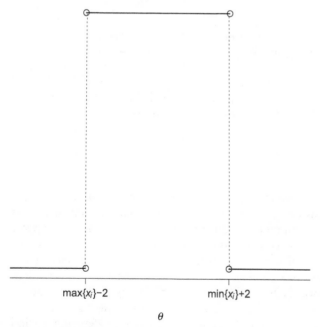

Uniform Likelihood

max$\{x_i\}$–2   min$\{x_i\}$+2

θ

FIGURE 4.2 The likelihood surface for $\mathcal{L}(\theta \mid \mathbf{x})$ where the probability model is $X \sim$ Unif$(\theta - 2, \theta + 2)$.

---

[1] The MLE is given as $\hat{\theta} = \max\{|x_1|, \ldots, |x_n|\}$.

[2] In fact the MLE is any $\theta \in [x_* - 2, x^* + 2]$ where $x_* = \min\{x_1, \ldots, x_n\}$ and $x^* = \max\{x_1, \ldots, x_n\}$.

results. Applying the theoretical results from Chapter 2 to such output can lead to erroneous conclusions.

4.1.2 Profile Likelihood

Likelihood functions with many parameters (i.e., most of them) become difficult to conceptualize. In some applications, we may only care about a subset of model parameters, viewing the rest as *nuisance parameters* – those that must be estimated for completeness but in which we have no interest. Even when we are interested in all the estimated parameters, it is difficult to visualize the likelihood surface for all parameters jointly. We examine the surface in one dimension at a time. To do this effectively we need to focus on the parameters' functional interdependence. *Profile* or *concentrated* likelihood is one of the most common ways of doing this.

> **Definition 4.1** (Profile Likelihood). Suppose we have likelihood function $\mathcal{L}(\theta)$ where θ is a vector. We partition θ into $\{\theta_1, \theta_2\}$, where interest centers on θ_1. The *profile likelihood*, $\mathcal{L}_p(\theta_1)$ is defined as
>
> $$\mathcal{L}_p(\theta_1) \equiv \max_{\theta_2} \mathcal{L}(\theta_1, \theta_2)$$
>
> $$\equiv \mathcal{L}(\theta_1, \hat{\theta}_2(\theta_1)).$$

In other words, the profile likelihood function returns, for each value of θ_1, the maximum value of the likelihood function for the remaining parameters, θ_2. Maximizing the profile likelihood will return the MLE for θ_1. We can plot profile likelihoods, construct likelihood ratios, and even build likelihood-based confidence intervals. We have already seen a profile likelihood once: Figure 1.4 displays the profile likelihood for a regression coefficient treating the other coefficients and the variance as nuisance parameters.

4.2 NUMERICAL OPTIMIZATION

Notwithstanding some of the examples presented in earlier chapters, finding the MLE and taking advantage of all its various properties is almost always accomplished using a computer. In calculating the MLE, most computer programs iterate some numerical optimization procedure. These algorithms update and recalculate until the change in the current value falls below some threshold or *tolerance*. At this point the algorithm is said to have *converged*. In many of the standard models discussed in this book, finding extrema is not too difficult. But in more complicated analyses, especially using highly customized likelihoods, a unique maximum and the ability of a particular algorithm to find it is not guaranteed.

The workhorse for finding the extrema of log-likelihood functions are *hill-climbing* algorithms. Such algorithms use the information contained in the derivative of a function to "climb" to the maximum (or descend to the minimum). Although there are now many hill-climbing algorithms, most are based on the logic of Newton's method, also known as the Newton-Raphson algorithm.

4.2.1 Newton-Raphson

The Newton-Raphson (N-R) algorithm is a general procedure for finding the root(s) of equations of the form $g(\theta) = 0$. For scalar θ, given an initial guess θ_0, the algorithm updates by relying on a linear (Taylor series) expansion of the target function:

$$g(\theta) \approx g(\theta_0) + g'(\theta_0)(\theta - \theta_0) = 0$$

solving for θ yields the next step in the algorithm

$$\theta_1 = \theta_0 - \frac{g(\theta_0)}{g'(\theta_0)},$$

where $g'(\theta_0) = \frac{d}{d\theta}g(\theta)\Big|_{\theta=\theta_0}$. The algorithm stops when $\theta_n = \theta_{n-1}$.

For vector $\boldsymbol{\theta}$, recall that the MLE is the solution to the score equation, $S(\boldsymbol{\theta}) = 0$. Given an initial $\boldsymbol{\theta}_0$, the Taylor expansion is

$$S(\boldsymbol{\theta}) \approx S(\boldsymbol{\theta}_0) - \frac{\partial}{\partial \boldsymbol{\theta}}S(\boldsymbol{\theta}_0)(\boldsymbol{\theta} - \boldsymbol{\theta}_0) = 0$$

$$\approx S(\boldsymbol{\theta}_0) - H(\boldsymbol{\theta}_0)(\boldsymbol{\theta} - \boldsymbol{\theta}_0) = 0.$$

The updated value, $\boldsymbol{\theta}_1$, is therefore

$$\boldsymbol{\theta}_1 = \boldsymbol{\theta}_0 - H(\boldsymbol{\theta}_0)^{-1}S(\boldsymbol{\theta}_0).$$

Intuitively, the N-R algorithm climbs to the MLE by moving in the direction indicated by the gradient, with the step size weighted by the curvature of the likelihood surface at our current point. The algorithm will iterate until $|\boldsymbol{\theta}_n - \boldsymbol{\theta}_{n-1}| < \varepsilon$, where ε sets the tolerance.

Stabilization, Fisher Scoring, & Iteratively (Re)weighted Least Squares (IWLS)

Newton-Raphson will converge so long as the Hessian matrix is invertible. When $\boldsymbol{\theta}_0$ starts near $\hat{\boldsymbol{\theta}}$, this typically happens quickly and with few problems. But if our starting values are far away from where we want to end up, then we may encounter issues. Given a starting value, $\boldsymbol{\theta}_0$, the next step in the Newton-Raphson algorithm is determined by $S(\boldsymbol{\theta}_0)$. If we are far from the top of the hill, then $|S(\boldsymbol{\theta}_0)|$ could be quite large, leading to a large step. This step could be sufficiently large in magnitude that the estimate jumps over the MLE. One way to stabilize convergence is by adjusting the size of the step by some factor, $\delta \in (0, 1]$. The algorithm is now:

$$\theta_1 = \theta_0 - \delta H(\theta_0)^{-1} S(\theta_0).$$

Other stabilization procedures can be used in place of or in addition to adjusting the step size. Most software packages allow users to adjust the step size in addition to supplying different starting values and setting the tolerance.

Given a regular likelihood there should be no problem inverting the Hessian matrix, but in some situations $H(\theta_0)$ may turn out to be negative or difficult to invert, especially if we are far from the MLE. Replacing the observed Fisher information, $-H(\theta) = I(\theta)$, in the updating step with the expected Fisher information, $\mathcal{I}(\theta)$, can solve this problem, in addition to speeding up convergence. Optimizers that replace observed with expected Fisher information are said to follow *Fisher scoring*. In the context of the Generalized Linear Model (see Chapter 7), where observed and expected Fisher information are the same, Fisher scoring is automatic. The default optimizer for $\mathcal{R}$'s glm function, Iteratively (re)Weighted Least Squares (IWLS), uses the Fisher scoring approach. Standard summary output from glm reports the number of Fisher scoring (i.e., N-R) iterations.

4.2.2 Other Algorithms

The N-R and related methods have the notable drawback of requiring recalculation of the first and second derivatives of the log-likelihood at every iteration. Moreover, N-R is only useful for problems where the likelihood is regular in the neighborhood of the MLE. Derivative-based hill-climbing approach may not be available for nonstandard problems. "Quasi-Newton" algorithms such as BFGS (implemented in $\mathcal{R}$ as part of the optim function) approximate the Hessian using information in the gradient. This can accelerate convergence.

Complex or highly-sculpted likelihoods may have several local optima that can trap hill-climbing algorithms. A variety of other algorithms are available. Among the most interesting (and computationally intensive) are *simulated annealing* and *Markov Chain Monte Carlo-MLE* (MCMC-MLE). While they differ in many important ways, both involve procedures that iteratively and stochastically propose new values of θ. The new value is probabilistically accepted based on a particular rule and information about the current value of the likelihood function. Both methods intentionally allow the algorithm to sample points in the parameter space that are "worse" (i.e., of lower likelihood) than the previous iteration. While this makes the algorithms more computationally expensive it also allows them to jump across the parameter space and reduces the chances of becoming stuck at a local maximum or saddle point.

4.2.3 Expectation Maximization (EM)

In a famous paper – cited over 46,000 times as of this writing – Dempster et al. (1977) develop a general optimization algorithm with application to a variety of more complicated likelihood-based estimation problems, including missing data (Chapter 12) and mixture models. This algorithm goes by the name of *Expectation Maximization* (EM). EM appears frequently in custom and nonstandard estimation problems, so we outline the basic logic of EM here.

Suppose we are interested in a model that can be expressed as $\mathcal{L}(\theta \mid \mathbf{X}_c)$, but we are missing some information: the *complete data*, $\mathbf{X}_c$, is only partially observed. We define the *observed data* as $\mathbf{X}_o \subset \mathbf{X}_c$. This might happen because some covariates were not measured or reported for some of the units in $\mathbf{X}_c$. We call $\log \mathcal{L}(\theta; \mathbf{X}_o)$ the *observed data log-likelihood*, while $\log \mathcal{L}(\theta; \mathbf{X}_c)$ is the *complete data log-likelihood*. Starting from an initial guess, θ_0, EM arrives at $\hat{\theta} = \arg \max \log \mathcal{L}(\theta; \mathbf{X}_c)$ by iterating the following steps:

E-step Given the observed data and a particular iteration, θ_n, find the expected value of the complete data log-likelihood,

$$Q(\theta \mid \mathbf{X}_o, \theta_n) \equiv \mathrm{E}\left[\log \mathcal{L}(\theta; \mathbf{X}_c) \mid \mathbf{X}_o, \theta_n\right].$$

M-step Find the maximizer of the expected complete data log-likelihood, given the observed data and θ_n,

$$\theta_{n+1} = \arg \max_{\theta} Q(\theta).$$

EM's "trick" is to use the value of θ at the current iteration, combined with the likelihood function, to fill in the missing values in the observed data. EM's tremendous popularity is testament to its flexibility and the ubiquity of missing data problems. EM has drawbacks, however: It can be slow to converge; it does not readily produce uncertainty estimates around $\hat{\theta}$; and it can get trapped at local maxima.

In case you were wondering ... 4.2 Mixture distribution/mixture model

A *mixture distribution* is a distribution or mass function that is composed of multiple subpopulations described by different probability distributions. For example, let $g_j(x; \theta_j)$ be a distribution function with parameter vector θ_j and assume that there are J total subpopulations. We can express the mixture distribution as

$$f(x; w_j, \theta_j) = \sum_{j=1}^{J} w_j g_j(x; \theta_j),$$

where the parameters w_j are the *mixing parameters* or weights such that $\sum_{j=1}^{J} w_j = 1$. When J is known (or assumed), we have a *finite mixture model*. In such a case we can construct a likelihood:

$$\mathcal{L}(w_j, \boldsymbol{\theta}_j \mid \mathbf{x}) = \prod_{i=1}^{n} \left[\sum_{j=1}^{J} w_j g_j(x_i; \boldsymbol{\theta}_j) \right].$$

Treating the w_j as "missing data," we can use EM to maximize the likelihood (although there are other tools as well).

Mixture distributions and models are widely applied in categorization and machine learning problems, notably text analysis.

4.3 ESTIMATION CHALLENGES

Real-world applications of likelihood-based models can encounter a variety of challenges in estimation. We describe some of the most common and offer suggestions for troubleshooting.

4.3.1 Optimizer Fails to Converge

Numerical optimization techniques can run into problems depending on the data, model estimated, and optimizing algorithm. When the algorithm fails to converge it can be a simple computational issue or a symptom of a bigger problem. Here we highlight the most common problems and offer some guidance toward solutions, should you encounter them.

4.3.2 Starting Values

Most numerical optimizers need jumping off points in the form of starting values for the parameters. Unfortunately, if you had ideal starting values, you might not need the algorithm at all. Practically, most algorithms will start pretty well if least squares estimates are used to generate a set of starting values, but some problems may be too complex for this simple solution. If you are totally in the dark, you might try a grid search or sample from a variety of starting values to ensure that the solution is not dependent on where the algorithm starts.

4.3.3 Algorithm Choice

The choice of optimizer seems esoteric, but it might actually be important in some problems. There are two major types of algorithms: those that allow you to specify the first and second derivatives, and those that try to figure them out without your intervention. The former generally are much faster because they have more information to deal with and can straightforwardly work out where the maxima (minima) will be located. If you can supply only first-order conditions, then the BHHH algorithm is a good choice; BFGS and DFP are good algorithms when you don't have good starting values and don't know the formulas for the Hessians. One strategy is to start with the coarse algorithms, and use the results from these to serially move to better and better algorithms, carrying along the final estimates from one run as starting values for the next, and also supplying the calculated Hessian from the preceding run into the call for the current run.

4.3.4 Scaling of Variables

The scale of the variables should not matter in principle, but it can matter for numerical calculations, and especially for minimization (maximization) problems. If you have variables with vastly different scales (e.g., GDP in dollars and population in billions of individuals), it is quite plausible that coefficients for some variables will disappear into machine rounding during iterative fitting. As a result, the first- and second-order conditions will deliver incorrect or misleading information to the optimizing function, since for some changes in parameter estimates it will appear that the log likelihood will not change. This is because the actual change is being masked by the scale of an estimated coefficient. In general, variables should be within about three orders of magnitude. Standardizing variables to have a mean of 0 and a standard deviation of 1 can be particularly helpful in more complicated models with covariates on vastly different original scales. Gelman et al. (2008) suggest scaling of variables in logistic regression to have a mean of 0 and a standard deviation of 0.5; see also Gelman (2008).

4.3.5 Step Sizes

Most optimizing algorithms internally calculate the size of the change for the next iteration, but if the step is too big the optimizer can get stuck in a loop, continually skipping over the maximum (minimum), or go in the wrong direction, whether off to $\pm\infty$ or simply to a lower "hill" (and the wrong answer). Fortunately, most computer programs allow you the flexibility of specifying the step size. Shrinking the step size is one possible solution to this problem, albeit at the cost of more computational cycles.

4.3.6 Flat Likelihoods

A "flat likelihood" is generally a failure of model specification, implying that there is no unique solution to the maximization problem. This is most commonly a problem of perfect collinearity in covariates (which some programs identify and drop) or complete separation (see Section 4.5.1), but it could also be a failure to program a completely identified statistical model, implying that different combinations of values for covariates are equally likely, given the data. Flat likelihoods also arise in more complex likelihood functions, especially ones with multiple modes. The flat area of the likelihood could trap the optimizer even when there is a unique and identifiable maximum. The best solution is to plot the likelihood surface in a variety of directions, if at all possible. From here it may make sense to give the optimizer different starting values (away from the plateau) or increase the step size (so the optimizer can jump off the flat area).

4.3.7 Absence of Single Maximum

Similar to flat likelihoods, some likelihood surfaces are multimodal. Multimodality can trap the optimizer at a local optimum when a superior alternative exists. Multimodality is again more common in complicated, highly sculpted likelihoods. It can be hard to diagnose without visualizing the likelihood in some way. Solutions involve combinations of those given above: give the optimizer several sets of starting values, increase the step size, and try different algorithms.

4.4 DIFFERENT SOFTWARE YIELDS "DIFFERENT" RESULTS

Suppose you are interested in replicating a statistical finding reported in published research. The author has been kind enough to post or share her data with you. She may have even shared her STATA .do file. You estimate the model in $\mathcal{R}$ and the table of numbers displayed differs from what you see in the published result. What gives? Is STATA wrong? Is there a coding error in $\mathcal{R}$? Both? Neither?

Very often the answer is "neither." Different results from different software packages can be the result of different parameterizations for the same model. For example, STATA's `ologit` command, which estimates the ordered logit model discussed in Chapter 8, uses a parameterization which omits the constant (intercept), whereas the commonly used $\mathcal{R}$ functions do estimate an intercept. The models are mathematically identical and will yield the same interpretations on the scale of the response variable – another reason to focus interpretation there rather than on complicated transformations of specific coefficients. Similarly, some software packages may make different default decisions about how to treat categorical variables (e.g., which level is the "reference category"). Looking into the documentation is the only way to sort out how this works.

If serious differences remain across statistical platforms, then the next place to look is at the default settings for dealing with missing data, perfect separation, and similar issues. Some software packages will fit models with little or no warning that there is a problem. For example, the Rauchhaus (2009) example later in this chapter was initially fit in STATA. STATA, unlike $\mathcal{R}$, automatically drops covariates for which there is perfect separation. Furthermore, Rauchhaus's model was fit using STATA's `xtgee` function; this function does not generate a warning that perfect separation was detected, leading to material differences in estimates across computing platforms.

A third place to look for the explanation is in the default choice of optimization algorithm, especially for more complicated or customized likelihood problems. Different optimizers with different default tolerances, etc., can generate different answers. Whether this is an indication of a problem or simple rounding differences requires further investigation by the analyst. If different optimization algorithms are giving wildly different answers, then this is a symptom of problems described above (multiple modes, etc.). A closer inspection of the likelihood surface is in order.

4.5 MODELING CHALLENGES APPEAR AS ESTIMATION PROBLEMS

4.5.1 (Near-)Perfect Separation

Perfect separation occurs when some covariate in a model (or, less commonly, linear combination of covariates) perfectly predicts an outcome, or so nearly so that the computer can't tell the difference. Perfect separation occurs most commonly in models for categorical data (such as the binary logit), but it illustrates a more general issue. This problem is easiest to see when considering a single covariate, X, that can take on two values, "high" or "low." In our data there are no observed successes when X is "high." Knowing that observation i has $x_i =$ high is sufficient to tell us that $y_i = 1$.

Perfect separation can also happen with covariates that are continuous if there is some threshold that cleanly divides all the 1s and 0s. For example, if we are using age to predict whether someone voted in the last US presidential election (which was about a year ago at the time of publication), then (almost?) all survey respondents reporting an age less than 19 will not have voted. The consequence of perfect separation is that the optimizer will never converge, instead attempting to estimate an infinite coefficient (and standard error).

A recent example received some attention in the literature on nuclear deterrence and stability. Rauchhaus (2009) looks at the incidence of conflict at the country dyad-year level, finding that if both countries in the dyad are nuclear-capable, then the risk of escalation to war is substantially lower than if only one or neither of the countries is armed with nuclear weapons. Bell and Miller (2015) criticize this article on the basis of its handling of perfect separation, among other issues.

We fit the Rauchhaus (2009) model in $\mathcal{R}$ as a standard logit using glm, with $\mathcal{R}$ issuing the following warning:

```
Warning message:
glm.fit: fitted probabilities numerically 0 or 1 occurred
```

This is a generic warning, indicating that the optimizer called by glm() is spinning off towards $\pm\infty$, forcing the predicted probability to one of the boundaries. This happens most commonly under situations of perfect separation. In particular, this means there is probably no unique set of parameters that maximizes the likelihood. If a model with a single covariate, for example, gives perfect separation with an estimate $\hat{\beta} = 0.3$, that model will also give the same perfect separation with $\hat{\beta} = 0.3 \times 100$.

The results presented in Table 4.1 give an additional hint as to the problem: the twonukedyad variable, representing an indicator variable for dyads in which both countries are nuclear-capable, has an enormous standard error relative to the estimated coefficient. But this standard error is not infinite.

Table 4.2 looks at this variable more directly. The contingency table shows that being a nuclear dyad is a perfect predictor of the absence of war. Zorn (2005) refers to such patterns as "quasi-complete separation" since twonukedyad is only a perfect predictor of nonwar.

What is to be done here? The most common solution – the one built in to STATA – is to simply drop the variable on which there is perfect separation. Many have noted that this is clearly suboptimal, since the offending variable

TABLE 4.1 *Estimation of the Rauchhaus (2009) logit model. Note the enormous standard error for* twonukedyad.

	$\hat{\beta}$	$\sigma_{\hat{\beta}}$	t-Ratio	p-Value
Constant	−3.85	1.13	−3.42	0.00
onenukedyad	0.91	0.37	2.47	0.01
twonukedyad	−13.28	522.99	−0.03	0.98
logCapabilityRatio	−0.65	0.12	−5.23	0.00
Ally	−0.44	0.35	−1.25	0.21
SmlDemocracy	−0.07	0.03	−2.35	0.02
SmlDependence	−119.86	48.97	−2.45	0.01
logDistance	−0.69	0.13	−5.19	0.00
Contiguity	2.95	0.38	7.69	0.00
MajorPower	2.36	0.39	5.97	0.00
NIGOs	−0.03	0.01	−2.52	0.01
n	455,619			
AIC	932			

TABLE 4.2 *Contingency table showing the incidence of war between dyad-years of different levels of nuclear capacity from Rauchhaus (2009).*

	< 2-nuke dyad	2-nuke dyad
no war	610,402	806
war	102	0

is, in essence, *too good* of a predictor. One estimation strategy is the so-called Firth logistic regression (Firth, 1993), which is a penalized likelihood approach. Bell and Miller (2015) use Firth regression and show that Rauchhaus's finding disappears.

4.5.2 Rare Events (and Small Samples)

The example above also serves to illustrate another challenge in model fitting for categorical data, the so-called *rare events* problem, in which the frequency of observations in a particular category is dwarfed by the number of trials. The problem is most extensively studied in the context of binary data where the number of 1s is quite small relative to n. In the conflict data just considered, there were 102 dyad-years of observed wars against 611,402 nonwars, or about one war for every 6,000 nonwars. Data with rare events are, ironically, seen in political science with some regularity. The number of major protests are small relative to the number of daily or yearly opportunities; the number of revolutions or regime changes is even less frequent. The number of people who choose to run for public office is small relative to the population, etc.

The consistency of the MLE is an *asymptotic* property. In small samples, the MLE, including the logit model, can be biased (Firth, 1993; McCullagh and Nelder, 1989). King and Zeng (2001) show that data with rare events are analogous to small samples, since a dataset with only 102 events gives relatively little information about event occurrence even when there are over 600,000 observed trials. But there is the issue of absolute versus relative infrequency of events. The issue of small-sample bias is one of absolute infrequency. If we had a dataset with 2,000 observed wars, we would no longer face a small-sample problem, even if that would still represent less than 0.3% of the observed dyad-years. That said, extremes in relative infrequency can also induce computational problems in some circumstances.

Rare events can be approached from several directions. One way is to alter the assumed link function, using an asymmetric one, such as the *cloglog* approach mentioned earlier or even the generalized extreme value distribution. Another approach, advocated by King and Zeng (2001), imposes a direct bias correction on the intercept. Penalized likelihood such as Firth regression can also models for binary data in the face of rare events. Finally, there are various Bayesian estimation frameworks beyond the scope of this text.

4.6 CONCLUSION

Estimating models using maximum likelihood is often fast and painless. But one of the strengths of the likelihood approach is its flexibility in accommodating more complicated data structures and custom-designed models. As a result, some understanding of the topography of a likelihood function and of details around numerical optimization is a good thing. This chapter introduced the basics of profile likelihood and outlined some of the more common optimization procedures.

Understanding what is happening inside your statistical software is important not just for understanding the output on your screen. Some problems that initially appear to be computational in nature are, in fact, features of the data at hand, something the should be explored rather than ignored or swept under the rug. We highlighted perfect separation and rare events as frequently encountered examples in the context of model for binary or other categorical data.

4.7 FURTHER READING

Applications

Perfect separation is a common problem in political science data; recent examples include Ahlquist (2010a); Barrilleaux and Rainey (2014); and Mares (2015, ch. 9). Chalmers (2017) uses both rare events and Firth logit in modeling banks' decisions to lobby the Basel Committee.

Past Work

Heinze and Schemper (2002) provide an applied discussion in support of Firth regression. Zorn (2005) provides an applied, political-science-focused discussion of perfect separation problems.

Advanced Study

Pawitan (2013) provides an extended discussion of profile likelihoods and likelihood-based confidence intervals and inference.

Mebane and Sekhon (1998, 2011) develop and implement a flexible optimization algorithm that has seen some use in the numerical optimization of more complicated likelihood functions.

When looking at separation and rare events, Gelman et al. (2008) take a Bayesian approach and propose a proper but uninformative Cauchy prior over the regression coefficients. See Rainey (2016) for more on the limitations of Firth regression and the importance of priors when using Bayesian methods to address perfect separation.

Kordas (2006) uses a binary quantile regression framework for modeling unbalanced and rare events binary data. Wang and Dey (2010) discuss the use of the Generalized Extreme Value distribution for modeling rare events using a more flexible, asymmetric link function.

Software Notes

The $\mathcal{R}$ library ProfileLikelihood (Choi, 2011) calculates, plots, and constructs likelihood-based confidence intervals from profile likelihoods for specified parameters for many commonly used models.

The $\mathcal{R}$ libraries maxLik (Henningsen and Toomet, 2011) and bbmle (Bolker and R Development Core Team, 2016) provide wrapper functions and easier access to a number of $\mathcal{R}$'s numerical optimization algorithms for maximum likelihood estimation. rgenoud implements the Mebane and Sekhon GENOUD algorithm.

Penalized and Firth regression are implemented in logistf (Heinze and Ploner, 2016) and brglm (Kosmidis, 2017). King and Zeng's rare events logit model is implemented within the Zelig library (Imai et al., 2009). Gelman et al.'s Bayesian approach to separation and rare events are implemented in the bayesglm() function in the arm library (Gelman and Su, 2016).

PART II

MODEL EVALUATION AND INTERPRETATION

5

Model Evaluation and Selection

Building statistical models in terms of systematic and stochastic components implies that, when the estimation is completed, the researcher has constructed a working model of the data-generating process. Such models embody more than just decisions about covariates. The researcher also makes decisions about the functional form linking covariates to the systematic component, the process governing random variation, and the degree to which we believe that different observations are independent of one another. Before worrying about particular parameters or other estimates, we must first convince both ourselves and our audiences that the model itself is a useful one. Models, as we all know, should be evaluated based on their relative usefulness for specific, well-defined purposes.

We begin this chapter with a caricature of current social science practice in evaluating and disseminating the results of statistical modeling. We do this to highlight common pitfalls and motivate what continues to be a shockingly underutilized model evaluation tool: out-of-sample prediction. We then describe the mechanics of predicting out-of-sample and demonstrate its use in real research problems.

5.1 CURRENT PRACTICE

Unfortunately, current publication practice demands output that often fails to fully exploit the underlying statistical models while also failing to display results in the most memorable and easily understood formats. Rather, readers are confronted with the Big Ugly Table of Numbers (BUTON), presenting estimated coefficients and their associated standard errors for a handful of models, perhaps fit to differing subsets of the available data. That is, most scholarly output consists of coefficient point estimates along with some measure of the uncertainty in these estimates. Scholars proceed apace to draw inferences by calculating t- or z-statistics and comparing these values to arbitrary thresholds that are, nevertheless, imbued with near-magical importance. Based on the values of these statistical tests, scholars adorn the BUTON with stars, crosses, dots, accents, and other decoration.

5.1.1 BUTON

BUTONs are ubiquitous. Several appear in this book; Table 5.2 later in this chapter is a good example. This table satisfies at least one basic idea about presenting your research: science should be transparent; procedures and results should be widely available. Of course, it is important to also share the data, so that these results may be replicated by other scholars in different laboratories around the world, using different computers and different programs. In addition to these kinds of standard numerical displays, many scholars will include a variety of useful model diagnostics and "goodness-of-fit" statistics such as likelihood ratios, R^2, BIC, F- and other Wald tests. All these pieces of information are conditional on the sample used to fit the model; they tell us little about the extent to which the model is highly tuned to a particular data set.

BUTON are rarely compelling when trying to convince readers of a particular model's benefits. Why? Here are three easy exercises to illustrate the problem:

1. Think of your favorite empirical study. Write down a coefficient and a standard error from that model. On paper. Without looking. Put the answers here:

   $\hat{\beta}$:   ; $\sigma_{\hat{\beta}}$:

2. Okay, try this one. Write down the estimated coefficient from any article you read in the past week. Put your answer here: $\hat{\beta}$:

3. What was the estimated intercept for the model from last week's homework? Answer: $\hat{\beta}_0$:

All those coefficients, all those standard errors. Like so many through the years, they are forgotten. This suggests that having a table of numbers somewhere for the careful scholar to review is important, but presenting a large table of numbers is unlikely to be compelling or memorable. The current publishing norm is to present tables of regression output, explaining it as you go. Nevertheless, this is frequently not the best option for making your analysis stick in your readers' minds. Nor is it necessarily a good strategy for your own model checking. It seems a sad waste of effort to reduce hard modeling work to simple tabular summaries, especially when the estimated models contain all the necessary components to build a simulation of the process you began studying in the first place. We want to take advantage of the models' richness to explore how we expect our dependent variables to behave in different situations of substantive relevance.

Since tables will continue to be produced – and rightly so – some care in their production seems merited. Some basic principles for constructing tables are:

- Tables are best for cataloging and documenting your results. Fill them with details for those carefully studying your work. Think of them as entries in the scientific record.
- BUTON are not well suited for quickly transmitting the crux of your findings in the body of an article or in a presentation to a wide audience.
- Tables should facilitate precise, analytical comparisons.
- Comparisons should flow from left to right.
- There should be enough white space to allow the eyes to construct focused comparisons easily.
- There should be no unnecessary rules (i.e., lines) that separate columns or rows within the table.
- Tables are most useful for reporting data: counts of things, or percentages.
- Numbers should be right justified to a common number of decimal places to facilitate comparisons.
- Tables should present information only as precisely as necessary; entries should reflect a reasonable degree of realism in the accuracy of measurement. This means 8% or 8.3% is generally better than 8.34214%. Items that yield extremely large ($9.061e+57$) or small ($5.061e-57$) quantities should be rescaled or, in the latter case, simply called 0.
- Rows and columns should be informatively and adequately labeled with meaningful English-language text, in groups or hierarchies if necessary.
- Entries in the table should be organized in substantively meaningful ways, not alphabetically.
- Give the table an informative title and footnotes to detail information inside the tabular display.

5.1.2 Graphical Displays

Fortunately things have begun to improve and many scholars create detailed appendices containing many BUTON that then appear on the Web alongside data archives. For example, Prorok's article in the 2016 *American Journal of Political Science* includes no big table of numbers, except in the supporting information, which is found on the publisher's website. This is becoming more common and is entirely sensible.

There is also an old and growing movement to display our data and results graphically whenever possible (Cleveland and McGill, 1984; Gelman et al., 2002; Kastellec and Leoni, 2007). The coefficient or ropeladder plots displayed in Figure 3.4 are but one example of such tools. Graphical displays, when done well, can convey much more information in a smaller area than tables. Readers tend to be faster and more accurate in making comparisons when using graphs compared to tables (Feliciano et al., 1963). Subsequent recall of relationships or trends tends to be better when presented graphically. Maps (or map-like visualizations) are particularly memorable (Saket et al., 2015).

But presenting figures alone is not the answer, either (Gelman, 2011). Academic researchers (much less lay audiences or policy makers) routinely misinterpret confidence intervals of the sort displayed in Figure 3.7. Researchers can also produce graphics that are information-sparse, communicating relatively little compared to a table containing the same information. For example, Mutz and Reeves (2005) use experiments to study the impact of televised incivility upon political trust. They use bar charts to display their findings. These charts appear as Figure 3 in their article, commanding a prominent place and appearing in color in the journal's digital edition. The figure's number is apt because their display contains just three pieces of information. Three comparisons of interest appear in 31 square inches; the entire page is 62 square inches. Compared to displays such as Figure 3.3 this is a low content-to-space ratio.

In designing compelling graphical displays Tufte (1992) has excellent advice, including

- Show the data,
- Encourage comparisons,
- Maximize the data-to-ink ratio,
- Erase non-data and redundant data-ink,

to which we add,

- Give the graphical display an informative caption to detail information inside the display.

5.1.3 What's Left Out?

The dominant modes of scholarly communication – journals and books – impose constraints. Journal articles and books have page limits, printing costs, and black-and-white images. The constraints imposed by publication imply that only a relatively small subset of all the analysis we do for a particular project is ever disseminated. As a result, readers usually have no idea what models or findings were *omitted* from the reported tables. When combined with the fact that traditional outlets also tend not to publish "null" findings, we wind up with well-documented publication biases (Gerber and Malhotra, 2008; Gerber et al., 2001), among other problems.

Even if there were no constraints, and we all published arbitrarily long (and colorful) blog entries detailing all our analysis, we would still face the cognitive and resource limitations of our audiences. How many readers are really willing to dig through an online appendix of many models and terse equations? Are the paper's findings really sufficiently important that it is reasonable to expect audiences and reviewers to spend that much time and effort? Astute consumers of our analysis recognize this fact and understand the incentives we all face, leading them to be understandably skeptical of our results. How can a reader be reassured that the models we choose to present aren't simply the result of a specification search? Credible, reproducible, and transparent methods for model selection help.

Reproducibility, Transparency, and Credibility

Over the last decade, several incidents drew attention to the reproducibility problems in social scientific research. In one example, enterprising PhD students discovered an error in calculations conducted directly in the Excel spreadsheet program (Herndon et al., 2014), leading to the revision of an influential study in economics. In perhaps the most widely reported incident, another team of then-graduate students discovered scientific fraud by reanalyzing study data (Broockman et al., 2015), resulting in the retraction of a study published in *Science*. This came as quite a shock to much of the social science community, but the so-called crisis of reproducibility has been well-known for at least a decade (Ioannidis, 2005).

Several organized responses to doubts about reproducibility have emerged. Recently http://retractionwatch.com/ appeared as a resource for monitoring publications that have been (or should be) withdrawn from the published body of knowledge. In the world of cancer biology, there is an ongoing project to independently replicate a subset of experimental results from a number of high-profile papers published between 2010 and 2012 (https://osf.io/) while building a framework for reproducible research. A team of over 270 researchers in psychology has come together in a systematic effort to reproduce the results of 100 published studies in major psychology journals, with sobering results to date (Open Science Collaboration, 2015).

The solution to this broad problem is complicated, but researchers can take concrete steps to make sure that their own research is reproducible and that they don't wind up reading about their research on retractionwatch.com. First, we need to keep a record of everything. In today's world, this means version control. Second, we need to keep a backup of every change, ideally off-site or in the cloud. Third, we want a work flow that will minimize error by being repeatable so that we can redo calculations and graphics if data or ideas about which model is most appropriate should change. This means working from files with scripts, not clicking buttons. Storing data and performing analysis in spreadsheet programs is a recipe for disaster. Fourth, we want a way to integrate statistical analysis and writing. Cutting and pasting is not the solution, nor is manual entry of results into your textual report. Fifth, it is important to have a way to annotate our procedures and our data, for others and for yourself. Sixth, it is important to share our data – not just our conclusions – with others.

5.1.4 Sign, Significance, and the Perils of p-Values

Social science theories are still generally too coarse to generate strong pre-dictions about, say, the functional form a relationship should take, or what exactly the "null" hypothesis should be in a particular application. As a result, we generally state our hypotheses as something like "The conditional mean of Y should be increasing in X_f," where f denotes the covariate favored by the theoretical argument. We then fit models, including X_f, and if β_f, the regression parameter for X_f, is the right sign and the standard error is small enough, we declare the relationship "significant," scarcely acknowledging the fact that this "significance" is entirely conditional on the model.

> **In case you were wondering ... 5.1 Frequentist p-values**
>
> Given a statistical model with parameter θ and an hypothesized value of the parameter, θ_h, the p-value is the probability of observing a value at least as extreme as the one obtained with the actual data at hand if θ_h were true. Researchers view small p-values as reason to reject the hypothesis that $\theta = \theta_h$.
>
> Researchers claim *statistical significance* (at the α level) if the p-value for a favored parameter in a particular model is less than some arbitrary threshold, α. If α is unstated, then social science convention holds $\alpha = 0.05 = \frac{1}{20}$.

Current practice takes as given that a small p-value for β_f is a sufficient reason to prefer a model that includes X_f. This claim to statistical significance is usually based on the (unstated) null hypothesis that the "true" value of the regression coefficient is 0.0 and some statistical theory telling us that the estimates are normally distributed in sufficiently large samples. In many instances, model selection is implicit, i.e., authors present several models but then discuss only one in any detail.

Authors sometimes proceed to describe the "substantive significance" of their findings, i.e., the size of the marginal effect implied by their chosen model for the variable of interest. Substantive significance is hard to evaluate. The now-standard approach is for an author to pick a model that she likes and compare the change in the expected value of the outcome over some range of the covariate of interest. If this difference in expected values is "big," then the author claims to have identified an important relationship. Authors may even present a whole collection of models as "robustness checks," presumably as evidence that no matter how one fits the model, a similar relationship between the covariate of interest and the response obtains.

Notwithstanding all the claims about the sign, significance, and magnitude of a relationship, explicit justification for the selected model is rare. There are myriad examples in the literature that discuss in detail the statistical significance of estimated regression coefficients in different models but fail to comment on the comparative fit of these same models. Indeed, we observe authors arguing for or against models that are practically indistinguishable from one another *as models*.

This practice of fitting models based on theory (perhaps post hoc) and then filtering results based on the p-values for some covariates is problematic. There is a well-established literature that points away from the uncritical use of p-values in model selection for three reasons. First, p-values do not have the same interpretation after measurement and model selection as they do ex ante. Second, any statement of magnitude is conditional on the model employed, as is any claim to statistical significance. *Identifying "significance," substantive or otherwise, therefore requires that authors first justify their preferred models and the comparison scenarios.* Only then can we meaningfully turn to the magnitude of the difference implied by the chosen models, covariates, and scenarios. Third, using p-values ignores the issue of *model* uncertainty. Any statement about parameter values is conditional on the model and its underlying assumptions. If we are uncertain about which of a variety of possible models is most appropriate, then using p-values to justify selection is nonsensical.

Theory, by itself, is a weak justification for preferring a particular model specification, especially if one of the researchers' goals is to "test" that exact theory. Rather, evaluating model performance can be viewed as an integral part of the research enterprise: a good and useful theory should lead to better prediction. If the data support the theoretical claim, then the theoretically motivated model specification should outperform feasible (and simpler) competitors. Unfortunately, standard practice often provides no explicit reason to prefer the models presented compared to competitors; p-values on regression coefficients do not help in making this determination. We argue that out-of-sample prediction is a sensible, flexible, and powerful method for adjudicating between competing models and justifying model selection.

An Example: Trade and the World Trade Organization, Part I

As an example, consider the vigorous empirical debate over whether the World Trade Organization (WTO) and its precursor, the General Agreement on Trade and Tariffs (GATT), alter countries' patterns of trade in goods and services. Rose (2004) kicked off the debate. He pools annual dyadic trade flows for the post–World War II period and regresses it on the dyad-year's WTO status, along with numerous other covariates. He finds no evidence for a consistent relationship between a dyad's GATT/WTO status and trade flows. Subramanian and Wei (2007), Tomz et al. (2007), and Goldstein et al. (2007) claim to overturn Rose's null findings by arguing for more-nuanced measurement of trade and GATT/WTO participation. Rose's bilateral trade data set, pooled over 1949–99, has 234,597 observations, while Goldstein et al. (2007)'s expanded data set has $n = 381,656$. In such a context, statistical significance for specific coefficients is a weak criterion by which to evaluate a model; it is highly unlikely that any relationship in these data is exactly 0.0. The danger of overfitting here is not trivial; these authors use models with country, dyad and/or year effects along with a slate of covariates running into the double digits. Nevertheless, the bulk of the debate revolves around whether the GATT/WTO variables are statistically significant. None of the authors challenging Rose present evidence for why we should prefer a model with GATT/WTO variables included; presumably the existence of significant coefficient estimates is justification enough. The substantive debate is much impoverished by the participants' focus on *p*-values, failing to engage the models in a predictive sense.

5.2 THE LOGIC OF PREDICTION, OUT-OF-SAMPLE

The logic of out-of-sample prediction is simple: to the extent our statistical models capture underlying social processes, they should be able to predict instances not used to calibrate the model in the first place, assuming the underlying DGP has not changed. Two comparisons are relevant for evaluating the model. The first involves comparing the model's in-sample fit to its ability to predict new data. This is a way of guarding against overfitting. The second compares models against each other as a way of justifying model selection.

Overfitting refers to an estimated model that is sculpted to the data in hand where that data is not necessarily characteristic of all the data that might be observed. Overfitting is a common threat to models that are reasonably complex, especially in observational studies. With enough parameters we can perfectly fit the observed data. But such a model is not likely a very useful one nor a correct description of the data-generating process. To anneal our description of the data-generating process against the threat that the estimated model is tuned entirely to the observed data, we can test the model's ability to predict data not used to fit the model in the first place.[1] These data for validating the model can literally be "new" in the sense that they were observed after fitting the model. But it is more common that we consciously hold back some of our data for later use in the model evaluation phase.[2]

A model that fits about as well in-sample as out-of-sample indicates that the model can generate predictions that are in line with the data-generating process (which is almost never observed in nonexperimental studies). It also enables greater confidence that the estimated model was not overly influenced by some particular features of the data used to calibrate the model. We can

---

[1] This is also related to Type-I error: testing an hypothesis using the data that suggested the hypothesis in the first place is unlikely to reject a null.

[2] What constitutes "new" data poses thorny questions in environments where agents are observing and learning from each other while acting strategically. How best to implement and evaluate out-of-sample prediction in such circumstances requires particular care. See, for example, Gleditsch and Ward (2013) for the case of interstate conflict.

think of this second point, broadly, as a generalization of the concept of influence diagnostics (leverage statistics), including "hat" quantities such as DF-fit, DF-β, and others that decompose the fit into the individual observations' contributions to summary statistics.

Simply performing equivalently in- and out-of-sample does not mean a model is "good." It merely means that it has not been overly sculpted to a particular set of observations. In the second set of comparisons we seek to make judgments about how useful a particular model is by evaluating predictive performance (out-of-sample) relative to other models. If our favored model is no better than feasible and simpler alternatives at predicting new data, then we have little reason to prefer that model, regardless of whether our theoretically inspired specification has "significant" coefficients for special covariates. If we have little reason to believe that the favored covariate is an important part of the underlying data-generating process, then it makes little difference that its regression coefficient conforms to theoretical expectations in an overfit model. Even with well-designed and executed experiments, where the researcher partly controls the DGP, and we can recover estimates of causal relationships, out-of-sample prediction can be helpful. One of the commonly cited weaknesses of experimental interventions is the difficulty in sorting out how well findings generalize to other contexts where exposure is nonrandom. Advance in this domain typically proceeds through a process of comparing competing models, ideally using new data (Clarke, 2006).

A direct consequence of the possibility of overfitting is that statistical significance for a particular parameter does *not* imply that that a model including that parameter predicts better out-of-sample than one without. In fact, the more complicated model may even perform more poorly (Lo et al., 2015; Ward et al., 2010). This issue becomes more salient as the size of the data set increases. In an observational study with twenty observations, statistical significance at five percent, for example, requires systematic patterning and very little error; in a binomial model you could be wrong one time in twenty. The same study with 20,000 observations imposes fewer requirements, since it is unlikely that any regression parameter has a true value of exactly 0. In the binomial case, one in twenty with 20,000 as the number of observations yields 1,000 plausible errors within the five-percent range. With 200,000 observations, it is difficult for an estimated parameter not to achieve "significance," largely because we may expect variation sufficient for precise estimates.

5.2.1 The Process of Evaluating Out-of-Sample Predictions

In out-of-sample prediction, interest centers on evaluating a model's prediction error, often referred to as *generalization error* or *generalization performance*. To estimate this quantity, we must identify a *training set* (the data used to fit the model), a *test set* (the data used to evaluate model's predictions), a model, and a loss function, which measures the model prediction's deviation from the actual value in the test set. Good models will have good performance in the training *and* test data sets.

More formally, suppose we observe our outcome of interest, y, and covariates X for a set of n units. We can partition our data into our training set, S, and our test set, V, such that $n = S \cup V$ and $S \cap V = \emptyset$. We also have a model for Y_i, denoted $M(\mathbf{x}_i; \theta)$, and is a function of the covariates and parameters, θ. The term $\hat{\theta}_S$ is the parameter estimate based on S, the observations in the training set.

For continuous Y we denote a prediction based on $M(\mathbf{x}_i; \hat{\theta}_S)$ as $\hat{y}_i$. The most commonly used loss function for continuous Y is squared error loss:

$$\text{Loss}(y_i, \hat{y}_i) = (y_i - \hat{y}_i)^2 = (y_i - M(\mathbf{x}_i; \hat{\theta}_S))^2.$$

Less commonly used is absolute error:

$$\text{Loss}(y_i, \hat{y}_i) = |y_i - M(\mathbf{x}_i; \hat{\theta}_S)|.$$

In the case that Y is categorical, falling into one of G possible categories, there are several frequently employed loss functions. In situations where the models generate predicted probabilities for being in a category g we can sum across categories in a manner analogous to squared error or absolute loss. For the absolute error case, in which $\mathbb{1}_g(y_i)$ is the indicator function for category g and $M_g(\mathbf{x}_i; \hat{\theta}_S) = \hat{M}_g$ is the predicted probability of being in category g, we get

$$\text{Loss}(y_i, M(\mathbf{x}_i; \hat{\theta}_S)) = \sum_{g=1}^{G} |(\hat{M}_g - \mathbb{1}_g(y_i))|.$$

Also commonly used is the bounded loss function, which takes on a value of unity whenever $\hat{y}_i \neq y_i$ and 0 otherwise. The predicted category, $\hat{y}_i$ is typically the category with the largest predicted probability: $\hat{y}_i = \arg\max_g \hat{M}_g$. Finally, there is deviance given as

$$\text{Loss}(y_i, M(\mathbf{x}_i; \hat{\theta}_S)) = -2 \sum_{g=1}^{G} \mathbb{1}_g(y_i) \log \hat{M}_g.$$

The quantity of interest is the expected prediction error, or Err in the notation of Hastie et al. (2008):

$$\text{Err} = \text{E}\left[\text{Loss}\left(Y, M(X, \hat{\theta}_S)\right)\right],$$

where expectations are taken over all that is random (partition of training and test set, etc.).

Cross-Validation
The question naturally arises as to where the test and training sets come from in real-world applications. In a data-rich environment we might consider actually

withholding some of the data for later use as the test set. Or we might expect a new sample to arrive later in time. But both of these are relatively uncommon in the social sciences. Cross-validation is a way to use the data we do have as both training and test sets, just not at the same time.

Initial work on cross-validation followed the thinking of Seymour Geisser, who believed that the inferential framework of hypothesis testing was misleading. Instead, he believed that using prediction-based tools would lead to the selection of better, i.e., more useful models, even if these models were not the "true" models.

More specifically, k-fold cross validation divides the data randomly into k disjoint subsets (or folds) of approximately equal size.[3] The division into subsets must be independent of all covariates for estimating generalization error. Each of the k subsets will serve as the test set for the model fit using the data in the remaining $k - 1$ subsets as the training set. For each observation, we calculate the prediction error based on the predicted value generated by the model fit to the training data. More formally, if $\kappa(i)$ is the fold containing observation i and $-\kappa(i)$ is its complement, then the k-fold cross-validation estimate of *Err* is given by

$$\text{Err}_{\text{CV}}(M, \mathbf{y}, \mathbf{X}) = \frac{1}{n} \sum_{i=1}^{n} \text{Loss}(y_i, M(\mathbf{x}_i; \hat{\boldsymbol{\theta}}_{-\kappa(i)})).$$

Alternatively we can write the k-fold cross validation estimate as the average of prediction errors within each of the k folds:

$$\text{CV}_j(M, \mathbf{y}, \mathbf{X}) = \frac{1}{|\kappa_j|} \sum_{i \in \kappa_j} \text{Loss}(y_i, M(\mathbf{x}_i; \hat{\boldsymbol{\theta}}_{-\kappa(i)}))$$

$$\text{Err}_{\text{CV}}(M, \mathbf{y}, \mathbf{X}) = \frac{1}{k} \sum_{j=1}^{k} \text{CV}_j(M, \mathbf{y}, \mathbf{X}),$$

where κ_j denotes the set of observations i in each fold $j \in \{1, 2, \ldots, k\}$, and $|\kappa_j|$ denotes the cardinality, or number of observations, of this set.

What about k? One choice is "leave-one-out" cross-validation, in which $k = n$. Leave-one-out has some nice properties but has higher variance and is computationally more expensive than setting k to some smaller value. Shao (1993) shows that leave-one-out cross-validation will not lead to the selection of the "true" model as $n \to \infty$ but leaving out a larger number of observations will – if we are willing to entertain the notion of a "true" model. As a result, cross-validation setting $k = 5$ or 10 is fairly common. Under such a decision there may be some bias in our estimate of Err, but the bias is upwards. As n grows large the distinction becomes less relevant. In comparing models,

---

[3] Note that we are temporarily departing from our notation convention in other chapters, where k was used to denote the number of covariates in a model. Here we follow the literature on cross-validation and use k to denote the number of "folds."

the important consideration is using the same k for all the cross-validation estimates. The exact value of k is less important.

We clearly prefer models with lower prediction error. How big of a difference in prediction error is "big enough?" Currently, a general description of the distribution cross-validation estimator does not exist. But we can estimate the empirical variance of the cross-validation Err:

$$\text{var}\,[\text{Err}_{CV}] = \frac{1}{k}\text{var}\,[CV_1, \ldots, CV_k]\,.$$

The square root of this quantity is the standard error of the cross-validation estimate of prediction error. Hastie et al. (2008) suggest the "one standard error rule" in which we select the most parsimonious model whose cross-validation-estimated prediction error is within one standard deviation of the model with the smallest prediction error. Put another way, if a simpler model's prediction error falls within one standard deviation of a more complicated model's prediction error then the simpler model is to be preferred.

When should cross-validation occur, and how does it relate to model building more generally? Hastie et al. (2008) argue that "In general, with a multi-step modeling procedure, cross-validation must be applied to the entire sequence of modeling steps. In particular, samples must be 'left out' before any selection or filtering steps are applied." (p. 245–249). It is important to note, however, that they are discussing cross-validation in the context of machine learning, where there are a very large number of predictors and little to inform model selection (e.g., some genomics applications). Most social science applications, on the other hand, present arguments justifying the inclusion of specific predictors or decisions about functional form (e.g., "interaction terms"). In such situations, some model selection has already been accomplished. Cross-validation can then be used to compare competing models and justify model choices without necessarily building models from scratch for each of the k folds.

Example of Cross-Validation

We look to the Fearon and Laitin (2003) classic article on civil wars for an example. We display the BUTON for a reestimation of their logistic regression model in Table 5.1.

For exposition we conduct a two-fold cross-validation. We randomly split the data in two sets denoted κ_1 and κ_2. We first fit the model using just the data in κ_1. Using those estimated coefficients, along with covariate data, we produce an in-sample predicted probability for κ_1 and an out-of-sample predicted probability for the cases in κ_2. We then refit the model, reversing the roles for κ_1 and κ_2, producing both in-sample and out-of-sample predicted probabilities for each observation. From here we can construct a variety of displays and undertake various calculations summarizing the differences, if any. A ROC plot summarizing in-sample and out-of-sample predictive performance is one example, shown in Figure 5.1. The model's out-of-sample predictive

TABLE 5.1 *Logistic regression of civil war onset, replicating Fearon and Laitin (2003).*

	β	$\sigma_{\hat{\beta}}$
Intercept	−6.75	0.73
Prior war	−0.90	0.31
GDP per capita	−0.34	0.07
Population	0.26	0.07
% mountainous	0.23	0.08
Noncontiguous state	0.35	0.28
Oil exporter	0.91	0.28
New state	1.59	0.34
Instability	0.60	0.24
Democracy	0.02	0.02
Ethnic fractionalization	0.07	0.37
Religious fractionalization	0.40	0.51
n	6,402	
$\log \mathcal{L}$	−483	
AIC	990	
BIC	1,071	

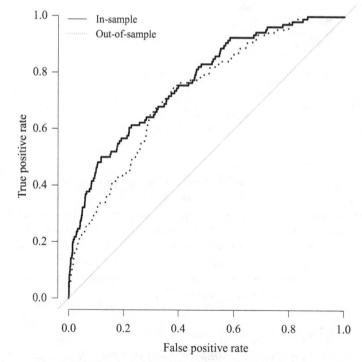

FIGURE 5.1 ROC plot of twofold cross-validation of the Fearon and Laitin replication from Table 5.1.

R Code Example 5.1 Twofold CV

```
library (pROC)
flmdw <- read.csv("flmdw.csv")
infitset<-sample(rownames(flmdw),size=dim(flmdw)[[1]]/2) #divide the sample
totalset<-rownames(flmdw)
intestset<-setdiff(totalset,infitset)
fl.trainset<-flmdw[infitset,]
fl.testset<-flmdw[intestset,]
#estimate
training.fit<- glm(as.factor(onset) ~ warl + gdpenl + lpopl1 +
    lmtnest + ncontig + Oil + nwstate + instab + polity21 +
    ethfrac + relfrac, family = binomial(link = logit),
    data = fl.trainset)
pi.train <- predict(training.fit, type="response") #in-sample predictions
pi.test <- predict(training.fit, type="response",
    newdata = fl.testset) #out-of-sample predictions

flmdw$is.fit<-flmdw$oos.fit<-NA
flmdw[infitset,"is.fit"]<-pi.train
flmdw[intestset,"oos.fit"]<-pi.test
training.fit2<- glm(as.factor(onset) ~ warl + gdpenl + lpopl1 +
    lmtnest + ncontig + Oil + nwstate + instab + polity21 +
    ethfrac + relfrac, family = binomial(link = logit),
    data = fl.testset)
pi.train2 <- predict(training.fit2, type="response")
pi.test2 <- predict(training.fit2, type="response", newdata = fl.trainset)
flmdw[intestset,"is.fit"]<-pi.train2
flmdw[infitset,"oos.fit"]<-pi.test2

#plot
par(bty="n", las=1)
plot.roc(flmdw$onset,flmdw$is.fit, xlab="False positive rate",
    ylab="True positive rate", lwd=3,
    legacy.axes=T, se=T)
plot.roc(flmdw$onset,flmdw$oos.fit ,add=T, lty=3, lwd=3)
legend("topleft", legend=c("In-sample", "Out-of-sample"),
    lty=c(1,3), bty="n")
```

performance is marginally worse than in-sample. Code Example 5.1 demonstrates how we undertake two-fold cross-validation "by hand."

For the sake of simplicity in this two-fold cross-validation example, we did not utilize the estimated models' descriptions of our estimation uncertainty. To do this we could redraw many coefficient vectors from the multivariate normal distribution to produce many predictions, both in- and out-of sample, building up distributions of predictions. Doing so, we would discover that, in this case, the model's in- and out-of-sample predictions overlap considerably.

5.2.2 Variations on a Theme

Cross-validation is part of a class of *resampling* tools that take advantage of modern computing power to repeatedly analyze subsamples of a common data set in order to build up information about a quantity or distribution of interest. The bootstrap, jackknife, and randomization tests are other tools in this class.

Bootstrap Estimation

The bootstrap differs from cross-validation, although both rely on randomly sampling the data we have to build up distributional insights for complicated problems. Bootstrapping is an estimation method, whereas cross-validation is typically a post-estimation tool for formal evaluation.

Bootstrap methods involve repeatedly estimating a statistic of interest on a series of random subsamples from the observed data. Importantly, bootstrapping relies on sampling *with replacement*, whereas cross-validation partitions the data into disjoint subsets. Thus, bootstrap methods aim to build up distributional information about the statistic of interest (calculating standard errors, for example).

Suppose we have a data set with 1,000 observations, and we are interested in the model $Y \sim f(y; \theta)$. We could find bootstrap estimates of the standard errors around $\hat{\theta}$ by randomly selecting 100 observations (with replacement), estimating the regression model, and storing the estimate of $\hat{\theta}$. Repeating this procedure many times builds up a distribution for $\hat{\theta}$. This distribution is treated as the sampling distribution, because it is. The goal is to derive robust estimates of population parameters when inference to the population is especially problematical or complicated.

Jackknife

The jackknife is an even older resampling technique designed to build up sampling information about a statistic. The jackknife involves iteratively removing each data point and calculating the statistic on the $n-1$ remaining observations and then averaging across all these values. The jackknife is similar to leave-one-out cross-validation in that it serially leaves a single observation out of the estimation and then computes an average of the statistics being examined from the $n-1$ jackknifed subsample statistics. The variance of the averages calculated on the resamples is an estimate of the variance of the original sample mean but robust in small samples as well.

Permutation and Randomization Tests

Permutation and randomization tests are yet other reanalysis techniques designed to test whether differences between groups of observations "matter" under the maintained hypothesis that they should not. As an example, consider a researcher-controlled experiment with n subjects in which $s < n$ receive a stimulus, while the other $n - s$ do not. The researcher then measures the outcome of interest and proceeds to make comparisons. The so-called sharp null hypothesis maintains that the effect of the treatment is exactly 0.0 for all subjects. Under this assumption, we should be able to shuffle which subjects are labeled as having received the stimulus and still retrieve approximately the same outcome distributions as what was observed. In "shuffling" the label, the same proportion of the subject pool is labeled as "stimulated," we merely alter which subjects those are. In other words, we are sampling without replacement. In a permutation test, the researcher actually generates all $\binom{n}{s}$ distinct ways of assigning stimulus to s subjects out of n, constructing the distribution of the statistic of interest under the sharp null. We can then determine exactly where in this distribution our observed data fall, generating exact p-values.

Permutation tests can become cumbersome in even moderate samples. For example, a study with 30 subjects, half of whom receive a stimulus, has 155,117,520 different combinations. In order to determine whether our observed data are "surprising," we do not necessarily need to construct all possible permutations. We can simply do many of them. When inference is based on such a random sample of all possible combinations, we refer to a *randomization test*.

5.2.3 Out-of-Sample Prediction: Trade and the WTO, Act II

The participants in the trade-and-WTO debate introduced in Section 5.1.4 rely on the augmented "gravity model," estimated in the following log-linear form:

$$\log y_{ijt} \sim f_{\mathcal{N}}(\mu_{ijt}, \sigma_{ij}^2) \qquad \forall \quad j \neq i$$

$$\mu_{ijt} = \mathbf{x}_{ijt}^{\mathsf{T}} \boldsymbol{\beta},$$

where i and j index countries and t indexes time. Interest centers on the trading pair or "dyad," ij. In this example, all models treat dyad-years as conditionally independent. The dependent variable, Y, is averaged bilateral trade; X is a matrix of possibly time-varying covariates, including year indicator variables. The parameters $\boldsymbol{\beta}$ and σ_{ij}^2 are to-be estimated quantities. The subscripts on σ^2 indicate the commonly recognized problem that repeated measurements on the same dyad should show some dependence; this is most commonly addressed by using a sandwich estimator and "clustering" standard errors at the dyad level.

We begin by replicating the Rose (2004) and Tomz et al. (2007) (TGR) analysis. For the sake of direct comparison, we use the same slate of covariates as Rose and TGR and the data set provided on Tomz's website. In addition to indicators for dyad-level GATT/WTO involvement, X includes the log great circle distances between countries, the log product of real GDP, the log product of real GDP per capita, the log product of land area, and indicators for colonial ties, involvement in regional trade agreements, shared currency, and the Generalized System of Preferences, shared language, shared borders, shared colonizing powers, whether i ever colonized j, whether i was ever a territory of j, the number of landlocked countries in the dyad, and the number of island nations in the dyad.

TGR measure GATT/WTO participation based on whether countries were formal members, "non-member participants," or out of the system entirely. An "F-F" dyad is one where both countries are formal GATT/WTO members; "F-N" dyads are those where one is a formal member and one is a non-member participant; "F-O" dyads have one formal member and one country out of the system. "N-N," "N-O," and "O-O" dyads are defined analogously.

We will base our comparisons on four models. In Model 1 we fit a benchmark gravity model using only GDP, per capita GDP, and distance as covariates. Model 2 augments the benchmark model with TGR's five variables encoding the dyad's GATT/WTO status. Model 3 is Rose's "default" gravity model reported in Rose (2004, 104) but excluding any variables identifying GATT/WTO participation. In the fourth model we replicate TGR's model 3 (Tomz et al., 2007, 2012), which includes a series of variables accounting for the GATT/WTO status of the dyad.[4] We refer to this model as TGR-3.

To evaluate these competing models we compare cross-validated out-of-sample predictive performance. Table 5.3 displays the mean-squared prediction error for each model under two prediction scenarios. First, we conducted five-fold cross validation using all the data; these results are the first column in Table 5.3. As a substantive matter, TGR argue that the GATT effect is most pronounced in the pre-1967 period. We therefore repeat the cross-validation but using only data prior to 1967. These results are in the second column. We see that including GATT/WTO variables buys very little in terms of predictive performance out-of-sample. Comparing Models 1 and 2, we see that the addition of the GATT/WTO covariates improves model performance by less than 1%, with a similar result when comparing Model 3 with TGR-3. In the pre-1967 period, the inclusion of the GATT/WTO covariates improves model performance by about 1%.

Table 5.3 also reports the standard error of the cross-validation for the model with the smallest MSE in each column. Using the one standard error rule we have no reason to prefer the TGR-3 model over Model 3 in the full data set. In the pre-1967 period, TGR-3's predictive performance is one standard error better than Model 3, yet still represents a 1% improvement.

Participants in the trade-GATT/WTO debate fit models to similar data and then based their knowledge claims on the (non)significance of GATT/WTO covariates without first comparing model fit. In our reestimations, we recover TGR's "significant" GATT/WTO coefficients given a null hypothesis of $\beta = 0.00$ and $\alpha = 0.05$. But this is weak evidence in such a huge data set. Using an out-of-sample prediction heuristic, we find that the more-complicated TGR-3 model is nearly indistinguishable from simpler alternatives in terms of its ability to predict trade flows not already included in fitting the model. We see

---

[4] From our estimation and based on TGR's discussion of their findings, there appears to be a typographical error in the original table; estimates and standard errors for "Formal member and non-member participant" and "Both non-member participants" were transposed. Correct estimates are reported in Table 5.2.

TABLE 5.2 *Linear regression of bilateral trade flows 1948–99,*
replicating Tomz et al. (2007).

	(1)	(2)	(3)	(4-TGR3)
Distance	−1.237	−1.251	−1.120	−1.129
	(0.020)	(0.005)	(0.022)	(0.022)
GDP	0.815	0.837	0.916	0.926
	(0.007)	(0.002)	(0.009)	(0.010)
GDPpc	0.506	0.479	0.321	0.312
	(0.012)	(0.003)	(0.014)	(0.014)
GATT/WTO: F-F		0.469		0.173
		(0.022)		(0.067)
GATT/WTO: F-N		0.712		0.410
		(0.024)		(0.071)
GATT/WTO: N-N		1.305		0.796
		(0.042)		(0.142)
GATT/WTO: F-O		0.136		0.064
		(0.023)		(0.065)
GATT/WTO: N-O		0.304		0.327
		(0.030)		(0.090)
GSP			0.857	0.851
			(0.032)	(0.032)
Regional FTA			1.200	1.187
			(0.106)	(0.110)
Currency union			1.116	1.114
			(0.122)	(0.123)
Common language			0.315	0.312
			(0.040)	(0.040)
Shared border			0.528	0.517
			(0.111)	(0.110)
Num. landlocked			−0.271	−0.269
			(0.031)	(0.031)
Num. island			0.041	0.018
			(0.036)	(0.036)
Land area			−0.097	−0.093
			(0.008)	(0.008)
Common colonizer			0.584	0.523
			(0.067)	(0.067)
Currently colonized			1.078	0.937
			(0.234)	(0.234)
Ever had colonial rel.			1.162	1.153
			(0.117)	(0.115)
Common country			−0.015	−0.019
			(1.081)	(1.071)
$\bar{R}^2$	0.62	0.62	0.65	0.65
AIC	1,005,451	1,002,665	986,246	985,288
BIC	1,006,031	1,003,298	986,951	986,044

Note: All models include a constant, year dummies, and report dyad-clustered
standard errors in parentheses. $n = 234,597$.

TABLE 5.3 *Out-of-sample predictive performance for models of international trade. Cell entries are mean-squared prediction errors, and quantities in parentheses are standard errors for models with the smallest MSE in each column.*

	CV (all years)	CV (pre-1967)
Model 1	4.35	1.79
Model 2	4.31	1.74
Model 3	4.05	1.59
Model 4 (TGR-3)	4.04 (0.02)	1.57 (0.01)

little reason to believe that, among these competitors, the models including GATT/WTO covariates should be privileged over those that do not.

5.2.4 Benefits of Cross-Validation

In-sample fit statistics are not necessarily informative about how well the model describes the data-generating process. Cross-validation is a general approach that helps overcome these shortcomings.

Clearly, using real test sets of data are preferable to constructed test sets. But we go through a lot of trouble and expense to collect the data we do have. It is a shame to spend it all in one place. Cross-validation, retrodiction, and forecasting help the researcher to determine how well something is fitting outside of the null hypothesis testing framework for inference. Indeed, you can use cross-validation heuristically, to examine which variables, for example, will most degrade your ability to accurately use your estimated model to generate precise predictions. It is sometimes the case that deleting a highly significant variable may have little impact on the predictive power of a model, while another variable is an extremely powerful predictor.

Cross-validation uses the power of resampling to address problems in analyzing data that are not a random sample from some larger population. Much of the data analyzed in the social sciences falls into this bucket, all the more so in "big data" applications. The standard inferential framework may be less informative than a predictive one if we are dealing with all the existing data anyway.

Finally, cross-validation allows us to frame the results in terms of the substantive questions driving the results, rather than in terms of a BUTON containing numbers that no one will remember tomorrow.

5.3 CONCLUSION

This chapter provided some tools for model selection and evaluation, in contrast to current practice, in which model selection is often implicit and small *p*-values are prized. Model selection is a broad topic, and we have only scratched the surface. But the key point is that we cannot declare victory simply because we fit a model with "significant" results. It is easy to overfit the data and build a model that *only* describes the data already in hand. That is almost never the goal, because the researcher already has that data and can make models arbitrarily close to perfect with those data. The issue is whether the estimated model will be useful for additional data.

We must also compare models to one another and justify our preferred specifications *prior to* making inference about any parameters. Out-of-sample prediction is a powerful tool for annealing results against overfitting. Cross-validation is the most common way of conducting out-of-sample tests.

Most statistical software packages contain functionality for out-of-sample prediction, but it is often worthwhile to design predictive exercises to speak directly to questions of substantive interest. Existing software's default settings for loss function or method of dividing the data may not be best for a particular application. In certain circumstances we may want to see how a model works in specific kinds of cases, not necessarily in all of them. By dividing your sample into different sets and using a cross-validation strategy, we can probe the dependencies between the model and the data. If it is possible to keep some data isolated from the estimation process altogether, then all the better.

We are not, however, arguing for a pure data-mining approach, absent substantive knowledge and theoretical reflections. A good theory should lead us to specify models that predict better, but better-predicting models do not necessarily reflect a "true" or even causal set of relationships. We must also be careful in constructing out-of-sample prediction exercises when there are dependencies in the data (e.g., temporal correlation) or when we have reason to believe that the fundamental processes at work may have changed. As a result, the prediction heuristic is general, powerful, simple to understand, and relatively easy to build in a computer. But it will not solve all our model-building problems nor will it obviate the need for careful reflection on how the data were obtained.

5.4 FURTHER READING

Applications

Hill and Jones (2014) use cross-validation to systematically evaluate a variety of competing empirical models of government repression. Grimmer and Stewart (2013) show how cross-validation and other out-of-sample methods are critical to the burgeoning field of machine learning, especially in the context of text analysis. Titiunik and Feher (2017) use randomization inference in examining the effects of term limits in the Arkansas legislature. Ho and Imai (2006) use randomization inference in the context of California's complicated candidate randomization procedure to determine whether appearing on the first page of a ballot affected vote share in the 2003 recall election.

Previous Work

On the misinterpretation of confidence intervals and p-values, see Belia et al. (2005); Cumming et al. (2004); Hoekstra et al. (2014).

See Singal (2015) for a detailed description of the *Science* retraction of the LaCour and Greene study. Important recent articles about reproducibility in the social sciences have begun to appear (Benoit et al., 2016; Laitin and Reich, 2017; Miguel et al., 2014). Many political science journals now require publicly visible data repositories and more (Bueno de Mesquita et al., 2003; DA-RT, 2015; Gleditsch et al., 2003; King, 1995).

Many current recommendations on research reproducibility stem from Knuth's invention of *literate programming* (1984), which was a way of integrating textual documentation with computer programs. Gentleman and Temple Lang (2007) expanded this idea to statistical programming, and recently Xie (2015) further updated these ideas with the use of *markdown* and *pandoc* (MacFarlane, 2013).

Regarding the WTO-trade dispute, Park (2012) and Imai and Tingley (2012) revisit the Goldstein et al. (2007) findings in the context of other methodological discussions. Both show the GATT/WTO finding to be fragile. Ward et al. (2013) dispute the assumption of dyadic conditional independence in gravity models of international trade, arguing for models that incorporate higher-order network dependencies in the data.

Advanced Study

On the interpretation and (mis)use of p-values in model selection, see Freedman (1983); Gill (1999); Raftery (1995); Rozeboom (1960).

Model selection need not imply that we choose one "winner." Rather, in a Bayesian framework, we can average across models (Bartels, 1997; Raftery, 1995). This approach has received renewed interest in political science (Montgomery et al., 2012a,b; Nyhan and Montgomery, 2010).

Hastie et al. (2016) is the canonical text for cross-validation and applied machine learning. Arlot and Celisse (2010) provide a recent review of the state of the art. Stone (1977) shows that choosing models based on leave-one-out cross validation is asymptotically equivalent to minimizing the AIC, whereas Shao (1997) links *k-fold* cross-validation to the BIC. Hastie et al. (2008) observe that leave-one-out cross validation is approximately unbiased as an estimator of the expected prediction error. Markatou et al. (2005) presents some inferential approaches for cross-validation results in the linear regression case. Efron and Tibshirani (1998) gives a detailed treatment of the bootstrap and jackknife procedures; see also Davison and Hinkley (1997). Gerber and Green (2012) provide extensive discussion of randomization and permutation inference in political science.

Software Notes

There are many cross-validation and related routines in $\mathcal{R}$. The cv.glm function in the boot library (Canty and Ripley, 2016) produces cross-validation estimates for many of the models explored in this book. One disadvantage of this implementation is that it simply returns another single number summary, which, while informative, can be improved upon. The crossval function in the bootstrap package (Tibshirani and Leisch, 2017) requires some user manipulation but has more flexibility. Both boot and bootstrap enable bootstrap and jackknife resampling. cvTools (Alfons, 2012) and caret (Kuhn, 2016) contain cross-validation functionality as well. The ri (Aronow and Samii, 2012) package enables randomization and permutation inference.

6

Inference and Interpretation

After settling on a set of defensible model specifications we can undertake the process of interpretation. Conventional practice emphasizes statistical inference using null hypotheses, point estimates, and p-values for specific parameters. With the possible exception of simple linear models, such practice communicates relatively little. In more complicated, nonlinear models of the sort described in this book, basing inference on null hypothesis testing for particular parameters can be misleading. In this chapter, we focus on model interpretation rather than parameter inference. Model interpretation involves describing a model's implications – and our uncertainty about them – using directly interpretable and substantively important quantities of interest. We derive these implications by constructing plausible and substantively relevant scenarios and then using the model, along with likelihood theory, to generate simulations of the data-generating process.

6.1 THE MECHANICS OF INFERENCE

At a general level, *statistical inference* is the process of making knowledge claims based on the analysis of observed data. Part of the power of statistical inference is the ability to quantify, communicate, and interpret our uncertainty about these claims. To do this, many scholars examine the Big Ugly Table of Numbers (BUTON) produced by their statistical program. If the scholar's null hypothesis is that the parameter of interest, β_f, equals zero, and if the ratio of a point estimate to its standard error is greater than 1.96, then the scholar claims a "statistically significant" finding. That is, the scholar makes a knowledge claim in which the hypothesis that $\beta_f = 0.0$ has been rejected in favor of some other, such as $\beta_f > 0$. The scholar then proceeds to adorn his/her BUTON with ***.

119

The claim of statistical significance is shorthand for saying "if $\beta_f = 0.0$, and we were to repeatedly generate new independent, random samples and calculate a $\hat{\beta}_f$ for each, then we should see $\hat{\beta}_f$ values at least as large as the one we just calculated less than 5% of the time." You can see why we have developed a shorthand phrase. Alternatively, the author might construct a 95% *confidence interval* around $\hat{\beta}_f$, which has a similar interpretation.

In case you were wondering ... 6.1 Frequentist confidence intervals

Given observed data and a statistical model with parameter θ, we construct an estimate, $\hat{\theta}$. The $100(1-\alpha)\%$ *confidence interval* (CI) around $\hat{\theta}_j$ is the set of values, C, such that, for any $x \in C$ the p-value of $|\hat{\theta}_j - x|$ is $\geq \alpha$.

The MLE is asymptotically normally distributed, so the asymptotic 95% confidence interval around the MLE is

$$\left\{ x : \hat{\theta}_j - 1.96se(\hat{\theta}_j) \leq x \leq \hat{\theta}_j + 1.96se(\hat{\theta}_j) \right\}.$$

Confidence intervals are frequently misinterpreted. A 95% frequentist CI does *not* mean there is a 95% probability that true θ lies in the interval.[a]

---
[a] Bayesian credible regions, however, do have such an interpretation, although the Bayesian understanding of "probability" differs.

Importantly, however, this line of inference only works if there is a sense in which our data can be considered a random sample of cases. One way this might hold is when we have such a large population that we can actually randomly draw a set of cases to analyze. Another way to achieve this is to randomly assign cases different values of the covariate, X_f, so the observed data are but one realization of many possible random assignments.[1] However, many studies are observational, and the statistical inference framework developed for experiments and samples from larger populations is not entirely satisfactory.

An Example: World Trade and Democratization I
Ahlquist and Wibbels (2012) use world trade volumes as a tool for examining the relationship between income inequality and regime transitions. Rather than a random sample, Ahlquist and Wibbels gather data for all available country-years from 1875–2001, excluding the periods of World War I and II. Existing theoretical arguments implied that the relationship between trade and

---
[1] Permutation tests and randomization inference, discussed in Chapter 5, exploit this exact property.

TABLE 6.1 *Probit regression of democratic transitions 1875–2001, a reestimation of Ahlquist and Wibbels (2012).*

	(1)	(2)
Labor endowment	−0.116	−0.500
	(0.175)	(0.175)
World trade	−0.020	−0.027
	(0.012)	(0.012)
Labor endowment × world trade		0.014
		(0.006)
Global % democracies	0.020	0.018
	(0.004)	(0.004)
Neighborhood % democracies	0.470	0.467
	(0.202)	(0.202)
Prior democratic failure	0.324	0.312
	(0.061)	(0.061)
Communist	−0.620	−0.616
	(0.227)	(0.227)
Gold Standard	0.171	0.105
	(0.146)	(0.146)
Interwar	−0.163	−0.241
	(0.235)	(0.235)
Post–Bretton Woods	0.394	0.419
	(0.216)	(0.216)
Neighborhood democratic transition	0.386	0.373
	(0.133)	(0.133)
n	8,347	8,347
$\log \mathcal{L}$	−621	−619
AIC	1,279	1,278
BIC	1,406	1,419

Note: Estimated model is a dynamic probit; interaction terms with lagged dependent variable omitted for simplicity, as is the constant term. Robust standard errors are reported, following Ahlquist and Wibbels (2012).

the transition from an autocratic to a democratic government should depend on a country's labor endowment, so Ahlquist and Wibbels fit a variety of probit models that include a multiplicative interaction term between labor endowment and trade. Table 6.1 is a streamlined presentation of their theoretically preferred model alongside a simpler alternative that omits the interaction term.[2]

---

[2] Ahlquist and Wibbels estimate a dynamic probit model that accounts for transitions out of democracy as well. We omit those terms from the table here for simplicity; they are readily available in the original paper or with the data and code accompanying this volume.

Looking at in-sample performance using the AIC and BIC, they find that the models with and without the interaction term perform almost identically, providing little little reason to prefer the more-complicated version. Nevertheless, a standard form of inference might proceed to look at the point estimate and standard error of the endowment × trade term and notice that $0.014/0.006 \approx 2.3$, which implies a (two-sided) p-value of about 0.03. What knowledge claims are we to make with this result?

6.2 INTERPRETING MODELS AND PRODUCING SCENARIOS OF INTEREST

To make knowledge claims based on a model, we need to interpret the model in its domain of intended use. This means describing and evaluating the model's *implications*, not simply looking at stars next to particular parameters. Model implications, then, are statements about how we expect the outcome variable to behave under different conditions, along with statements of our uncertainty about those outcomes.

Our uncertainty comes from three sources. *Fundamental uncertainty* is the idea that the world, or at least our perceptions and measurements of it, have a fundamentally stochastic character. This is captured in the model's stochastic term, $Y \sim f$, in which we assume that the stochastic nature of our measurement and observation can be described using a particular probability model, such as the normal or Bernoulli distribution. *Estimation uncertainty* stems from the fact that we have limited data and, as such, our parameter estimates are subject to variability or revision upon observing more data. Estimation uncertainty in the likelihood framework is usually described using the large sample theory outlined in Chapter 2 and contained in the covariance matrix that we obtain when fitting models to actual data. Finally, there is *model uncertainty*, something we discussed in the previous chapter, when we emphasized that model evaluation and selection must occur prior to any interpretation.

6.2.1 Quantities of Interest

Quantity of interest is the generic name for the value we are going to use to interpret our model. As we learned in Chapter 3, the parameters of statistical models frequently fail to have direct and useful interpretations. It is the researcher's job to transform an estimated model into something informative to both ourselves and audiences. It is almost always easiest to understand a model when its implications are presented on the scale of the dependent variable. Predicted probabilities are more transparent than log-odds or odds ratios. Wages or incomes are easier to understand and communicate than elasticities.

In generating implications on the scale of the response, there are two primary quantities of interest: the *expected value* and the *predicted value*, where both are conditional on fixed covariate values and the estimated model parameters. The difference between the two is that the predicted value incorporates fundamental uncertainty, whereas the expected value does not.

Examples will help. Recall the linear regression of log CO_2 on log per capita GDP, reported in Table 1.2. In this model we estimated that

$$Y_i \sim f_{\mathcal{N}}(\mu_i, 2.112^2)$$
$$\mu_i = -0.08 + 1.04X_i.$$

Suppose we are interested in the model's predictions of India's CO_2 emissions if its per capita GDP were 10% larger than in 2012, i.e., if $x_i = \log(1.1 * 4{,}921.84)$. The expected amount of CO_2 is then $\exp(1.04*\log(1.1*4{,}921.84) - 0.08) = \exp(8.86) = 6{,}915.3\text{kT}$. The predicted amount, however, will take account of the fundamental uncertainty, as represented by the normal distribution with variance estimated at 2.112^2. To do this, we can take a draw from $\mathcal{N}(8.86, 2.112^2)$. One such draw is 6.71; $\exp(6.71) = 821$, which represents one predicted value.

As a second example, recall the exercise in Chapter 3 in which we estimated the predicted probability of a woman being in the paid labor force when she had a college degree, holding the other covariates at their central tendencies. Based on a logistic regression model we calculated this expected value as $\text{logit}^{-1}\left(\bar{\mathbf{x}}_{\neg\text{coll}}\hat{\boldsymbol{\beta}}\right)\Big|_{\text{coll}=1} = 0.75$. A predicted value in this case must be either 0 or 1. To generate a predicted value that accounts for fundamental uncertainty, we would sample from a Bernoulli distribution with $\theta = 0.75$. Or flip an appropriately weighted coin.

Exploring how expected values change under different values of covariates helps interpret the systematic component of the model we fit. This is frequently of primary interest. And, in general, we will not generate a single predicted value; we will take advantage of our computing power and generate many, the average of which will necessarily converge on the expected value. Nevertheless, the predicted values are useful for understanding how much fundamental uncertainty remains after we have fit our model. Does fundamental uncertainty still swamp whatever systematic relationship we have? If so, this is usually reason for both some humility in our claims and a need for more research, including gathering more data.

6.2.2 Scenarios

In calculating our expected and predicted quantities, we must choose specific values for the covariates in the model. Since our model posits a description of the data-generating process, these vectors of covariate values represent scenarios, or possible situations that we are interested in. These scenarios are sometimes referred to as *counterfactuals*, since they provide an answer to the question: "What would we expect to happen if an independent variable took on a value different from what we observe in the data?" Counterfactuals are ultimately at the heart of causal inference in randomized experiments in which we interpret the (average) effect of the treatment as what we would expect to happen to the control group were we to administer the treatment to them.

In the context of model interpretaton, the question remains, "What is a good scenario?" Good and useful scenarios should:

- Address a concrete and important substantive issue that motivated the research. If we are interested in the effect of natural disasters on support for democracy in poor countries versus rich ones, then we should construct a scenario that holds national income at a low level and at a high level, not necessarily near the mean of the data set.
- Be compared to other scenarios. Construct several scenarios of theoretical or policy relevance to provide a picture of the model's implications in its intended domain of application. One scenario is almost never enough.
- Be simple enough for meaningful comparisons to be made. This usually means only varying one thing at a time.
- Include descriptions of our uncertainty about the model's implications. Remember that we have estimation uncertainty (the variance-covariance matrix) and fundamental uncertainty as reflected in the stochastic component of our models. Both of these are directly accessible from the model in our computers. Uncertainty over the models themselves is the most difficult to quantify and express.
- Keep the scenarios "close to" our experience (more later in this chapter). A useful baseline typically involves estimating what happens near the center of our data, i.e., holding variables at their central tendencies.
- Respect the structure of the data. If a variable of interest is only observed or available in discrete chunks, then the scenarios of interest should reflect this. For example, in Figure 3.7 the scenarios we report reflect the fact that senators are up for election every other year, inducing inherent discreteness in the time-to-election variable.
- Avoid extreme changes – unless that's what we're interested in. Unless we are toggling indicator variables, it usually does not make much sense to take the variable of interest from its minimum value to its maximum value. For example, if we're interested in the relationship between income per capita on regime transitions, using the GDP per capita of the Democratic Republic of Congo and Luxembourg is unlikely to provide much insight for a world in which income per capita changes relatively smoothly and slowly.

6.2.3 Interpolation, Extrapolation, and Convex Hulls

Some of the advice above can be restated in a more formal fashion. King and Zeng (2006a,b) make the important point that the further our counterfactual scenarios are from the support of the data used to estimate the model, the more *model dependent* the implied predictions become. As our modeling assumptions increasingly determine our predictions, our uncertainty about these "extreme counterfactuals" is understated since the calculated confidence bands fail to incorporate our uncertainty about the model itself. As model uncertainty comes to dominate, our inferences about model predictions become increasingly tenuous.

The difference between interpolation and extrapolation provides a relatively intuitive criterion for whether our counterfactuals deviate too far from our experience. To define these terms we must first understand the *convex hull* of our data. The convex hull is the smallest convex set that can contain all the data points. The easiest way to get a feel for the hull is to visualize it, as in Figure 6.1. Statisticians have long defined *interpolation* as a way of constructing new data points that are inside the convex hull of the data, wheras *extrapolation* involves going outside the hull and necessarily further from our recorded experience.

Once we move out of two dimensions, calculating and visualizing convex hulls becomes difficult, but software exists to assist us.

Our perspective is that predictions involving scenarios within the convex hull of the data, i.e., interpolation, are better for describing a model's implications. But pressing policy problems may require that we pose questions beyond the realm of our recorded experience, i.e., our data. Should we disregard the data we do have and the models we can fit in these situations? Probably not. Nevertheless, an important first step in making such

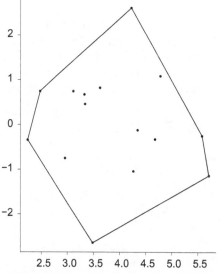

FIGURE 6.1 Visualizing the convex hull in 2 dimensions.

predictions is recognizing that the scenario of interest is in fact quite far from our observed experience and, as such, predictions are more likely to depend on modeling decisions. A second step, then, would be to conduct *sensitivity analysis*, generating predictions from a variety of models that perform well in the observed data set to produce some sense of the prediction uncertainty.

An Example: World Trade and Democratization II

Ahlquist and Wibbels chose to interpret their model by comparing a labor-scarce autocracy to a labor-abundant one at different levels of world trade. To set appropriate values, they chose the labor endowment values for Argentina (scarce) and China (abundant) in 1980. They hold other covariates at their mean or modal values. They then consider 150 different world trade values within the historical interquartile range, 15%–30% of world GDP.

We compare Ahlquist and Wibbels' counterfactual scenarios to their data to see which are similar to observed experience and which are outside the convex hull. Summary results appear in Table 6.2. In both the labor-scarce and the labor-abundant examples, all 150 scenarios fall inside the convex hull. We also see that the labor-scarce scenarios based on Argentina's labor endowment are, on average, closer to the observed data than the labor-abundant scenarios based on China. This is unsurprising since China's labor endowment value in 1980 of 4.2 put it at about the 87th percentile of all observed values in the data set, closer to the hull. Argentina's value of 0.5 was almost exactly the 25th percentile.

6.2.4 Simulating Estimation Uncertainty

Interpreting models in terms of scenarios and expected (or predicted) values requires that we incorporate our estimation uncertainty. Sometimes these values can be derived analytically, but there is no need to restrict either our modeling decisions or our interpretation to simple or easy-to-calculate objects. With existing computing power we can easily generate many samples of our model

TABLE 6.2 *Model dependence and the Ahlquist and Wibbels interpretation scenarios.*

	Labor Scarce	Labor Abundant
Labor endowment value	0.5	4.2
Number of scenarios	150	150
% scenarios in convex hull	100	100
Avg. % observed data "nearby"	29	18

Note: Data points "nearby" are within one geometric variance of the scenario point. The distance measure is Gower's G^2.

parameters from distributions reflecting our estimation uncertainty. We can then combine each of these samples with our scenarios and models to build up distributions for any quantity we may be interested in.

In regular likelihood problems we can use the theory from Chapter 2 to sample from the multivariate normal distribution, just as we did in Chapter 3. To review, we do the following:

1. Fit the model of interest and store the estimated parameters, $\hat{\theta}$, along with the covariance matrix, $\text{cov}(\hat{\theta})$;
2. Construct a scenario embodied in the vector of covariates, $\mathbf{x}_s$;
3. Draw a parameter vector, $\tilde{\theta}$, from $\mathcal{N}\left(\hat{\theta}, \text{cov}(\hat{\theta})\right)$;
4. Calculate the quantity of interest based on $\mathbf{x}_s$ and $\tilde{\theta}$. In the models explored in this book this means calculating the linear predictor, $\mathbf{x}_s^\mathsf{T}\hat{\beta}$, and then mapping that quantity into $E[Y]$. In the logit case this was $\text{logit}^{-1}(\mathbf{x}_s^\mathsf{T}\hat{\beta})$;
5. Repeat steps 3–4 many times to build up the distribution for the quantity of interest under this scenario;
6. Calculate important quantiles (e.g., 0.025 and 0.975) from this distribution or display the distribution;
7. Return to step 2 and construct a different scenario;
8. Once finished, we can display the model implications, along with the estimation uncertainty around them.

In nonstandard or more customized applications when large-sample likelihood theory does not apply, we can apply the logic of bootstrap resampling to repeatedly resample from our existing data to fit models and calculate quantities of interest.

Interpreting Interactive and Conditional Relationships

Much has been written on the use and interpretation of models containing multiplicative (or other nonlinear) terms. This literature rightly points out that direct examination of coefficient point estimates is insufficient for interpreting conditional relationships. The basis for this discussion is couched in terms of marginal effect calculations and standard errors in linear regression. If $E[Y_i] = \mathbf{x}_i^\mathsf{T}\beta = \beta_0 + \beta_1 x_{i1} + \beta_2 x_{i2} + \beta_3 x_{i1} x_{i2}$, then

$$\frac{\partial E[Y_i]}{\partial x_{i1}} = \beta_1 + \beta_3 x_{i2}.$$

It follows that

$$\text{var}\left(\frac{\partial E[Y_i]}{\partial x_{i1}}\right) = \text{var}\left(\beta_1 + \beta_3 x_{i2}\right)$$

$$= \text{var}\left(\beta_1\right) + x_{i2}^2 \text{var}\left(\beta_3\right) + 2x_{i2}\text{cov}\left(\beta_1, \beta_3\right),$$

from which we can easily calculate the standard error of the marginal effect. Several observations emerge from these expressions:

- Both the relationship between X_1 and Y and our uncertainty about it depends on X_2. It therefore makes no sense to declare the conditional relationship to be "significant," since our confidence intervals may contain 0 at some values of X_2 but not others.

- It often makes no sense to talk about "main effects" and "interaction effects." There is simply the marginal or predicted effect; any instance in which $x_{i2} = 0$ is simply a special case. The one exception here is when X_1 or X_2 are binary variables encoded as 0 and 1.

- There is almost never an instance in which it makes sense to include an interactive term without the constitutive terms.

These calculations for the standard error of the marginal effect only apply to linear regression. But the observations echo points raised in Chapter 3 about marginal effects in a logit context. This means that our strategy of specifying scenarios of interest, simulating from the model's sampling distribution, and then constructing displays of the model's predicted consequences encompasses the interpretation of interactive, conditional, and other relationships that are nonlinear in the covariates. We do not need to derive marginal effects (and variance) expressions for each specific class of models; we can simulate them directly. But our discussion of model validation and selection adds another important observation: before engaging in model interpretation and hypothesis testing, analysts proposing models with conditional, nonlinear, or other complicated functional relationships have a special burden to show that their more-complicated models out-perform their model's simpler cousins.

An Example: World Trade and Democratization III

Ahlquist and Wibbels (2012) estimated models with a "significant" interaction term between world trade and labor endowment. To interpret this model they constructed a series of counterfactual scenarios, allowing us to compare the model's predicted probability of democratic transition as a function of world trade in labor-abundant and labor-scarce autocracies. In these scenarios, they varied world trade across its interquartile range. "Labor scarce" was defined as the value observed in Argentina in 1980 while "labor abundant" was the value observed in China in the same year. All these scenarios were found to be in the convex hull of the data.

Ahlquist and Wibbels then proceed to calculate predicted probabilities – expected values – for each of these 300 scenarios and simulate from the sampling distribution to describe their estimation uncertainty. Figure 6.2 reproduces their key interpretive results, with the solid line representing the labor-scarce and the dashed line depicting the labor-abundant autocracy. The shaded regions represent the 95% confidence intervals around the predictions. If the data were consistent with the literature's predictions, the plot would look like an "X," with the risk of transition increasing in world trade for the labor-abundant scenario, and the reverse for the labor-scarce. While the risk of a transition decreases for labor-scarce autocracies as trade increases, there is no discernible relationship between trade and democratization in labor-abundant autocracies. The confidence intervals overlap substantially for all values of trade, making it difficult to sustain the claim that there is an important conditional relationship at work here, notwithstanding the small *p*-value on the interaction term. Had the authors simply declared victory based on theory and a small *p*-value on an interaction term, erroneous inference could have occurred.

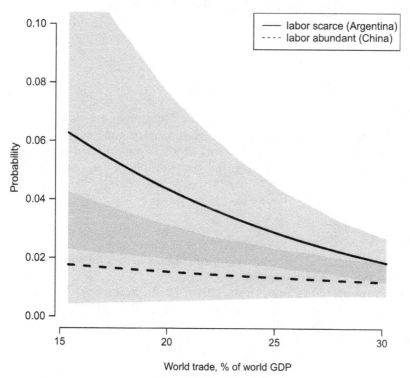

FIGURE 6.2 The relationship between world trade and the probability of a democratic transition in labor-abundant and labor-scarce autocracies. Reproduced from Ahlquist and Wibbels (2012), figure 4.

6.3 CONCLUSION

Conventional statistical inference focuses on deciding whether particular model parameters are sufficiently far away from an arbitrary "null" value, based on estimation uncertainty and a particular model of data sampling. While useful, this mode of reasoning can be misleading or miss the point entirely, especially when the data do not conform to an actual sample from a population or a researcher-controlled experiment. Moreover, in many models the parameters do not have ready interpretations applicable to the substantive question at hand, meaning statements of statistical significance, as the primary mode of inference, do not have immediate meaning to audiences.

A more readily accessible form of inference explores a model's implications by using substantively relevant scenarios to compare predicted outcomes under different conditions. Model interpretation is almost always most effective when communicated on the scale of the dependent variable, whether as an expected or predicted value. By incorporating (and displaying) estimation uncertainty around these implications we can develop a richer understanding of both the size of a model's predicted "effects" as well as the level of uncertainty around them.

6.4 FURTHER READING

Applications

Shih et al. (2012) provide an excellent interpretation and presentation of conditional effects from interaction terms in a custom-designed model for rank data. They explicitly consider the convex hull in their interpretive scenarios.

Previous Work

King et al. (2000) discuss the construction and display of meaningful quantities of interest for model interpretation.

Ai and Norton (2003); Berry et al. (2010, 2012); Brambor et al. (2006); Braumoeller (2004); and Kam and Franzese (2007) all discuss the inclusion and interpretation of multiplicative interaction terms in the linear predictor.

Advanced Study

Cox (2006) provides a detailed discussion of the theory, practice, and history of statistical inference.

Software Notes

Tomz et al. (2001) developed the stand-alone CLARIFY package for calculating quantities of interest and estimation uncertainty around them. This functionality has been incorporated into $\mathcal{R}$'s Zelig library.

There are several $\mathcal{R}$ packages for calculating convex hulls. The basic chull function only handles two-dimensional data. Stoll et al. (2014) developed WhatIf that allows us to compare proposed scenarios to the convex hull of our data. The geometry package (Habel et al., 2015) also contains functionality for calculating the convex hull in more than two dimensions.

THE GENERALIZED LINEAR MODEL

7

The Generalized Linear Model

7.1 THE GENERALIZED LINEAR MODEL

In Part III, we focus on the most widespread modeling framework applying likelihood principles: the *Generalized Linear Model* (GLM). Any GLM has the following components:

- A specified probability model, $Y_i \sim f$ where f is a member of the *exponential family* of distributions,
- A *linear predictor* term, $\mathbf{x}_i^\mathsf{T} \boldsymbol{\beta}$,
- A *link function*, $g(\cdot)$, such that $E[Y_i] = g^{-1}(\mathbf{x}_i^\mathsf{T} \boldsymbol{\beta})$.

In the language we have been using so far, the probability model describes the stochastic component of Y while the linear predictor represents the systematic component. The linear predictor and the link function emphasize that GLMs are models of the mean or expected response, conditional on covariates and parameters. The inverse link function serves to map the linear predictor values into intervals appropriate to the assumed probability model; it links the linear predictor with the conditional mean.

In case you were wondering ... 7.1 Which "GLM"?

The Generalized Linear Model is not be confused with the "General Linear Model," "General Linear Methods" or "Generalized Least Squares."

General Linear Methods are a collection of tools for solving differential equations; they are outside the scope of this text.

Generalized Least Squares is a generalization of OLS to situations in which residuals are correlated. We introduced some of these ideas in Section 2.4.1 in the context of robust standard errors.

The General Linear Model is the matrix generalization of standard OLS-based linear regression to the situation of q outcomes:

$$\mathbf{Y} = \mathbf{X}\boldsymbol{\beta} + \boldsymbol{\varepsilon}$$

where $\mathbf{Y}$ is now a $n \times q$ matrix of response variables, $\mathbf{X}$ is $n \times k$ design matrix, $\boldsymbol{\beta}$ is a $k \times q$ matrix of to-be-estimated regression parameters, and $\boldsymbol{\varepsilon}$ is a $n \times q$ matrix of errors, assumed to follow multivariate normal distribution.

Nelder and Wedderburn (1972) coined the term "Generalized Linear Model" and, more importantly, built out the mathematics of the exponential family, developed the concept of a linear predictor and a link function, and showed that IWLS can be used to find the MLE for models in the exponential family.

7.2 THE EXPONENTIAL FAMILY

The *exponential family* is a class of probability distribution and mass functions that can be written in certain mathematically convenient forms. It is important to distinguish the exponential *family* from the exponential *distribution*. To further confuse matters, the exponential distribution is also a member of the exponential family.

In case you were wondering ... 7.2 Exponential distribution

Suppose $X \in [0, \infty)$. We say that X follows the exponential distribution with rate parameter λ, $X \sim f_e(x; \lambda)$, if

$$f_e(x) = \lambda \exp(-\lambda x),$$

with $E[X] = \lambda^{-1}$ and $\text{var}(X) = \lambda^{-2}$.

Definition 7.1 (Exponential Family). A distribution or mass function $f(x; \boldsymbol{\theta})$ is of the *exponential family* if it can be written as

$$f(x; \boldsymbol{\theta}) = \exp\left[\eta(\boldsymbol{\theta})^{\mathsf{T}} h(x) - A(\boldsymbol{\theta}) + c(x)\right]$$

for some functions $\eta(\boldsymbol{\theta})$, $h(x)$, $A(\boldsymbol{\theta})$ and $c(x)$. The function $h(x)$ returns a vector of "sufficient statistics" of the same length as $\eta(\boldsymbol{\theta})$.

An extension of the exponential family commonly used in GLMs is the *exponential dispersion model*.

Definition 7.2 (Exponential dispersion model). A distribution function $f(x; \theta, \phi)$ is said to be of the *natural exponential dispersion family* if it can be written of the form

$$f(x; \theta, \phi) = \exp \left[\frac{x\theta - A(\theta)}{\phi} + c(x, \phi) \right]$$

for some functions $A(\theta)$ and $c(x, \phi)$.

Written in this form, we refer to θ as the *canonical parameter* and ϕ as the *dispersion parameter*. The key feature of exponential family distributions is that they can be factored into terms containing only data (x), only parameters (θ, ϕ), or constants that do not depend on either θ or the data. This implies that distributions in the exponential family have a particular relationship between their mean and variance. Specifically, for scalar θ, $E[X] = \mu = \frac{dA(\theta)}{d\theta}$ while $\text{var}(X) = \phi \frac{d^2 A(\theta)}{d\theta^2}$. It is this relationship that makes modeling and estimation more convenient. Products of exponential family distributions are themselves in the exponential family. So it follows that the joint distribution of i.i.d. samples from an exponential family distribution is also in the exponential family.

Many of the most commonly used distributions are members of the exponential family, including the normal, log-normal, Bernoulli, beta, χ^2, Dirichlet, gamma, and Poisson. Distributions where the support for the distribution involves θ (e.g., the uniform distribution) are not in the exponential family. Neither are the Cauchy nor t-distributions.

7.3 PAST EXAMPLES AS GLMS

In Chapter 3 we derived the Bernoulli GLM. The Bernoulli distribution can be written as

$$\begin{aligned} f_B(x; \theta) &= \theta^x (1-\theta)^{1-x} \\ &= \exp \left[\log(\theta^x (1-\theta)^{1-x}) \right] \\ &= \exp \left[x \log \theta + (1-x) \log(1-\theta) \right] \\ &= \exp \left[x \log \frac{\theta}{1-\theta} + \log(1-\theta) \right] \\ &= \exp \left[x\text{logit}(\theta) + \log(1-\theta) \right]. \end{aligned}$$

From here we see that the Bernoulli distribution is in the exponential family, with dispersion fixed at 1. This expression also makes it easy to see how we arrive at the logit as the link function for the Bernoulli GLM.

In deriving the normal-linear model in Chapter 1, we actually specified a GLM in which $Y_i \sim f_N(y_i; \theta_i)$ and where $\theta_i = (\mu_i, \sigma^2)$. To see that the normal distribution (with unknown mean and variance) is of the exponential family, note that we can factor the distribution to be

$$f_N(y; \mu, \sigma^2) = \exp \left[\frac{y\mu - \mu^2/2}{\sigma^2} - \frac{\log 2\pi\sigma^2}{2} - \frac{y^2}{2\sigma^2} \right],$$

so for the normal distribution, we have canonical parameter μ and dispersion parameter σ^2.

For the normal GLM, $E[Y_i] = \mu_i = \mathbf{x}_i^\mathsf{T}\boldsymbol{\beta}$. Since the normal distribution has support over the entire real line it can take any real number as a mean value. The link function for the normal GLM is correspondingly the identity $\mathbf{I}_n\mathbf{X}\boldsymbol{\beta} = \mathbf{I}_n^{-1}\mathbf{X}\boldsymbol{\beta} = \mathbf{X}\boldsymbol{\beta}$, where $\mathbf{I}_n$ is the $n \times n$ identity matrix.

7.3.1 GLMs in $\mathcal{R}$

The syntax of the $\mathcal{R}$ function `glm` is built on the theory of the GLM. In particular, `glm` requires that the user:

- Supply a linear predictor term in the form of an $\mathcal{R}$ formula. In the Mroz example in Chapter 3 we specified `lfpbin~young.kids + school.kids + age + college.woman + wage`.
- Choose a probability model using the `family` argument. In the Mroz example we specified `family=binomial`.
- Choose a link function (or write your own). In the Mroz example we chose the logit link, `family=binomial(link='logit')`, but others are available, including the probit and complementary log-log.

In summarizing a model fit with `glm`, $\mathcal{R}$ returns information about the dispersion parameter for that family. For example, using `glm` to estimate the LPM described in Table 3.4, $\mathcal{R}$ returns

```
(Dispersion parameter for Gaussian family taken to be
    0.2155109)
```

As we have just seen, in the normal model the dispersion parameter corresponds to σ^2. Thus $0.22 = \hat{\sigma}^2$ in the Mroz LPM example. The square root of this quantity for a linear-normal GLM corresponds to the standard error of the regression. Table 3.4 reports a regression standard error of 0.46, which is approximately $\sqrt{0.2155109}$. In fitting the logit model for the Mroz example the code chunk in Section 3.4.2 shows that $\mathcal{R}$ reports the dispersion parameter fixed at 1, as the binomial GLM requires.

7.4 "QUASI-" AND "PSEUDO-"LIKELIHOOD

The functional relationship between the mean and variance among exponential family distributions has direct application in the "quasilikelihood" framework, sometimes called "pseudolikelihood." Rather than specify a full probability model (and thus a likelihood function), a quasilikelihood only requires a model for the mean and a function that links the mean to the variance:

$$E[Y_i] = \mu_i(\beta) = g^{-1}(\mathbf{x}_i^\mathsf{T}\boldsymbol{\beta}),$$
$$\text{var}(Y_i) = \phi V(\mu_i).$$

Definition 7.3 (Quasilikelihood). The *quasilikelihood function* $Q(y_i; \mu_i)$ is defined by the relation

$$\frac{\partial Q_i}{\partial \mu_i} = \frac{y_i - \mu_i}{\phi V(\mu_i)},$$

where $V(\mu_i)$ is assumed known. If $\mu_i \equiv g^{-1}(\mathbf{x}_i^\mathsf{T}\boldsymbol{\beta})$, then the quasilikelihood can be expressed with the relation

$$\frac{\partial Q_i}{\partial \beta_j} = \frac{y_i - \mu_i}{\phi V(\mu_i)}\frac{\partial \mu_i}{\partial \beta_j}. \tag{7.1}$$

Equation 7.1 defines the *quasiscore* function, $U(\boldsymbol{\beta})$, which is a vector of length k. Setting $U(\boldsymbol{\beta}) = 0$ gives a set of *quasiscore* or estimating equations. The $\hat{\boldsymbol{\beta}}$ that satisfies the quasiscore equations gives the quasilikelihood estimates of $\boldsymbol{\beta}$.

Based on the quasiscore we can derive the quasi-information as

$$-\frac{\partial U}{\partial \boldsymbol{\beta}} = \frac{\mathbf{D}\mathbf{V}^{-1}\mathbf{D}}{\phi}, \tag{7.2}$$

where $\mathbf{V}$ is a diagonal matrix with ith entry $V(\mu_i)$ and $\mathbf{D}$ is the $n \times k$ matrix with (i,j) element $\partial \mu_i(\beta)/\partial \beta_j$. The dispersion parameter is typically estimated as

$$\hat{\phi} = \frac{1}{n-k}\sum_{i=1}^{n}\frac{(y_i - \hat{\mu}_i)^2}{V(\hat{\mu}_i)}. \tag{7.3}$$

Using methods analogous to those in Chapter 2, it can be shown that if the model for the mean is correct, then the maximum quasilikelihood estimator is consistent for β and asymptotically normal, with covariance matrix given by the inverse quasi-information. Note the close correspondence between this variance formula and the "sandwich" covariance estimator from Section 2.4.1. The chief difference is the form of the "meat" in the sandwich and the inclusion of the dispersion parameter.

In the quasilikelihood world the specification of the variance function determines the "family." For example, if $V(\mu_i) = \mu_i(1 - \mu_i)$, then we have a quasibinomial model (see Chapter 3). If $V(\mu_i) = \mu_i$, then we have a quasipoisson (see Chapter 10).

Because of the functional relation between the mean and variance in the exponential family, the quasiscore equation turns out to be exactly the score equation for the log-likelihood of a particular distribution. As a result, the $\hat{\boldsymbol{\beta}}$ from maximum likelihood will equal the $\hat{\boldsymbol{\beta}}$ from a quasilikelihood estimation among the exponential family. In fact, the consistency of the quasilikelihood estimates relies on the functional connection between the mean and variance that the exponential family provides. What differs between MLE and quasi-likelihood is the covariance matrix and therefore the standard errors. The chief benefit of a quasilikelihood approach is the ability to partially relax some of the distributional assumptions inherent in a fully-specified likelihood. For example, quasilikelihood allows us to account for overdispersion in binary or count data. But the quasilikelihood does not calculate an actual likelihood, so likelihood-based quantities like the AIC and BIC as well as likelihood-based tests are not available.

7.5 CONCLUSION

This brief chapter introduced the concept and notation of the Generalized Linear Model, something we have already seen in the context of linear and logistic regression. The GLM provides a unified way of specifying and estimating a variety of models with different distributional assumptions. So long as we are hypothesizing probability models that rely on distributions in the exponential family, we can decompose our model building into the specification of a linear predictor term – covariates and regression parameters – and the link function that maps the linear predictor into the expected value.

Subsequent chapters in this part of the book introduce commonly used GLMs for outcomes that are integer counts as well as ordered and unordered categorical variables. Other GLMs exist for outcomes that are strictly positive, negative, or bounded, as well as many others, a testament to the flexibility of the exponential family of distributions. But it is also important to recognize that GLMs are not the only ways we can apply the method of maximum likelihood. We take up more complicated modeling tools in the last part of the book.

7.6 FURTHER READING

Advanced Study

McCullagh and Nelder (1989) is the canonical citation for the GLM. A variety of subsequent texts have expanded on these ideas, including Agresti (2002).

Wedderburn (1974) introduced quasilikelihood. A widely used extension of these ideas appears in the theory and implementation of Generalized Estimating Equations (GEE) (Hardin and Hilbe, 2012; Ziegler, 2011). Zorn (2000) summarizes the GEE approach with applications to political science.

8

Ordered Categorical Variable Models

8.1 MOTIVATION

Many variables that social scientists study are neither continuous nor binary, but rather consist of a (usually small) set of categories that are ranked from low to high. The most familiar example is the five point scale that is widely used in surveys such as the American National Election Study (ANES). Survey designers frequently phrase questions so that respondents must choose among five ordered choices ranging from strongly disagree (at the low end) to strongly agree (at the high end). Intermediate categories are Agree, Don't Know, and Disagree. This assumes an underlying dimension, y^*, in which the various responses are ordered, but we lack a meaningful metric for distance. How far is "disagree" from "strongly agree"?

$$y^* \longleftarrow \text{Strongly Agree} \text{------} \text{Agree} \text{------} \text{Don't Know} \text{------} \text{Disagree} \text{------} \text{Strongly Disagree} \longrightarrow y^*$$

Sometimes data for which we do have a meaningful distance metric are reported in ordered bins or categories. Age, for example, is often measured in chunks (under 18, 18–24, etc.). Income, especially when solicited as a self-reported value on a survey, is another variable frequently measured in coarse, ordinal categories. Even if the underlying variable is continuous and might be measured at the interval (or even ratio) level, binning the data into categories usually fails to preserve the metric information. Ordinal data instead represent ranks such that we can use inequality operations but not arithmetic ones. We can tell which of two responses is greater, but we cannot say by how much.

If we could measure the distances between adjacent categories, then we could treat the categorization scheme as if it were a continuous variable. In the absence of such information, treating ordered categories as continuous – by calculating a mean or fitting an OLS model – requires strong assumptions. There are numerous published studies where the authors proceed anyway, sometimes leaving these assumptions as implicit.

Treating ordered data as continuous can lead to problems similar to those we identified with the linear probability model for binary data. Fortunately the likelihood framework allows us to relax assumptions about the metric content of our data. We do this by positing a latent but unobserved continuous variable that is only reported in discrete bins if the underlying value falls between particular cutpoints. The challenge becomes one of estimating the thresholds that divide one category from another.

8.2 THE ORDERED LOGIT MODEL

In modeling ordinal data we generalize the latent variable model introduced in Chapter 3. Suppose our observed data, Y, can take on one of M possible ordered categorical values. We again imagine that the observed Y is an imperfect or imprecise observation of some underlying continuous latent variable, Y^*, such that $y_i < y_j \Rightarrow y_i^* < y_j^*$. Recall that in constructing the latent variable model for the binary case, we assumed, arbitrarily, that we observed a "0" if $y_i^* \leq 0$ and "1" otherwise. In other words, we fixed a threshold, $\tau = 0$. In the binary case where $M = 2$ we needed only one threshold. With $M > 2$ we need to estimate not only the regression parameters but also the thresholds which will divide the underlying latent variable into the observed ordered categories. As usual our approach involves specifying stochastic and systematic components:

$$Y_i^* \sim f_L(\mu_i, 1)$$
$$\Updownarrow$$
$$Y_i^* = \mu_i + \varepsilon_i, \quad \varepsilon_i \sim f_L(0, 1)$$
$$\mu_i = \mathbf{x}_i^\mathsf{T} \boldsymbol{\beta}$$
$$Y_i = m \iff \tau_{m-1} < Y_i^* \leq \tau_m \quad \forall \quad m \in \{1, \ldots, M\},$$

where τ_m are the threshold parameters that divide the unobserved, latent variable into observed, modeled categories. We commonly assume that $\tau_0 = -\infty$ (the probability of being less than the lowest category is 0) and $\tau_M = +\infty$ (the probability of being in some category is 1). This leads to a stochastic component with the following form:

$$\begin{aligned}
\Pr(Y_i = m | \mathbf{x}_i) &= \Pr(\tau_{m-1} < Y_i^* \leq \tau_m | \mathbf{x}_i) \\
&= \Pr(\tau_{m-1} < \mathbf{x}_i^\mathsf{T} \boldsymbol{\beta} + \varepsilon_i \leq \tau_m) \\
&= \Pr(\tau_{m-1} - \mathbf{x}_i^\mathsf{T} \boldsymbol{\beta} < \varepsilon_i \leq \tau_m - \mathbf{x}_i^\mathsf{T} \boldsymbol{\beta}) \\
&= \Pr(\varepsilon_i \leq \tau_m - \mathbf{x}_i^\mathsf{T} \boldsymbol{\beta}) - \Pr(\varepsilon_i \leq \tau_{m-1} - \mathbf{x}_i^\mathsf{T} \boldsymbol{\beta}).
\end{aligned}$$

The assumption that the errors are logistic implies that[1]

$$\Pr(\varepsilon_i \le \tau_m - \mathbf{x}_i^{\mathsf{T}}\boldsymbol{\beta}) = \Lambda(\tau_m - \mathbf{x}_i^{\mathsf{T}}\boldsymbol{\beta}) = \frac{\exp(\tau_m - \mathbf{x}_i^{\mathsf{T}}\boldsymbol{\beta})}{1 + \exp(\tau_m - \mathbf{x}_i^{\mathsf{T}}\boldsymbol{\beta})}$$
$$= \Pr(Y^* \le \tau_m) = \Pr(Y \le m),$$

where Λ is the logistic cumulative distribution function (cdf).

It follows that we simply difference the logistic cdf for adjacent categories to find the probability that Y_i falls in any specific category m:

$$\Pr(Y_i = m) = \frac{\exp(\tau_m - \mathbf{x}_i^{\mathsf{T}}\boldsymbol{\beta})}{1 + \exp(\tau_m - \mathbf{x}_i^{\mathsf{T}}\boldsymbol{\beta})} - \frac{\exp(\tau_{m-1} - \mathbf{x}_i^{\mathsf{T}}\boldsymbol{\beta})}{1 + \exp(\tau_{m-1} - \mathbf{x}_i^{\mathsf{T}}\boldsymbol{\beta})}.$$

The cutpoints serve an important purpose: they slice up the density of the underlying latent variable into categories. Suppose we have five observed categories, following the Likert scale widely employed in surveys, where $m \in \{SD, D, DK, A, SA\}$.

$$\Pr(Y_i = m) = \begin{cases} \Lambda(\tau_{SD\text{-}D} - \mathbf{x}_i^{\mathsf{T}}\boldsymbol{\beta}) & \text{for} \quad m = SD \\ \Lambda(\tau_{D\text{-}DK} - \mathbf{x}_i^{\mathsf{T}}\boldsymbol{\beta}) - \Lambda(\tau_{SD\text{-}D} - \mathbf{x}_i^{\mathsf{T}}\boldsymbol{\beta}) & \text{for} \quad m = D \\ \Lambda(\tau_{DK\text{-}A} - \mathbf{x}_i^{\mathsf{T}}\boldsymbol{\beta}) - \Lambda(\tau_{D\text{-}DK} - \mathbf{x}_i^{\mathsf{T}}\boldsymbol{\beta}) & \text{for} \quad m = DK \\ \Lambda(\tau_{A\text{-}SA} - \mathbf{x}_i^{\mathsf{T}}\boldsymbol{\beta}) - \Lambda(\tau_{DK\text{-}A} - \mathbf{x}_i^{\mathsf{T}}\boldsymbol{\beta}) & \text{for} \quad m = A \\ 1 - \Lambda(\tau_{A\text{-}SA} - \mathbf{x}_i^{\mathsf{T}}\boldsymbol{\beta}) & \text{for} \quad m = SA. \end{cases}$$

$$(8.1)$$

This is illustrated in Figure 8.1, which shows example cutpoints defining the observed categories in a hypothetical example. The figure also illustrates how covariates and regression parameters are translated into the observed categories. The two curves represent the distributions for two hypothetical observations, i and j. We can see that $\mathbf{x}_j^{\mathsf{T}}\boldsymbol{\beta} > \mathbf{x}_i^{\mathsf{T}}\boldsymbol{\beta}$. This has the effect of shifting the probability mass to the right, implying more of the mass is above the higher thresholds for observation j. This means that Y_j is more likely to be in the higher categories than Y_i.

Equation 8.1 is the basic probability statement for the model, which yields a likelihood that is simply the product of the binary logit models that switches between adjacent categories for each observation:

$$\mathcal{L}(\{\beta_1, \ldots, \beta_k\}, \{\tau_1, \ldots, \tau_m\} | \mathbf{Y}, \mathbf{X})$$
$$= \prod_{i=1}^{n} \prod_{m=1}^{M} \left[\Lambda(\tau_m - \mathbf{x}_i^{\mathsf{T}}\boldsymbol{\beta}) - \Lambda(\tau_{m-1} - \mathbf{x}_i^{\mathsf{T}}\boldsymbol{\beta}) \right]^{\mathbb{1}_{im}},$$

---

[1] Recall that $\Pr(V \le v) = \int_{-\infty}^{v} f(r)dr$, which implies that $\Pr(u < V \le w) = \int_{-\infty}^{w} f(r)dr - \int_{-\infty}^{u} f(r)dr = F(w) - F(u)$ where $f(\cdot)$ is the density function, and $F(\cdot)$ is the cumulative distribution function for the random variable V.

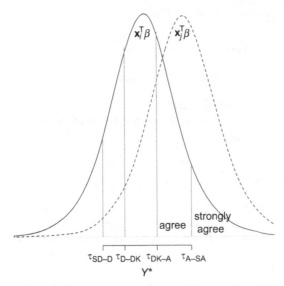

FIGURE 8.1 Visualizing how cutpoints divide the density of a continuous latent variable into discrete ordered categories. The curves represent Y^* for two observations, i and j.

where $\mathbb{1}_{im}$ is an indicator variable equal to 1 if and only if $y_i = m$ and 0 otherwise.

This translates easily to the log-likelihood as

$$\log \mathcal{L}(\boldsymbol{\beta}, \boldsymbol{\tau} | \mathbf{Y}, \mathbf{X}) = \sum_{i=1}^{n} \sum_{m=1}^{M} \mathbb{1}_{im} \log[\Lambda(\tau_m - \mathbf{x}_i^{\mathsf{T}} \boldsymbol{\beta}) - \Lambda(\tau_{m-1} - \mathbf{x}_i^{\mathsf{T}} \boldsymbol{\beta})]. \quad (8.2)$$

One additional mathematical consideration involves the question of how to anchor the scale of the latent variable or, put another way, whether to estimate an intercept. To see this, note that we can conceptualize the τ parameters as a series of intercepts, i.e., probabilities of being in each category when all independent variables are set to 0.0. If we estimate an intercept along with a threshold for each of the categories (i.e., $M-1$ cut points), then the model is not identified. In order to identify the model either the intercept or a cutpoint must be dropped. $\mathcal{R}$'s polr function (from the MASS library) omits the intercept. These differences are purely technical; they have no bearing on the model's fit to the data or the interpretation of the regression parameters.

As with the standard logit model, the ordered logit likelihood can be maximized with respect to the regression parameters and cutpoints. As usual we calculate the variance-covariance matrix from the inverse of the Hessian matrix.

8.2.1 What about the Ordered *Probit* Model?

Just as in the binary case, the distinction between ordered logit and probit is driven by assumptions about the stochastic component of the model or, equivalently, the error process. In the ordered logit we assumed that the errors followed a standard logistic distribution. If we assume the errors follow the standard normal distribution, then we have an ordered probit model. Using the convention that Φ denotes the cumulative distribution function for the standard normal, we can express the log-likelihood for an ordered probit model as

$$\log \mathcal{L}(\boldsymbol{\beta}, \boldsymbol{\tau} | \mathbf{Y}, \mathbf{X}) = \sum_{i=1}^{n} \sum_{m=1}^{M} \mathbb{1}_{im} \log \left[\Phi(\tau_m - \mathbf{x}_i^\mathsf{T} \boldsymbol{\beta}) - \Phi(\tau_{m-1} - \mathbf{x}_i^\mathsf{T} \boldsymbol{\beta}) \right].$$

(8.3)

Just as in the binary case, the choice between logit and probit is virtually always inconsequential.

8.2.2 Results and Interpretation

Results from ordered logit and probit models are frequently presented using the standard BUTON of coefficient and standard error estimates. This is unfortunate since the point estimates from ordered logit models are even less straightforward on their own than in the binary logit case. This is largely because these models have multiple categories for the dependent variable. Each category is itself modeled as a nonlinear function of covariates and parameters.

Scholars will also sometimes report odds ratios, although these remain difficult to explain in front of others (e.g., in job talks). For completeness, however, the change in the odds of $Y \leq m$ (versus greater than m) associated with a δ-unit change in covariate X_j equals $\exp(-\delta \hat{\beta}_j)$. Using tabular displays for interpreting things like odds ratios for ordered outcomes becomes quite complicated because each level of the dependent variable must be discussed separately.

Another way of looking at model implications is to consider marginal effects in the form of the partial derivative of the probability of any particular outcome value with respect to a particular covariate $j \in \{1, 2, \ldots, k\}$. This is given as

$$\left. \frac{\partial \Pr(Y = m)}{\partial x_j} \right|_{\bar{\mathbf{x}}} = \frac{\partial \Lambda(\hat{\tau}_m - \bar{\mathbf{x}}^\mathsf{T} \hat{\boldsymbol{\beta}})}{\partial x_j} - \frac{\partial \Lambda(\hat{\tau}_{m-1} - \bar{\mathbf{x}}^\mathsf{T} \hat{\boldsymbol{\beta}})}{\partial x_j}$$

$$= \hat{\beta}_j \left[f_L(\hat{\tau}_m - \bar{\mathbf{x}}^\mathsf{T} \hat{\boldsymbol{\beta}}) - f_L(\hat{\tau}_{m-1} - \bar{\mathbf{x}}^\mathsf{T} \hat{\boldsymbol{\beta}}) \right]. \quad (8.4)$$

A change in x_j shifts the density up or down the axis, while the positions of the cutpoints stay the same. For a positive $\hat{\beta}_j$ the "mass of probability" in the middle category first gets larger, then smaller as we increase x_j. Mathematically, this means that the change in the probability of observing a "middle category" response as a function of X_j, is not directly observable from the sign of $\hat{\beta}_j$.

Predicted probabilities and first differences are also straightforward to calculate, as we show below:

$$\Pr(\widehat{Y_i = m}|\mathbf{x}_i) = \Lambda(\hat{\tau}_m - \bar{\mathbf{x}}_i^{\mathsf{T}}\hat{\boldsymbol{\beta}}) - \Lambda(\hat{\tau}_{m-1} - \bar{\mathbf{x}}_i^{\mathsf{T}}\hat{\boldsymbol{\beta}}). \tag{8.5}$$

As always, the most informative presentations of results will not just rely on point estimates but also incorporate the full measure of uncertainty.

8.3 EXAMPLE: CATEGORICAL ASSESSMENTS OF POLITICAL IDEOLOGY

The ANES includes a variety of interesting questions, many of which are ordered, categorical variables. We use the pilot study from 2016 to illustrate the ordered logit model. The variables are delineated, briefly, in Table 8.1.

We fit an ordered logit model to respondents' ratings of Obama's conservatism as a function of how much one pays attention to politics, party identification, age, educational level, income, and race. Standard $\mathcal{R}$ results appear in Table 8.2, a BUTON.

What can we tell from these results? First, categories can be distinguished from each other. We see this by looking at the τ_m; the distances between the cutpoints are large relative to their standard errors. There is a significant and substantively large negative relationship between party identification and perceptions of Obama's conservatism. Party identification is coded from 0 (Strong Democrat) to 7 (Strong Republican), which implies that Republican identifiers are more likely to perceive Obama to be politically liberal than Democratic identifiers. Thus, $\exp(-1 * -0.39) = 1.47$, which shows that a respondent one "unit" more Republican is more likely to place Obama in category m or lower by a factor of 1.5. Interest in politics, income, and age

TABLE 8.1 *Selected variables and descriptors from 2016 ANES pilot study.*

Obama L-C	Barak Obama's perceived conservatism, 7-point scale (7 = very conservative)
age	respondent's age in years
education	respondent's education level, 7-point scale (7 = advanced degree)
income	respondent's family income (binned)
party ID	respondent's partisan allegiance, 7-point scale (7 = strong Republican)
follow politics	extent to which respondent follows politics, 4-point scale (1 = most of the time)
white	Did the respondent self-identify as white?

TABLE 8.2 *Ordered logit analysis of 2016 ANES data. What determined the liberal–conservative assessment of Barak Obama?*

	$\hat{\beta}$	$\sigma_{\hat{\beta}}$
follow politics	0.62	0.08
party ID	−0.39	0.03
age	−0.01	0.004
education	−0.03	0.04
income	−0.04	0.02
white	−0.10	0.14
cutpoints	$\hat{\tau}_m$	$\sigma_{\hat{\tau}_m}$
1|2	−1.58	0.34
2|3	−0.51	0.33
3|4	0.34	0.33
4|5	1.95	0.35
5|6	2.73	0.37
6|7	3.58	0.42
n	998	
$\log \mathcal{L}$	−1,400	
AIC	2,823	
BIC	2,882	

also appear to be strong predictors of respondents' perceptions of Obama's conservatism. But it is hard to be very precise about these relationships without some exponentiation, alas.

The logic of calculating first differences suggests that a plot may be useful. We examine the model's predicted probabilities of falling into each outcome category as over different levels of party identification while holding the other covariates at fixed levels. Specifically, we do this calculation for a 49-year-old white respondent with more than 12 years of schooling but no higher degree, with annual family income between $40,000–$49,000, and who claims to follow politics "most of the time."

Figure 8.2 illustrates these results, which are obtained using the $\mathcal{R}$ code displayed in the box for Example 8.1. We can then plot these predicted probabilities across the range of party ID, as displayed in Figure 8.2.

Figure 8.2 displays a common feature of models for ordered categorical data: the effect of a covariate on the probability of falling into the extreme categories is monotonic, but a covariate's effect on the probability of falling into intermediate categories is not. Figure 8.1 shows why this occurs: the covariates shift the location of each individual's latent Y_i^* but the

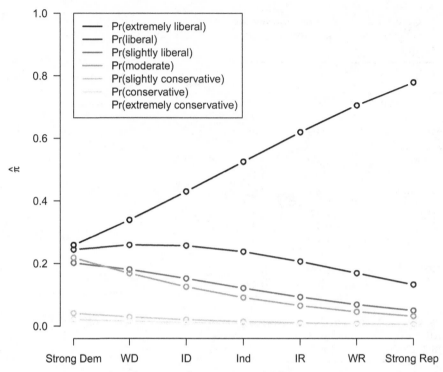

FIGURE 8.2 Party identification and perceptions of Obama's conservatism, calculated from the ordered logistic regression reported in Table 8.2.

cutpoints remain fixed. A change in a covariate that shifts the probability distribution to the right will unambiguously put more of the mass beyond the highest threshold and less of it below the lowest, but what happens in between depends on the magnitude of the shift and the point where we started.

Figure 8.2 echoes Figure 3.3, only without including any way of evaluating the uncertainty in point estimates. Including error bars or shaded regions for all predicted outcome categories here would make the figure hopelessly unreadable. We can build on the uncertainty estimates produced during model fitting, though we may be required to choose specific levels of the outcome variable to focus on for visual clarity. We do just that in Figure 8.3, presenting the differences between self-identified weak democrats and independents in finding Obama to be "moderate" and "liberal." As always in nonlinear models, we hold all other covariates at fixed values. Here we use their central tendencies. The densities reflect our estimation uncertainty around these quantities.

Code Example 8.1 produces these estimates and graphics.

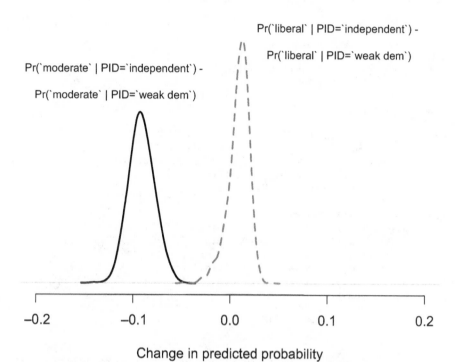

Change in predicted probability

FIGURE 8.3 First differences: Comparing weak democrats against independents in their predicted probabilities of identifying Obama as "moderate" (solid) and "liberal" (broken), calculated from the ordered logistic regression reported in Table 8.2. Probability densities reflect the estimation uncertainties around these quantities.

8.4 PARALLEL REGRESSIONS

An alternative way of conceptualizing the ordered logit/probit model is as the constrained estimation of a system of logit/probit models. To see this, note that we can reexpress our ordered categorical variable, Y_i, as a series of binary variables, $\tilde{Y}_{im}$, such that $\tilde{y}_{im} = 1 \Leftrightarrow y_i \leq m$ for some category, m. We might then be interested in fitting the system of equations

$$\Pr(Y_i \leq 1) = \text{logit}^{-1}\left(\tau_1 + \mathbf{x}_i^\mathsf{T}\boldsymbol{\beta}_1\right)$$

$$\vdots$$

$$\Pr(Y_i \leq M - 1) = \text{logit}^{-1}\left(\tau_{M-1} + \mathbf{x}_i^\mathsf{T}\boldsymbol{\beta}_{M-1}\right)$$
$$\Pr(Y_i = M) = 1 - \text{logit}^{-1}\left(\tau_{M-1} - \mathbf{x}_i^\mathsf{T}\boldsymbol{\beta}_{M-1}\right).$$

The system of logit models fit to each of these $\tilde{Y}_m$ is called the *cumulative logit* model.

$\mathcal{R}$ Code Example 8.1 *Ordered logit first differences*

```
library (MASS)
# requires anes.sub data from repository.
attach(anes.sub)
polr.out <- polr(as.ordered(Obama.LR)~ follow.politics + pid +
                 age + education +income + white,
                 data=anes.sub, method="logistic", Hess=T)
beta <- coef(polr.out)
tau <- polr.out$zeta
#create predicted probabilities
X <- cbind(median(follow.politics), #scenario of interest
           min(pid):max(pid),       #across range of party ID
           median(age), median(education),
           median(income), median(white)
           )
p1 <- plogis(tau[1] - X %*% beta)
p2 <- plogis(tau[2] - X %*% beta) - plogis(tau[1] - X %*% beta)
p3 <- plogis(tau[3] - X %*% beta) - plogis(tau[2] - X %*% beta)
p4 <- plogis(tau[4] - X %*% beta) - plogis(tau[3] - X %*% beta)
p5 <- plogis(tau[5] - X %*% beta) - plogis(tau[4] - X %*% beta)
p6 <- plogis(tau[6] - X %*% beta) - plogis(tau[5] - X %*% beta)
p7 <- 1.0 - plogis(tau[6] - X %*% beta)
```

Note that in this general specification each equation has its own set of slope parameters, β_m. The ordered logit and probit models estimate these equations simultaneously, with the constraint that slope parameters are equal across equations, i.e., $\beta_m = \beta \ \forall \ m$. The intercepts ($\tau_m$) vary across equations, as they must if we are to discriminate between categories. This assumption of common slope parameters across levels of the response variable goes by the name "parallel regressions" or, in the logit case, "proportional odds." The phrase parallel regressions describes how the impact of the covariates may shift the predicted probability curves to the right or the left but does not change the basic slope of these curves across any two categories. This means that the partial derivative for the probability that Y is in any category with respect to the covariate information should be equal:

$$\frac{\partial \Pr(y \leq m \mid x)}{\partial x} = \frac{\partial \Pr(y \leq m - 1 \mid x)}{\partial x} = \frac{\partial \Pr(y \leq m - 2 \mid x)}{\partial x} = \cdots$$

For better or worse, the parallel regressions assumption is rarely examined in practice, so the extent to which violations are substantively important is not well-explored. But it is possible for a covariate to increase the probability of being in category 2 relative to 1 and yet have a null or even negative relationship at other levels. An inappropriate constraint could result in missing this relationship. The parallel regressions assumption is easier to satisfy when

$\mathcal{R}$ Code Example 8.2 *Interpreting ordered logit*

```
#scenarios
X.wd <- cbind(median(follow.politics), 1, #PID=1 weak democrat
            median(age), median(education), median(income), TRUE)
X.ind <- cbind(median(follow.politics), 3, #PID=3 independent
            median(age), median(education), median(income), TRUE)

#coefficient vectors. Note inclusion of cutpoints
draws<-mvrnorm(1000, c(coef(polr.out),polr.out$zeta),
        solve(polr.out$Hessian))
B<-draws[,1:length(coef(polr.out))]
Taus<-draws[,(length(coef(polr.out))+1):ncol(draws)]

#predicted probabilities
pi.lib.wd<- plogis(Taus[,2] - B%*%t(X.wd)) - plogis(Taus[,1] - B%*%t(X.wd))
pi.lib.ind <- plogis(Taus[,2] - B%*%t(X.ind)) - plogis(Taus[,1] - B%*%t(X.ind))
pi.mod.wd<- plogis(Taus[,4] - B%*%t(X.wd)) - plogis(Taus[,3] - B%*%t(X.wd))
pi.mod.ind <- plogis(Taus[,4] - B%*%t(X.ind)) - plogis(Taus[,3] - B%*%t(X.ind))

#differences
fd.lib<- pi.lib.ind - pi.lib.wd
fd.mod<- pi.mod.ind - pi.mod.wd

#plotting
plot(density(fd.mod, adjust=1.5), xlim=c(-0.2,0.2),ylim=c(0,50),
    xlab="Change in predicted probability", bty="n", col=1,
    yaxt="n", lwd=2, main="", ylab="")
lines(density(fd.lib, adjust=1.5), col=grey(0.5), lwd=2, lty=2)
text(x=0.11, y=42, labels="Pr('liberal' | PID='independent') -
    \n Pr('liberal' | PID='weak dem')",cex=.8)
text(x=-.12, y=35, labels="Pr('moderate' | PID='independent') -
    \n Pr('moderate' | PID='weak dem')",cex=.8)
detach(anes.sub)
```

there are just a few categories but becomes more difficult to meet as the number of categories grows.

The parallel regressions assumption can be tested in several ways. One way is to fit $m - 1$ binary regressions after expanding the ordinal dependent variable into $m - 1$ binary $\tilde{Y}_m$. With these regression results in hand, the equality of $\hat{\beta}_m$ can be examined with standard Wald-type tests or simply visualized. A somewhat easier test to execute is to compare the ordered logit/probit model with a cumulative logit or a multinominal logit/probit. We provide an example of the former below. Multinomial models are discussed in Chapter 9.

8.4.1 Example: Genocide Severity

Krain (2005) examined the effectiveness of military intervention in slowing or stopping killing during genocides. His results suggested that interventions that directly challenged the perpetrator or specifically aided the targets were the only efficacious types of military responses. Krain's dependent variable, magnitud,

TABLE 8.3 *The distribution of observations over Krain's 11-point scale of genocide magnitude.*

Category	0	0.5	1	1.5	2	2.5	3	3.5	4	4.5	5
Frequency	45	27	20	21	16	25	34	53	19	7	6

is an ordered categorical variable describing the magnitude of genocide, where the category coded 0 implies the lowest severity of genocide, and 5 is used to flag the highest severity levels. Table 8.3 displays the frequency of cases in each of the eleven categories.

In his analysis Krain treats the outcome variable as ordered categories, which is, strictly speaking, correct. But when there is a large number of categories it is common to use continuous regression models such as least squares, especially if there is roughly the same number of observations in each category. We revisit this decision by comparing Krain's ordered logit specification to a simpler OLS model. We also interrogate the parallel regressions assumption.

Table 8.4 displays the BUTON for an OLS and ordered logit specification. The results for the ordered logit model are identical to those presented by Krain in his article (model 1, in table 3, pg. 379). Note that the likelihood ratio, AIC, and BIC all indicate that the simpler OLS model with fewer parameters is a better in-sample fit than the ordered logit. Looking at the estimated cutpoints, we also see that they are all very close together relative to their standard errors, particularly below category 3.5. This indicates that the model has a hard time distinguishing between adjacent categories in these data. With eleven categories the assumption of a continuous response appears reasonable.

8.4.2 Parallel Regressions and Genocide Severity

We can use two different graphical heuristics to examine the parallel regressions assumption in the Krain genocide severity example.

Figure 8.4 plots the means of the regressors at different levels of the response variable.[2] If the included regressors are able to differentiate one category from another, then we should expect to see a strong trend across the levels of the dependent variable. If the parallel regressions assumption holds, then this trend should be linear, and the conditional means should line up neatly along the broken trend line. In Krain's data, this does not appear to hold. Covariates that appear as "significant" in Table 8.4 – duration of genocide (genyr) and state failure (stfl) – appear to have nonlinear relationships with the levels of Y.

A second strategy is to fit the cumulative logit regressions without any constraint and examine the stability of the coefficients across the levels of the response variable. A response with eleven categories implies ten simultaneous

---

[2] Note that we have rescaled the response variable to be in integer increments, e.g., $\{0, 1, \ldots, 10\}$, rather than increments of 0.5.

TABLE 8.4 *The correlates of genocide severity, a reanalysis of Krain (2005).*

	OLS	Ordered logit
Intervention	0.23 (0.22)	0.13 (0.30)
Contiguity	0.39 (0.22)	0.57 (0.30)
Genocide severity	0.42 (0.06)	0.72 (0.10)
Genocide duration	−0.05 (0.02)	−0.07 (0.03)
State failures	0.44 (0.19)	0.54 (0.27)
Regime type	−0.01 (0.02)	−0.01 (0.02)
Ethnic fractionalization	0.78 (0.38)	0.49 (0.51)
Economic marginalization	0.0004 (0.001)	−0.0004 (0.002)
Cold War	0.03 (0.24)	−0.27 (0.36)
Cutpoints		$\hat{\tau}_m$
Constant	0.50 (0.41)	
0|0.5		−0.33 (0.57)
0.5|1		0.34 (0.56)
1|1.5		0.80 (0.56)
1.5|2		1.25 (0.57)
2|2.5		1.60 (0.58)
2.5|3		2.12 (0.59)
3|3.5		2.84 (0.60)
3.5|4		4.35 (0.62)
4|4.5		5.45 (0.65)
4.5|5		6.29 (0.72)
n	273	273
$\log \mathcal{L}$	−450	−565
AIC	920	1,167
BIC	960	1,236

equations using the cumulative logit conceptualization. Table 8.5 displays how the dependent variables, the $\tilde{Y}_m$, are constructed.

Figure 8.5 displays the results. The vertical axis is the $\hat{\beta}_k$. If parallel regression holds, then these estimates should be approximately equal. The plots are scaled so that the vertical axis distance roughly covers ±2 standard errors from the maximum and minimum coefficient estimates. Again, we see unusual and unstable patterns in the regression coefficients, even those like state failure (stfl) that appeared as significant in the ordered logit fit.

The results here are consistent with the imprecisely estimated threshold parameters reported in Table 8.4, implying that several of the categories are difficult to distinguish from one another. We might fit the OLS model, as above, or consider combining some categories together, especially where thresholds are imprecisely estimated. But either way this application violates the parallel regressions assumption.

TABLE 8.5 *Coding Krain's response variable for the cumulative logit.*

		$\tilde{Y}_{im} = 1$	$\tilde{Y}_{im} = 0$
eq. 1	$\tilde{Y}_{i,0}$	0	0.5, 1, 1.5, 2, 2.5, 3, 3.5, 4, 4.5, 5
eq. 2	$\tilde{Y}_{i,0.5}$	0,0.5	1, 1.5, 2, 2.5, 3, 3.5, 4, 4.5, 5
eq. 3	$\tilde{Y}_{i,1}$	0,0.5,1	1.5, 2, 2.5, 3, 3.5, 4, 4.5, 5
eq. 4	$\tilde{Y}_{i,1.5}$	0,0.5,1, 1.5	2, 2.5, 3, 3.5, 4, 4.5, 5
eq. 5	$\tilde{Y}_{i,2}$	0,0.5,1, 1.5, 2	2.5, 3, 3.5, 4, 4.5, 5
eq. 6	$\tilde{Y}_{i,2.5}$	0,0.5,1, 1.5, 2, 2.5	3, 3.5, 4, 4.5, 5
eq. 7	$\tilde{Y}_{i,3}$	0,0.5,1, 1.5, 2, 2.5, 3	3.5, 4, 4.5, 5
eq. 8	$\tilde{Y}_{i,3.5}$	0,0.5,1, 1.5, 2, 2.5, 3, 3.5	4, 4.5, 5
eq. 9	$\tilde{Y}_{i,4}$	0,0.5,1, 1.5, 2, 2.5, 3, 3.5,4	4.5, 5
eq. 10	$\tilde{Y}_{i,4.5}$	0,0.5,1, 1.5, 2, 2.5, 3, 3.5,4, 4.5	5

8.4.3 Extensions

Several extensions to the ordered logit/probit model have been proposed to partially relax the parallel regressions assumptions and allow for other nuances like unequal variances across units. These models, going by names like *partial proportional odds* and *generalized ordered logit* have not seen exensive use in the social science for several reasons. First, an even more general and flexible approach, the multinomial model taken up in the next chapter, is widely understood. The main cost of the multinomial model is that it estimates many more parameters than an ordered alternative. With datasets growing bigger and computers becoming ever faster, the relative cost of the multinomial alternative is falling fast. Second, most of these models require theoretical or other reasons for contraining some predictors to respect the parallel regressions assumption, while others do not. Or, as with the heterokedastic probit model, some covariates must be used to model scale parameters, often with little improvement to model fit. Rarely do we have theories at this level of precision. Third, interpretation of these hybrid ordered models is more complicated, including the fact that it is possible for certain models to generate negative predicted probabilities (McCullagh and Nelder, 1989).

8.5 ORDERED CATEGORICAL VARIABLES AS REGRESSORS

Computer programs, including $\mathcal{R}$, do not care on which side of the regression equation categorical variables appear. Analysts, however, will often model an ordered variable using ordered logit or probit when it is an outcome, yet treat the same variable as if it were continuous when including it as a regressor. We did just that for both the model reported in Table 8.2 and those in Table 8.4. In the former we treated the respondents' self-reported party identification as an interval-level variable while modeling the same respondent's perception of

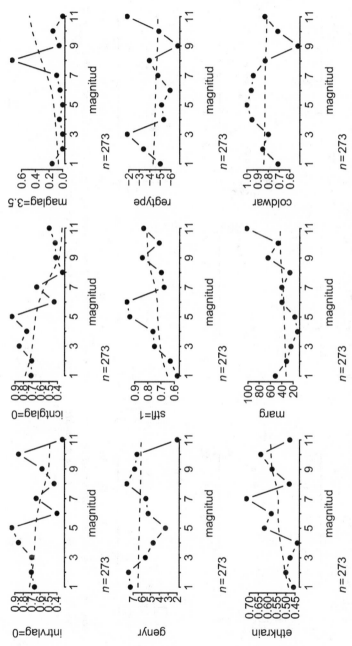

FIGURE 8.4 *Plot of the conditional means of the regressors at different levels of the response variable,* magnitud. *If the parallel regressions assumption holds, the means will show a strong trend across values of the response variable and line up neatly. The broken line is the loess smoother describing this trend.*

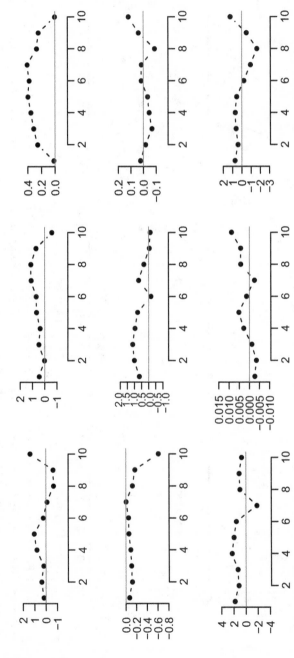

FIGURE 8.5 *Plot of the estimated regression coefficients from* $M - 1$ *regressions on* $\tilde{Y}_m$, *the indicators that* $Y \leq m$. *If the parallel regressions assumption holds, the estimated coefficients should be stable across levels of* $\tilde{Y}$.

Obama as categorical (but ordered). In the latter we reproduced Krain's model, in which he included a one-year lagged version of the genocide magnitude variable as a predictor, again treating it as continuous even though that same variable was treated as ordered categorical on the left side of the regression.

The difference between an ordered categorical variable and one that is "continuous" can be subtle. We do not wade into complicated issues of measurement and scaling here. Rather, we take an applied (some might say naïve) approach. Whether a variable is better treated as an ordered categorical variable or an interval-scaled measure will depend on the quantities of interest, coarseness or fineness of the coding scheme, available degrees of freedom, and, ultimately, predictive power. Deciding on the best modeling approach to take will benefit from the tools and heuristics described in Chapter 5.

8.5.1 An Example: Child Mortality and Democracy

Suppose we are interested in the relationship between democracy and infant mortality, a common measure of human well-being. We gather data on child mortality rates for a cross-section of countries in the year 2000. The measure we use for democracy here is the "constraints on the executive" (XCONST) variable from Polity IV (Marshall et al., 2016), an ordinal scale ranging from few restrictions to many. In Figure 8.6 we display the distribution of (log) mortality for different levels of XCONST. It appears that child mortality drops significantly when the executive is highly constrained (categories 6 and 7).

We first follow common practice and fit an OLS regression model treating XCONST as if it were simply an interval-scaled variable. We obtain the results presented in the first column of Table 8.6, in which there appears to be a substantively large and "significant" negative association between (log) child mortality and XCONST.

In the second column we treat XCONST as a purely categorical variable; all XCONST coefficients represent comparisons against XCONST=1. In this case we see that *only* category 7 (most constrained) of XCONST shows a substantively large negative relationship with child mortality relative to category 1.[3] Clearly, conclusions based on the first model were somewhat misleading. Consistent with Figure 8.6, it does not appear that the negative relationship holds equally and constantly across all levels of XCONST.

One way of thinking about what we have done so far is that in the first model, we privileged ordering over the categories, whereas in the second model, we gave greater analytical weight to the categories (particularly the comparison against category 1) and ignored the ordinal information. What

[3] But note that categories 6 and 7 can be distinguished from 2–5.

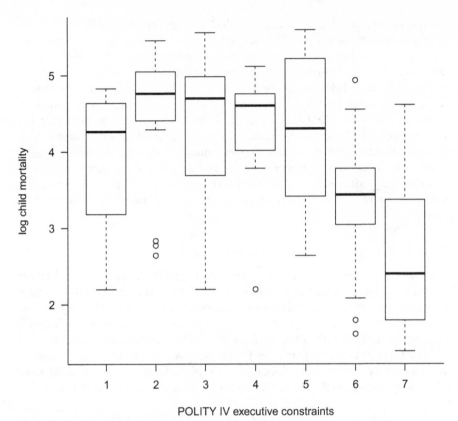

POLITY IV executive constraints

FIGURE 8.6 Child mortality and constraints on the executive.

happens if we try to balance both, respecting the categorical, ordinal nature of the variable? In $\mathcal{R}$ we simply declare the variable to be of class `ordered`. In this case we also choose to use "successive differences" contrasts, reporting results in the third column of Table 8.6. In this model, coefficient estimates represent the "effect" of going from one level of a variable to the next, e.g., the expected change in child mortality associated with going from XCONST=2 to XCONST=3. In fact, the coefficient estimates in the last column are simply the differences of coefficients for adjacent categories from the second model. Note that using this encoding of XCONST does not in any way alter the model fit, since we are not bringing any new information to bear. This encoding simply alters how we interpret the coefficients from the model. On this basis we see that moving from 5 to 6 and 6 to 7 both reduce infant mortality.

There are several other things worth noting here. First, the two models treating XCONST as a categorical variable fit the data equally well. Second, by the AIC and (penalized) R^2 criteria, the second and third models

TABLE 8.6 *OLS regression of (log) infant mortality on different encodings of executive constraints (XCONST).*

	Continuous	Categorical	Ordered
XCONST	−0.30		
	(0.04)		
XCONST=2		0.59	
		(0.37)	
XCONST=3		0.40	
		(0.35)	
XCONST=4		0.30	
		(0.46)	
XCONST=5		0.37	
		(0.35)	
XCONST=6		−0.58	
		(0.37)	
XCONST=7		−1.29	
		(0.32)	
$XCONST_{2-1}$			0.59
			(0.37)
$XCONST_{3-2}$			−0.19
			(0.30)
$XCONST_{4-3}$			−0.09
			(0.41)
$XCONST_{4-4}$			0.07
			(0.41)
$XCONST_{6-5}$			−0.95
			(0.31)
$XCONST_{7-6}$			−0.72
			(0.28)
Constant	5.07	3.91	3.88
	(0.21)	(0.29)	(0.09)
n	140	140	140
Adjusted R^2	0.26	0.37	0.37
AIC	411	393	393
BIC	420	417	417

using categorical treatments of XCONST fit the data better in-sample than the one treating XCONST as continuous. On a BIC basis, the decision is less clear. Using a five-fold cross validation heuristic, we find that the first model returns an MSE of 1.07; the other two return MSEs of 0.926, an improvement of almost 14% in out-of-sample predictive performance. Better modeling of the categorical data on the right hand side of the regression has helped us better understand the relationship between the variables of interest here.

8.6 FURTHER READING

Applications

Walter (2017) uses ordered logit to analyze European Social Survey data reporting people's perceptions of labor market risk. Kriner and Shen (2016) analyze an experiment on the presence of the draft on support of military action.

Past Work

McKelvey and Zaviona (1975) present an early introduction to the ordered probit in the social sciences. Fullerton (2009) develops a typology of the various types of logit-based models for ordered categorical outcome variables.

For a nuanced exploration of an ordered categorical variable commonly treated as interval-scaled (Polity scores), see Treier and Jackman (2008).

Advanced Study

On the "generalized ordered logit" that constrains some regression parameters to be equal across categories while allowing others to vary, see Peterson and Harrell (1990); Williams (2016).

Software Notes

See Venables and Ripley (2002) for more extended discussion of contrasts in $\mathcal{R}$ and how they are constructed. Successive differences contrasts are part of the MASS library, as is the polr function. The ordinal package (Christensen, 2015) implements a variety of models for ordinal data, including partial proportional odds and heterokedastic ordered logit. The oglmx package (Carroll, 2017) implements heteroskedastic ordered logit and probit models.

9

Models for Nominal Data

9.1 INTRODUCTION

In Chapter 8 we extended the latent variable model for binary outcomes to incorporate ordered response variables. We managed this by adding a set of estimated "thresholds" that served to map the assumed probability density into discrete but ordered categories. Our ability to do this relies on the "parallel regressions" assumption: the relationship between covariates and the outcome variable is constant across different categories of the outcome.

Unordered, polychotomous dependent variables are simply variables in which the categories cannot be ordered in any mathematically meaningful way. These are also called *nominal* variables having more than the two categories found in a dichotomous variable. There are lots of good examples in the social sciences: vote choice (Christian Democrat, Social Democrat, Greens, etc.); occupation (doctor, lawyer, mechanic, astronaut, student, etc.); marital status (single, married, divorced, etc.); college major (art history, modern history, Greek history, etc.); language (French, German, Urdu, etc.); ethnicity (Serb, Croat, Bosniak, Avar, Lek, etc.); and many, many others. Sometimes these nominal groups can represent ascriptive categories. But often these groups are the objects of some choice process. This, in turn, has consequences for how we think about a statistical model and find relevant covariates. For example, there may be covariates relevant to the *choice*, such as price, color, or party platform. Or we might be interested in covariates relevant to the *chooser* or choice process, like income, age, or gender.

Constructing likelihood-based models for nominal variables builds on a generalization of the binomial distribution, the appropriately named *multinomial*. From there we develop a set of linear predictors that allow us to incorporate both covariates and link functions that map the linear predictor into the appropriate interval.

In case you were wondering ... 9.1 Categorical and multinomial distributions

Let S be some finite set with cardinality M. Define Z_i such that, for any $m \in S$, $\Pr(Z_i = m) = p_m$, $\sum_{m \in S} p_m = 1$, and $\Pr(Z_i = l) = 0 \;\forall\; l \notin S$. We say that Z_i follows a *categorical distribution*, with probability mass function denoted

$$Z_i \sim f_c(z_i; p_1, \ldots, p_M).$$

We can write the expectation of a categorical variable using the notion $\mathbb{1}_m$ to be the indicator variable taking on 1 if $Z_i = m$ and 0 otherwise. $\mathrm{E}[\mathbb{1}_m] = p_m$ and $\mathrm{var}(\mathbb{1}_m) = p_m(1 - p_m)$. The covariance between any two categories, $a, b \in S$, is given as $\mathrm{cov}(\mathbb{1}_a, \mathbb{1}_b) = -p_a p_b$. The Bernoulli distribution is a special case of the categorical distribution in which $M = 2$.

Now suppose we have n independent realizations of Z_i. Let $n_j \leq n, j \in S$ denote the number of realizations in category j such that $\sum_{j \in S} n_j = n$. Let $Y = (n_1, \ldots, n_M)$. We say that Y follows a multinomial distribution with parameter vector $\theta = (n, p_1, \ldots, p_M)$ and probability mass function

$$Y \sim f_m(\mathbf{y}; \theta) = \frac{n!}{\prod_{j \in S} n_j!} \prod_{j \in S} p_j^{n_j},$$

with $\mathrm{E}[Y] = (np_1, \ldots, np_M)$ and $\mathrm{var}(Y) = (np_1(1-p_1), \ldots, np_M(1-p_M))$. The covariance between any two categories, $a, b \in S$, is given as $\mathrm{cov}(\mathbb{1}_a, \mathbb{1}_b) = -np_a p_b$. The binomial distribution is a special case of the multinomial distribution in which $M = 2$.

9.2 MULTINOMIAL LOGIT

The multinomial logit model describes nominal outcomes such that the influence of each independent variable differs by outcome category. As a running example, consider data from the 2013 Australian National Election Survey describing how survey respondents voted for various parties in the lower house of parliament. Respondents could choose between the two major parties, Labor and Liberal, as well as the National Party, the Green Party, and "other," a residual category that included spoiling a ballot (Australia has compulsory voting). For our purposes we will simplify this to three categories, Labor, Coalition (Liberal and National), and Other. We are interested in how respondents' measured attributes relate to their vote choice. To derive a likelihood we build on the categorical distribution.

Suppose we have n survey respondents indexed by i. The outcome variable, Y_i, can take one and only one of M values, which we consider to be unordered categories. For example, we might have $Y_i \in \{L,C,O\}$. We *index* the elements of this set with j. For example $y_i = C$ would imply $j = 2$. Applying the categorical distribution, $\Pr(Y_i = m) = p_{im}$ and $\sum_{h=1}^{M} p_{ih} = 1$.

We want to allow p_{im} to vary as a function of $k - 1$ observation-level covariates along with a constant. That is, the response variable is an $n \times 1$ vector where element i records the category in which i falls. In our example, each cell is respondent i's vote intention. The covariate data is the typical $n \times k$ matrix in which each row represents an observation's values on $k - 1$ independent variables (plus a 1 for the intercept). In our example, covariates include income (in \$AU 10,000), union membership, religious affiliation (Protestant as reference), sex, and age.

Because covariates are observed at the level of the unit, i, and not the category, m, regression coefficients differ across outcome categories. This must be the case because a covariate that increases the chances that i chooses Labor must necessarily reduce the probability that she chooses at least one of the other options. In other words the multinomial model posits a different $\boldsymbol{\beta}_m$ specific to each outcome category.

We want to connect our linear predictor term, $\mathbf{x}_i^{\mathsf{T}} \boldsymbol{\beta}_m$, to the probabilities, p_{im}. Probabilities must be nonnegative, so we can use an exponential setup: $p_{im} = \exp(\mathbf{x}_i^{\mathsf{T}} \boldsymbol{\beta}_m)$. To ensure that probabilities sum to 1 across outcome categories, we divide by the sum across all M categories:

$$\Pr(Y_i = m) \equiv p_{im} = \frac{\exp(\mathbf{x}_i^{\mathsf{T}} \boldsymbol{\beta}_m)}{\sum_{h=1}^{M} \exp(\mathbf{x}_i^{\mathsf{T}} \boldsymbol{\beta}_h)}. \tag{9.1}$$

The expression in Equation 9.1 is unidentified. To fix the model, we must choose a *baseline* or *reference* category against which other categories are compared. Computationally this is accomplished by constraining the $\boldsymbol{\beta}_m$ for a particular category, usually the first, to be zero. This results in the following restatement of the basic multinomial model:

$$\Pr(Y_i = m \mid \mathbf{x}_i) = \frac{\exp(\mathbf{x}_i^{\mathsf{T}} \boldsymbol{\beta}_m)}{1 + \sum_{j=2}^{M} \exp(\mathbf{x}_i^{\mathsf{T}} \boldsymbol{\beta}_j)}. \tag{9.2}$$

Inspecting Equation 9.2 reveals an important insight: the multinomial logit model is essentially $M - 1$ different binary logits estimated simultaneously. It differs from actually estimating a series of binary logits in that we constrain the probabilities to sum to unity, gaining efficiency through joint estimation. But, unlike the ordered model considered in the previous chapter, the multinomial model does not constrain the $\boldsymbol{\beta}_m$ to be constant across categories; we estimate $M - 1$ different sets of regression parameters, each of which describes the log odds of being in category m versus the reference category. It then follows that any multinomial model can be reestimated with a different reference category. This will not change the overall fit of the model or its implications, but it will generally change the regression coefficients that you see on your computer screen and their immediate interpretations. But, as we will see later in this section, we can still recover pairwise comparisons across categories not used as a baseline.

Thinking of the multinomial model as a set of binary models also highlights another important fact: multinomial models are very demanding of the data. Multinomial models burn degrees of freedom rapidly as we estimate $M - 1$ parameters for every new explanatory variable. In a multinomial framework all the problems of perfect separation and rare events that we encountered in binary data are amplified. With so many more predictor–outcome combinations, small numbers of observations in any of these cells can arise more easily.

The multinomial likelihood can be formed following our usual steps and using $\mathbb{1}_{ij}$ as an indicator variable taking on 1 when observation i is in the jth category and 0 otherwise. For notational simplicity, the equations include sums over all M categories. To identify the model, let $\boldsymbol{\beta}_1 = 0$ so $\exp(\mathbf{x}_i^{\mathsf{T}}\boldsymbol{\beta}_1) = 1$.

$$\mathcal{L}_i = \prod_{h=1}^{M} \left(\frac{\exp(\mathbf{x}_i^{\mathsf{T}}\boldsymbol{\beta}_h)}{\sum_{\ell=1}^{M} \exp(\mathbf{x}_i^{\mathsf{T}}\boldsymbol{\beta}_\ell)} \right)^{\mathbb{1}_{ih}},$$

$$\mathcal{L} = \prod_{i=1}^{n} \frac{\prod_{h=1}^{M} \left(\exp(\mathbf{x}_i^{\mathsf{T}}\boldsymbol{\beta}_h) \right)^{\mathbb{1}_{ih}}}{\sum_{\ell=1}^{M} \exp(\mathbf{x}_i^{\mathsf{T}}\boldsymbol{\beta}_\ell)},$$

$$\log \mathcal{L} = \sum_{i=1}^{n} \sum_{h=1}^{M} \mathbb{1}_{ij}\mathbf{x}_i^{\mathsf{T}}\boldsymbol{\beta}_h - \log \left(\sum_{\ell=1}^{M} \exp(\mathbf{x}_i^{\mathsf{T}}\boldsymbol{\beta}_\ell) \right).$$

This likelihood is nice in all the standard ways: globally concave and quickly converging, producing (in the limit) estimates that are consistent, normal, and efficient.

9.2.1 A Latent Variable Formulation

Like the binary logit model, the multinomial model can be derived in a latent variable framework. Suppose an individual, i, chooses among discrete alternatives in the set S, with a utility $U_i(m)$, associated with each choice, m. Like all of statistics, each utility has a stochastic part and a systematic part. That is, $U_i(m) = \mu_i(m) + \epsilon_{im}$. The systematic part is a function of variables associated with the individual and might consist of different weights for each of these characteristics across alternatives: $\mu_i(m) = \mathbf{x}_i^\mathsf{T} \boldsymbol{\beta}_m$. Being clever, the individual chooses among the alternatives so as to maximize utility:

$$
\begin{aligned}
\Pr(Y_i = m) &= \Pr(U_i(m) > U_i(d) \;\; \forall \;\; d \neq m \in S) \\
&= \Pr(\mu_i(m) + \epsilon_{im} > \mu_i(d) + \epsilon_{id} \;\; \forall \;\; d \neq m \in S) \\
&= \Pr(\mathbf{x}_i^\mathsf{T} \boldsymbol{\beta}_m + \epsilon_{im} > \mathbf{x}_i^\mathsf{T} \boldsymbol{\beta}_d + \epsilon_{id} \;\; \forall \;\; d \neq m \in S) \\
&= \Pr(\epsilon_{im} - \epsilon_{id} > \mathbf{x}_i^\mathsf{T} (\boldsymbol{\beta}_d - \boldsymbol{\beta}_m) \;\; \forall \;\; d \neq m \in S). \quad (9.3)
\end{aligned}
$$

If the difference between the stochastic component and that of any alternative is greater than the difference in the systematic parts, it has the highest utility, because either ϵ_{im} is large or $\mathbf{x}_i^\mathsf{T} \boldsymbol{\beta}_m$ is large, or both. The expression in Equation 9.3 relies on differences between coefficient vectors across categories, so once again we see that model identification requires that we fix one category as the baseline. To complete the model we need to choose an expression for the stochastic component, i.e., we specify the distribution of the error terms, ϵ_{im}. If we choose a multivariate normal distribution we arrive at the multinomial probit model. If we use a standard *type-I extreme value* distribution (EV-I), and the errors are i.i.d. across categories, we arrive at the multinomial logit model already introduced.

In case you were wondering ... 9.2 Extreme value distributions

We say that a random variable, V, follows a *generalized extreme value distribution* with parameter vector $\boldsymbol{\theta} = (\mu, \sigma, \eta)$:

$$
V \sim f_{GEV}(v; \mu, \sigma, \eta)
$$

$$
\Pr(V \le v) = \begin{cases} \exp\left(-\left(1 + \eta \frac{v - \mu}{\sigma}\right)^{1/\eta}\right) & \eta \neq 0, \\ \exp\left(-\exp\left(-\frac{v - \mu}{\sigma}\right)\right) & \eta = 0 \end{cases}.
$$

The case where $\eta = 0$ is called the *type-I extreme value distribution*, also known as the *Gumbel, log-Weibull,* and the *double exponential* distribution. $E[V] = \mu + \sigma\gamma$ and $\text{var}(V) = \frac{\pi^2}{6}\sigma^2$, where γ is Euler's constant. Setting $\mu = 0$ and $\sigma = 1$, we have the standard type-I extreme value distribution, and we write $V \sim f_{EV_1}(v; 0, 1)$.

The choice of EV-I appears arbitrary. The following theorem justifies this choice by linking the EV-I distribution to the logistic distribution we are already familiar with from Chapters 3 and 8.

Theorem 9.1. *If* $A, B \overset{i.i.d.}{\sim} f_{EV_1}(0, 1)$ *then* $A - B \sim f_L(0, 1)$.

Proof The proof involves the convolution of two type-I extreme value distributions. Let $C = A - B$.

$$F_C(c) = \Pr(C \le c) = \Pr(A - B \le c)$$

$$= \int_{b=-\infty}^{\infty} \Pr(A \le c + b) f_{EV_1}(b; 0, 1) db$$

$$= \int_{b=-\infty}^{\infty} F_{EV_1}(c + b; 0, 1) f_{EV_1}(b; 0, 1) db$$

$$= \int_{b=-\infty}^{\infty} \exp(-\exp(-(c + b))) \exp(-b - \exp(-b)) db$$

$$= \int_{b=-\infty}^{\infty} \exp(-b - \exp(-b)(1 + \exp(-c))) db.$$

Let $u = \exp(b)$. This leads to:

$$F_C(c) = \int_{u=0}^{\infty} \frac{1}{u^2} \exp\left(\frac{1}{u}(-1 - \exp(-c))\right) du.$$

Let $v = \frac{1}{u}(-1 - \exp(-c))$. We now have

$$F_C(c) = \frac{1}{1 + \exp(-c)} \int_{v=-\infty}^{0} \exp(v) dv = \frac{1}{1 + \exp(-c)}.$$

The last expression is the CDF for the standard logistic distribution.   □

From Theorem 9.1 we see that each pairwise difference between alternatives follows a logistic distribution, just as in the binary logit model. Once again we see that a multinomial logit model can be viewed as a collection of $M-1$ binary logits.

9.2.2 IIA

IIA stands for the *independence of irrelevant alternatives*. IIA is an assumption about the nature of the choice process: under IIA, an individual's choice does not depend on the availability or characteristics of inaccessible alternatives. IIA is closely related to the notion of transitive (or acyclic) preferences.

Returning to the Australian election example, suppose a voter is asked whether she prefers the Labor Party or the Liberal Party and she responds with "Liberal." The interviewer then reminds her that the Green Party is also fielding candidates, and she switches her choice. IIA says that the only admissible switch she could make is to the Green Party. She cannot say Labor because she could have chosen Labor before (when it was only Labor v. Liberal) but decided not to. More formally, IIA says that if you hold preferences {Liberal ≻ Labor} when those are the only two options, then you must also hold preferences {Green ≻ Liberal ≻ Labor} or {Liberal ≻ Labor≻ Green} or {Liberal ≻ Green ≻ Labor} when the Green party is available. Orderings like {Labor ≻ Liberal ≻ Green}, in which Labor and Liberal switch positions once Green becomes available, are not admissible under the IIA assumption.

The multinomial model implies that

$$\frac{\Pr(Y_i = m)}{\Pr(Y_i = d)} = \frac{\exp(\mathbf{x}_i^\mathsf{T}\boldsymbol{\beta}_m)}{\sum_{\ell=1}^M \exp(\mathbf{x}_i^\mathsf{T}\boldsymbol{\beta}_\ell)} \frac{\sum_{\ell=1}^M \exp(\mathbf{x}_i^\mathsf{T}\boldsymbol{\beta}_\ell)}{\exp(\mathbf{x}_i^\mathsf{T}\boldsymbol{\beta}_d)},$$

$$= \frac{\exp(\mathbf{x}_i^\mathsf{T}\boldsymbol{\beta}_m)}{\exp(\mathbf{x}_i^\mathsf{T}\boldsymbol{\beta}_d)},$$

$$= \exp[\mathbf{x}_i^\mathsf{T}(\boldsymbol{\beta}_m - \boldsymbol{\beta}_d)]. \tag{9.4}$$

That is, the log ratio of the probabilities for any two alternatives m and d is just the values of the covariates times the difference between the two alternatives' coefficient vectors. Importantly, this means that *the ratio of the probabilities of choosing any two outcomes is invariant with respect to the other alternatives.* It only depends on the characteristics of the alternatives in question:

$$\frac{\Pr(Y_i = m|M_R)}{\Pr(Y_i = d|M_R)} = \frac{\Pr(Y_i = m|M_S)}{\Pr(Y_i = d|M_S)} \forall m, d \in R \subseteq S.$$

In other words, the IIA assumption is baked in to the standard multinomial model. The IIA assumption buys us enormous computational simplicity: rather than having to evaluate an M-dimensional integral, we can construct a series of binary logits. This assumption may or may not hold in applied settings. Violations of IIA imply that our model of the data-generating process is inaccurate.

Diagnosing IIA Violations

There are tests for violations of the IIA assumption. If the IIA assumption holds, then a model omitting any particular choice should return $\hat{\boldsymbol{\beta}}_m$'s for the remaining alternatives similar to those estimated under the full model. Conversely, if the $\hat{\boldsymbol{\beta}}_m$'s vary a lot when an alternative is omitted, the data likely violate IIA. A common statistical test built on this insight is known as the Hausman-McFadden test (Hausman and McFadden, 1984). The test statistic takes the form:

$$H = (\hat{\boldsymbol{\beta}}_r - \hat{\boldsymbol{\beta}}_u)^\mathsf{T}[\hat{\mathbf{V}}_r - \hat{\mathbf{V}}_u]^{-1}(\hat{\boldsymbol{\beta}}_r - \hat{\boldsymbol{\beta}}_u) \tag{9.5}$$

$$H \,|_{H_0} \sim \chi^2,$$

where $\hat{\boldsymbol{\beta}}_r$ are the estimates from the restricted model (i.e., the model with an omitted alternative), $\hat{\boldsymbol{\beta}}_u$ is the vector of estimates for the unrestricted model (i.e., the one with all the alternatives included), and $\hat{\mathbf{V}}_r$ and $\hat{\mathbf{V}}_u$ are the estimated variance-covariance matrices for the two sets of coefficients, respectively.[1] Under the null hypothesis that IIA holds, the test is distributed

---

[1] Let $\boldsymbol{\beta}_m$ be the coefficients for the choice category that is omitted from the restricted model but included in the unrestricted one. For these vectors and matrices to be conformable, we omit all the $\boldsymbol{\beta}_m$ elements from $\hat{\boldsymbol{\beta}}_u$ and $\hat{\mathbf{V}}_u$.

χ^2 with degrees of freedom equal to the rank of $\mathbf{V}_r$, typically the number of estimated parameters in the restricted model. The logic of the test is as follows: if IIA holds, then both the restricted and unrestricted models will be consistent, but the unrestricted model will be more efficient (smaller variance). If IIA does not hold, however, then the unrestricted model is consistent (assuming nothing else has been left out), but the restricted model is not.

While IIA tests can be useful they should be viewed as heuristics rather than dispositive. The Hausman-McFadden test can actually return negative values. In the original paper Hausman and McFadden interpret this as evidence that IIA is satisfied, but such values clearly do not satisfy the asymptotic properties of the test statistic, thus p-values are meaningless in such cases. If there are many categories, and each one is tested sequentially for IIA violations, then we have the traditional multiple testing problem. Cheng and Long (2007) argue that IIA tests are underpowered and can give conflicting results in practice. In Section 9.5 we discuss modeling extensions that relax the IIA assumptions. Deciding whether these models are appropriate in any particular application usually requires more than a simple Hausman test. Comparisons across competing models can help.

9.3 AN EXAMPLE: AUSTRALIAN VOTERS IN 2013

We are now in a position to examine the Australian survey data from the 2013 election. We will fit the model twice, once with "Labor" as the reference category and once with "Coalition." Results in the form of a BUTON appear in Table 9.1.

Table 9.1 shows that multinomial models produce a lot of output since we are estimating $k \times (M - 1)$ parameters, one for each covariate category except the baseline. The size of the BUTON can therefore grow very quickly. Altering the reference category alters the coefficients you see but not their implications in terms of $\hat{p}_{im}$. To see this, examine the Coalition and Labor columns. Entries in the Coalition column describe how a covariate relates to the probability of choosing Coalition relative to Labor, while the coefficients in the Labor column describe the reverse relationship. As we would expect, the coefficients are exactly equal in absolute value but opposite in sign.

9.3.1 Evaluation

Before interpreting the output of a multinomial model, we have several tools available to describe model fit. With multinomial models we, of course, have access to the usual in-sample test statistics as well as the AIC and BIC. Most statistical software packages report the likelihood ratio model diagnostic comparing a null model ($M - 1$ intercepts) to the one specified. This tells us whether all coefficients estimated are equal to 0 for all M outcomes and k variables. This is typically not very informative, like most null models.

TABLE 9.1 *Multinomial logistic regression on vote choice in the 2013 Australian elections. The left half of the table uses Labor as the reference category, whereas the right uses Coalition.*

	Coalition	Other	Labor	Other
(Intercept)	−0.32	−0.33	0.32	−0.01
	(0.21)	(0.25)	(0.21)	(0.24)
income	0.05	0.01	−0.05	−0.03
	(0.01)	(0.01)	(0.01)	(0.01)
union member	−1.03	−0.21	1.03	0.82
	(0.10)	(0.11)	(0.10)	(0.12)
Catholic	−0.24	−0.35	0.24	−0.11
	(0.11)	(0.15)	(0.11)	(0.14)
not religious	−0.71	0.37	0.71	1.08
	(0.11)	(0.13)	(0.11)	(0.12)
other religion	−0.21	0.23	0.21	0.44
	(0.13)	(0.16)	(0.13)	(0.15)
female	−0.05	0.05	0.05	0.10
	(0.08)	(0.10)	(0.08)	(0.10)
age	0.02	−0.01	−0.02	−0.02
	(0.00)	(0.00)	(0.00)	(0.00)
n	3,342			
$\log \mathcal{L}$	−3,316			
AIC	6,664			
BIC	6,762			

In general, model evaluation is best conducted by comparing models to one another. Within the multinomial framework we can check individual sets of estimated coefficients by comparing an unrestricted model to a restricted version that excludes some specific variable $j \in \{1, 2, \ldots, k\}$. In the multinomial context, this restriction takes the form $\beta_{jm} = 0 \ \forall \ m$, a test of whether variable j is jointly significant across the $M - 1$ outcome categories. The corresponding likelihood ratio is distributed χ^2 with $M - 1$ degrees of freedom for each of the variables excluded.

The multinomial model allows us to test whether we have "too many" categories given our ability to distinguish between groups. In our Australian election example, if our covariates are unable to distinguish between Coalition and Other, then (for fixed covariates) we can combine the two categories, gaining efficiency and simplifying our model considerably. For concreteness, let's consider the model with Labor as the baseline. There are k covariates (including the intercept). An inability to distinguish Coalition and Other can be expressed as the null hypothesis

$$\hat{\beta}_{jC} = \hat{\beta}_{jO} \ \ \forall \ \ j \in \{2, 3, \ldots, k\}.$$

$\mathcal{R}$ Code Example 9.1 *Wald test for combining categories in a multinomial logit*

```
# the myoz data from the online repository is needed here.
library(nnet)  #where the multinom() function lives
mnl.fit<-multinom(vc.simp ~   income2 + union + religion.simp +
   sex + age, Hess=T, model=T, data=myoz, maxit=200) #model
Beta<-as.vector(t(coef(mnl.fit)))       #vectorizing coefficients
A<-rbind(                               #constraint matrix
   c(0,1,0,0,0,0,0,0,0,-1,0,0,0,0,0,0), #income_c - income_o
   c(0,0,1,0,0,0,0,0,0,0,-1,0,0,0,0,0), #union_c - union_o
   c(0,0,0,1,0,0,0,0,0,0,0,-1,0,0,0,0), #Catholic_c - Catholic_o
   c(0,0,0,0,1,0,0,0,0,0,0,0,-1,0,0,0), #no relig_c - no relig_o
   c(0,0,0,0,0,1,0,0,0,0,0,0,0,-1,0,0), #other relig_c - other relig_o
   c(0,0,0,0,0,0,1,0,0,0,0,0,0,0,-1,0), #female_c-female_o
   c(0,0,0,0,0,0,0,1,0,0,0,0,0,0,0,-1)  #age_c-age_o
   )
wt<-t(A%*%Beta)%*%solve(A%*%vcov(mnl.fit)%*%t(A))%*%(A%*%Beta) #Wald test
pchisq(wt, df=dim(A%*%Beta)[1], lower.tail=FALSE)
```

Stated in words, all coefficients (except the intercepts) for outcomes C and O are equal. This can be restated as a simple linear constraint: the differences in coefficients (except the intercepts) for each of the two outcomes are zero under the null, which leads naturally to a Wald test. Code Example 9.1 calculates the model in Table 9.1 and then performs the Wald test that the Coalition and Other can be combined. This produces a p-value ≈ 0, leading to the conclusion that we *can* distinguish Coalition from Other.[2]

Do Australian voters' choices between Labor and Coalition depend on the presence of Other alternatives? We can use Equation 9.6 to conduct a the Hausman-McFadden test for IIA. Leaving out the Other category gives us a test statistic of -2, implying that preferences between Labor and Coalition are not affected by the presence of Other, as IIA requires.

Prediction Heuristics

Alongside these hypothesis tests we can take advantage of a variety of tools for describing how well a multinomial model predicts outcomes, whether in- or out-of-sample. Many of the tools below are generalizations of those described for binary outcomes. All start by generating predicted probabilities for each observation across all M categories: $\hat{\mathbf{p}}_i = (\hat{p}_{i1}, \ldots, \hat{p}_{iM})$. From these predictions it is common to define $\hat{y}_i = \arg_m \max\{\hat{p}_{im}\}$, i.e., observation i is classified into the category with the highest predicted probability.

One of the simplest diagnostic tools, a *confusion matrix*, derives from a comparison of $\hat{y}_i$ and y_i. Table 9.2 displays an in-sample version of this matrix for the model in Table 9.1. From the table we can see that the model

---

[2] This test can also be constructed as a likelihood ratio in which we constrain all the coefficients except the intercept for one of the *categories* to be 0.

TABLE 9.2 *Confusion matrix for the classifications from the multinomial logistic regression in Table 9.1.*

		Predicted		
		Labor	Coalition	Other
Actual	Labor	396	665	20
	Coalition	246	1,305	21
	Other	243	419	27

TABLE 9.3 *The category-by-category "one-versus-all" confusion matrices.*

		Predicted	
		Labor	non-Labor
	Labor	396	685
	non-Labor	489	1,772
		Coalition	non-Coalition
Actual	Coalition	1,305	267
	non-Coalition	1,084	686
		Other	non-Other
	Other	27	662
	non-Other	41	2,612

is underpredicting Other and overpredicting Coalition and Labor. This is unsurprising since the distribution of observations is unbalanced across the three categories, with Other less frequently observed.

From the confusion matrix we can calculate a variety of interesting and useful quantities. For example, the overall accuracy of the model – also called the correct classification rate – is defined as the sum of the main diagonal of the confusion matrix divided by the total number of observations. In this example the model yields accuracy of 0.52. This implies error rate of 0.48. We can also construct M binary, "one-versus-all" confusion matrices in which we examine correct and incorrect prediction for each category separately. These are displayed in Table 9.3.

From the one-versus-all tables we can construct category-specific error rates and accuracy measures weighted by the prevalence of that category in the data. The *per-class error rate* and its mean across all three categories is displayed in Table 9.4. Note that the mean per-class error rate is substantially smaller than the overall error rate of 0.48 because averaging over the one-versus-all matrices has the effect of upweighting categories that are more prevalent in the sample.

Code Example 9.2 produces all the above calculations and tables.

TABLE 9.4 *Per-class error.*

Labor	Coalition	Other	Mean Error
0.35	0.40	0.21	0.32

$\mathcal{R}$ Code Example 9.2 *Predictive diagnostics for multinomial logit*

```
pmnl<-predict(mnl.fit)
conmat<-table(mnl.fit$model[,1],pmnl,
  dnn=list("actual","predicted"))    #confusion matrix
sum(diag(conmat))/sum(conmat)        #overall accuracy
oneVall <- lapply(1:ncol(conmat),    #one v. all matrices
  function(i){
    v <- c(conmat[i,i],                   #true positives
      rowSums(conmat)[i] - conmat[i,i], #false negatives
      colSums(conmat)[i] - conmat[i,i], #false positives
      sum(conmat)-rowSums(conmat)[i]- colSums(conmat)[i] + conmat[i,i]);
    return(matrix(v, nrow = 2, byrow = T,
      dimnames=list(
        c(paste("actual",colnames(conmat)[i]),
          paste("actual non",colnames(conmat)[i])),
        c(paste("predicted",colnames(conmat)[i]),
          paste("predicted non",colnames(conmat)[i]))
      )
    )
  )
 }
)
pcerr<-lapply(oneVall, function(x) #per class error
  return(1-sum(diag(x))/sum(x))
)

smat <- matrix(0, nrow = 2, ncol = 2)
for(i in 1 : ncol(conmat)){smat<- smat + oneVall[[i]]}
1-sum(diag(smat))/sum(smat) #mean per class error
```

As with binary classifiers, we can generate ROC curves or separation plots, but in higher dimensions they become harder to interpret. One strategy is to simply generate separate ROC curves for each category. Figure 9.1 displays exactly such "one-versus-all" ROC plots. Multiple plots present a challenge similar to the per-class error: it is not obvious how to weigh each binary comparison when evaluating multiple models that may perform differently in their abilities to distinguish between particular categories. Higher dimensional ROC manifolds can be constructed and some have advocated for calculating single-number generalizations to the AUC (Li and Fine, 2008). Our take is that single-number summaries often mask important nuance, even in simple binary cases. That problem is accentuated in the more-complicated multinomial setting. Careful, problem-driven consideration of the costs of misclassification for particular categories, combined with a suite of diagnostic quantities, will enable a nuanced evaluation of competing models for nominal data.

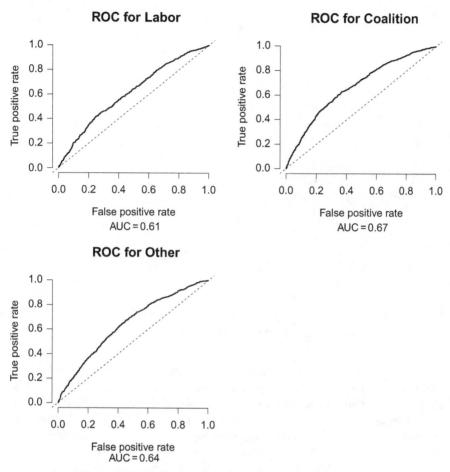

FIGURE 9.1 "One-v.-all" ROC curve diagnostics for the multinomial logit in Table 9.1.

9.3.2 Interpretation

How does one interpret the (really big) table of numbers generated from multinomial models? We proceed in the same way as in earlier chapters: simulate outcomes from the assumed data-generating process described by the model under meaningful scenarios. As usual, we include the systematic and stochastic components in all their glory. Here this means using the fundamental probability statement of the multinomial model from Equation 9.2. From there we can construct graphical displays, tables of first differences, or calculated marginal effects. With multiple outcome categories there are multiple comparisons that should be reflected in any interpretation.

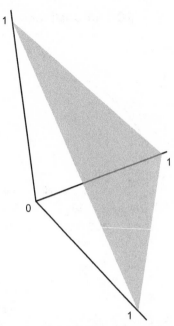

FIGURE 9.2 The three-dimensional unit simplex.

In the special – although common – case in which $M = 3$, a *ternary plot* is a useful way to display predicted probabilities. Ternary plots take advantage of the *probability simplex* to view a three dimensional object (a vector of predicted probabilities) in a convenient two-dimensional plane. This is possible because probabilities of choosing among the three options, e.g., Labor, Coalition, and Other, must sum to unity. Given predicted probabilities for any two categories, we can infer the third. The shaded triangular region in Figure 9.2 depicts exactly this three-dimensional probability simplex.

Ternary plots take the three-dimensional vector and plot it in the unit simplex triangle. Thus points on the vertices represent certainty that a respondent will choose that category. Points in the interior display the combination of probabilities simultaneously. In Figure 9.3 we construct a ternary plot in order to interpret how union membership relates to vote choice in the 2013 Australian election. In this plot we first construct a relevant scenario: a male, Protestant with income and age equal the median among union members. We then sample coefficient vectors from the multivariate normal distribution and generate predicted probabilities for each sample, one for a union member and one for a nonmember. We then plot these predicted probabilities along with the 95% confidence region. From here we can see that union members are substantially more likely to vote Labor than nonmembers. The difference between the groups is large relative to the estimation uncertainty.

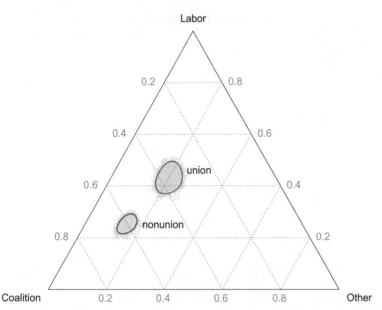

FIGURE 9.3 Using ternary plots to interpret multinomial logit models when $M = 3$. The curves define 95% confidence regions for predicted vote choice among Australians in 2013 as a function of union membership, other covariates fixed.

A second possibility for displaying results – one that generalizes beyond $M = 3$ – is shown in Figure 9.4. Here we plot cumulative probabilities, where the vertical height of each band reflects the predicted probability of falling into the category at particular levels of the covariate. In this case we are interested in displaying how vote choice in Australia is expected to vary across voters aged 20–70. The figure shows how support for the Coalition increases with age. The increase in support for the Coalition among older voters comes at the expense of Other and, especially, Labor. A strength of this plot is its clear display of trade-offs across categories at different levels of the covariates. A weakness is a failure to show estimation uncertainty.

We can also unstack the predicted probabilities to show estimation uncertainty, as in Figure 9.5. In this figure we are interested in looking at how vote choice relates to income. We construct a scenario in which we examine a nonunion, Protestant female of median age (among women). We vary income between its 20th and 80th percentiles. In this scenario we see that higher income respondents are much more likely to support the Coalition and less likely to support Labor. Chosing "Other" is unrelated to income.

Other Interpretation Strategies
While graphical displays accounting for uncertainty are useful, you will likely encounter other interpretation approaches in your reading. One such strategy

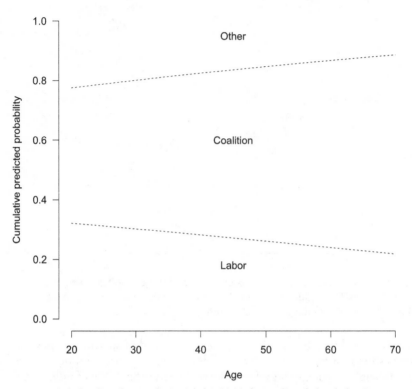

FIGURE 9.4 Predicted vote choice in the 2013 Australian federal elections across age cohorts. Older voters are more likely to support the Liberal-National Coalition.

is the dreaded *odds ratio*. Since the multinomial logit is a log-odds model, it may be useful to note that the log of the ratio of two probabilities is a linear function of the independent variables:

$$\log \left[\frac{\Pr(Y_i = m | \mathbf{x}_i)}{\Pr(Y_i = d | \mathbf{x}_i)} \right] = \mathbf{x}_i^{\mathsf{T}} (\hat{\boldsymbol{\beta}}_m - \hat{\boldsymbol{\beta}}_d).$$

Since we set the coefficients of one category – the baseline – to zero for identification, we can calculate the log odds that i is in m relative to the baseline using:

$$\log \left[\frac{\Pr(Y_i = m | \mathbf{x}_i)}{\Pr(Y_i = 1 | \mathbf{x}_i)} \right] = \mathbf{x}_i^{\mathsf{T}} \hat{\boldsymbol{\beta}}_m.$$

This approach is linear in the parameters. We can calculate hypothetical changes in the odds ratio for category m associated with a particular covariate x_j by exponentiation (i.e., $\exp(\hat{\beta}_{m,j})$). In this way we can inspect Table 9.1

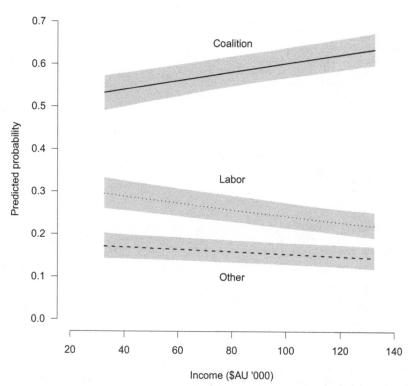

FIGURE 9.5 Predicted vote choice in the 2013 Australian federal elections for different income levels. Higher income voters were more likely to support the Liberal-National Coalition and less likely to vote for Labor.

and see that a Catholic has 21% lower odds of voting for the Coalition over Labor relative to a Protestant ($\exp(-0.24) = 0.79$); this relationship is large relative to the estimated standard error. However, such statements are cumbersome because the model is about comparing several categories. Simply exponentiating coefficients (or their differences) privileges some comparisons over others. Standard errors and statements of significance may vary depending on the comparison made. For example, looking back at Table 9.1, we see that Catholic is a "significant" predictor of voting for Labor relative to Other (left half), but it is not a "significant" predictor of voting for the Coalition relative to Other (right half). Relying on just the BUTON to view and interpret the implications of a multinomial model may not be the most effective means of communicating the model's substantive implications to audiences. It certainly fails to display many quantities that may be of interest to both readers and analysts.

R Code Example 9.3 *Ternary plots and confidence regions*

```
B<-mvrnorm(1000,
  mu=c(coef(mnl.fit)[1,],coef(mnl.fit)[2,]),
  Sigma=vcov(mnl.fit))
X.u<-c(1,median(myoz$income2[myoz$union=="Yes"]),
  1,0,0,0,0,median(myoz$age[myoz$union=="Yes"]))
X.nu<-c(1,median(myoz$income2[myoz$union=="Yes"]),
  0,0,0,0,0,median(myoz$age[myoz$union=="Yes"]))

k<-dim(coef(mnl.fit))[2]
denom.u<- 1+exp(B[,1:k]%*%X.u)+exp(B[,(k+1):(2*k)]%*%X.u)   #denominator of
  multinomial
denom.nu<-1+exp(B[,1:k]%*%X.nu)+exp(B[,(k+1):(2*k)]%*%X.nu)#denominator of
  multinomial
pp.coal.u<-exp(B[,1:k]%*%X.u)/denom.u
pp.other.u<-exp(B[,(k+1):(2*k)]%*%X.u)/denom.u
pp.coal.nu<-exp(B[,1:k]%*%X.nu)/denom.nu
pp.other.nu<-exp(B[,(k+1):(2*k)]%*%X.nu)/denom.nu
union.pp<-cbind(pp.coal.u, pp.other.u, (1-pp.coal.u-pp.other.u))
nounion.pp<-cbind(pp.coal.nu, pp.other.nu, (1-pp.coal.nu-pp.other.nu))
colnames(union.pp)<-colnames(nounion.pp)<-c("Coalition", "Other", "Labor")

library(compositions)
#Getting ellipse radius for CR
#See van den Boogaart and Tolosana-Delgado 2013 p. 83
df1 = ncol(union.pp)-1
df2 = nrow(union.pp)-ncol(union.pp)+1
rconf = sqrt( qf(p=0.95, df1, df2)*df1/df2 )
rprob = sqrt( qchisq(p=0.95, df=df1) )

plot(acomp(union.pp), col = grey(0.8))
plot(acomp(nounion.pp), col = grey(0.8), pch=3, add=T)
isoPortionLines(, col=grey(0.5), lty=2, lwd=.7)
ellipses(mean(acomp(union.pp)),var(acomp(union.pp)),r=rprob,col="red", lwd=2)
ellipses(mean(acomp(nounion.pp)),var(acomp(nounion.pp)),r=rprob,col="blue",
  lwd=2)
text(.35,.2,"non\n union")
text(.52,.4,"union")
```

Another approach to interpretation – marginal effects calculations – does include comparisons across multiple outcome categories. To see this, we calculate the partial derivative for a particular covariate $j \in \{1, 2, \ldots, k\}$:

$$\frac{\partial \Pr(Y_i = m)}{\partial x_{ij}} = \Pr(Y_i = m | \mathbf{x}_i) \left[\beta_{jm} - \sum_{d \in S} \beta_{jd} \times \Pr(Y_i = d | \mathbf{x}_i) \right].$$

This expression depends not only on the values of the other covariates but also on all the other regression coefficients, $\beta_d, d \neq m$. As a result, the marginal effect of a particular covariate for a specific category may not have the same sign as an estimated coefficient for covariate j appearing in a BUTON. A full accounting of marginal effects would require yet another BUTON in which we display the marginal effects of each variable for each category, each of which is conditional on a specific scenario embodied in $\mathbf{x}_i$. Whether a particular marginal effect is large relative to estimation uncertainty will depend on the scenario chosen, the coefficient for the variable of interest, and all the other coefficients in the model. As a result, this approach to interpretation is often best avoided.

9.4 CONDITIONAL MULTINOMIAL LOGIT

Thus far we have described categorical outcomes in terms of the characteristics of the "chooser," i. But the multinomial model can be flipped around. Suppose we are instead interested in how attributes of the categories relate to choices. In the voting example we might consider how party platforms or candidate attributes might make them more or less attractive to voters.

To formalize this version of the model, suppose we again have $k - 1$ covariates. But now we let $\mathbf{w}_{im}$ be a k-vector with values describing how category m is experienced by individual i. The key distinction here is that regressors now vary across choice categories; they can also vary across individuals. For example, in the Australian survey data, outcome-level covariates might include the distance between a voter's left-right placement and that for each party; whether the respondent voted for party m in the last election; or whether party m contacted the voter in the course of this election campaign. All these clearly differ across parties for each respondent as well as across respondents. This leads to an altered model formulation:

$$\Pr(Y_i = m) = \frac{\exp(\mathbf{w}_{im}^\mathsf{T}\boldsymbol{\delta})}{\sum_{h=1}^{M} \exp(\mathbf{w}_{ih}^\mathsf{T}\boldsymbol{\delta})}.$$

The parameter vector $\boldsymbol{\delta}$ has a constant and a regression coefficient for each of $k - 1$ regressors. This formulation goes by the name *conditional (multinomial) logit*.[3] Note that in the conditional logit model the *covariate values* differ across categories and the parameters are constant, whereas in the multinomial model the covariate values are fixed for each individual across choice categories, and the parameters differ. Another way to see this is to consider the ratio of the probabilities of choosing m over d under the conditional logit:

$$\frac{\Pr(Y_i = m)}{\Pr(Y_i = d)} = \exp[(\mathbf{w}_{im} - \mathbf{w}_{id})^\mathsf{T}\boldsymbol{\delta}]. \tag{9.6}$$

---

[3] Note a "conditional logit" model means different things in different disciplines. In economics, political science, and sociology "conditional logit" usually refers to the model described in this section, following McFadden (1974). In epidemiology, "conditional logit" refers to a matched case-control logit model, sometimes called "fixed effects/panel logit" in other disciplines. It is possible to show that the McFadden conditional logit is a special case of the fixed effects version, but we do not take that up here. Note that STATA has different model commands for each of these.

Equation 9.6 is just a restatement of the IIA condition. Comparing Equation 9.4 to Equation 9.6 highlights the difference between in the multinomial and conditional logit specifications.

Of course the multinomial and the conditional logits can each be viewed as special cases of the other. Their log-likelihood and methods of interpretation are nearly identical. It is also possible to build a model that combines both category- and chooser-specific covariates:

$$\Pr(Y_i = m) = \frac{\exp(\mathbf{w}_{im}^\mathsf{T}\boldsymbol{\delta} + \mathbf{x}_i^\mathsf{T}\boldsymbol{\beta}_m)}{\sum_{h=1}^{M}\exp(\mathbf{w}_{ih}^\mathsf{T}\boldsymbol{\delta} + \mathbf{x}_i^\mathsf{T}\boldsymbol{\beta}_h)}.$$

To illustrate these models, we reanalyze the 2013 Australian election data, including a party-level covariate that also differs by respondent: whether party m personally contacted the respondent. We fit two models. The first is a conditional multinomial logit including only the contact variable; we allow for differing intercepts across categories. The second is a combined model that includes the party-level contact variable as well as the same individual-level covariates as above. Coalition is the reference category for both models. The resulting BUTON for coefficients appears as Table 9.5.

The models in Table 9.5 present a useful revision to the model in Table 9.1. Using the BIC, we see that the mixed conditional/multinomial model outperforms both the conditional logit and the multinomial logit in Table 9.1. The new contact variable is precisely estimated away from zero. To a first approximation, a respondent is about 43% more likely to vote for a party that contacted her than one that did not ($\exp(0.36) \approx 1.43$). Adding in other covariates does not alter this basic conclusion. Other coefficient estimates are nearly identical to those in the multinomial model.

9.4.1 A Note on Data Structure

In terms of estimation, the trick involved in going from a multinomial model to a conditional or mixed multinomial involves the structure of the data set. In the pure multinomial model with just individual-specific covariates, the data are in a standard rectangular matrix in which the rows are individuals and the columns are variables. Table 9.6 displays a clip of the 2013 Australia election data in this form. Note how the contact variable is broken out by response category.

In order to estimate a conditional or mixed model, however, we need to think of the response category as the unit of analysis. But these response categories are now grouped by the individual or "case." Table 9.7 displays the same clip of the 2013 Australia data in this form. Each row is a person-category; each person accounts for M rows of the data set. The data set is now one $M \times k$ matrix for each individual, stacked on top of one another. Note that the category-level contact variable has been collapsed to a single column.

TABLE 9.5 *Conditional and mixed conditional-multinomial logistic regression on vote choice for the 2013 Australian elections. Coalition is the reference category.*

	Conditional	Mixed
Contact	0.36	0.33
	(0.06)	(0.06)
Labor: intercept	−0.32	0.32
	(0.04)	(0.21)
Other: intercept	−0.72	0.04
	(0.05)	(0.24)
Labor: income		−0.05
		(0.01)
Other: income		−0.03
		(0.01)
Labor: union member		1.02
		(0.10)
Other: union member		0.81
		(0.12)
Labor: Catholic		0.24
		(0.11)
Other: Catholic		−0.11
		(0.14)
Labor: not religious		0.71
		(0.11)
Other: not religious		1.09
		(0.12)
Labor: other religion		0.22
		(0.13)
Other: other religion		0.43
		(0.15)
Labor: female		0.06
		(0.08)
Other: female		0.11
		(0.10)
Labor: age		−0.01
		(0.00)
Other: age		−0.02
		(0.00)
n	3,342	3,342
$\log \mathcal{L}$	−3,476	−3,302
AIC	6,957	6,639
BIC	6,976	6,743

TABLE 9.6 *A typical rectangular data structure for a multinomial model. Note the inclusion of the choice-specific variables.*

							Contact		
Respondent	Vote Choice	Income	Union	Religion	Sex	Age	Labor	Coalition	Other
1	Labor	20.0	No	Protestant	Female	43	1	1	0
2	Labor	20.0	No	Protestant	Male	61	1	1	1
3	Other	15.5	Yes	None	Male	52	1	1	1
4	Coalition	7.5	No	Protestant	Female	69	1	1	1
5	Other	1.2	No	Other	Female	61	1	1	1
6	Labor	9.5	Yes	None	Female	20	0	0	0
...	...	...	...	...	...	...	...	...	...
3,342	Other	9.5	Yes	None	Female	40	1	1	0

TABLE 9.7 *A grouped-response data structure enabling conditional and mixed logit estimation. Each row is a person-category.*

Respondent	Category	Vote Choice	Contact	Income	Union	Religion	Sex	Age
1	Coalition	FALSE	1	20	No	Protestant	Female	43
1	Labor	TRUE	1	20	No	Protestant	Female	43
1	Other	FALSE	0	20	No	Protestant	Female	43
2	Coalition	FALSE	1	20	No	Protestant	Male	61
2	Labor	TRUE	1	20	No	Protestant	Male	61
2	Other	FALSE	1	20	No	Protestant	Male	61
...	...	...	...	...	...	...	...	...
3,342	Coalition	FALSE	1	9.5	Yes	None	Female	40
3,342	Labor	FALSE	1	9.5	Yes	None	Female	40
3,342	Other	TRUE	0	9.5	Yes	None	Female	40

The data in Tables 9.6 and 9.7 contain exactly the same information. Reformatting only serves computational convenience. Understanding how the data are organized is important for understanding how to effectively sample from the limiting distribution of the parameters and generate predicted probabilities.

Viewing the data in grouped-response format has the additional benefit of highlighting the connection between a conditional or mixed multinomial logit model and panel data. A panel data set in which each individual is observed repeatedly is also typically organized as stacked individual-level matrices. In fact a "conditional logit" is one way of analyzing binary panel data, something we take up further in Chapter 11.

9.5 EXTENSIONS

All of the models above rely on the IIA assumption. The IIA, in turn, results from the assumption that (1) the errors are independent across *categories*, (2) the errors are identically distributed, and (3) the errors all follow as EV-I distribution. A variety of alternatives have been developed to partially relax IIA or, equivalently, allow for unequal variance or correlation across the outcome categories. In formulating the likelihood, all these models continue to maintain the assumption of (conditional) independence across individuals, i.

9.5.1 Heteroskedastic Multinomial Logit

The *heteroskedastic multinomial logit* model, sometimes called the *heteroskedastic extreme value* model, allows the error variance to differ across outcome categories. This model might be useful in situations in which we are worried that a change in a covariate might produce different rates of substitution across choices (Bhat, 1996).[4]

Formally, we can restate the latent variable formulation as $U_i(m) = \mu_i(m) + \sigma_m \epsilon_{im}$, where $\epsilon_{im} \sim f_{EV_1}(1,0)$.[5] To fix the model we require that $\sigma_1 = 1$ for the reference category. In this way we can write

$$\Pr(Y_i = m) = \frac{\exp\left[(\mathbf{w}_{im}^\mathsf{T}\boldsymbol{\delta} + \mathbf{x}_i^\mathsf{T}\boldsymbol{\beta}_m)/\sigma_m\right]}{\sum_{h=1}^{M} \exp\left[(\mathbf{w}_{ih}^\mathsf{T}\boldsymbol{\delta} + \mathbf{x}_i^\mathsf{T}\boldsymbol{\beta}_h)/\sigma_h\right]}. \tag{9.7}$$

Fitting the heteroskedasic model entails estimating an additional $M - 1$ scale parameters. Reestimating the mixed model in Table 9.5, allowing for heteroskedasticity, yields scale parameters that are indistinguishable from 1 and a BIC of 6,759.[6] In the 2013 Australia election data there is no benefit for this additional complication.

---

[4] In a conditional multinomial logit, the "marginal rate of substitution" between outcomes in terms of outcome-level covariates k and l is $\frac{\delta_k}{\delta_l}$.

[5] Or, equivalently, assume that $\epsilon_{im} \sim f_{EV_1}(1,\sigma_m)$.

[6] Recall that the standard multinomial model fixes $\sigma = 1$. So, when evaluating the $\hat{\sigma}_j$ from a heteroskedastic model we are interested in the null hypothesis that $\sigma_j = 1$.

9.5.2 Nested Logit

The *nested logit* model partially relaxes the assumption that outcome categories are uncorrelated with each other. With this model we imagine that the choice set has subcomponents or nests. Formally, S can be partitioned into D disjoint subsets, $A_1, A_2, \ldots, A_D$. Under nested logit we retain the IIA assumption *within* nests but not across them. The *cross-nested logit* allows for choices to appear in more than one nest, but we do not take this up further in this volume.

One way for nested choice to arise in the real world is when people make choices sequentially: past choices affect the subsequent choice options. For example, Figure 9.6 displays part of the ballot confronting California voters in 2003. They were first asked to decide whether the incumbent governor, Gray Davis, should be removed from office. They were then asked who should replace him, presenting voters with a list of 135 candidates, including actors Arnold Schwarzenegger and Gary Coleman along with infamous publisher Larry Flynt. Voters were presented with the sets $A = \{$"Gray Davis", "not Gray Davis"$\}$ and then presented with $B = \{$"Gary Coleman", $\ldots\}$.

Conceptually the nested logit involves modeling $\Pr(Y_i = m)$ as the probability that the nest containing m is chosen times the probability that m is selected from among the choices in that nest:

$$\Pr(Y_i = m) = \Pr(A_d) \times \Pr(Y_i = m | m \in A_d) \quad \forall d \in \{1, \ldots, D\}. \tag{9.8}$$

The nested logit can be extended to several partitions and several layers of nesting, but we will only consider two layers here.

To fix the model, we can decompose each part of the product in Equation 9.8.[7] Let $V_{im} = \mathbf{w}_{im}^{\mathsf{T}} \boldsymbol{\delta} + \mathbf{x}_i^{\mathsf{T}} \boldsymbol{\beta}_m$. This is simply the linear predictor term, but in the context of a choice situation, we can think of V_{im} as being the systematic part of i's utility function, evaluated for category m. The probability of choosing m out of all the elements of the nest A_d is simply a multinomial logit:

$$\Pr(Y_i = m | m \in A_d) = \frac{\exp(V_{im}/\lambda_d)}{\sum_{j \in A_d} \exp(V_{ij}/\lambda_d)}. \tag{9.9}$$

Equation 9.9 is similar to the expression for the heteroskedastic model in Equation 9.7, only here the error variances differ across nests rather than across categories. In the standard multinomial model the parameter $\lambda_d = 1$. To the extent that λ_d approaches 0 there is more homogeneity within the categories in nest d.[8]

Let $W_d = \mathbf{q}_d^{\mathsf{T}} \boldsymbol{\alpha}_d$ be any nest-level covariates (if such things exist) and associated parameters. We also define $Z_d = \log \sum_{m \in A_d} \exp(V_{im}/\lambda_d)$. Z_d is called the *inclusive value* or *log-sum*, and λ_d is the inclusive value or log-

---

[7] The nested logit model can also be derived from the latent variable constructing by assuming that the M−vector of errors, ϵ_i, follows a Generalized Extreme Value distribution.

[8] A λ_d outside the $(0,1]$ interval is commonly viewed as evidence of model misspecification.

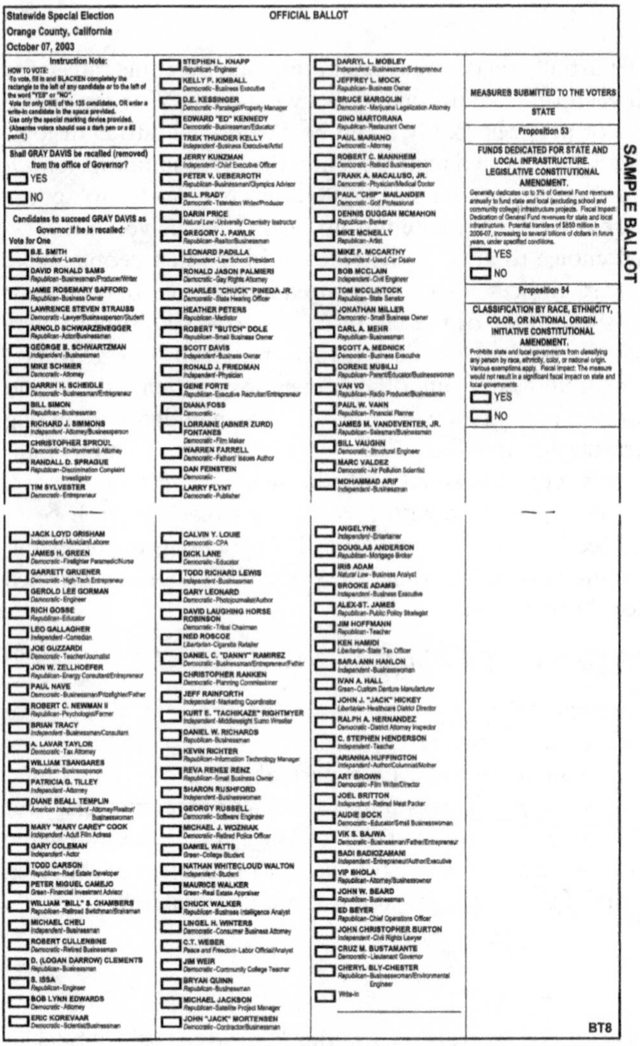
Statewide Special Election
Orange County, California
October 07, 2003
OFFICIAL BALLOT
SAMPLE BALLOT

Instruction Note:
HOW TO VOTE:
-To vote, fill in and BLACKEN completely the rectangle to the left of any candidate or to the left of the word "YES" or "NO".
-Vote for only ONE of the 135 candidates, OR enter a write-in candidate in the space provided.
-Use only the special marking device provided. (Absentee voters should use a dark pen or a #2 pencil.)

Shall GRAY DAVIS be recalled (removed) from the office of Governor?
YES
NO

Candidates to succeed GRAY DAVIS as Governor if he is recalled:
Vote for One

B.E. SMITH — Independent-Lecturer
DAVID RONALD SAMS — Republican-Businessman/Producer/Writer
JAMIE ROSEMARY SAFFORD — Republican-Business Owner
LAWRENCE STEVEN STRAUSS — Democratic-Lawyer/Businessperson/Student
ARNOLD SCHWARZENEGGER — Republican-Actor/Businessman
GEORGE B. SCHWARTZMAN — Independent-Businessman
MIKE SCHMIER — Democratic-Attorney
DARRIN H. SCHEIDLE — Democratic-Businessman/Entrepreneur
BILL SIMON — Republican-Businessman
RICHARD J. SIMMONS — Independent-Attorney/Businessperson
CHRISTOPHER SPROUL — Democratic-Environmental Attorney
RANDALL D. SPRAGUE — Republican-Discrimination Complaint Investigator
TIM SYLVESTER — Democratic-Entrepreneur
STEPHEN L. KNAPP — Republican-Engineer
KELLY P. KIMBALL — Democratic-Business Executive
D.E. KESSINGER — Democratic-Paralegal/Property Manager
EDWARD "ED" KENNEDY — Democratic-Businessman/Educator
TREK THUNDER KELLY — Independent-Business Executive/Artist
JERRY KUNZMAN — Independent-Chief Executive Officer
PETER V. UEBERROTH — Republican-Businessman/Olympics Advisor
BILL PRADY — Democratic-Television Writer/Producer
DARIN PRICE — Natural Law-University Chemistry Instructor
GREGORY J. PAWLIK — Republican-Realtor/Businessman
LEONARD PADILLA — Independent-Law School President
RONALD JASON PALMIERI — Democratic-Gay Rights Attorney
CHARLES "CHUCK" PINEDA JR. — Democratic-State Hearing Officer
HEATHER PETERS — Republican-Mediator
ROBERT "BUTCH" DOLE — Republican-Small Business Owner
SCOTT DAVIS — Independent-Business Owner
RONALD J. FRIEDMAN — Independent-Physician
GENE FORTE — Republican-Executive Recruiter/Entrepreneur
DIANA FOSS — Democratic-
LORRAINE (ABNER ZURD) FONTANES — Democratic-Film Maker
WARREN FARRELL — Democratic-Fathers' Issues Author
DAN FEINSTEIN — Democratic-
LARRY FLYNT — Democratic-Publisher
DARRYL L. MOBLEY — Independent-Businessman/Entrepreneur
JEFFREY L. MOCK — Republican-Business Owner
BRUCE MARGOLIN — Democratic-Marijuana Legalization Attorney
GINO MARTORANA — Republican-Restaurant Owner
PAUL MARIANO — Democratic-Attorney
ROBERT C. MANNHEIM — Democratic-Retired Businessperson
FRANK A. MACALUSO, JR. — Democratic-Physician/Medical Doctor
PAUL "CHIP" MAILANDER — Democratic-Golf Professional
DENNIS DUGGAN MCMAHON — Republican-Banker
MIKE MCNEILLY — Republican-Artist
MIKE P. MCCARTHY — Independent-Used Car Dealer
BOB MCCLAIN — Independent-Civil Engineer
TOM MCCLINTOCK — Republican-State Senator
JONATHAN MILLER — Democratic-Small Business Owner
CARL A. MEHR — Republican-Businessman
SCOTT A. MEDNICK — Democratic-Business Executive
DORENE MUSILLI — Republican-Parent/Educator/Businesswoman
VAN VO — Republican-Radio Producer/Businessman
PAUL W. VANN — Republican-Financial Planner
JAMES M. VANDEVENTER, JR. — Republican-Salesman/Businessman
BILL VAUGHN — Democratic-Structural Engineer
MARC VALDEZ — Democratic-Air Pollution Scientist
MOHAMMAD ARIF — Independent-Businessman

MEASURES SUBMITTED TO THE VOTERS
STATE
Proposition 53
FUNDS DEDICATED FOR STATE AND LOCAL INFRASTRUCTURE. LEGISLATIVE CONSTITUTIONAL AMENDMENT.
Generally dedicates up to 3% of General Fund revenues annually to fund state and local (excluding school and community college) infrastructure projects. Fiscal Impact: Dedication of General Fund revenues for state and local infrastructure. Potential transfers of $850 million in 2006-07, increasing to several billions of dollars in future years, under specified conditions.
YES
NO
Proposition 54
CLASSIFICATION BY RACE, ETHNICITY, COLOR, OR NATIONAL ORIGIN. INITIATIVE CONSTITUTIONAL AMENDMENT.
Prohibits state and local governments from classifying any person by race, ethnicity, color, or national origin. Various exemptions apply. Fiscal Impact: The measure would not result in a significant fiscal impact on state and local governments.
YES
NO

JACK LOYD GRISHAM — Independent-Musician/Laborer
JAMES H. GREEN — Democratic-Firefighter Paramedic/Nurse
GARRETT GRUENER — Democratic-High-Tech Entrepreneur
GEROLD LEE GORMAN — Democratic-Engineer
RICH GOSSE — Republican-Educator
LEO GALLAGHER — Independent-Comedian
JOE GUZZARDI — Democratic-Teacher/Journalist
JON W. ZELLHOEFER — Republican-Energy Consultant/Entrepreneur
PAUL NAVE — Democratic-Businessman/Prizefighter/Father
ROBERT C. NEWMAN II — Republican-Psychologist/Farmer
BRIAN TRACY — Independent-Businessman/Consultant
A. LAVAR TAYLOR — Democratic-Tax Attorney
WILLIAM TSANGARES — Republican-Businessperson
PATRICIA G. TILLEY — Independent-Attorney
DIANE BEALL TEMPLIN — American Independent-Attorney/Realtor/Businesswoman
MARY "MARY CAREY" COOK — Independent-Adult Film Actress
GARY COLEMAN — Independent-Actor
TODD CARSON — Republican-Real Estate Developer
PETER MIGUEL CAMEJO — Green-Financial Investment Advisor
WILLIAM "BILL" S. CHAMBERS — Republican-Railroad Switchman/Brakeman
MICHAEL CHELI — Independent-Businessman
ROBERT CULLENBINE — Democratic-Retired Businessman
D. (LOGAN DARROW) CLEMENTS — Republican-Businessman
S. ISSA — Republican-Engineer
BOB LYNN EDWARDS — Democratic-Attorney
ERIC KOREVAAR — Democratic-Scientist/Businessman
CALVIN Y. LOUIE — Democratic-CPA
DICK LANE — Democratic-Educator
TODD RICHARD LEWIS — Independent-Businessman
GARY LEONARD — Democratic-Photojournalist/Author
DAVID LAUGHING HORSE ROBINSON — Democratic-Tribal Chairman
NED ROSCOE — Libertarian-Cigarette Retailer
DANIEL C. "DANNY" RAMIREZ — Democratic-Businessman/Entrepreneur/Father
CHRISTOPHER RANKEN — Democratic-Planning Commissioner
JEFF RAINFORTH — Independent-Marketing Coordinator
KURT E. "TACHIKAZE" RIGHTMYER — Independent-Middleweight Sumo Wrestler
DANIEL W. RICHARDS — Republican-Businessman
KEVIN RICHTER — Republican-Information Technology Manager
REVA RENEE RENZ — Republican-Small Business Owner
SHARON RUSHFORD — Independent-Businesswoman
GEORGY RUSSELL — Democratic-Software Engineer
MICHAEL J. WOZNIAK — Democratic-Retired Police Officer
DANIEL WATTS — Green-College Student
NATHAN WHITECLOUD WALTON — Independent-Student
MAURICE WALKER — Green-Real Estate Appraiser
CHUCK WALKER — Republican-Business Intelligence Analyst
LINGEL H. WINTERS — Democratic-Consumer Business Attorney
C.T. WEBER — Peace and Freedom-Labor Official/Analyst
JIM WEIR — Democratic-Community College Teacher
BRYAN QUINN — Republican-Businessman
MICHAEL JACKSON — Republican-Satellite Project Manager
JOHN "JACK" MORTENSEN — Democratic-Contractor/Businessman
ANGELYNE — Independent-Entertainer
DOUGLAS ANDERSON — Republican-Mortgage Broker
IRIS ADAM — Natural Law-Business Analyst
BROOKE ADAMS — Independent-Business Executive
ALEX-ST. JAMES — Republican-Public Policy Strategist
JIM HOFFMANN — Republican-Teacher
KEN HAMIDI — Libertarian-State Tax Officer
SARA ANN HANLON — Independent-Businesswoman
IVAN A. HALL — Green-Custom Denture Manufacturer
JOHN J. "JACK" HICKEY — Libertarian-Healthcare District Director
RALPH A. HERNANDEZ — Democratic-District Attorney Inspector
C. STEPHEN HENDERSON — Independent-Teacher
ARIANNA HUFFINGTON — Independent-Author/Columnist/Mother
ART BROWN — Democratic-Film Writer/Director
JOEL BRITTON — Independent-Retired Meat Packer
AUDIE BOCK — Democratic-Educator/Small Businesswoman
VIK S. BAJWA — Democratic-Businessman/Father/Entrepreneur
BADI BADIOZAMANI — Independent-Entrepreneur/Author/Executive
VIP BHOLA — Republican-Attorney/Businessowner
JOHN W. BEARD — Republican-Businessman
ED BEYER — Republican-Chief Operations Officer
JOHN CHRISTOPHER BURTON — Independent-Civil Rights Lawyer
CRUZ M. BUSTAMANTE — Democratic-Lieutenant Governor
CHERYL BLY-CHESTER — Republican-Businesswoman/Environmental Engineer
Write-in
BT8

FIGURE 9.6 An example of sequential choices confronting voters, from the 2003 California gubernatorial recall election.

sum coefficient commonly reported. With these expressions we can now define another logit,

$$\Pr(A_d) = \frac{\exp(W_d + \lambda_d^{\mathsf{T}} Z_d)}{\sum_{\ell=1}^{D} \exp(W_\ell + \lambda_\ell^{\mathsf{T}} Z_\ell)}.$$

The nested logit requires that we pre-specify the set of nests or meta categories. In most situations there are several possible nesting structures, and it may not be obvious which is "correct." In the California recall example, state law held that only those voting in favor of the recall could cast valid votes for the successor, conforming to the nested logit structure and providing an obvious way to construct a nesting structure. This provision was challenged in court and found unconstitutional during the 2003 recall campaign. As a result, in the actual election, voters could vote for *both* the retention of Gray Davis as well as his successor, a violation of the nesting assumption. In the 2013 Australian election data, we might imagine that voters first decide whether to vote for a mainstream party (Labor or Coalition) or to cast a protest vote (Other). Alternatively, we might imagine that voters first decide whether to vote left (Labor, Other) or right (Coalition). Evaluating these options involves another layer of model selection, requiring tools such as likelihood ratios, BIC, and out-of-sample evaluation. In the particular case of the Australian survey data, there is no benefit to including either of these nesting structures, based on the BIC.

9.5.3 Multinomial Probit

Recall the random utility specification: $U_i(m) = \mu_i(m) + \epsilon_{im}$. If we assume

$$\epsilon_i = (\epsilon_{i1}, \ldots, \epsilon_{iM}) \sim \mathcal{N}(0, \Sigma),$$

we arrive at the multinomial probit model. The covariance matrix $\Sigma_{M \times M}$ allows for arbitrary correlation across choice categories. In other words, the multinomial probit does not require the IIA assumption. But the cost is a much heavier computational burden. To see this, note the choice probability for individual i:

$$\Pr(Y_i = m) = \Pr(U_i(m) > U_i(d) \quad \forall \ d \neq m \in S)$$

$$= \Pr(\epsilon_{im} - \epsilon_{id} > \mu_i(d) - \mu_i(m) \quad \forall \ d \neq m \in S).$$

Since one category is fixed as a reference, this second expression involves numerically evaluating an $(M-1)$-dimensional integral. In general the researcher must place some constraints on the covariance matrix to identify the model.

9.5.4 Random Coefficients and Mixed Logit

The *mixed logit* model is a further generalization of the multinomial logit model that allows us to model arbitrary dependence across categories and relax the IIA assumption. The easiest way to conceive of a mixed logit is as a "random coefficient" model. That is, we imagine that the regression parameters are heterogeneous across the population but governed by some underlying distribution. We can then average across the possible values of the β to recover the choice probabilities across categories. In this model the $\boldsymbol{\beta}$ varies according to some distribution, with its own parameters given by $\boldsymbol{\theta}$. It is common to assume a normal distribution, implying that $\boldsymbol{\theta} = (\boldsymbol{\mu}_{\boldsymbol{\beta}}, \boldsymbol{\Sigma}_{\boldsymbol{\beta}})$, although others are feasible.

The mixed logit retains the logit probability, but treats it as a function of $\boldsymbol{\beta}$. That is,

$$\Pr(Y_i = m | \boldsymbol{\beta}) = \frac{\exp(\mathbf{x}_{im}^{\mathsf{T}} \boldsymbol{\beta}_i)}{\sum_{\ell=1}^{M} \exp(\mathbf{x}_{i\ell}^{\mathsf{T}} \boldsymbol{\beta}_i)}.$$

But now we must specify the distribution for $\boldsymbol{\beta}$ and then integrate over it in the process of maximization:

$$\Pr(Y_i = m) = \int_{\boldsymbol{\beta}} \Pr(Y_i = m | \boldsymbol{\beta}) f(\boldsymbol{\beta} | \boldsymbol{\theta}) d\boldsymbol{\beta}.$$

The necessity of integrating over $\boldsymbol{\beta}$ complicates estimation substantially, but simulation methods and modern computing power combine to make this problem surmountable. Mixed logit is widely viewed as the most flexible approach to relaxing IIA in the context of nominal data. It can accommodate a wider variety of distributional assumptions than the multinomial probit and, in many cases, is faster to estimate. Refitting the models from Table 9.5 as a mixed logits, treating the contact variable random, and following a normal distribution adds nothing. The original models are preferred on a BIC and likelihood ratio basis. In the 2013 Australia data there is no evidence of violations of IIA necessitating further complications.

9.6 CONCLUSION

In this chapter we generalized our treatment of binary and ordered categorical variables to include multi-category, unordered outcomes. The standard model is the multinomial logit, which can accomodate covariates describing attributes of both the outcome categories as well as the units. The multinomial logit model relies on the assumed IIA, which may be too restrictive for some applications. Several extensions provide ways to relax this assumption.

The generality of the multinomial model comes at a cost. Multinomial models ask a lot of the data, estimating a large number of parameters. These models can become quite rich – and complex – very rapidly with the inclusion of additional covariates or outcome categories. Decisions about what to include or leave out necessitate a hierarchy of model evaluation decisions. Once estimated, the presentation and interpretation of model results also entails additional care and effort, all the more so when the models involve nested outcome categories or hierarchical, random coefficients.

9.7 FURTHER READING

Applications

Eifert et al. (2010) use multinomial logit to analyze the choice of identity group in a collection of African countries. Glasgow (2001) profitably uses the mixed logit to analyze voter behavior in multi-party UK elections. Martin and Stevenson (2010) use the conditional logit to examine coalition bargaining and government formation.

Past Work

Alvarez and Nagler (1998) present an early systematic comparison of several of the models described in this chapter; also see Alvarez (1998).

Advanced Study

Train (2009) is the more-advanced text on the specification and computation of a variety of mulitnomial models. Bagozzi (2016) presents a "zero-inflated" multinomial model with application to international relations. Mebane and Sekhon (2004) discuss and extend the use of the multinomial model in the context of counts across categories. See van den Boogaart and Tolosana-Delgado (2013) on the calculation and plotting of confidence ellipses for compositional data.

Software Notes

In $\mathcal{R}$, the multinom function in the nnet package (Ripley and Venables, 2016; Venables and Ripley, 2002) only handles rectangular data and only fits a standard multinomial model with individual-level covariates. The mlogit (Croissant, 2013) and mnlogit (Hasan et al., 2016) libraries contain tools for restructuring data sets and estimating all the models discussed in this chapter. The MNP library (Imai and van Dyk, 2005) fits a Bayesian multinomial probit. The compositions library (van den Boogaart et al., 2014) has a variety of functions for working with compositional data such as the probability simplex.

10

Strategies for Analyzing Count Data

10.1 INTRODUCTION

According to legend, the mathematician and logician Leopold Kronecker believed that mathematics should be entirely based on whole numbers, noting, "God made the natural numbers; all else is the work of man." Counts of discrete events in time and space are integers. These counts could be the number of bombs falling in a particular neighborhood, the number of coups d'état, the number of suicides, the number of fatalities owing to particular risk categories, such as traffic accidents, the frequency of strikes, the number of governmental sanctions, terrorist incidents, militarized disputes, trade negotiations, word counts in the speeches of presidential candidates, or any wide range of political and social phenomena that are counted.

Models of dependent variables that are counts of events are unsurprisingly called *event count models*. Event count models describe variables that map only to the nonnegative integers: $Y \in \{0, 1, 2, \ldots\}$. While grouped binary or categorical data can be thought of as counts, such data sets are generally not analyzed with count models.[1] Count data have two important characteristics: they are discrete and bounded from below.

Using ordinary least squares to directly model integer counts can lead to problems for the same reason it does with binary data. The variance of a count increases with the mean (there is more error around larger values), implying inherent heteroskedasticity. More worryingly, OLS will generate predictions that are impossible to observe in nature: negative counts and non-integer values. Some try to salvage a least squares approach by taking the logarithm of the dependent variable. This strategy, however, requires a decision about what to do with the zero counts, since $\log(0) = -\infty$. One option is to simply discard

---

[1] A major exception is the analysis of vote totals across candidates or parties. See, for example, Mebane and Sekhon (2004).

the zero-count observations and instead only model the positive counts. This has numerous drawbacks, including the potential to discard a large proportion of the observed data. A second approach is to add some constant to the outcome before taking logs. Aside from its arbitrariness, this approach has its drawbacks, including exacerbating problems with nonconstant variance and complicating interpretation. In this chapter we introduce a series of models that are explicitly designed to model event count data as what they are – integer counts.

10.2 THE POISSON DISTRIBUTION

Imagine a situation in which we are interested in the occurrence of concrete events, but we are unable to observe specific instances (or non-instances). Rather, we only observe the number of events occurring within some observational window. This window could be spatial (number of bombs that fell in a quarter square kilometer) or temporal (number of children born in January). We denote the size of this window, sometimes called the *exposure interval*, as h. The average number of events in any particular exposure interval is the *arrival rate*, denoted λ. Thus the probability of an event occurring in the interval $(t, t+h]$ is λh and, conversely, the probability of no event occurring in this interval $(t, t+h]$ is $1 - \lambda h$. When events occur independently – the occurrence of one event does not influence the probability that another will occur – and with a constant arrival rate we say they follow a *Poisson process*.

In case you were wondering ... 10.1 Poisson distribution

Let $Y \in \{0, 1, 2, \ldots\}$. We say that Y_i follows a *Poisson distribution* with parameter vector $\boldsymbol{\theta} = (\lambda, h)$:

$$Y \sim f_P(y; \lambda, h)$$
$$\Pr(Y = y) = \frac{\exp(-\lambda h)(\lambda h)^y}{y!},$$

with $\lambda > 0, h > 0$, and $E[Y] = \text{var}(Y) = h\lambda$.

If all the observational intervals are of the same length then we can standardize $h = 1$ and the probability mass function reduces to:

$$\Pr(Y = y) = \frac{\exp(-\lambda)\lambda^y}{y!},$$

with $E[Y] = \text{var}(Y) = \lambda$.

Siméon Denis Poisson (1781–1840) was a French mathematician, famous for correcting Laplace's equations for celestial mechanics. He discovered a probability distribution for discrete events, occurring in fixed intervals. He derived his invention in terms of the "law of rare events" in which he described the behavior of a binomial distribution as $n \to \infty$ and $p \to 0$. Poisson used the distribution in an analysis of "criminal and civil matters," an early study of public policy (Poisson, 1837).

Given the probability model, it is straightforward to incorporate covariates x_i into a model for the mean. Because $E[Y] > 0$, we need a link function that maps onto positive values. The exponential is the most commonly employed transformation for achieving this. Thus,

$$E[Y_i] \equiv h\lambda_i = he^{x_i^T \beta}.$$

From this expression it is easy to see that the natural log is the (canonical) link function for the Poisson GLM. We can also see why the Poisson model is sometimes referred to as "log-linear." The log of the mean is linear in the covariates and regression parameters. Setting $h = 1$ for simplicity and incorporating this expression into the Poisson mass function yields:

$$\Pr(Y_i = y|x_i) = \frac{\exp[-\exp(x_i^T\beta)][\exp(x_i^T\beta)]^y}{y!}.$$

The likelihood is straightforward to derive:

$$\mathcal{L}(\beta|X,y) = \prod_{i=1}^{n} \frac{\exp[-\exp(x_i^T\beta)][\exp(x_i\beta)]^{y_i}}{y_i!}$$

$$\log \mathcal{L} = \sum_{i=1}^{n} \left[-\exp(x_i^T\beta) + y_i x_i^T\beta - \log(y_i!) \right]$$

The last term, $-\log(y_i!)$, is ignorable. This log-likelihood is regular and well-behaved, so the standard tools apply. We can also derive the score equation for the Poisson model:

$$\frac{\partial \log \mathcal{L}}{\partial \beta} = \sum_{i=1}^{n} y_i x_i^T - x_i^T \exp(x_i^T\beta)$$

$$= \sum_{i=1}^{n} (y_i - \exp(x_i^T\beta))x_i = 0. \tag{10.1}$$

Equation 10.1 will appear below because we can also view it from an estimating equation or quasi-likelihood approach.

10.2.1 An Example: Means and Mediation

In a classic early application of the Poisson distribution, Bortkiewicz (1898) found that Prussian Army deaths from horse kicks were distributed as a Poisson

TABLE 10.1 *OLS and Poisson regression of the number of times a country served as a mediator in an international conflict between 1950 and 1990. The last two models account for unequal "exposure" across countries by including an offset term.*

	OLS			Poisson		
	log $(y_i + 0.01)$	log $(y_i + 10)$			Exposure Offset	Exposure
GDPpc 1990	0.33	−0.02	0.01	0.07	0.06	0.06
	(0.16)	(0.05)	(0.01)	(0.01)	(0.01)	(0.01)
UNSC member	34.59	3.98	1.02	2.35	2.18	2.17
	(4.19)	(1.39)	(0.14)	(0.11)	(0.10)	(0.11)
log duration						1.11
						(0.19)
Intercept	0.78	−1.85	2.43	0.42	−3.03	−3.42
	(1.04)	(0.35)	(0.04)	(0.08)	(0.08)	(0.66)
n	146	146	146	146	146	146
$\log \mathcal{L}$	−526	−366	−35	−585	−563	−563
AIC	1,059	737	75	1,176	1,132	1,134
BIC	1,071	749	82	1,185	1,141	1,146

process. Bercovitch and Schneider (2000) is a more recent example of count data in security studies. They study mediation in the international system, developing a model of the factors that lead countries to act as mediators in international disputes. We use their data to explore a Poisson model, simplifying their argument considerably. The basic argument is that rich and powerful countries are more likely to be requested as mediators. Their data contain 146 countries, observed over the period from 1950 to 1990. The dependent variable is the number of times that a country received a mandate to mediate in an international conflict. Mediation count is taken to be a log-linear function of whether or not the country is a member of the United Nations Security Council (UNSC) and its per capita Gross Domestic Product ($US '000) in 1990.

The first three columns of Table 10.1 display standard BUTON output for the OLS regressions. The first is an OLS on the unmolested dependent variable. The second and third add constants – 0.01 and 10, respectively – to the outcome before taking logarithms. The results in the table show how adding arbitrary constants can alter the model fit and interpretation. For example, the standard OLS says that a UNSC member is expected to have mediated 35 more disputes than a nonmember, whereas the log-transformed model implies that a UNSC member will have mediated exp(3.98) = 49 more disputes. This is a serious discrepancy that is not reflected in any uncertainty estimates. Comparing the second and third models, we see that indicators of model fit shift dramatically simply with the addition of a constant; this is unsurprising; adding a fixed

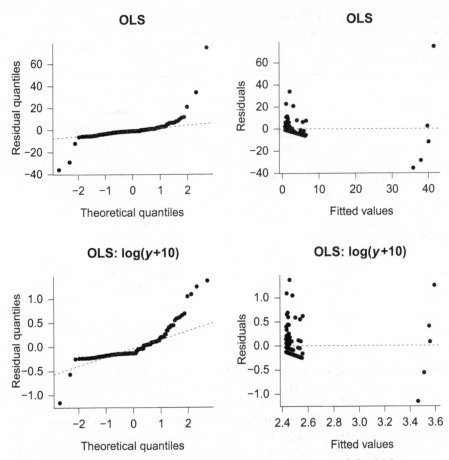

FIGURE 10.1 Diagnostic plots for the standard OLS regression and the OLS on log(y_i + 10) reported in Table 10.1. There is clear evidence of non-normality of heteroskedasticity in the residuals, becoming worse as a constant is added to the outcome variable and then transformed.

amount is easily absorbed by the intercept and has the effect of artificially reducing residual variance.[2]

Figure 10.1 displays residual quantiles and fitted-residual plots for the standard OLS model as well as the OLS on log(y_i + 10). Both clearly indicate that the OLS residuals are non-normal (with fat tails) and severely heteroskedastic, as we would expect from count data. Adding a constant and transforming the data has the drawback of exacerbating both these problems.

---

[2] Technically the log-likelihoods and related quantities for the second and third models are not comparable since they are fit to "different" outcome variables. This distinction is rarely appreciated in applied work; the constant added to y is often not explicitly stated.

The last three columns of Table 10.1 present results from a series of Poisson regressions. The first of these fits a model with the same linear predictor as the OLS regression. Based on the AIC and BIC, the OLS model might be preferable to the Poisson. But the general expression for the Poisson distribution takes into account the extent of "exposure" for each subject. In the mediation example, countries that have been around longer have had more opportunities to be requested as mediators. If observations have different exposure windows, then their expected counts should differ proportionally. Differential exposure needs to be incorporated into the model. There are two approaches. The first is known as an *offset*: include the size of the exposure window, h_i, in the regression but constrain its coefficient to be 1.0:

$$\lambda_i = \exp[\mathbf{x}_i^T \boldsymbol{\beta} + \log(h_i)].$$

The second approach simply includes the exposure variable (in logs) in the regression equation and allows a coefficient to be determined empirically.

The last two columns of Table 10.1 reestimate the Bercovitch and Schneider example, taking account of each country's "exposure" with a variable indexing the number of years a country has been a member of the international system. The fifth column includes this log duration variable as an offset, while the model in the sixth estimates a parameter. Accounting for exposure improves model fit, based on the likelihood ratio and the information criteria. Comparing the models in the final two columns, we see little reason to estimate a parameter for the exposure variable. The log-likelihoods for the two models are identical. A Wald test on the log duration coefficient from the third model gives a p-value of $(1.11 - 1)/0.19 = 0.6$. In general, accounting for unequal exposure is important for count models. Failing to do so will tend to inflate the putative impact of covariates.

10.2.2 Interpretation

As with many of the models we have seen in this volume, the relationship between a covariate and the response is nonlinear and depends on the value of other covariates in the model. Suppose we have $k - 1$ covariates in the model. The marginal effect of particular regressor, X_j, on $E[Y_i]$ is

$$\frac{\partial \lambda_i}{\partial x_{ij}} = \beta_j \exp[\mathbf{x}_i^T \boldsymbol{\beta}]. \tag{10.2}$$

In such situations we can follow our usual strategy: construct meaningful scenarios; sample from the limiting distribution of the parameters; and combine the two to generate predicted values, along with our estimation uncertainty.

In Figure 10.2 we do just that, presenting both the predicted and expected number of mediations as a function of per capita GDP and membership on the UNSC. For each of these scenarios, the black line represents the expected

$\mathcal{R}$ Code Example 10.1 *Fitting Poisson regression models with offsets*

```
bs<-read.csv("mediation.csv",header=T)
# medteam: number of mediations, including team mediations
# council: 1=member of UN Security Council
# gdp90: gdp per capita in constant dollars (needs to be rescaled)
bs$pop90<-bs$pop90/100000
bs$gdp90<-bs$gdp90/1000
bs.out<-glm(medteam~ gdp90 + council, data=bs,family="poisson")
offset.out<-glm(medteam ~ gdp90 + council + offset(log(duration)),
    data=bs,family="poisson")
#bs.out<-glm(medteam ~ gdp90 + council, offset = log(duration),
#    data=bs,family="poisson") #equivalent
duration.out<-glm(medteam ~ gdp90 + council + log(duration),
    data=bs,family="poisson")
```

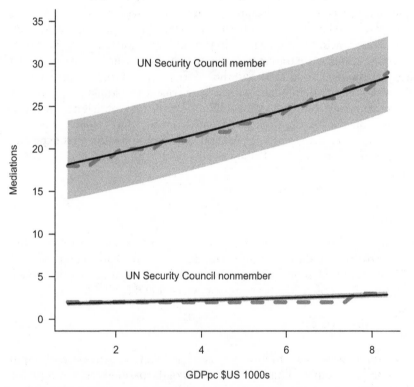

FIGURE 10.2 The expected and predicted number of international mediations as a function of per capita GDP and UNSC membership. Black lines are expected values and gray lines are predicted counts. Gray regions are 95% confidence bands around the expected value.

value ($\hat{\lambda}_i$), while the red line represents the predicted value – an integer. Gray bands are 95% confidence intervals around the expected value. In constructing these scenarios we vary GDP per capita from its 20th to 80th sample percentile values. We set duration in the international system at its sample median value for UNSC nonmembers. We set it to $\log 40 \approx 3.69$ for UNSC members, its minimum value for that group of countries. The plot shows that richer countries are more likely to be mediators and that UNSC members are about eight times more likely to be asked across income levels.

The log-linear construction of the Poisson model lends itself to other interpretive strategies that you may encounter in your reading. Since $\log \lambda_i = \mathbf{x}_i^\mathsf{T} \boldsymbol{\beta}$ we know that β_j is the change in $\log \lambda_i$ for a change in x_{ij}. The quantity $\exp(\hat{\beta}_j)$ therefore represents a multiplicative change in $\hat{\lambda}_i$, as shown in Equation 10.2. In the mediation example, $\exp(2.18) \approx 8.8$, so countries on the UNSC serve as mediators about nine times more frequently than countries not on the council. If a particular covariate is included on the log scale, then the coefficient of that covariate in a Poisson model has a direct interpretation in terms of elasticities, or a percent change in the outcome for a 1% change in the covariate. For example, if we included per capita GDP in logarithms (rather than thousands of dollars), then we obtain $\hat{\beta}_{GDP} = 0.20$; a ten-percent increase in per capita GDP is associated with a two-percent increase in the arrival rate of mediation requests.

10.3 DISPERSION

Intuitively we expect greater variation around the mean when there is a large number of expected events. We therefore expect count data to be inherently heteroskedastic. The Poisson distribution captures this fact; the variance increases with the mean, one-for-one. But this one-to-one relationship is quite restrictive and often violated in real-world data. The (very frequent) situation in which the variance of the residuals is larger than the mean is known as *over-dispersion*. *Under-dispersion* occurs when the variance is too small; it is much less commonly observed in social science data.

$$\text{Poisson Assumption} \leftrightarrow \mathrm{E}[Y] = \mathrm{var}(Y)$$
$$\text{Over-dispersion} \leftrightarrow \mathrm{E}[Y] < \mathrm{var}(Y)$$
$$\text{Under-dispersion} \leftrightarrow \mathrm{E}[Y] > \mathrm{var}(Y) \quad \leftrightarrow \quad 0 < \sigma < 1$$

Over-dispersion can arise for several reasons, all of which have consequences for model building and interpretation. At the simplest level, over-dispersion may simply be the result of a more variable process than the Poisson distribution is capable of capturing, perhaps due to heterogeneity in the underlying population. If this is the case then the model for the mean may still be adequate, but the variance estimates will be too small, perhaps wildly so. But over-dispersion may also arise for more complicated reasons that have both substantive and modeling implications. For example, over-dispersion may arise if there are an excess of zeros in the data or, most importantly, if events are positively correlated (previous events increase the rate of subsequent events), violating a basic assumption of the Poisson process. These challenges imply that the model for the mean is no longer adequate, and we should expect problems of inconsistency and potentially erroneous inference. In short, over-dispersion should be viewed as a symptom that needs to be investigated. The results of this investigation usually turn up substantively interesting aspects of the data-generating process.

10.3.1 Diagnosing Over-Dispersion

We can use the MLE to derive one heuristic for over-dispersion. First, note that

$$\log \mathcal{L} = \sum_{i=1}^{n} -\lambda + y_i \log \lambda$$

$$= -n\lambda + \log \lambda \sum y_i,$$

$$\frac{\partial}{\partial \lambda} \log \mathcal{L} = -n + \lambda^{-1} \sum y_i = 0$$

$$\Rightarrow \hat{\lambda} = \bar{y}.$$

Since the sample mean is the MLE for λ, and equi-dispersion implies that the mean and variance are equal, we can compare the sample mean and the sample variance. In the Bortkiewicz data on Prussian deaths by horse kick, we obtain a mean of 0.61 and a variance of 0.61. In the international mediation example, the sample mean is 3.5 and the variance is 126.

Graphical Methods

One visualization tool, the *Poissonness plot* (Hoaglin, 1980), examines the distribution of the dependent variable relative to theoretically expected values under a Poisson distribution.[3] The horizontal axis is the number of events, denoted y. The vertical axis is the so-called *metameter*. For the Poisson distribution the metameter for count value y is given as $\log y! n_y - \log n$, where n_y is the observed frequency of y events. If the data conform to the proposed distribution, the points should line up, similar to a quantile-quantile (Q-Q) plot for continuous distributions. Moreover, a regression of y on the metameter for y should have slope $\log(\lambda)$ and intercept $-\lambda$ under the Poisson distribution.

---

[3] Hoaglin and Tukey (1985) extend the Poissonness plot to the negative binomial and binomial. Each distribution has its own metameter calculation.

Poissonness Plot

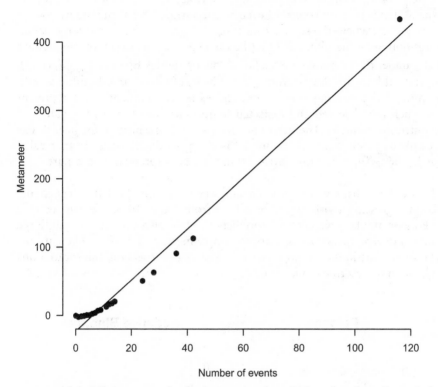

FIGURE 10.3 A Poissonness plot for international mediations data from Bercovitch and Schneider (2000). If the data follow a Poisson distribution, then the points should line up, and the slope of the regression should be $\log \lambda$, whereas the intercept should be $-\lambda$. With these data $\hat{\lambda} = 3.5$. The slope of the regression line is 3.7, and the intercept is -23.

Figure 10.3 displays a *Poissonness* plot for the international mediations data. The points clearly fail to line up on the regression line.[4] If these data followed a Poisson distribution we should observe an intercept of -3.5 and a regression slope of $\log 3.5 = 1.25$. Instead, we observe a slope of about 3.7 and an intercept of -23. Based on the *Poissonness* plot, the mediation data do not conform to the Poisson distribution. But a weakness of the plot is its inability to tell us anything about over-dispersion *per se* or about a particular model fit to those data.

---

[4] The outlier is, unsurprisingly, the United States. Excluding the United States implies a $\hat{\lambda} = 2.75$. The corresponding *Poissonness* plot yields an intercept of -12.5 and a slope of 2.7.

To address both these concerns, Kleiber and Zeileis (2016) advocate persuasively for a *hanging rootogram*, due to Tukey (1977). In a rootogram the horizontal axis is again counts of events. The vertical axis is the square root of the frequency, where the square root transformation ensures that large values do not dominate the plot. Let $E[n_y]$ be the expected frequency of event count value y under the proposed model. For a Poisson model, $E[n_y] = \sum_{i=1}^{n} f_P(y; \hat{\lambda}_i)$. The vertical bars are drawn from $\sqrt{E[n_y]}$ to $(\sqrt{E[n_y]} - \sqrt{n_y})$. In other words, the vertical boxes hang down from the expected frequency and represent how much the observed and expected frequencies differ at various values of the outcome variable. The zero line presents a convenient reference. A bar that fails to reach 0 means the model is overpredicting counts at that value $(E[n_y] - n_y > 0)$. A bar that crosses 0 implies underprediction at a particular value of y.

Figure 10.4 displays two rootograms. The plot on the left refers to the Poisson regression (with exposure offset) from Table 10.1. We can see that the Poisson model severely underpredicts 0 while also underpredicting large counts. It overpredicts counts near the sample mean of 3.5. Wave-like patterns and underpredictions of 0s are consistent with over-dispersion. But rootograms can be used to describe model fit more generally, whether in- or out-of-sample.

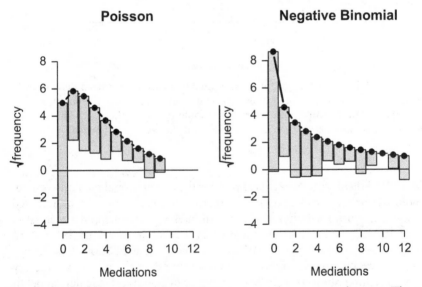

FIGURE 10.4 A hanging rootogram plotting expected versus actual counts. The curve represents the square root of the expected frequency of mediations under the specified model, while the vertical bars are drawn from the expected frequency to the observed frequency (both in square roots). The display on the left is from the Poisson model (with offset) from Table 10.1; the display on the right is from the negative binomial model in Table 10.2.

Formal Tests

There are several tests for over-dispersion. Most of them are constructed based on the assumptions that (1) the model for the mean is correct and (2) we can think of over-dispersion as taking the form

$$\text{var}(Y_i|\mathbf{x}_i) = h_i\lambda_i + \gamma w(h_i\lambda_i),$$

where $w()$ is some function. The most frequently used alternatives are $w(h_i\lambda_i) = h_i\lambda_i$ and $w(h_i\lambda_i) = (h_i\lambda_i)^2$. Cameron and Trivedi (1990) develop one regression-based test based on this logic. Define

$$\hat{e}_i = \frac{(y_i - h_i\hat{\lambda}_i)^2 - y_i}{h_i\hat{\lambda}_i}, \tag{10.3}$$

then we can estimate the OLS regression (omitting the intercept) $\hat{e}_i = \gamma \frac{w(h_i\hat{\lambda}_i)}{h_i\hat{\lambda}_i} + \varepsilon_i$. For over-dispersion we are interested in testing the *one-tailed* hypothesis that $\gamma > 0$ against the null of equi-dispersion, $\gamma = 0$.[5] Applied to the Poisson model (with offset) from Table 10.1 and assuming $w(x) = x$, we obtain $\hat{\gamma} = 8.9$ with a one-sided p-value of 0.005, consistent with over-dispersion.

Gelman and Hill (2007) describe a version of the Pearson χ^2 test that takes advantage of the fact that the standard deviation of the Poisson is equal to the square root of the mean. Define the standardized (or Pearson) residuals from a Poisson model as

$$z_i = \frac{y_i - h_i\hat{\lambda}_i}{\sqrt{h_i\hat{\lambda}_i}}.$$

If the Poisson assumption is correct, then each z_i is a standard normal random variable. This implies that $\sum z_i^2 \sim \chi^2_{n-k}$, which has an expected value of $n - k$ under the null hypothesis of equi-dispersion. In the case of over-dispersion, however, the mean of $z_i > 0$ and the corresponding sum of squares will be larger than $n - k$. In the Poisson example above (with offset), the sum of the standardized residuals is a hefty 1,448, rather than the expected 143. This yields a p-value ≈ 0, indicating over-dispersion.

10.4 MODELING OVER-DISPERSION

We found over-dispersion in the international mediation data. So what to do? That depends on our confidence in the model for the mean. If we believe that the model for the mean is correct and our conditional independence assumptions hold, then ignoring over-dispersion will not bias coefficient estimates. Over-dispersion does, however, induce bias and inconsistency into

---

[5] A joint test for either over-dispersion or under-dispersion corresponds to a two-tailed test against the null that $\gamma = 0$.

our estimated standard errors. We need to allow more flexibility in the model. Two immediate approaches present themselves: quasi-likelihood and the negative binomial model. These approaches often give similar results when evaluated on the scale of the outcome variable, but not always, as we shall see.

10.4.1 Quasipoisson

One way to proceed is with a quasi-likelihood approach in which we specify a model for the mean and a variance function rather than a full probability model (see Section 7.4). If our model for the mean is $\lambda_i = \exp(\mathbf{x}_i^T \boldsymbol{\beta})$ and our variance function is $\phi V(\lambda_i) = \phi \lambda_i$, then the set of quasiscore equations reduces to Equation 10.1. This implies that the solution to the Poisson score equations and the solution to the quasiscore equations where the mean is modeled as $\exp(\mathbf{x}_i^T \boldsymbol{\beta})$ is the same. In other words, the Poisson MLE for $\hat{\boldsymbol{\beta}}$ are the same as the quasipoisson estimates. As a result the quasipoisson approach will not alter point estimates of predicted outcomes.

Where quaispoisson and the full Poisson GLM differ is in the standard errors. In the quasipoisson setup we estimate the dispersion parameter, ϕ, using Equation 7.3, which is exactly the formula for the Pearson residuals we used earlier divided by $n - k$. Quasipoisson standard errors are then calculated from Equation 7.2. With $\phi > 1$ the quasipoisson standard errors will be larger than those from the Poisson GLM. While we do not have access to the maximized likelihood or information criteria from the quasipoisson model, we can still generate predicted counts and use simulation techniques to generate uncertainty estimates.

10.4.2 The Negative Binomial Model

Another approach for addressing over-dispersion is to specify a more-flexible distribution as the basis for deriving the log-likelihood. The most commonly used model is the *negative binomial*. One way to derive this model is to view λ_i as a random variable. But, conditional on λ_i, Y_i is still Poisson. In other words, we imagine that there is heterogeneity in the rate parameter that the Poisson model is too restrictive to capture. To fix the model we must pick a distribution for λ_i. Since we want a distribution that yields strictly positive numbers and has the flexibility to accommodate over-dispersion, we typically use the one-parameter *gamma* distribution.[6]

---

[6] The choice of the gamma distribution is somewhat arbitrary. Its primary convenience is that it yields a closed-form expression for the marginal distribution of Y_i. In Bayesian terminology, the gamma distribution is the conjugate prior for the Poisson.

> **In case you were wondering ... 10.2 The gamma function and distribution**
>
> The *gamma function,* denoted $\Gamma(\cdot)$, is a generalization of the factorial to non-integer (and complex) arguments. $\Gamma(x+1) = x!$ for positive integer x.
>
> The *gamma distribution* has several parameterizations. We use the "shape/rate" version. Let $Y \in (0, \infty)$. We say that Y follows a *gamma distribution* with parameter vector $\theta = (a, b)$ if
>
> $$Y \sim f_\Gamma(y; a, b) = \frac{b^a y^{a-1}}{\Gamma(a)} \exp(-by),$$
>
> with *shape* parameter $a > 0$ and *rate* or *inverse scale* parameter $b > 0$. $E[Y] = \frac{a}{b}$ and $\text{var}(Y) = \frac{a}{b^2}$.
>
> Fixing $a = b = \alpha$ yields the *one-parameter gamma* distribution, $f_\Gamma(y; \alpha)$, with expected value of 1 and a variance of α^{-1}.

The negative binomial probability model can be built in parts

$$Y_i \mid \lambda_i \sim f_P(\lambda_i),$$
$$\lambda_i = \exp(\mathbf{x}_i^\mathsf{T} \boldsymbol{\beta} + u_i),$$
$$= \exp(\mathbf{x}_i^\mathsf{T} \boldsymbol{\beta}) \exp(u_i),$$

where u_i is an error term in the expression for the Poisson mean, λ_i. If we let $\mu_i = \exp(\mathbf{x}_i^\mathsf{T} \boldsymbol{\beta})$ and $v_i = \exp(u_i)$ we can complete the model:

$$\lambda_i = \mu_i v_i,$$
$$v_i \sim f_\Gamma(\alpha).$$

The v_i are now unit-mean multiplicative error terms for the Poisson mean. As before, $E[Y_i] = \lambda_i$, but now $E[\lambda_i] = \mu_i$, implying that $E[Y_i] = \mu_i$. The μ_i are typically modeled in a log-linear fashion as $\exp(\mathbf{x}_i^\mathsf{T} \boldsymbol{\beta})$. Integrating over v_i gives us the marginal distribution for Y_i, which is a negative binomial distribution.

> **In case you were wondering ... 10.3 The negative binomial distribution**
>
> Let $Y \in \{0, 1, 2, \ldots\}$. We say that Y follows a *negative binomial distribution* with parameter vector $\theta = (\mu, \alpha)$, where $\mu > 0$ and

$\alpha > 0$, if

$$Y \sim f_{Nb}(y; \mu, \alpha)$$

$$\Updownarrow$$

$$\Pr(Y = y \mid \mu, \alpha) = \frac{\Gamma(y + \alpha)}{y! \Gamma(\alpha)} \left(\frac{\alpha}{\alpha + \mu} \right)^{\alpha} \left(\frac{\mu}{\alpha + \mu} \right)^{y}. \qquad (10.4)$$

The negative binomial has $E[Y] = \mu$ and $\text{var}(Y) = \mu(1 + \alpha^{-1}\mu) = \mu + \alpha^{-1}\mu^2$.

Via the parameter α, the negative binomial allows the variance to be greater than the mean. Cameron and Trivedi (2013) refer to the version just described as the NB2 model, with the 2 referring to the variance's quadratic dependence on the mean. They develop other versions as well. For example, if we substitute $\alpha'\mu_i$ for α in Equation 10.4, then we arrive at the NB1 model, with $\text{var}(Y) = \mu(1 + 1/\alpha')$. More generally, substituting $\alpha\mu^{p-2}$ for α in Equation 10.4 yields the NBp model, with $\text{var}(Y) = \mu(1 + \alpha^{-1}\mu^{p-1})$. Greene (2008) provides a general expression of the NBp log-likelihood:

$$\mu_i = \exp(\mathbf{x}_i \top \boldsymbol{\beta}),$$

$$r_i = \frac{\alpha}{\alpha + \mu_i},$$

$$q_i = \alpha\mu_i^{2-p},$$

$$\log \mathcal{L}(\boldsymbol{\beta}, \alpha \mid \mathbf{X}, \mathbf{y}, p) = \sum_{i=1}^{n} \log \Gamma(y_i + q_i) - \log \Gamma(q_i) - \log \Gamma(y_i + 1)$$

$$+ q_i + \log r_i + y_i \log(1 - r_i). \qquad (10.5)$$

The NB2 model is by far the most commonly used. Differences between NB1 and NB2 appear to be small in most applications. As these models are not nested versions of one another, choosing between them is best accomplished using information criteria and out-of-sample fit heuristics. All these versions of the negative binomial estimate the k regression parameters along with α, which governs the mean-variance relationship.

While both the quasipoisson and negative binomial models allow for over-dispersion, they approach it differently. The quasipoisson model directly estimates a dispersion parameter from the data and uses it to adjust standard errors while retaining the Poisson estimating equation for $\boldsymbol{\beta}$. The negative binomial model retains the $\phi = 1$ assumption of the Poisson and instead uses α to acount for over-dispersion; α is *not* a dispersion parameter in the exponential family sense. This fact is directly visible in the $\mathcal{R}$ summary output for the negative binomial glm: Dispersion parameter for Negative Binomial(0.3326) family taken to be 1, where 0.3326 is the estimate for α^{-1}. As we can see from Equation 10.5, the negative binomial likelihood differs from the Poisson even when the linear predictor terms are identical. Model estimates and implications can differ between the two.

Within the negative binomial class of models, the α parameter is a weight in a polynomial function of the mean. As the underlying polynomial changes, α also changes. As a result the α from an NB2 is not directly comparable to α' from an NB1, etc., notwithstanding the fact that most texts use the same notation across model parameterizations. However, all NBp models collapse to a simple Poisson as $\alpha \to \infty$. Because the Poisson is a limiting case of the negative binomial we can implement another over-dispersion test by constructing a likelihood ratio between a Poisson and negative binomial model.[7]

10.4.3 Mediations

We return to the international mediations example to examine how the quasipoisson and negative binomial models perform. Table 10.2 displays results

TABLE 10.2 *Quasipoisson and negative binomial regression of the number of times a country served as a mediator in an international conflict between 1950 and 1990. All models include offsets to account for unequal "exposure" across countries.*

	Quasipoisson	NB2	NB1
1990 GDPpc	0.06	0.01	0.01
	(0.03)	(0.03)	(0.02)
UNSC	2.18	2.51	1.86
	(0.33)	(0.82)	(0.35)
Intercept	−3.03	−2.76	−2.51
	(0.25)	(0.22)	(0.24)
ϕ	10.12		
α^{-1}		0.33	
		(0.06)	
α'			11.42
			(2.85)
n	146	146	146
$\log \mathcal{L}$		−280	−280
AIC		568	567
BIC		578	579

[7] Because we obtain a Poisson distribution at the boundary of the negative binomial parameter space the likelihood ratio between a Poisson and negative binomial model has a nonstandard distribution, with half of its mass at 0 and half as a χ_1^2. As a result, the critical value for a test at the a level is the χ_i^2 value associated with a $2a$ test. For example, the critical value for a 95% test is 2.71 rather than the 3.84 normally associated with a χ_1^2.

for a quasipoisson, NB2, and NB1 models. All three models include an offset for log duration to account for unequal exposure windows.

The quasipoisson returns exactly the $\hat{\beta}$ from the third model in Table 10.1. What has fundamentally changed are the standard errors, which are substantially larger, reflecting more uncertainty, owing to the over-dispersion that is no longer being ignored. In general, ignoring over-dispersion will lead to dramatically underestimated standard errors. Note that the estimated dispersion parameter for the quasipoisson, $\hat{\phi}$, is exactly the sum of squared Pearson residuals calculated for the over-dispersion test divided by the residual degrees of freedom, 1,477/143.

Based on the information criteria, both of the negative binomial models represent large improvements over the OLS and Poisson models in Table 10.1. The right panel of Figure 10.4 displays the rootogram for the NB2 model, which clearly fits the data better than the Poisson alternative. It is far more accurate in its predictions of 0s and does not show the wave-like pattern of over- and underprediction across outcome values of the Poisson specification. The negative binomial models are preferable to the Poisson or quasipoisson. But, based on the in-sample fit statistics, the two negative binomial models are nearly identical, a common occurrence.

Consistent with the over-dispersion in the data the negative binomial models return substantial estimates for α. In $\mathcal{R}$ the glm.nb function fits the NB2 model and uses the parameterization and notation in Venables and Ripley (2002). In their parameterization of the negative binomial distribution they use "θ," which is equivalent to α^{-1} in our notation.[8] We can recover an approximate standard error for $\hat{\alpha}$ from glm.nb output by calculating $\hat{\sigma}_\theta/\hat{\theta}^2$. In the NB2 case we therefore recover $\hat{\alpha} = 3, \sigma_{\hat{\alpha}} = 0.52$.

In the mediation example the negative binomial models give substantively different results from the quasipoisson; per capita GDP is not a strong predictor of mediation demand once we account for over-dispersion. Differences between the quasipoisson and negative binomial sometimes arise due to differences in the weights attached to large counts in the fitting of the model (Ver Hoef and Boveng, 2007). But in this example the negative binomial model fits the data substantially better than the (quasi)Poisson. This divergence can happen when the process generating over-dispersion is more complicated than simple heterogeneity in the underlying population. For example, the negative binomial distribution and over-dispersion can result from positive contagion across events (Gurland, 1959; Winkelmann, 1995), something that appears to be at work here.

Interpretation of the negative binomial models follows our usual procedures. For example, take China, a member of the UNSC but relatively poor during this

---

[8] The dbinom (and other associated functions) in $\mathcal{R}$ can take several parameterizations of the negative binomial distribution. In our notation the mu argument to dbinom corresponds to μ and size corresponds to α.

time. Had China not been on the UNSC, the model predicts that it would have been requested as a mediator between two and three times ($\hat{\lambda} = 2.54$) with a standard error of 0.49). But China as a UNSC member is expected to have been asked to mediate 31 times. Doubling China's per capita GDP has no effect on these predictions.

10.4.4 Under-Dispersion

While under-dispersion is less common than over-dispersion, it does arise. Under-dispersed count data can be thought of as having some kind of negative contagion. For example, the neighboring counties to a toxic waste site will be less likely to create their own, for a variety of reasons.

Many of the same tools used for diagnosing over-dispersion can be repurposed for under-dispersion. We can examine the mean of the sample relative to its variance. We can use the Cameron-Trivedi regression-based test in Equation 10.3, only specifying an alternative hypothesis of $\gamma < 0$. Note, however, that dispersion tests relying on a likelihood ratio comparing a Poisson model to a negative binomial will *not* capture under-dispersion.

We can model under-dispersed data using the quasipoisson approach (in which case we should recover $\hat{\phi} \in (0,1)$). The quasipoisson model for under-dispersion entails all the same restrictions and drawbacks we encountered for over-dispersion. Several fully parameterized likelihood approaches exist. King (1989a) details the "continuous parameter binomial" (CPB) for under-dispersion and the generalized event count model that estimates dispersion directly. The generalized Poisson model enables estimation of over-dispersion and some forms of under-dispersion (Hilbe, 2014). The generalized Poisson distribution entails some restrictions that limit the degree of under-dispersion that it can capture. The Conway-Maxwell-Poisson (Conway and Maxwell, 1962) is a relatively recent addition to the applied literature; its two-parameter structure does not readily accommodate a linear predictor for the mean, making it difficult to construct easily interpretable regression models (Sellers et al., 2012).

10.5 HURDLING 0S AND 1S

As we have seen, the Poisson model's restriction that the mean equal the variance can result in underestimates of both the observed number of large events and 0s when the assumption fails to hold. This over-dispersion can be dealt with using the negative binomial model. But what if we observe more zeros than a negative binomial model would expect? There are two basic conceptual approaches here.

Suppose we believe that there are multiple processes that determine whether we observe a zero. For example, a survey respondent might be asked to estimate the number of times she visited the public library in the past month. She might answer zero because she never uses the public library. But she might also have answered zero because, while she is a library user, she did not go in the past month owing to inclement weather. These two situations are fundamentally different. Among one group, the weather might be a covariate that would help to understand library usage. In the other it has no bearing at all. The data are therefore composed of two distinct subpopulations: "never-users" and "conditional users." There will be a large number of zeros in the data originating from two distinct processes. A Poisson or Negative Binomial model will understate the number of zeros in the data, resulting in the problem of *zero inflation*.

A related situation occurs when the process that generates a zero outcome is fundamentally different than the process generating other outcomes. For example, we might not observe any protest events due to severe government repression, but more protest when repression is moderate. The number of strikes and demonstrations in the German Democratic Republic during the 1960s and 1970s was essentially zero, owing mainly to a repressive and thoroughly pervasive state "security system." However, once strikes and demonstrations did begin in the mid-1980s, they occurred somewhat frequently, irrespective of the level of repression, which itself diminished. It is easy to imagine that the first (and subsequent) demonstrations in East Germany during the 1980s was determined by a different set of forces than those which were responsible for the total absence of such public demonstrations during the 1970s. In short, the number of zeros in observed data may be due to the fact that the zeros were generated by a different process than that which generated the counts of events (including some of the zeros, plausibly). This situation is commonly referred to as a *hurdle process*; the hurdle we need to clear to observe that first event is systematically "higher" (or "lower") than the hurdles between subsequent events.

Hurdle and mixed-population/zero-inflation processes are not uncommon in the social sciences. Two models have been developed to take advantage of these situations. The first – the *hurdle Poisson* or negative binomial model – involves one expression (and set of covariates) to describe the zeros in an observed count, while permitting another to model the positive counts, given that we have observed a nonzero value. The second class of models – *zero-inflated Poisson* and zero-inflated negative binomial – can be thought of as a switching model that is controlled by an indicator variable that switches between two states, conditional on the data.

Both the hurdle and zero-inflation models are examples of a more-general modeling strategy that combines multiple distributions in the same model. The key distinction between the two models is that the hurdle model assumes that if the "hurdle" is crossed, we will certainly observe some number of events greater than 0; it is a conditional model. The zero-inflation model does not make this assumption; it is a "split population" or mixture model (see In case you were wondering... 4.2). Both, however, are amplifications of the approach for modeling binary data with the Bernoulli distribution combined with distributions for count data. In many applied settings both models give very similar results. But this is not always the case, as we will see.

10.5.1 How Many 0s Are Too Many?

Bagozzi et al. (2017) are interested in how climactic conditions – droughts – relate to the targeting of civilians in civil conflicts. They combine remote-sensing data on droughts with geolocated instances of rebel attacks against civilians in agricultural regions of developing countries, 1995–2008. Data are at the 0.5° × 0.5° grid-cell level, and the outcome of interest is the total number of recorded atrocity events in a grid cell between 1995 and 2008. Figure 10.5 displays the distribution of this variable; the vertical axis is on the square root scale to enable us to see the nonzero frequencies. Clearly zeros dominate these data.

There are 26,566 cells that enter the analysis. The mean of the dependent variable is 0.092, so a Poisson distribution predicts that we should observe about 24,231 zeros in these data. There are 25,836 – about 1,605 more than expected. Is that "too many?" After all, these data also display a variance of

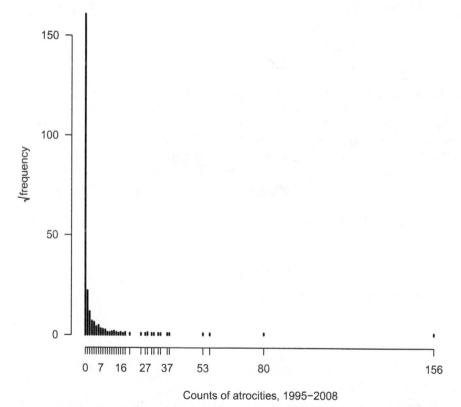

FIGURE 10.5 The observed frequency of rebel atrocities against civilians (on the square root scale) between 1995 and 2008 in 26,566 0.5° × 0.5° grid cells. Cells are agricultural regions in developing countries.

2.1, implying over-dispersion. Perhaps a model accounting for over-dispersion is sufficient to "explain" these excess zeros. It turns out that there is no single test to answer this question. Instead, we must actively develop and compare competing models.[9]

10.5.2 Hurdle Models

The *hurdle Poisson* and *hurdle negative binomial* use a standard logit model to describe whether there were any atrocities in a grid cell and then employ a truncated count model to describe the number of atrocities committed *given that there was at least one*. We can express this model by imagining that $Y_i = \pi_i Y_i^*$, where $\pi_i \in \{0, 1\}$. We can then formulate the hurdle Poisson model as

$$\pi_i = \begin{cases} 0 & \text{for} \quad y = 0, \\ 1 & \text{for} \quad y > 0, \end{cases}$$

$$\text{stochastic}: \pi_i \sim f_B(\theta_i),$$

$$Y_i^* \sim f_P(y_i; \lambda_i \mid y_i > 0),$$

$$\text{systematic}: \theta_i = \text{logit}^{-1}(\mathbf{z}_i^\mathsf{T} \boldsymbol{\delta}),$$

$$\lambda_i = \exp(\mathbf{x}_i^\mathsf{T} \boldsymbol{\beta}).$$

This specification highlights four things. First, the hurdle model is conventionally set up such that crossing the hurdle (i.e., $y_i > 0$) is coded as a "success" for the logit portion. Second, different vectors of covariates (with different regression parameters) can govern the "hurdle" ($\mathbf{z}_i$) and the count ($\mathbf{x}_i$) processes. Third, the hurdle model can also accommodate *too few* zeros relative to our expectations. Fourth, the process describing positive counts is a *zero-truncated* Poisson distribution. Specifically,

$$f_P(y_i; \lambda_i \mid y_i > 0) = \frac{f_P(y_i \mid \lambda_i)}{1 - f_P(0 \mid \lambda_i)}$$

$$= \frac{\lambda_i^{y_i}}{(\exp(\lambda_i) - 1) y_i!}.$$

Thus the probability statement for Y_i is

$$\Pr(Y_i = y_i) = \begin{cases} 1 - \theta_i & \text{for} \quad y_i = 0, \\ \theta_i \frac{\lambda_i^{y_i}}{(\exp(\lambda_i)-1) y_i!} & \text{for} \quad y_i > 0, \end{cases}$$

---

[9] The Vuong test is used to test non-nested models; it has been frequently employed as a way to test for excess zeros in count models (Desmarais and Harden, 2013). But there is controversy about its applicability in these situations (Wilson, 2015), so we emphasize broader model-selection heuristics.

from which we can then derive the likelihood:

$$\mathcal{L}(\boldsymbol{\beta}, \boldsymbol{\delta} | \mathbf{X}, \mathbf{y}) = \prod_{i=1}^{n} \left[1 - \text{logit}^{-1}(\mathbf{z}_i^{\mathsf{T}} \boldsymbol{\delta}) \right]^{(1-\pi_i)}$$

$$\times \left[\text{logit}^{-1}(\mathbf{z}_i^{\mathsf{T}} \boldsymbol{\delta}) \frac{\exp(\mathbf{x}_i^{\mathsf{T}} \boldsymbol{\beta})^{y_i}}{(\exp(\exp(\mathbf{x}_i^{\mathsf{T}} \boldsymbol{\beta})) - 1) y_i!} \right]^{\pi_i}.$$

The hurdle negative binomial model is derived similarly, replacing the Poisson with the negative binomial distribution. The hurdle Poisson allows for some over-dispersion,[10] but the negative binomial is more flexible in its ability to model the variance of the integer counts.

10.5.3 Zero Inflation

The zero-inflated Poisson (ZIP) and zero-inflated negative binomial (ZINB) envision a sample composed of two different subpopulations, the "always-zeros" and those who are "eligible" for the event. Both subpopulations can generate observed zeros, but only the "eligible" can produce observed positive counts. In our earlier library example, the population was composed of "never-users" and those who sometimes go. Never-users will always say "0," while some library users simply did not have the ability or inclination to go last month. We can account for the separate processes or "split population" by adding additional probability mass at zero. The idea is relatively simple: model the zeros as a mixture of always zeros and count-model zeros. We use a Bernoulli model to estimate the probability that a particular zero is an always-zero.[11] Observations with positive counts follow one of our two integer count distributions, the Poisson or negative binomial. The ZIP mass function has the following form:

$$\pi_i = \begin{cases} 1 & \text{for} \quad y = 0, \\ 0 & \text{for} \quad y > 0, \end{cases}$$

$$\text{stochastic}: \pi_i \sim f_B(y_i \mid \theta_i),$$

$$Y_i^* \sim f_P(y_i \mid \lambda_i),$$

$$\text{systematic}: \theta_i = \text{logit}^{-1}(\mathbf{z}_i^{\mathsf{T}} \boldsymbol{\delta}),$$

$$\lambda_i = \exp(\mathbf{x}_i^{\mathsf{T}} \boldsymbol{\beta}).$$

---

[10] This is owing to the fact that the variance of a zero-truncated Poisson random variable, X, is $E[X](1 + \lambda - E[X])$, where $E[X] = \frac{\lambda \exp(\lambda)}{\exp(\lambda)-1}$. As a result, the variance is not restricted to be exactly equal to the mean, but they are tied together.

[11] The model developed here uses a logit link, but probit, cloglog, or others are feasible.

Note two important differences between the ZIP and the hurdle model. First, the ZIP/ZINB is conventionally parameterized such that a zero is counted as a "success" for the Bernoulli part of the model. In other words, the Bernoulli model describes the probability that an observation is an always-zero as opposed to the probability of crossing the hurdle. Second, the ZIP/ZINB does not truncate the count distribution. As a result, the ZIP probability statement differs from the hurdle Poisson model:

$$\Pr(Y_i = y_i) = \begin{cases} \theta_i + (1 - \theta_i) f_P(0|\lambda_i) & \text{for} \quad y_i = 0, \\ (1 - \theta_i) \frac{\exp(-\lambda_i)\lambda_i^{y_i}}{y_i!} & \text{for} \quad y_i > 0. \end{cases}$$

In the ZIP/ZINB, θ is the mixing parameter. The ZIP likelihood is

$$\mathcal{L}(\boldsymbol{\beta}, \boldsymbol{\delta}|\mathbf{X}, \mathbf{y}) = \prod_{i=1}^{n} [\theta_i + (1 - \theta_i)\exp(-\lambda_i)]^{\pi_i} \left[(1 - \theta_i)\frac{\exp(-\lambda_i)\lambda_i^{y_i}}{y_i!} \right]^{1-\pi_i}.$$

Inserting the expressions for θ_i and λ_i, simplifying, and taking logarithms produces the ZIP log-likelihood:

$$\log \mathcal{L}_{\text{ZIP}} = \pi_i \sum_{i=1}^{n} \log \left(\exp(\mathbf{z}_i^{\mathsf{T}}\boldsymbol{\delta}) + \exp(-\exp(\mathbf{x}_i^{\mathsf{T}}\boldsymbol{\beta})) \right)$$

$$+ (1 - \pi_i) \sum_{i=1}^{n} (y_i \mathbf{x}_i^{\mathsf{T}}\boldsymbol{\beta} - \exp(\mathbf{x}_i^{\mathsf{T}}\boldsymbol{\beta}))$$

$$- \sum_{i=1}^{n} \log(1 + \exp(\mathbf{z}_i^{\mathsf{T}}\boldsymbol{\delta})) - (1 - \pi_i) \sum_{i=1}^{n} \log y_i!.$$

This expression is difficult to maximize largely because the first sum yields a complicated gradient with no closed form. Introducing a latent/unobserved variable indicating whether i is an always-zero can separate the $\boldsymbol{\delta}$ from the $\boldsymbol{\beta}$ in the maximization problem. We can proceed using EM to iteratively maximize the log-likelihood (see Section 4.2.3).

10.5.4 Example: Droughts and Atrocities

Based on the hypothesis that some areas are simply not prone to rebel violence against civilians, whereas others are, Bagozzi et al. (2017) use ZINB models for their analysis of atrocities. Using a simplified version of their data we fit NB2, hurdle negative binomial, and ZINB models. Covariates include national-level average democracy (Polity IV), cell population, percent urban, indicators for drought and civil conflict, and a spatial lag of the dependent variable.[12] The BUTON appears as Table 10.3.[13]

Examining the model-fit statistics we see, clear evidence that the ZINB model is preferred to both the NB2 and the hurdle model. The zero-inflation hypothesis – that there are some observations that are effectively immune to atrocities in this period – is in better agreement with these data.

The hurdle and ZINB models frequently give very similar results. Not entirely so in this example. Aside from model fit statistics, inspection of the drought coefficients in the models for zeros highlights this (recall that the ZINB and hurdle models code successes in opposite ways!). In the zero-inflation model, drought is not a strong predictor of a cell being an always-zero, yet in the hurdle model, drought is a strong predictor of crossing from a zero to a positive count. Both models, however, predict that droughts increase the number of events.[14]

The ZINB model also illustrates how covariates can influence the predicted outcomes through two channels: whether an observation is likely to be always-zero and how many events are predicted to occur. In these data, drought and the proportion of land in urban settlements affect atrocities through their increase in the count; they are not good predictors of whether a cell is an always-zero, given the other covariates in the model.

10.6 SUMMARY

Understanding how we can model count data begins with the Poisson distribution. But the Poisson's assumption of equal dispersion means that it is rarely sufficient, since social science data are often overdispersed and frequently characterized by an inflated number of zeros, and may also have "natural" thresholds between successive numbers of events. As a result, it is often useful to employ a simple mixture model in which a binomial (or other) process is combined with a Poisson process, to capture the full range of the data-generating processes.

---

[12] The spatial lag is the total number of atrocities in immediately adjacent cells. Cells differ in area, becoming smaller as we move away from the equator. We might imagine that this would allow for different observational windows. Including cell area as an offset made no difference, so we omit it. But good for you if the issue concerned you.

[13] The `zeroinfl` and `hurdle` procedures in $\mathcal{R}$ return `log(theta)` and its standard error. Recall that `theta` corresponds to α^{-1} in our notation for the negative binomial distribution. By the invariance property of the MLE, we know that $\widehat{\log\theta} = \log\hat{\theta}$. We also know that the MLE is asymptotically normal. So we can apply the delta method to calculate the approximate standard error for θ as $\hat{\theta}\sigma_{\widehat{\log\theta}}$. These are the quantities reported in ZINB and hurdle columns of Table 10.3.

[14] Moving drought from 0 to 2 increases the number of predicted events from 0.03 to 0.04 in the ZINB and from 0.01 to 0.02 in the hurdle model, with no neighbors experiencing atrocities but with some civil conflict and all other covariates set to sample means.

                              Strategies for Analyzing Count Data

TABLE 10.3 *NB2, zero-inflated, and hurdle negative binomial regressions on counts of anti-civilian atrocities in the developing world, 1995–2008. Observations are 0.5° × 0.5° grid cells.*

Count Model	NB2	ZINB	Hurdle NB
Intercept	−9.28	−7.41	−15.30
	(0.33)	(0.43)	(42.67)
Spatial lag	29.45	24.06	4.89
	(1.44)	(1.98)	(1.53)
Conflict	0.16	0.07	0.09
	(0.01)	(0.01)	(0.02)
Drought	0.11	0.14	0.26
	(0.04)	(0.04)	(0.07)
log population	0.47	0.39	0.29
	(0.03)	(0.03)	(0.05)
Polity	−0.02	−0.05	−0.04
	(0.01)	(0.01)	(0.01)
Urban	0.08	0.10	0.06
	(0.02)	(0.03)	(0.03)
α^{-1}	0.07	0.10	0.00
	(0.00)	(0.01)	(0.00)

Zero Model	NB2	ZINB	Hurdle NB
Intercept		6.87	−8.96
		(1.05)	(0.29)
Conflict		−3.70	0.16
		(0.92)	(0.01)
Drought		0.16	0.14
		(0.12)	(0.03)
log population		−0.50	0.42
		(0.09)	(0.02)
Polity		−0.18	−0.03
		(0.03)	(0.01)
Urban		0.01	0.05
		(0.05)	(0.02)
n	26,566	26,566	26,566
$\log \mathcal{L}$	−4,194	−4,064	−4,272
AIC	8,405	8,157	8,572
BIC	8,470	8,272	8,687

10.7 FURTHER READING

Applications

Nanes (2017) uses negative binomial models to describe Palestinian casualties in the West Bank and Gaza. Edwards et al. (2017) use both OLS and negative binomial models to describe the number of US cities and counties that are split by Congressional districts.

Past Work

King (1988) is an early discussion of count models in political science. King (1989b); King and Signorino (1996) develop an alternative "generalized event count" model for over- and under-dispersion. Land et al. (1996) compare Poisson and negative binomial models with semiparametric versions. Zorn (1998) compares zero-inflated and hurdle models in the context of the US Congress and Supreme Court.

Advanced Study

The classic text in this field is Cameron and Trivedi (2013). Greene (2008) describes the likelihoods and computation for the NBp and related models; see also Hilbe (2008). Mebane and Sekhon (2004) discuss and extend the use of the multinomial model in the context of counts across categories for multiple units.

Software Notes

The `countreg` package (Zeileis and Kleiber, 2017) collects many of the models and statistical tests for count data previously scattered across multiple libraries, including `pscl` (Zeileis et al., 2008). The VGAM package (Yee, 2010) enables generalized Poisson regression. Friendly (2000) describes many useful graphical displays for count data, including the rootogram and distribution plots. Many of the tools described in that volume are collected in the vcd $\mathcal{R}$ library (Meyer et al., 2016). This likelihood ratio test for the negative binomial model relative to a Poisson is implemented as `odTest` in $\mathcal{R}$'s `pscl`, `AER`, and `countreg` libraries.

PART IV

ADVANCED TOPICS

11

Strategies for Temporal Dependence
Duration Models

Up to this point in the book we have derived likelihood functions and evaluated models under the assumption that the Y_i are conditionally independent, i.e., $\Pr(y_1, y_2, \ldots, y_n | \boldsymbol{\theta}) = P(y_1 | \theta_1) \times P(y_2 | \theta_2) \times \ldots P(y_n | \theta_n)$. This are many threats to this assumption. For example, observations close together in space may all be influenced by some neighborhood-specific factor, such as a leaky nuclear reactor. This is known as spatial dependence. Dependence can also arise when events or observations take place over time.

There are several ways of thinking about temporal dependence. For example, we can consider frequency rather than time (Beck, 1991). Another approach considers specific values or events in a temporal sequence. In such time series we have repeated observations of some unit i at fixed intervals $t, t + 1, \ldots$. We are concerned that there might be correlation across them, often referred to as serial (auto)correlation (Hamilton, 1994). Time series models, such as an autoregressive integrated moving average (ARIMA) and many others, typically organize the data to examine their characteristics in the time domain. There is a vast and highly developed literature on these topics. We do not pursue them here because that would require an entire volume. Instead, we concentrate on a third approach to temporal dependence: modeling the time between or until discrete events.

11.1 INTRODUCTION

Social scientists are frequently concerned with how long things last and how often they change. How long will one nation be at war with another? How long is a leader's tenure in office? How long after an election until a government is formed? How long can we expect a worker to remain unemployed? Analysis of this sort of data goes by different names across disciplines. In political science and sociology, models of these processes are most commonly called *event history* models; in economics they are referred to as *duration* models; in demography and health sciences the models are referred to as *survival* models; and in engineering they are called *failure time* or *hazard* models. Whatever they are called, these approaches are concerned with modeling what we will call *spells*, i.e., the length of time an observation spends in a particular condition (typically called a state) before either it transitions to different condition or the study period ends.

The basic idea behind duration models is to assume that spell durations can be viewed as a random variable, T. This permits the use of a probability density for a spell of length t. In turn, we can model the expected value of that distribution as a function of covariates, which may also vary over time.

The definition of what constitutes being in a spell is akin to a categorical variable. The most basic duration models employ a binary categorical variable, but more complex models for multiple, competing risks and the like have analogues in ordered or multinomial categorical data. The major wrinkle that justifies the development of an entirely new class of models for duration data is the problem of *censoring*.

As an example, consider a population of countries. We are concerned with the length of time a country spends at war. When observing conflict, we end up with two types of observations: those for which the duration of the conflict is known, i.e., we observe the entire spell from beginning to end, and those for which the duration of conflict is unknown because the observation period ends before the conflict is observed to end. Event history models account for both types of observations in the likelihood function.

In this chapter, we concentrate on duration models, binary time-series cross-section (BTSCS) data, and the semi-parametric Cox proportional hazards model. We then develop an overview of parametric event history models, such as the Weibull, on our way to a specialized form, the split-population event history model. The Cox model has rapidly become the standard in most empirical applications due to its less-restrictive assumptions about the baseline hazard rate and its flexibility in incorporating more complicated functional forms.

11.2 DATA STRUCTURES AND THINKING ABOUT TIME

More than most analysis problems, categorical time series data require us to think ahead about the types of models we are likely to fit before we set up our data in a format to be analyzed. Two key issues are (1) whether we consider time discrete or continuous and (2) whether to use the spell as the unit of analysis as opposed to some putatively natural unit of time such as a year. The latter decision will largely be driven by whether we wish to include time-varying covariates, i.e., explanatory variables that change through time – perhaps within a spell – in our models. Most social science data are collected in fixed intervals, such as years, not in terms of episodes that have a beginning and an end.

11.2.1 Discrete and Continuous Time

If we imagine transitions from one state to another can occur at any arbitrary moment, then we are thinking in continuous time. If events can only occur within specific intervals, then time is discrete. Discrete time is made from continuous time. The world we actually inhabit is one of continuous time, and few political processes are constrained to occur at specific discrete intervals. Nevertheless, actual measurement regularly coarsens time into discrete units or observational periods (days, weeks, years, etc.). Put another way, time is continuous, but our data are almost always discrete. Many texts make much of the distinction between discrete time and continuous time models. Our take is that this is less of a concern since our data are almost always discrete and grouped. The practical question involves the length of spells relative to our temporal precision in observing transitions from one state to another. The longer the spell relative to the time aggregation unit, the closer we are to observing continuous time. For example, if the average spell length is a year and a half and our data are at the annual level, then we clearly have a discrete process. If instead we have daily data, we observe transitions that are relatively finely grained moments in time.

If our observation of transitions is fine-grained, then it makes sense to consider time to be continuous, modeling the spell as the unit of analysis. Why? Recall the models of conflict that we covered in Section 4.5.1: for most dyads, in most years there is no conflict. We saw that most models for discrete processes were not terribly good at predicting both conflict and nonconflict. The challenge here is that there are so many nonconflict episodes relative to conflictual ones, i.e., our data are "zero-inflated." A highly accurate model is one that simply produces 0, since there are so few 1s. Similarly, if we observe a survival process at the daily level and most spells are years long, then we will have many time periods in which no events occur. It makes sense, then, to consider the length of the spell as our outcome of interest, especially if we have covariates that are not changing within a spell. Alternatively, if we have data aggregated to a high level relative to the length of a spell, then a discrete time approach is probably called for.

11.2.2 Organizing Data as a Spell-Level

Event history analysis (in continuous time) takes all data to be organized into spells. Table 11.1 gives an example of how this might look, taken from King et al.'s (1990) paper on cabinet durations. The key novelty here is the censoring variable, indicating whether a unit survived until the end of the observation period. Note that all covariates are constant within spells.

TABLE 11.1 *Spell organization of data.*

Case	Duration in Months	X_1	X_2	X_3	X_4	Censored?
1	7.00	93.00	1.00	1.00	5.00	Yes
2	27.00	62.00	1.00	1.00	1.00	Yes
3	6.00	97.00	1.00	1.00	1.00	Yes
4	49.00	106.00	1.00	1.00	1.00	No
5	7.00	93.00	1.00	1.00	4.00	Yes
⋮	⋮	⋮	⋮	⋮	⋮	
314	48.00	60.00	0.00	1.00	1.00	No

11.2.3 Continuous Time with Time-Varying Covariates: Counting Process

If we want to include covariates that may change within a spell, then we need to set up data in a different format, referred to as a *counting process*, due to Andersen and Gill (1982). Setting up data as a counting process is useful for more-complicated event history models, including those for time-varying covariates, repeated, and multiple events. The first step is to define the *risk set*, i.e., the units and time periods at risk for the transition or event of interest. We must then identify the intervals at which the covariates change value and the times when the events of interest occur. The counting process is formulated as a [start,stop] interval. The censoring variable indicates that a unit has exited the risk set, either due to an event of interest or because the observational period ended.

Table 11.2 displays some of the data used in Ahlquist (2010b), organized as a counting process. The `status` variable indicates whether the event of interest occurs in that period.

The counting-process construction in Table 11.2 reflects stacked time series data, also known to some as time-series cross-section (TSCS), and to others as a panel.[1] The primary difference from here is in modeling strategies. The BTSCS (discrete time) approach, discussed in the next section, uses `status` as the dependent variable and the number of periods since an event occurred for that unit as a measure of time. Models developed under the assumption of continuous time require the counting process (`start` and `stop`) in addition to the censoring indicator.

Before turning to this, we present briefly the data structure of duration models in Figure 11.1. The top row of this illustration is a vector of numbers

---

[1] The distinction between panel and TSCS data depends on whether n (the number of units) is much greater than the number of time periods, T. When $n >> T$ we are in a panel world. $T >> n$ is referred to as TSCS data. The distinction is not hard-and-fast and derives from whether a particular estimator relies on asymptotics in T or n to derive its properties. See Beck and Katz (1995).

TABLE 11.2 *Counting process data, from Ahlquist (2010b).*

Index	id	Country	Event Time	Start	Stop	Status	tsle.ciep	lag.infl	lag.unemp	growth	enpp
1	AUS1974Q1	Australia	1	0	1	0	36.00	16.38	2.13	3.79	2.52
2	AUS1974Q2	Australia	2	1	2	0	44.00	16.55	2.10	3.79	2.52
3	AUS1974Q3	Australia	3	2	3	0	4.00	15.90	2.11	3.79	2.52
4	AUS1974Q4	Australia	4	3	4	0	12.00	15.25	2.64	3.79	2.52
...		...		...		...		...		...	
36	AUS1982Q4	Australia	36	35	36	0	65.00	9.12	7.02	2.92	2.64
37	AUS1983Q1	Australia	37	36	37	1	74.00	8.54	8.72	-3.00	2.23
...		...		...		...		...		...	
2,381	USA1999Q1	United States	101	100	101	0	12.50	1.29	4.43	3.39	1.99
2,382	USA1999Q2	United States	102	101	102	0	25.00	1.44	4.29	3.39	1.99
2,383	USA1999Q3	United States	103	102	103	0	37.50	1.62	4.25	3.39	1.99
2,384	USA1999Q4	United States	104	103	104	0	50.00	1.80	4.25	3.39	1.99

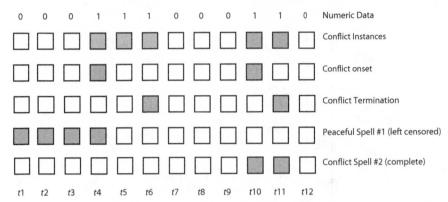

FIGURE 11.1 An illustration of duration data using conflicts, onsets, durations, spells.

that represent whether a particular country in the sample set being analyzed has a conflict during a particular year. Much conflict data are organized as a collection of such vectors in BTSCS format. The second row is a visual representation of the same information, with filled squares representing conflicts, and empty ones shown for years in which there was no conflict in that country. The third row uses shading to identify the years in which there was an observed transition from peace to conflict whereas the fourth row identifies conflict termination–years of transition from conflict to peace. The row labeled `peaceful spell` #1 shows that the first four time periods make up the first spell of non-conflict until (and including) the year in which the peace ends and the conflict begins. This spell is left-censored because we do not observe when it begins. The final row encodes the years consisting of the second spell of conflict, one in which we observe both the onset and termination. Standard analyses often focus on the numeric data, but duration models focus on explaining the lengths of the spells; Standard analyses have covariates that are measured for each t, but duration models are really concerned, if at all, with what the covariates look like during the spells.

11.3 DISCRETE TIME: THE BTSCS APPROACH

The discrete time BTSCS setup closely mirrors the analysis of panel and time series, cross-section data with continuous response variables. BTSCS data represent repeated observations of a unit i over time, t. The outcome of interest is a simple dichotomous variable, Y_{it}, which takes on a value of 1 if the event of interest occurred for unit i in period t and 0 otherwise. Typically we have n units, each of which is observed for T periods. The data for each unit are stacked on top of one another, producing an outcome vector of length nT. Beck et al. (1998) point out that the aggregation of events by time induces a discrete (i.e., grouped) structure in time. For example, if we have yearly observations on law adoption by US states, we only observe whether a state adopts the law in a year; all adoptions within a year are considered equivalent.

Beck et al. (1998) argue that fitting a logit, probit, or complementary log-log model to this pooled, stacked data is both appropriate and equivalent to event history modeling so long as the analyst includes either (1) indicator variables for event time or (2) (cubic) splines in event time.[2] The event time indicators that Beck et al. have in mind are $T - 1$ dummy variables for the number of periods since that unit last experienced an event. These time dummies have the direct interpretation of a "baseline hazard," i.e., the probability of an event occurring in any particular interval given that it has not yet occurred and before we consider covariates. It turns out this is equivalent mathematically to a duration model, developed in the next section.

Formally, the logit model with time indicators is

$$Y_{it} \sim f_B(y_{it}; \theta_{it},)$$

$$\theta_{it} = \text{logit}^{-1}\left(\mathbf{x}_{it}^{\mathsf{T}}\boldsymbol{\beta} + \tau_t \mathbb{1}_{t_i}\right),$$

where $\mathbb{1}_{t_i}$ is a dummy variable that equals one whenever unit i has gone t periods without an event and zero otherwise.

This BTSCS approach is simple to implement when the data are organized as a panel, rather than as a collection of episodes. BTSCS models can be interpreted along the lines of simple binary GLMs. But these models do require explicit description of temporal dependence across observations in the form of time indicators or splines. Carter and Signorino (2010) highlight two problems here. First, splines are complicated and often implemented incorrectly, in addition to being difficult to interpret. Second, a common problem with the indicator-variable approach is the small number of observations with very high times-to-failure. These small numbers can induce perfect separation. Carter and Signorino (2010) propose using a simple cubic term in event time ($\tau_1 t_i + \tau_2 t_i^2 + \tau_3 t_i^3$) rather than splines or time dummies to get around these exact problems. In our experience a simple linear trend often works well.

The BTSCS approach does have weaknesses. It requires time-varying data but, at the same time, it does not require explicit consideration of censoring. The BTSCS approach does not direct attention to the time between events or how covariates may affect that interval, focusing instead only on the event occurrence. While the BTSCS approach continues to see use, there are also flexible and easy-to-estimate duration models to which we turn.

---

[2] Splines are piecewise polynomials, with the pieces defined by the number of "knots," or locations in which the values of the two polynomials on either side are constrained to be equal. Temporal splines have the advantage of using many fewer degrees of freedom (one per knot) than indicator variables for each period, but the number and location of the knots is not an obvious decision. We do not take up splines further here. We also note that there are many other ways of addressing this degrees of freedom problem than just splines.

11.4 DURATION MODELS

The combination of spells and censoring motivate the duration model. But it often turns out that it is mathematically convenient to model spells in terms of the *hazard rate* rather than durations. In this section we survey the basic pieces of duration models: the density function over t, the *survivor function*, the *hazard function*, and the *cumulative* (or integrated) *hazard function*. All the pieces of event history analysis – the density, survivor function and hazard rate – are mathematically dependent. Defining one determines the rest.

The terms "survival," "hazard," "failure," and "risk" are artifacts of these models' development in the context of time-to-failure analysis in engineering and patient survival in the health sciences. While these terms lend the discussion something of a sinister air, we emphasize that they are purely technical terms and imply no normative judgment about whether being in a spell is good or bad. To be clear, a "failure" or "event" simply refers to the end of a spell or, equivalently, a transition from one state to another, e.g., from war to peace or life to death. Similarly, a unit is "at risk" for failure if it is still in a spell, i.e., it is at risk for a transition from one state to another.

11.4.1 Survivor and Hazard Functions

Suppose we have n observational units indexed by i. For each unit we observe either the complete length of its spell or the length of its spell until the observation period is truncated. More formally, an observed failure time $T_i = \min\{Y_i^*, C_i^*\}$, where Y_i^* is some latent failure time and C_i^* is a latent censoring time.

For brevity we suppress subscripts until discussing the likelihood. Let T be a random variable representing spell duration. It therefore takes values in $[0, \infty)$. We can represent the probability that $T = t$, i.e., that i's spell is of length t, by specifying a density function $f(t)$, with corresponding distribution function $F(t)$.

Definition 11.1 (Survivor and hazard functions). Let $F(t) = \Pr(Y_i^* \leq t)$. We define the *survivor function*, $S(t)$:

$$S(t) = 1 - F(t) = \Pr(T > t).$$

The survivor function describes the probability that i's spell will be at least of length t. The survivor function allows us to specify the *hazard function*, $h(t)$:[3]

$$h(t) = \frac{f(t)}{S(t)} = \frac{f(t)}{1 - F(t)}. \tag{11.1}$$

---

[3] Formally, the hazard function is defined as a limit: $h(t) = \lim_{\Delta t \to 0} \frac{\Pr(t \leq T < t + \Delta t \mid T \geq t)}{\Delta t}$, making it easier to see that the hazard function is a conditional distribution.

The hazard function describes the probability that a spell will end by t given that it has survived until t. The value of the hazard function at t is referred to as the *hazard rate*. Empirically, the hazard rate is simply the proportion of units still at risk for failure at t that fail between t and $t + 1$. We can sum the hazard rates in continuous time to express the "accumulation" of hazard. This function, $H(t)$, is called the cumulative or integrated hazard rate.

Theorem 11.1 (Integrated hazard rate).

$$H(t) \equiv \int_0^t h(x)dx = -\log S(t).$$

Proof We know that

$$
\begin{aligned}
f(t) &= \frac{d}{dt}F(t) = \frac{d}{dt}(1 - S(t)) \\
&= -\frac{d}{dt}S(t).
\end{aligned}
\tag{11.2}
$$

Substituting Equation 11.2 into 11.1 we obtain

$$h(t) = \frac{-\frac{d}{dt}S(t)}{S(t)}.$$

So,

$$
\begin{aligned}
\int_0^t h(x)dx &= \int_0^t \frac{-\frac{d}{dx}S(x)}{S(x)}dx \\
&= -(\log S(t) - \log S(0)) \\
&= -\log S(t),
\end{aligned}
$$

where the second line results from an application of the chain rule: $\frac{d}{dx}\log f(x) = \frac{f'(x)}{f(x)}$. $\qquad\square$

11.4.2 A Likelihood

The problem in constructing a likelihood for survival data is that we generally do not observe failure times for all units. Units for which our observation window ends before we observe failure are *right-censored*. Units that begin their risk exposure prior to the beginning of the observation period are called *left-censored*. The models discussed herein are capable of incorporating both left- and right-censoring but, for brevity, we focus on the far more common right-censored case. These observations contribute information on survival up to the censoring point; they do not contribute any information about failure. Thus, if we define a censoring indicator δ_i, which equals 1 if i is censored and 0 otherwise, the generic form of the likelihood is

$$\mathcal{L} = \prod_{i=1}^{n} f(t_i)^{1-\delta_i} S(t_i)^{\delta_i}. \qquad (11.3)$$

Different parametric duration models derive from different distributional assumptions for $f(t)$. The exponential, Weibull, log-logistic, and log-normal models are the most common. Each has different implications for the hazard rate and its relationship to time, i.e., "duration dependence." The exponential model is a special case of the Weibull and assumes a baseline hazard rate to be flat with respect to time. In this model the risk of an event is *time independent*. The Weibull distribution implies a model that fits a baseline hazard that is monotonic (increasing, decreasing, or unchanging) though time. Log-normal and log-logistic models allow for hazard rates to be unimodal, i.e., increasing and then decreasing in time. All these models can be estimated and evaluated with all the standard tools and procedures associated with MLE.

11.4.3 Writing Down a Duration Model

There are two main ways of expressing duration models: as "accelerated failure time" (AFT) and the proportional hazards specification. The former is more common in fields that use parametric event history models, whereas the latter is more common in the social sciences. The difference between the two is that AFT models link covariates to survival times, while hazard models link covariates to the hazard rate. But since specifying a hazard function also specifies a survival function, the two are very similar. Parameter estimates from an AFT model are simply -1 times the parameter estimates from a hazard rate specification.

Accelerated Failure Time (AFT)
In AFT, models covariates act multiplicatively on the failure time. Thus, AFT models focus on the rate at which an observation continues in the current state.
The model is given:

$$S(t|X) = \psi \left(\frac{\log(t) - \mathbf{x}_i^\mathsf{T} \boldsymbol{\beta}}{\sigma} \right),$$

where ψ can be any standard survival distribution and σ is a scaling parameter. This can be rewritten:

$$\log(T_i) = \mathbf{x}_i^\mathsf{T} \boldsymbol{\beta} + \sigma u_i$$
$$\Updownarrow$$
$$T_i = \exp(\mathbf{x}_i^\mathsf{T} \boldsymbol{\beta} + \sigma u_i),$$

which directly models the survival times, T_i. The only question is what distributional assumption to impose on u_i.[4] For example, if we assume that

---

[4] σ can be factored out if it is constant for each observation.

$u_i = \frac{1}{p}\epsilon_i$ and that ϵ_i is Type-I extreme value distributed, then we have the Weibull model. If we impose the constraint that $p = 1$, the exponential model results.

Proportional Hazards

The more common way of writing down duration models is in the hazard rate form. The exponential and Weibull models, as well as the Cox model described below, are often expressed in terms of hazard rates:

$$h_i(t) = h_0(t) \exp(\mathbf{x}_i^\mathsf{T} \boldsymbol{\beta}),\tag{11.4}$$

where $h_0(t)$ is the baseline hazard, possibly a function of time (but not covariates), and common to all units. The specification for h_0 determines the model. For example, if $h_0(t) = pt^{p-1}$, then we have the Weibull model; with $p = 1$ we again have the exponential.

In case you were wondering … 11.1 The Weibull distribution

Waloddi Weibull was a Swedish mathematician who described a two-parameter distribution now known as the Weibull distribution, even though Maurice Fréchet developed it much earlier. Fréchet published some of his papers in Esperanto.

We say $T \geq 0$ follows the Weibull distribution with parameters $\lambda > 0, p > 0$:

$$T \sim f_W(t; \lambda, p) = \begin{cases} \frac{p}{\lambda}\left(\frac{t}{\lambda}\right)^{p-1} \exp\left(-\left(\frac{t}{\lambda}\right)^p\right) & t \geq 0, \\ 0 & t < 0. \end{cases}$$

We refer to λ as the scale parameter and p the shape parameter. $E[T] = \lambda + \Gamma(1 + p^{-1})]$ and $\text{var}(T) = \lambda^2[\Gamma(1 + 2p^{-1}) - \Gamma(1 + p^{-1})^2]$. Note that when $p = 1$ the Weibull distribution reduces to the exponential distribution.

Given the Weibull density we can express the hazard and survivor functions as

$$h_W(t) = p\lambda^p t^{p-1},$$

$$S_W(t) = \exp(-(\lambda t)^p).$$

The distribution gives the time to failure in the sense that the failure rate is an exponential function of the length of time. Values of the shape parameter, p, bifurcate at 1; below that threshold the failure rate is decreasing, whereas above 1, it grows. Note that pt^{p-1} is the baseline hazard for a Weibull proportional hazards model.

The $\exp(\mathbf{x}_i^T \boldsymbol{\beta})$ expression represents unit-level differences that scale the baseline hazard up or down. In models that have the proportional hazards property, the intercept term is frequently omitted since it applies equally to all units and is therefore part of the baseline hazard rate. The multiplicative change in the hazard ratio – $\exp(\boldsymbol{\beta})$ – implies that $\boldsymbol{\beta}$ represents the change in the log hazard ratio. Positive coefficients imply increasing hazards (shorter survival times), whereas negative coefficients imply decreasing hazards (increasing survival times). In proportional hazards models it is often easier to interpret $\exp(\boldsymbol{\beta})$, since these are understandable in terms of proportional changes in the hazard ratio. For example, if $\exp(\hat{\beta}_1) = 1.4$, then a unit increase in x_1 increases the hazard rate by a factor of 1.4, or 40%.

From Equation 11.4 we can adduce an interpretation for the regression parameters $\boldsymbol{\beta}$ as well as demonstrate the *proportional hazards* property. To see both, suppose that we have only one covariate, x_1, and we want to compare the hazard rates for two different units, i and j, with covariate values of x_{i1} and x_{j1}, respectively.

$$\frac{h_i(t, x_1 = x_{i1})}{h_j(t, x_1 = x_{j1})} = \exp[(x_{i1} - x_{j1})\beta_1].$$

In comparing the hazard rates, the baseline hazard cancels out, which implies that the *hazard ratio* is fixed across time, a property referred to as proportional hazards. Put another way, proportional hazards implies a model where the "effect" of a covariate on the hazard rate is the same no matter when in a spell the covariate might change its value. The proportional hazards assumption is conceptually similar to the BTSCS assumption that the $\boldsymbol{\beta}$ are fixed through time and constant across observations. Note that the proportional hazards property is an *assumption* in several types of event history models, but it is one that can be tested.

11.5 THE COX MODEL

The preceding discussion begs the question of which among the many parametric models to use. Should the baseline hazard rate be decreasing, increasing, or fluctuating? Rarely is theory any guide. To the extent we fit models to test propositions, our ideas are generally about the relationship between covariates and the outcome. So the choice of baseline hazard is data-driven. We are then left with two starkly opposing solutions. The first, which we mention in passing, is to fit a variety of models and evaluate them on the basis of parsimony, predictive performance, or some other heuristic. The second is to refuse to specify the baseline hazard altogether, leaving the form of time dependence unspecified as a consequence. Pursuing this second option is the domain of the Cox proportional hazards model.

This Cox proportional hazard model can be expressed as

$$h_i(t) = h_0(t) \exp(\mathbf{x}_i^\mathsf{T} \boldsymbol{\beta}),$$

but while the parametric models assume a specific form for h_0, the Cox model leaves it unspecified. Since part of the model is left unspecified the Cox model is often referred to as "semi-parametric."

11.5.1 The Partial Likelihood

Without a baseline hazard, we cannot fully specify a likelihood function. But if we assume that the times between events contribute nothing to our understanding of the relationship between the covariates and the hazard rate, then we can use the ordered failure times to construct a *partial likelihood*, which has all the standard properties of a likelihood, and therefore can be maximized.

To derive the partial likelihood, assume for the moment that we have n observational units for which we observe n spells. Of these spells, u of them are uncensored, i.e., we observe the event. We can order the failure times as $t_1 < \ldots < t_u$. Note that these are all strict inequalities; we assume (for the moment) that there are no events occurring at the same moment. We then model the probability that an event happens to unit i at time t_j, conditional on there being an event at time t_j. The probability of an event happening to i, given that i has not yet failed, is simply the hazard rate for i. The probability of there being an event at t_j is simply the sum of all the hazards for all the units at risk for failure at t_j. If we denote R_j to be the risk set at time t_j, then the conditional probability can be expressed as

$$\frac{h_i(t_j)}{\sum_{l \in R_j} h_l(t_j)} = \frac{h_0(t_j) \exp(\mathbf{x}_i^\mathsf{T} \boldsymbol{\beta})}{\sum_{l \in R_j} h_0(t_j) \exp(\mathbf{x}_l^\mathsf{T} \boldsymbol{\beta})}$$

$$= \frac{\exp(\mathbf{x}_i^\mathsf{T} \boldsymbol{\beta})}{\sum_{l \in R_j} \exp(\mathbf{x}_l^\mathsf{T} \boldsymbol{\beta})}.$$

Thus the partial likelihood for the Cox model is given by

$$\mathcal{L}_P = \prod_{i=1}^{n} \left[\frac{\exp(\mathbf{x}_i^\mathsf{T} \boldsymbol{\beta})}{\sum_{l \in R_j} \exp(\mathbf{x}_l^\mathsf{T} \boldsymbol{\beta})} \right]^{1-\delta_i},$$

where, again, $\delta_j = 1$ if the case is right-censored. Comparing this expression to equation 11.3, there is an important difference: in the Cox partial likelihood the censored cases contribute information about the cases at risk for an event, but they contribute nothing to the estimation of failure times. This partial likelihood can be maximized with numerical techniques.

Tied Events

The derivation of the Cox model assumed that no two units failed in the same time interval. Indeed, if we were really observing events in continuous time, then the chances of two events actually occurring at the same instant are vanishingly small. However, data are aggregated in time slices (seconds, weeks, years). In practice ties occur regularly.

One of the great strengths of the Cox model is its flexibility in handling tied events. Several different methods have emerged to adjust the partial likelihood to accommodate ties. They go by the names *Breslow*, *Efron*, *averaged* or *exact partial*, and *exact discrete* or *exact marginal*. The Breslow method is the default method for most statistical packages *but not in* $\mathcal{R}$. It is generally held to be the least accurate, with this problem becoming more severe the more ties there are. The Efron method tends to work better (and is the default in $\mathcal{R}$). The two "exact" methods are the most precise, but can impose severe computational burdens if there are a lot of ties.

Residuals from Cox (and Other) Models

The concept of the empirical model residual becomes more complicated outside of the simple regression context. In event history models, it is even more complex because we have censored observations and, in the case of the Cox model, a semi-parametric model. It turns out that there are three different types of "residuals" that each have different uses. We outline their uses here, omitting technical discussions of their origins and properties:

Cox-Snell
: Cox-Snell residuals are used to examine overall model fit. They should be distributed as unit exponential. Residual plots allow us to visually examine whether this is (approximately) true for a particular model.

Schoenfeld
: Schoenfeld residuals are used for evaluating the proportional hazards property. Box-Steffensmeier and Jones (2004) note that Schoenfeld residuals can "essentially be thought of as the observed minus the expected values of the *covariates* at each failure time." (2004:121, emphasis added)

Martingale
: Martingale residuals are the most intuitive to think about but perhaps the most mathematically complex. They are given by the observed censoring indicator minus the expected number of events, as given by the integrated hazard rate. Martingale residuals are $\widehat{M}_i = \delta_i - \hat{H}_0(t_i) \exp\left(\mathbf{x}_i^{\mathsf{T}} \hat{\boldsymbol{\beta}}\right)$, where δ_i is an indicator of the event for observation i, and $\hat{H}_0(t_i)$ is the estimated cumulative hazard at the final time for observation i. Martingale residuals are plotted against included (or possibly excluded) covariates to evaluate whether they are included appropriately.

Deviance   Deviance residuals are Martingale residuals rescaled so as to be symmetric about 0 if the model is "correct."

Score   Score residuals are useful for identifying high-leverage observations.

11.5.2 An Example: Cabinet Durations

We illustrate some elements of event history analysis in $\mathcal{R}$ using the cabinet duration data from King et al. (1990). To begin, we load the `survival` library. In `survival` there are three basic steps to fitting a model:

1. Set up the data appropriately (spell-level or counting process).
2. Create a survival object using `Surv()`.
3. Fit the model as normal using the survival object as the response variable.

The King et al. (1990) data are organized at the spell level, containing 314 government cabinets in parliamentary democracies. The outcome variable is the duration of the government in months; covariates include a slate of variables capturing various aspects of the party system and political climate. Typical results are displayed in Table 11.3. Note the reporting of both $\hat{\beta}$ and $\exp(\hat{\beta})$.

What about the proportional hazards assumption? Figure 11.2 plots the Schoenfeld residuals against time; if the proportional hazards assumption holds, the slope of this relationship should be 0. There is no compelling visual evidence that the assumption is violated here.

These plots of residuals are helpful but largely subjective. A more formal test of the relationship between the residuals and time is available and presented

TABLE 11.3 *Cox model of government cabinet duration.*

	$\hat{\beta}$	$\exp(\hat{\beta})$	$\sigma_{\hat{\beta}}$
Majority Government	−0.49	0.62	0.13
Investiture	0.56	1.74	0.14
Volatility	−0.00	1.00	0.00
Polarization	0.03	1.03	0.01
Fractionalization	0.00	1.00	0.00
Crisis	−0.01	0.99	0.00
Formation Attempts	0.11	1.12	0.05
Opposition Party	−0.06	0.94	0.42
n	314		
$\log \mathcal{L}$	−1,293		
AIC	2,601		
BIC	2,630		

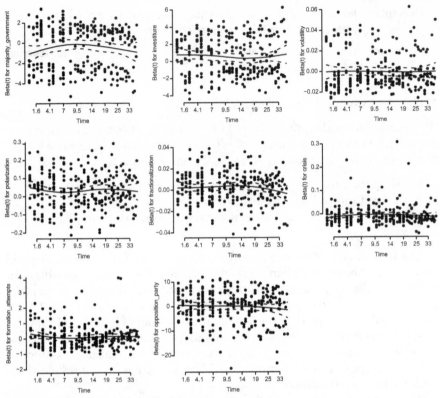

FIGURE 11.2 Schoenfeld residuals against adjusted time.

in Table 11.4. In none of the variables are we able to reject the null of no relationship. There is no reason to believe the proportional hazards assumption is violated here.

Interpreting Results

A quick glance at the (exponentiated) coefficients in the BUTON implies that, for example, requiring a vote of investiture increases the hazard of coalition termination by about 74%. Coalitions controlling a legislative majority have about a 38% longer survival time than those in the minority, all else constant. But, as usual, the nonlinear form of the model makes it difficult to envision what we mean by "all else constant." If we want to interpret the model on something like the scale of the dependent variable, more work is needed. We can construct meaningful scenarios and then generate model predictions on an interpretable scale.

TABLE 11.4 *Formal tests of the correlation of residuals with time.*

	ρ	χ^2	p-Value
Majority Government	0.00	0.01	0.94
Investiture	−0.05	0.52	0.47
Volatility	−0.01	0.05	0.81
Polarization	−0.01	0.01	0.89
Fractionalization	−0.06	0.86	0.35
Crisis	0.01	0.07	0.79
Formation Attempts	−0.03	0.26	0.61
Opposition Party	−0.06	1.23	0.26
GLOBAL	NA	2.93	0.93

Hazard rates are often difficult to understand or convey to audiences for two reasons: they are conditional, and the sign of estimated coefficients in a proportional hazards model is the opposite of its implications for survival. Presenting results on the survival scale is often easier to comprehend. Figure 11.3 displays the expected survival times for governments depending on whether the cabinet requires a vote of investiture. We see that only about 35% of governments requiring investiture are expected to survive for at least twenty months; the rate is about 55% for those not needing such a vote. Put another way, we expect about half of governments requiring an investiture vote to have fallen at around 15 months, compared to about 22 months for those not requiring a vote. This particular plot leaves off estimates of uncertainty around these predictions, but our standard simulation techniques are capable of generating them.

Code Example 11.1 produces the Cox analysis and graphics.

11.5.3 Pros and Cons of the Cox Model

The Cox model has much to recommend it. It avoids explicit modeling of duration dependence. It is flexible in its ability to handle ties, repeated events, and other complications. It has a relatively straightforward proportional hazards interpretation. Unless you care about the duration dependence directly, then Cox is often the model of choice.

The Cox model also has disadvantages. It avoids any need to model duration dependence and relies only on the ordering information, ignoring the duration between events. One month is the same as 50 months. The Cox model also has a tendency to overfit the data, since the baseline hazard is completely determined by the proportion of observations surviving in a period. That is, it is highly tuned to the data at hand. As a result, those focusing on out-of-sample prediction and extrapolation (e.g., engineers) often use parametric

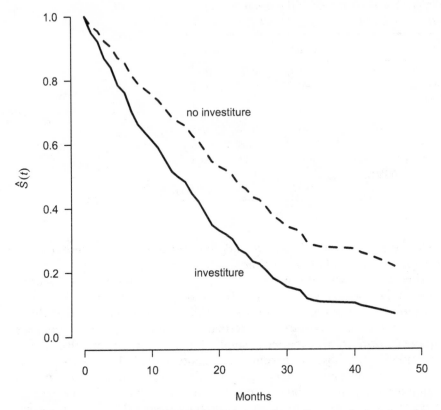

FIGURE 11.3 Expected government survival times depending on whether the cabinet requires a vote of investiture, with all over covariates held at central tendencies.

models. Extracting interpretation on the level of the dependent variable, often a good thing to do, can be quite difficult in more-complicated Cox models with stratified variables, competing risks, or "frailty" terms.[5] Finally, like most duration models it treats all observations as being determined by the same forces. New Zealand and the Ukraine would be subject to the same influences in terms of a model of civil conflict. It would seem that the baseline level of risk in the former is much less than in the latter. We now turn to a way to model this.

---

[5] Stratification in a Cox model estimates a separate baseline hazard rates for different values of the stratified variable. Competing risks models are those that model multiple types of transitions at once. "Frailty" models are a form of random coefficient or "random effects" Cox model in which observational units are heterogeneous in the propensity to survive.

R Code Example 11.1 *Fitting and interpreting Cox PH models*

```
library(survival)
library(foreign)
sdat <- read.dta("coalum2.dta")
cox.fit <- coxph(Surv(time=duration, event=censor12) ~ majority_government +
            investiture + volatility + polarization + fractionalization +
            crisis + formation_attempts + opposition_party, data=sdat)
cox.zph(cox.fit) #testing the proportional hazards assumption
deets <- coxph.detail(cox.fit)
times <- c(0,deets$time)  #observed failure times
h0 <- c(0,deets$hazard) #hazard evaluated a sample mean of covariates
x0 <- c(0)-cox.fit$mean
h0 <- h0*exp(t(coef(cox.fit))%*%x0) #baseline hazard
x.inv <- c(1,1,median(sdat$volatility), #investiture scenario
    mean(sdat$polarization),
    mean(sdat$fractionalization), mean(sdat$crisis),
    median(sdat$formation_attempts),mean(sdat$opposition_party))
x.ninv <- x.inv
x.ninv[2] <- 0  #no investiture scenario
h.inv <- h0*exp(t(coef(cox.fit))%*%x.inv)
h.ninv <- h0*exp(t(coef(cox.fit))%*%x.ninv)
Sinv <- exp(-cumsum(h.inv))   # survival function
Sninv <- exp(-cumsum(h.ninv)) # survival function
plot(times,Sinv, type="l", xlab="Months", lwd=2,
    ylab=expression(hat(S)(t)), bty="n", las=1,
    ylim=c(0,1), xlim=c(0,50))
lines(times,Sninv, lwd=2, lty=2)
text(x=20, y=c(0.2, 0.7), labels=c("investiture", "no investiture"))
```

11.6 A SPLIT-POPULATION MODEL

Suppose you are interested in modeling how long leaders stay in power, and whether the transition from one leader to the next is by regular, constitutional means, or by some irregular process, such as a coup d'état, revolution, or succession crisis. Consider the irregular transfer of power to be the event of interest. To model the timing until the onset of a problem event, we use a split-population duration approach. Initially developed in a health sciences context to examine the survival of medical patients under the assumption that some are "cured" and others remain at risk, split-population models assume a heterogeneous group of subjects. We can use them here to model the survival of polities, given some risk of irregular leader transition, war, or a similar type of failure event. This approach involves mixing different distributions, something we discussed in the context of the zero-inflated Poisson model (see Section 10.5.3).

The hypothesis that not every polity is at risk of irregular regime change motivates the split-population approach. For all practical purposes, countries like Germany, Canada, or Japan are highly unlikely to experience irregular transitions within the time period we consider here. However, many countries in

Africa and the Middle East experienced irregular transitions in the past decade. The important point from a modeling perspective is identifying countries, or in this case country-months, which are "at risk" of failure. From a policy perspective these are the places where estimating an expected duration until the next event makes sense.

Figure 11.4 illustrates the intuition behind this approach. As shown in the left panel, there are two types of polities. First are those that may have had an event but essentially are immune from further events (Country B). These include countries that never had any events but are not shown in this illustration. The second type of polity is at risk for future events (Country A). The split-population approach models first the separation of locations into type A or B, denoted by the *if* in the panel. The next part of the model determines the duration of time until the next event, denoted by *when*. The right panel illustrates the differences in base hazard rates under the assumption that all locations have the same risk profile (the standard Weibull) compared to the baseline risk that assumes the population of locations consists of two types: those at risk and those immune from risk.

The basic likelihood of this kind of situation may be thought of as a mixture of two distributions: a Bernoulli distribution determining whether a unit is at risk and then a second distribution describing duration. We define the variable $\pi_i(t)$ to be an indicator variable equal to one if t_i is part of a spell that ultimately ends in an observed event of interest and 0 otherwise. We can build the model as

$$T_i = \min\{Y_i^*, C_i^*\},$$
$$\pi_i \sim f_B(\theta_i),$$
$$\theta = \text{logit}^{-1}(z_i^\mathsf{T} \gamma),$$
$$T_i \sim f(t_i; \lambda),$$
$$\lambda = \exp(-\mathbf{x}_i^\mathsf{T} \boldsymbol{\beta}),$$
$$S(t_i|\mathbf{x}, \mathbf{z}) = \theta_i S(t) + (1 - \theta_i).$$

Building on Equation 11.3, we can derive the likelihood as a product of the risk and duration:

$$\mathcal{L} = \prod_{i=1}^{n} \left[\theta_i f(t_i)\right]^{1-\delta_i} \times \left[(1 - \theta_i)S(t_i)\right]^{\delta_i},$$

where $f(t_i)$ is the failure rate at time t_i, $S(t_i)$ is the survival function, and δ_i is the indicator of right-censoring. The split-population model is set up for two populations, one of them at risk for an event, the other "immune."

This likelihood function reflects a mixture of two equations: a first step classifying risk and immunity, and a second step describing expected duration in a spell. One advantage of this modeling approach is that it allows covariates to have both a long-term and a short-term impact, depending on whether they' appear in the $\mathbf{z}$ or the $\mathbf{x}$ vector. Variables that enter the at-risk equation

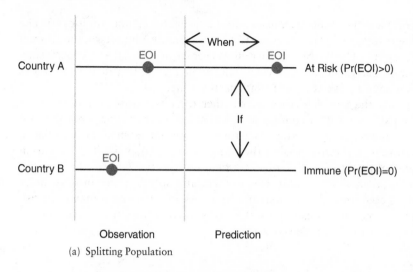

(a) Splitting Population

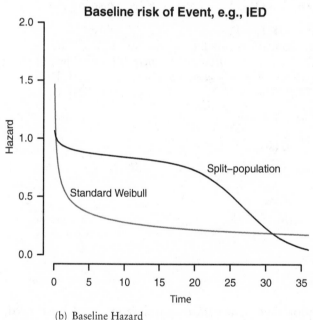

(b) Baseline Hazard

FIGURE 11.4 Country A is at risk; Country B is not at risk. Mixing these two yields a risk assessment that is too low while overestimating the risk decline. EOI refers to the Event Of Interest.

have a long-term impact because they change the probability of being at risk at all. Variables in the second duration equation can be thought of as having a short-term impact that modifies the expected duration until the next failure.

To complete the model we must choose a distribution function for $f(t)$. The $\mathcal{R}$ package spduration (Beger et al., 2017) currently admits two: the Weibull and log-logistic. The Weibull density allows for hazard rates that are increasing, constant, or decreasing over survival time, while the log-logistic density can fit rates that have a peak at a particular survival time.

Note that the model focuses on whether the observational unit at time t is in the risk set – e.g., a country at a particular point in time – not the unit *per se*. As the covariates change over time, so can our estimate of whether an observation is in the risk pool at that point in time. So, while it is helpful on a conceptual level to speak of observational units as being at risk or immune, in a technical sense we should refer to them at a specific point in time. In an analysis of countries, Canada may not be at risk in 2014, but it may be at risk in 2015 if some unanticipated disaster leads to conditions that we associated with country-months in the risk pool.

In case you were wondering ... 11.2 The Log-logistic distribution

Let $X \sim f_L(x; \mu, \sigma)$. If $T = \exp(X)$, we say T follows the *log-logistic* distribution, sometimes called the *Fisk* distribution. The log-logistic distribution has several different parameterizations. The one implemented in spduration uses scale parameter $\lambda > 0$ and shape paramter $p > 0$:

$$T \sim f_{lL}(t; \lambda, p) = \begin{cases} \frac{p\lambda(\lambda t)^{p-1}}{(1+(\lambda t)^p)^2} & t \geq 0, \\ 0 & t < 0. \end{cases}$$

Given the log-logistic density we can express the hazard and survivor functions as

$$h_{lL}(t) = \frac{p\lambda(\lambda t)^{p-1}}{1 + (\lambda t)^p},$$

$$S_{lL}(t) = \frac{1}{1 + (\lambda t)^p}.$$

To use the observation-time data with a split-duration model, we need, among other variables, a counter for each spell that indicates the number of months since the start time or previous failure time. This introduces an issue when we do not observe the previous failure time, i.e. left-censoring. For example, in a study of irregular regime changes, if we were to start all counters in 2001, the United Sates in 2004 would have the same counter value as Serbia, which had an irregular exit in October 2000 (Slobodan Milosevic). To mitigate this problem, we use a much earlier date as the start date for building the duration-related variables, if at all possible.

Survival data consist of two types of spells, those which end in an event of interest and those that are right-censored. The key assumption with the split-population approach involves the coding of spells or country-months as susceptible ($\pi_{it} = 1$). The split-duration approach "retroactively" codes $\pi_{it} = 1$ if period t is part of a spell that ended in an observed event in unit i. Spells that are right-censored take on $\pi_{it} = 0$, as do spells that end when an observation leaves the data set with no event taking place in the last spell (e.g., an observation ceases to exist). Treating right-censored spells as "cured" can be problematic, since they may later, after we observe more data, end in failure. The probabilistic model for π_i partially mitigates this by both incorporating the length of a censored spell and sharing information across cases known to be at risk as well as those coded as cured.

11.6.1 Interpretation of Split-Duration Estimates

Once estimated, there are several different quantities we can calculate from a split-population duration model. We focus on the *conditional hazard rate*, which describes the probability that a country will experience failure during a given time period, given that it has already survived without failure to that point, and considering that some countries will never experience failure. In fewer words, it is the split-duration model's best guess of a particular unit's failure during the time period in which we are interested. To fully understand this, we can break the conditional hazard rate for a country at a time t down into two components: the unconditional hazard rate and the probability that it is at risk of failure at all.

The *unconditional hazard rate* is the probability that an observation will experience a failure in a given time frame (say a month), given that it has survived without failure up until that month. We can estimate it based on historical data on previous events in other observations and previous events in the same observation. Thus the unconditional hazard rate for a particular month gives the probability of an event, given that it will have been some number of months at that point since the previous event occurred in that observation.

There are three things to note about the hazard rate. First, it is specific to a given observation and a given time since the last event. The hazard rate for events in one observation is likely to be different from the hazard rate our model estimates for another. Similarly, the hazard rate for six months from the last event will probably be different from the hazard rate at twelve months from the last event. Second, these changes in the hazard rate over time can follow specific shapes. They can be flat, meaning that the hazard of an event does not change over time. This is the case, for example, for the decay of radioactive elements. But the hazard rate for events could also have a bump in the beginning, indicating that these are more likely a short time after the last event, but less likely over time. In any case, a variety of shapes are possible. The third thing to note is that this unconditional hazard rate assumes that all observations are subject to experiencing the events. That hardly seems sustainable, since we know that some observations are immune to the particular risk under study. To that end, a split-population duration model also tries to group observations that are at risk separately from those that are effectively "cured."

The *risk probability* is an estimate that a given observation at a specific time falls into either the susceptible group ($\pi = 1$) or the cured group ($\pi = 0$). It is an estimate *at a given time* because it also depends on how much time has passed since the last event. To calculate the conditional hazard, we combine our estimated hazard rate with the estimated probability that a country at a given time is susceptible to an event. In other words, *conditional hazard = unconditional hazard × risk probability*. More formally, given the density distribution and estimated parameters we are interested in, the conditional hazard $h(t,\theta)$, where both the at-risk probabilities and hazard are conditional on survival to time t:

$$\theta(t) = \frac{1-\theta}{S(t) + (1-\theta)(1-S(t))}, \tag{11.5}$$

$$h(t,\theta) = \frac{f(t,\theta)}{S(t,\theta)} = \frac{\theta(t)f(t)}{(1-\theta(t)) + \theta(t)S(t)}. \tag{11.6}$$

Equation 11.6 shows that the conditional risk rate is decreasing over event time because, as time passes, the surviving cases increasingly consist of the immune $(1-\theta)$ that will never fail. In Equation 11.6 for the conditional hazard, the failure rate in the numerator is conditional on the probability that a case is in the risk set, given survival up to time t. The denominator is an adjusted survivor function that accounts for the fraction of cured cases by time t: $(1-\theta(t))$.

We estimate the probability of an event in (say) February 2014 to be the unconditional probability of that event when it has been so many (say, 23) months since the last event times the probability that the observation is in the "at risk" group given its characteristics and given that it has been 23 months since the last event. In this way we can get a probability estimate for an event that takes into account the changing hazard of events over time but which also corrects for the fact that some observations will never experience an event.

The coefficient estimates from a split-population model can be interpreted similar to how we viewed ZIP coefficients. The coefficients in the risk equation are logistic regression parameters that indicate whether a change in a variable increases or decreases the probability that a country-month is in the set of susceptible unites; exponentiated coefficients indicate the factor change in risk probability associated with a one-unit change in the associated variable. The duration part of the model is in AFT format, and for interpreting them it is convenient to think of the dependent variable as being survival time, or, equivalently, time to failure. A negative coefficient shortens survival and thus hastens failure (higher probability of an event at time t), while a positive coefficient prolongs survival and thus delays failure (lower probability of an event at time t).

11.6.2 An Example

In order to illustrate practical implementation of a split-population model, we adapt the Beger et al. (2017) reexamination of Belkin and Schofer (2003). Belkin and Schofer model coups d'état. They explicitly distinguish long-term structural risk factors for coups from short-term triggering causes that can explain the timing of a coup in an at-risk regime. The data we analyze include 213 coups. As examples, we fit a conventional Weibull model and Weibull and log-logistic split-population duration models, including Belkin and Schofer's index of structural coup risk in the risk equation. Table 11.5 is the requisite BUTON reporting coefficients from the duration equation and then estimates from the risk equation.[6] The duration models are in accelerated failure time format, and the coefficient estimates are on the log of expected time to failure. The negative coefficient for military regimes, for example, means that the expected time to a coup is shorter in military regimes than nonmilitary regimes, holding all other factors constant. In the risk equation, positive coefficients mean a higher risk of coup. Thus, military regimes have a higher risk of experiencing a coup. Looking at the AIC and BIC, we see that the split-population model outperforms the Weibull AFT model. The split-population models are indistinguishable, so we will continue to focus on the log-logistic form.

A plot of the conditional hazard is the probability of a coup at a time t, conditional on the covariates in the risk and duration equations and survival up to time t. We fix covariates at their sample means. These are shown in Figures 11.5 and 11.6. Figure 11.6 compares the conditional hazard with covariates held at mean values (panel A) and when covariates are set to a high-risk, military-regime values (panel B). The conditional hazard is much higher and steeper in B than in A, reflecting the increased risk of coup.

Code for estimating these models appears as Code Example 11.2.

Out-of-Sample Testing

One of the strengths of a parametric model is its ability to generate out-of-sample forecasts. In this case we use data from 1996 onwards as the test set, and prior data for training purposes. For the training data, we need to subset the training set first, so that coups in the test set do not influence the risk coding in the training data. For the test set, we add the duration variables and *then* subset the test set. Since the test set is later in time than the training set, there is no contamination of the risk coding, but if we subset the data before building the duration variables, we will start all duration counters at 1996, when in fact we can safely use the previous historic coup information.

---

[6] The AFT parameterization of the Weibull model does not report an intercept.

TABLE 11.5 *Weibull and split-population Weibull and log-logistic regression models of coups, 1960–2000.*

		Split Population	
Duration Model	Weibull	Weibull	log-Logistic
Intercept		3.22	2.40
		(0.17)	(0.21)
Instablity	−0.06	−0.09	−0.09
	(0.01)	(0.01)	(0.02)
Military regime	−2.33	−1.55	−1.13
	(0.17)	(0.19)	(0.21)
Regional conflict	6.03	5.08	−2.52
	(2.44)	(2.72)	(2.16)
$\log p$	−0.15	0.03	−0.45
	(0.05)	(0.05)	(0.06)
Risk Model			
Intercept		−0.44	2.93
		(3.89)	(1.87)
Risk index		1.65	0.59
		(0.83)	(0.32)
log GDPpc		0.35	−0.36
		(0.68)	(0.28)
Military regime		11.57	10.82
		(3.92)	(9.29)
Recent war		−2.19	−0.53
		(1.97)	(0.94)
Regional conflict		−5.30	−5.43
		(12.49)	(5.62)
South America		−0.55	2.10
		(2.18)	(1.45)
Central America		−1.02	−0.39
		(1.41)	(0.73)
n	4,250	4,250	4,250
Num. events	213	213	213
$\log \mathcal{L}$	−704	−662	−662
AIC	1,417	1,330	1,331
BIC	1,442	1,349	1,350

The default prediction in spdur is the conditional hazard, which can be thought of as a predicted probability. As a result, we can use the same tools for visualizing the performance of survival models that we used for other forms of binary classifiers, including the separation plot. Figure 11.7 displays the out-of-sample performance of both the Weibull and log-logistic models.

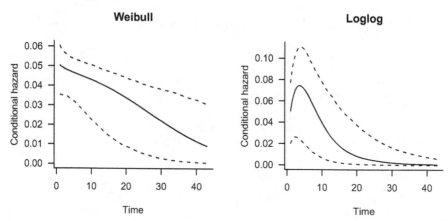

FIGURE 11.5 Conditional hazard rates for the split-population Weibull and log-logistic model of coups with all covariates held at sample means.

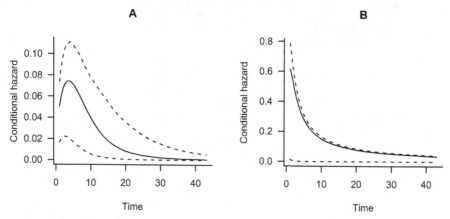

FIGURE 11.6 Plots of the hazard rate for the log-logistic model of coups. The left graph uses the default mean values for covariates, while graph B uses user-specified variable values for a high-risk military regime.

Code for conducting the out-of-sample forecasting exercise appears in Code Example 11.3.

11.7 CONCLUSION

This chapter introduced a framework for using likelihood principles when there is temporal dependence between observations. But rather than focusing on the serial approach that emphasizes repeated measurements over time, we focused on duration models that explicitly model time itself. We have developed the likelihoods and illustrated how they may be modified to address a variety of

R Code Example 11.2 *Split-population duration models*

```
data(bscoup)  #in spdur library.
bscoup$coup <- ifelse(bscoup$coup=="yes", 1, 0)
bscoup <- add_duration(bscoup, "coup", unitID="countryid",
   tID="year", freq="year", ongoing = FALSE) #formatting for duration model
weib_model <- spdur(
   duration ~ milreg + instab + regconf,
   atrisk ~ couprisk + wealth + milreg + rwar + regconf +
   samerica + camerica, data = bscoup, silent = TRUE)

loglog_model <- spdur(
   duration ~ milreg + instab + regconf,
   atrisk ~ couprisk + wealth + milreg + rwar + regconf +
   samerica + camerica, data = bscoup,
   distr = "loglog", silent = TRUE)

weib_aft <- aftreg(Surv(time=t.0, time2=duration, event=coup) ~
   milreg + instab + regconf, dist="weibull", param = "lifeExp",
   data=bscoup[rownames(bscoup)%in%rownames(weib_model$mf.dur),])
plot_hazard(weib_model, main = "A",bty="n",las=1)
plot_hazard(loglog_model, main = "A",bty="n",las=1)
plot_hazard(loglog_model,
            xvals = c(1, 1, 10, 0.05),
            zvals = c(1, 7, 8.64, 1, 1, 0.05, 0, 0),
            main = "B",bty="n",las=1)
```

Weibull

Loglog

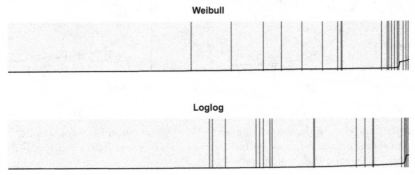

FIGURE 11.7 Out-of-sample separation plots.

questions – including population heterogeneity in the form of split-population models. In evaluating these models, we showed how hazard rates can be viewed as predicted probabilities, bringing us full circle from BTSCS to spells and back to binary data.

This chapter is far from a complete or canonical treatment of duration models. By focusing on intuition around temporal dependence and connect to likelihood principles and tools – including split populations and forecasting – we ignored other complications. One of these is left- and interval-censoring. Left-censoring means that an event happened prior to the beginning of data collection, but it is not known exactly when. Interval-censoring is most often

R Code Example **11.3** *Evaluating duration models out-of-sample*

```
coup_train <- bscoup[bscoup$year < 1996, ]   #training set
coup_train <- add_duration(coup_train, "coup", unitID = "countryid",
    tID = "year", freq = "year", ongoing = FALSE) #formatting for spdur
coup_test <- add_duration(bscoup, "coup", unitID = "countryid", tID = "year",
                          freq = "year", ongoing = FALSE)
coup_test  <- coup_test[coup_test$year >= 1996, ]
weib_model2   <- spdur(
    duration ~ milreg + instab + regconf,
    atrisk ~ couprisk + wealth + milreg + rwar + regconf + samerica +
      camerica,
    data = coup_train, silent = TRUE)

loglog_model2 <- spdur(
    duration ~ milreg + instab + regconf,
    atrisk ~ couprisk + wealth + milreg + rwar + regconf + samerica +
      camerica,
    data = coup_train, distr = "loglog", silent = TRUE)

weib2_test_p   <- predict(weib_model2, newdata = coup_test)
loglog2_test_p <- predict(loglog_model2, newdata = coup_test)
obs_y <- coup_test[complete.cases(coup_test), "coup"]
library("separationplot")
par(mfrow=c(2,1),mar=c(2,2,2,2))
separationplot(weib2_test_p,   obs_y, newplot = FALSE)
separationplot(loglog2_test_p, obs_y, newplot = FALSE)%\vspace*{-24pt}
```

ignored because it occurs so frequently in social sciences: an event occurred but exactly when in the interval is not recorded. Most country-year data are interval-censored. The basic issue is that the models assume that censoring is not endogenous, i.e., that it is not caused by the impending event.

We have also surveyed only a fraction of many distributional assumptions that can be made in duration analysis. Many others are used, including the log-normal, extreme value distributions as well as piecewise functions. Random effects or "frailty" are another way to approach heterogeneity, allowing individual parameters to vary by observation, in a way similar to random effects in other models. These are useful when there are recurrent events or when there are strata or clusters of observations that may be affected by similar factors.

11.8 FURTHER READING

Applications

Jones and Branton (2005) compare the BTSCS approach to the Cox model in the study of policy adoption across US states. Thrower (2017) uses the Cox model to investigate the duration of executive orders from the US president. Wolford (2017) also uses the Cox model to decribe the duration of peace among a coalition of victors in interstate wars.

248

Strategies for Temporal Dependence

Past Work

Freedman (2008) provides a critical primer to survival analysis from the perspective of medical research and experimentation. Box-Steffensmeier and DeBoef (2006); Box-Steffensmeier and Zorn (2001, 2002); and Box-Steffensmeier et al. (2003) introduce several of the more-complicated versions of the Cox model to political science audiences. Beck and Katz (2011) provide a broad reviews of the state of the art in the analysis of panel time series data.

Advanced Study

Therneau and Grambsch (2000) is an excellent resource for survival models. Kalbfleisch and Prentice (2002) present a detailed treatment as well. Box-Steffensmeier and Jones (2004) develop a political science-focused presentation of event history models. Park and Hendry (2015) argue for a revised practice in the evaluation of proportional hazards in the Cox model.

Time series analysis, much of which relies on the likelihood approach, is an area of vast research, with many texts available. The canonical text for analyzing time series and panel data remains Wooldridge (2010). Several recent contributions include Box-Steffensmeier et al. (2015); Brandt and Williams (2007); and Prado et al. (2017).

For an accessible introduction to spatial dependence in the context of regression models, see Ward and Gleditsch (2018). Beck et al. (2006) and Franzese and Hayes (2007) further discuss the interplay of spatial and temporal dependence.

Software Notes

Therneau and Grambsch (2000) underpins the survival library in $\mathcal{R}$. The eha package (Broström, 2012, 2017) provides other parameterizations of common survival models, including parametric models capable of handling time-varying covariates. flexsurv (Jackson, 2016) and rms (Harrell, Jr., 2017) are other alternatives that build on survival. The spduration library (Beger et al., 2017) implements the split-population survival model used in this chapter. See also smcure (Cai et al., 2012).

12

Strategies for Missing Data

12.1 INTRODUCTION

Missingness in data is like tooth decay. Everyone has it. It is easy to ignore. It causes serious problems. Plus, virtually no one likes to go to the dentist, which itself is painful and costly. While ignoring missing data is still widespread, developments in recent decades have made it easier to address the issue in a principled fashion. This chapter will review the problems of missing data and survey some techniques for dealing with it, focusing on one technique that can be inserted at the point of need: in the likelihood function.

Statistical modeling that ignores missingness in the data can result in biased estimates and standard errors that are wildly deflated or inflated (King et al., 2001; Molenberghs et al., 2014; Rubin, 1976). Yet many applied researchers still ignore this problem, even if it is well established (Lall, 2016). Principled approaches to missing data were first introduced in the 1970s, and now there are a variety of tools available. The general idea across all of them is to use some algorithm to fill in the missing data with estimates of what real data would look like were it available. Because these imputed values are uncertain, we want to do this many times and incorporate this uncertainty in our analysis. This means creating multiple "complete" data sets, which are then analyzed separately and combined to obtain final estimates of quantities of interest, accounting for the uncertainty due to the missing data (Rubin, 1996, 2004).

Data we collect from the real world, whether from the most carefully designed experiment or from the underfunded statistical agency of a poor country will, with near certainty, have some values that are missing. Missingness can arise due to individuals deciding not to answer certain questions or dropping out of a study altogether, human error, and data getting lost in the shuffle of paper and computer files. Or data can be systematically not reported. It may be that data are missing because they are collected asynchronously so that, for example, some data for a particular observation may be available at the beginning of a year but other data not available until the end. Some repository databases, such as those curated by the World Bank, may rely on collection mechanisms – such as national reporting agencies – that vary in their schedules. This can lead some data to be unavailable for various intervals of time. Another potential cause of missing data is that some reporting agencies may choose to delay the reporting of statistics if the data are perceived to be politically damaging. Additionally, natural disasters such as earthquakes and tsunamis disrupt data collection. Similarly, civil and international wars may cause some data to go unreported, either because the data were never generated or the institutions that gather and curate societal data were unavailable during the conflict.

Consider the example of Nigeria. During Nigeria's colonial period there was a national census in the early 1950s, yielding an estimate of about 32 million inhabitants. After independence, the national census became politicized and several attempted censuses were undertaken during the 1960s, yielding estimates between 50 and 60 million. After the Nigerian civil war ended in 1970, there were attempts to hold a census, but they were never completed because of the political controversy over which ethnic groups would be counted in which areas. It wasn't until the 1990s that Nigeria was able to conduct a census, and currently the population is estimated to be around 175 million. In many databases, Nigerian population was recorded as missing for the 1970s and 1980s. Obviously the Nigerian population didn't go missing, but as a result Nigeria was not included in many scholarly studies.

Missingness can take many forms and result from different events and circumstances. Each can lead to different patterns of missingness with different implications for analysis. But it is evident that social science data are rarely missing at random. Thus, we can often assume that the data are missing for reasons that we could, in principle, know or describe.

12.1.1 Concepts and Notation

To be concrete, *missingness* refers to observations or measurement that, in principle, could have been carried out but, for whatever reason, failed to occur; it is a gap in our data matrix. This is to be distinguished from a concept that has not yet been measured. While such data are certainly missing, they do not normally fall under the purview of the methods outlined in this chapter.

Missing data should also be distinguished from cells in data matrices that are ill-defined or nonsensical but that might be included in our data matrix for computational or other reasons. For example, we may have time-series cross-sectional data for a set of countries spanning 1960–2010. We wish for the data matrix to be balanced (having the same number of rows for each country) even though the data matrix contains countries that did not exist during certain parts of that time interval. It makes no sense to talk about the number or political parties in the Bangladeshi parliament in 1963; Bangladesh was not a nation-state until 1971. Thus rows in a data matrix for 1960–70 Bangladesh should not be considered missing; they are ill-defined. The missing data methods described in this chapter should not be applied to such situations.

The statistical methods examined in this book are for the most part designed with "rectangular" data in mind. We have a response vector (or matrix) y and covariate matrix X, where the rows represent observational units and the columns are the dimensions on which we have measured each unit. But if some of the entries in this matrix are missing, problems almost always arise. Missingness, if not addressed, can prevent us from fully utilizing all the data that people have gone to considerable expense to gather; it can limit the generalizability of what we learn from our analysis, but, perhaps more seriously, it can distort our results and mislead.

We will keep with the notation we have been using thus far, with some modifications. y continues to represent the response vector of length n, while X is the $n \times k$ matrix of covariates. We will denote $X_{obs} \subseteq X$ as the set of values in X that are observed, while $X_{mis} \subset X$ represent missing values. Note that $X_{obs} \cup X_{mis} = X$. We will define $M_{n \times k}$ as the missingness matrix such that $m_{ij} = 1$ if and only if $x_{ij} \in X_{mis}$ and 0 otherwise.

12.2 FINDING MISSINGNESS

In large databases it is common for every variable to have measurements that are missing on at least 5–10% of the units. Typically every unit has some missing values on one or more variables. For example, the *World Development Indicators* (2013) database contains information on over 7,000 variables for 214 countries over the period from 1960 to 2012. Many cells are missing. Looking at the data for a recent year that is deemed relatively complete – 2010 – and only variables that involved gross domestic product in some form, yields 177 variables for 209 countries. In this modern up-to-date slice of data, over half the data are missing (54%). Thus, the issue of missingness is especially problematic for observational studies, and for those employing matching strategies that derive from the completeness of the information set.

The first thing that should be undertaken is an analysis of what data are missing. This is typically overlooked. But more detail can be helpful. Before we can even begin to model the data we do have, an important step is understanding what's missing. Here we focus on visual tools for identifying the extent of missingness and any patterns therein.

A simple place to begin is by taking advantage of the fact that statistical packages typically have a special symbol reserved for encoding missing values. In $\mathcal{R}$ that symbol is NA. The Amelia (Honaker et al., 2011) and VIM (Kowarik and Templ, 2016) $\mathcal{R}$ libraries provide useful tools for examining missing data in large data sets. For example, Amelia's missmap generates colorblock matrices

Missingness Map

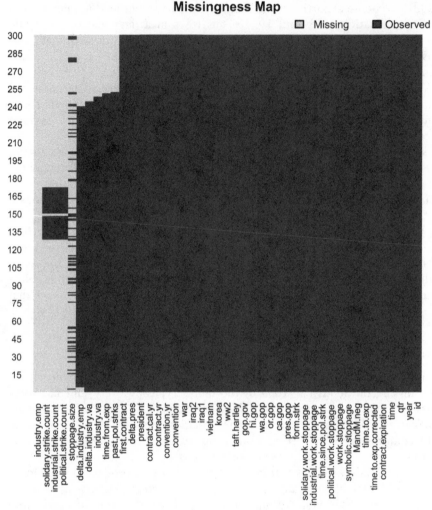

FIGURE 12.1 A "missingness map" displaying missing data by variable for an example data set.

showing missingness by variable. Figure 12.1 plots the missingness for an example data set. Note that the plot sorts the variables in order of decreasing missingness.

VIM has functions that provide different summaries of missingness. Figure 12.2 displays two useful plots. The left panel simply displays the proportion of observations that are coded as missing for a selection of variables, while the right panel is an "aggregation plot," displaying the frequency of missinginess for different combinations of variables. Consider the bottom row of the right panel. This row represents observations for which the variables boix.exchr,

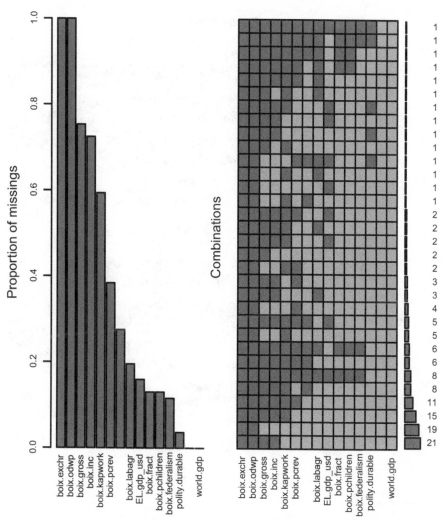

FIGURE 12.2 The left panel displays the proportion of observations missing for a selection of variables. The right panel displays the frequency of combinations of missing and non-missing variables.

`boix.odwp`, `boix.gross`, and `boix.inc` are missing, whereas the others are present. This combination occurs 21 times in this data set and is the most frequent single combination of missing/non-missing values.

A common data structure is time-series cross-section (TSCS) data in which we have repeated observations on the same observational units; thus we are interested in missingness along the temporal, observational unit, and a variable dimensions. `Amelia`'s missingness map allows us to visualize missingness in all three domains. An example appears as Figure 12.3. Note that the distance

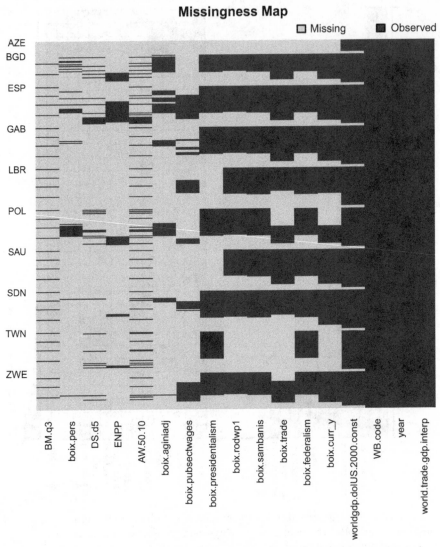

FIGURE 12.3 Visualizing missingness in TSCS data for a selection of countries and variables.

between observational units (the left axis) represents the number of time periods a particular unit was observed. In these example data Azerbaijan (AZE) has a relatively short period of observation, i.e., the time series is *unbalanced*.

A similar problem arises when the producers of data use numeric values to encode specific states. For example, the widely used Polity IV index measures

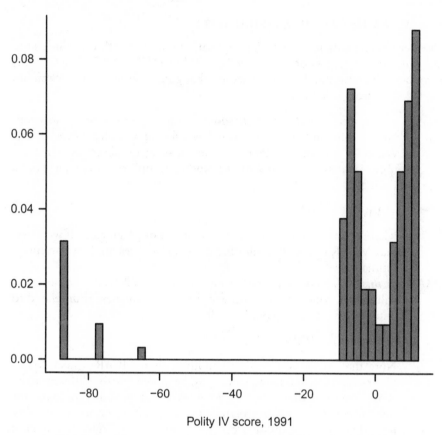

FIGURE 12.4 Polity IV uses numeric values to encode different kinds of missing data. Your computer does not know this.

democracy on a 21-point ordinal scale, but examining the histogram of Polity scores for 1991 displayed in Figure 12.4 indicates that something strange is going on.

It turns out that Polity uses the values $\{-66, -77, -88\}$ to encode interruptions, iterregnum, and regime-transition periods, respectively. Examining the data visually makes the unusual values apparent. What's more, it also forces the analyst to make a decision about how she wants to treat these observations. Simply ignoring the data and estimating models often leads to big problems.

The basic idea here is simple: in order to understand the data we do have, we need to have a good idea about the data we are missing. Inspecting the data carefully before analysis (not to mention reading codebooks) can save you many headaches, embarrassment, or worse down the road.

12.3 A TAXONOMY OF MISSING DATA

Whether missing data in a particular application is a serious threat to inference and prediction depends on how it arises. Rubin (1976; 1987; 2002; 2004) introduced the now-standard classification that guides the standard techniques employed to deal with missingness.

MCAR or *missing completely at random* is missingness where, the probability that any particular value is missing is independent of the values of any of the data, whether missing or observed. Thus the observed data can be treated as a random sample of the complete data. Formally,

$$f(\mathbf{M}|\mathbf{y}, \mathbf{X}, \boldsymbol{\theta}) = f(\mathbf{M}|\boldsymbol{\theta}),$$

where $f(\cdot)$ is the pdf of M and $\boldsymbol{\theta}$ is some set of parameters. If we know that MCAR holds, then ignoring missingness does not bias parameter estimates.

MAR or *missing at random* occurs when missingness is related to observed values but, conditional on observed data, missingness is unrelated to unobserved values. Again, formally,

$$f(\mathbf{M}|\mathbf{y}, \mathbf{X}, \boldsymbol{\theta}) = f(\mathbf{M}|\mathbf{y}_{obs}, \mathbf{X}_{obs}, \boldsymbol{\theta}).$$

Note that MAR is a weaker condition than MCAR. Under MAR, observations with missing values can be systematically different from those reporting data, but so long as the availability of data for one observation can be treated as independent of its availability for others and, conditional on the observed data, missingness does not depend on the values of the missing data, then the missingness is MAR.

NMAR or *not missing at random* is missingness that depends on the value of the missing data, even after conditioning on the observed values. Some mechanism is causing the missingness, a mechanism completely separate from that which generates the observed data. Missing values depend on unobserved variables.

It is impossible to tell whether missingness is M(C)AR or NMAR. There is no statistical test capable of telling you what your missing data want to say. Thus MCAR, MAR, or NMAR are more assumptions about the data than testable propositions. Assuming MCAR seems heroic. The important distinction here is that missingness that is MCAR or MAR is considered *ignorable* in so far as we can address the missingness without directly modeling the mechanism producing the missing values, whereas NMAR requires modeling of the process giving rise to the observed data. Ignorability does not imply that we can ignore the existence of gaps in our data matrix. It simply means that we can apply the methods described in this chapter.

12.4 COMMON STRATEGIES

There are a variety of strategies that have been developed to deal with these problems. Early approaches included deleting observations from calculations when they contain missing values, known as pair-wise deletion, or deleting whole rows from the data set if they contain *any* missing values on any relevant variables (so-called list-wise deletion). Note that list-wise deletion is the default response to missingness of most statistical software packages, only some of which issue warnings in the process. Another idea has been to replace missing values with the expected value for a given variable, i.e., mean replacement. As the amount of missing data increases, these approaches generally produce biased estimates and standard errors. More sophisticated approaches entail multiple imputation, but there is little evidence to suggest that these techniques are widely employed by analysis in medicine and the social sciences (Graham, 2009).

Why is multiple imputation not used more frequently? One issue is that there remains pervasive misunderstanding about what imputation does. For example, many researchers continue to believe that we cannot impute "the dependent variable," notwithstanding the fact that an imputation model does not care what status a variable will take in any subsequent analysis. Sometimes imputation produces results that seem counterintuitive. But, ultimately, imputation techniques are often multistage and complicated to implement. They require data imputation and the creation of multiple data sets, model estimation on each newly constructed data set, and, finally, one must combine and summarize estimation results from the multiple data sets. The imputation alone can be time consuming and computationally expensive. But not addressing data missingness leaves us open to potentially serious error.

12.4.1 Complete Case Analysis

Complete case analysis is exactly what it claims to be: analysis using only available data. This is what most statistical packages do automatically, some without warning or disclosure. This is what you get if you analyze na.omit(X) in $\mathcal{R}$. This is what most social scientists do in their reported findings, often with less disclosure than what is offered by statistical packages.

Complete case analysis has its benefits. It's easy to do, and almost everyone understands what's under analysis. Furthermore, *if* missingness is MCAR, then complete case analysis yields consistent (unbiased) estimates for both statistics of interest and their standard errors. But even if missingness is MCAR, complete case analysis is inefficient since we end up throwing away data. This efficiency problem can become acute, particularly when there are a large number of covariates. If we have 15 covariates, each with 10% missing (independently across covariates), then we end up using 0.9^{15} or 21% of the possible observations!

More problematic, however, is the fact that complete case analysis yields biased parameter estimates and invalid standard errors when the data are MAR or NMAR. Again, there is no way to be sure about the missingness mechanism; using complete case analysis *assumes* that missingness is MCAR.

12.4.2 Available Case Analysis

For some models, the statistics of interest (e.g., $\hat{\beta}$) can be calculated from some *sufficient statistics*. For example, the OLS estimator requires only the means, variances, and covariances of X and y. In calculating these quantities we can use all available data. For each $j \in \{1 \dots k\}$ we use $x_{j,obs}$ to calculate $\bar{x}_j$. Similarly, we use $x_{j,obs}$ and $x_{k,obs}$ to calculate $\text{cov}(x_j, x_k)$. In this way, we generally use more of the data than in complete case analysis (though even this isn't guaranteed). But there are several drawbacks as well. Probably the biggest drawbacks are that we still have not addressed the problem of bias. If missingness is not MCAR, then available case analysis suffers from all the problems of complete case analysis. In addition, since each of the statistics is calculated over different subsets of the data, we can end up with strange results, such as correlations outside the range of $[-1,1]$. Finally, available case analysis is not available beyond a small class of relatively simple models.

12.4.3 Mean Imputation

Simple mean imputation uses $x_{j,obs}$ to calculate $\bar{x}_{j,obs}$ and then substitutes $\bar{x}_{j,obs}$ into $x_{j,miss}$, so that every entry in $x_{j,miss}$ is the element $\bar{x}_{j,obs}$. This keeps the mean of each covariate x_j the same but generally reduces the variance and weakens the correlations between variables. Since we rely on (co)variation to estimate our models, this procedure generally induces bias into our statistical estimates and makes inference problematic or invalid *even if the missingness is MCAR*. What's more, including these imputed means increases our nominal sample size without including new information, further biasing our estimates of standard errors.

12.4.4 Conditional Mean Imputation

Conditional mean imputation uses some method (e.g., regression) to generate predicted values for the missing data, conditional on the other variables available in the data set. We can also include randomly generated residual values to make the (conditional) variance of the imputed values approximate what we see in the observed data. While this improves on simple mean imputation, it can still lead to bias even under MCAR. Furthermore, it fails to account for our estimation uncertainty in the regression model for missing data.

12.5 MULTIPLE IMPUTATION

A more-sophisticated approach to missing data takes advantage of powerful computers to better account for the uncertainty involved in imputing missing values. Rather than just imputing a single value for each piece of missing data, as in conditional mean imputation, multiple imputation generates multiple values for each missing value, thereby generating multiple "complete" data sets. We then run our analysis on *each* imputed data set as we would any complete data set and combine our estimates so that we account for our uncertainty in our estimation both within and across data sets.

Multiple imputation (MI) uses any method that replaces the set of missing values with multiple plausible values to obtain q complete data sets (Rubin, 1996). The most well-known application is in survey sampling, where it was developed. The responses of those who answered a particular set of questions provide information about the response of those who did not. Rubin (2004) originally suggested creating five imputations, but more recently authors recommended using closer to twenty imputations (Van Buuren, 2012). von Hippel (2009) has further modified Rubin's original suggestion and suggests an order-of-magnitude more imputed data sets depending on the amount of missingness.

12.5.1 MLE-EM and Bayesian Multiple Imputation

If we make some assumptions about the joint distribution of our data, we can construct a likelihood. The most common approach assumes a multivariate normal model for the observed and missing data. The normal model and has been shown to work pretty well, even in the presence of non-Gaussian data.

The joint density of $\mathbf{X}$ can be expressed as $\Pr(\mathbf{X}_{obs}, \mathbf{X}_{mis}, \boldsymbol{\theta})$, where $\boldsymbol{\theta}$ are unknown parameters of the density function. In an important result, Little and Rubin (2002) prove that we can obtain the maximum likelihood estimate of $\boldsymbol{\theta}$ from the distribution of the observed data *if* the missing data are MAR. The marginal distribution of the observed data is derived by integrating over the missing values:

$$\Pr(\mathbf{X}_{obs}, \boldsymbol{\theta}) = \int \Pr(\mathbf{X}_{obs}, \mathbf{X}_{mis}, \boldsymbol{\theta}) d\mathbf{X}_{mis}.$$

If we can calculate this integral, we can then construct a likelihood $\mathcal{L}(\boldsymbol{\theta}|\mathbf{X}_{obs})$. The trouble is that this integral almost never has a convenient solution, except in special circumstances. Little and Rubin (2002) use the EM algorithm (See Section 4.2.3) to find $\hat{\boldsymbol{\theta}}$. The algorithm consists of an E-step and an M-step; we start with a set of initial parameter values $\boldsymbol{\theta}_0$ and then iterate. Let $\boldsymbol{\theta}_t$ be the tth iteration of the algorithm:

E-step   Find the conditional expectation of the missing data, given the observed data and $\boldsymbol{\theta}_{t-1}$

M-step   Find θ_t by maximizing $\mathcal{L}(\theta|X_{obs}, \tilde{X}_{mis})$, where $\tilde{X}_{mis}$ are the current predicted values generated by the parameters θ_{t-1}

Once EM converges to the MLE of θ, we can sample from the multivariate normal distribution for the complete data to fill in X_{miss}. We do this repeatedly. Including a prior distribution over the parameters yields Bayesian multiple imputation, also known as data augmentation. Under a fully Bayesian set up, the imputation model generates draws from the posterior *predictive distribution* of the data. The tools in the Amelia II library (Honaker and King, 2010) employ a version of EM combined with a bootstrap step.

In case you were wondering … 12.1 Markov Chain Monte Carlo (MCMC)

A *Markov Chain* is a probabilistic model or process in which some system randomly transitions from one state to another; the transition probability depends only on the current state. A *Monte Carlo* method or simulation relies on a large number of random samples to estimate a numerical quantity. MCMC is a set of techniques for appropriately generating draws from a complicated, high-dimensional probability distribution. Although the individual draws in an MCMC are correlated, we will end up with a stationary distribution, independent of where we started, if the process goes on long enough.

MCMC is often used to numerically calculate the high-dimensional integrals that are common in Bayesian estimation problems. Because MCMC draws are correlated, estimation using MCMC usually allows for some *burn-in* (discarded initial draws) and *thinning* (only saving every nth draw).

12.5.2 MICE

An alternative approach is to focus on each variable and to look at its conditional distribution based on other variables. Multiple Imputation via Chained Equations (MICE) (Van Buuren, 2012) is a fully conditional specification method that starts with an initial guess of Y^{mis} (e.g., most often the mean). This "imputed" variable is used as dependent variable in a regression on all other variables. The obtained regression estimates are used to impute the missing observations. The estimates and parameters are then updated, cycling through the variables and imputing each one given the most current estimates. The procedure continues as long as some changes are being produced. A similar technique is used in the mi package in $\mathcal{R}$ (Su et al., 2011). Each variable is imputed based on an "appropriate generalized linear model for each variable's conditional distribution" (Kropko et al., 2014, 501).

One of the advantages of conditional model specification is that each variable is modeled based on a specific distribution. In practice, chained equations are very computationally demanding. A significant drawback of such conditional approaches is that they do not define a valid joint distribution for the data, which can lead to substantial difficulties in the convergence of the algorithms. The convergence of the imputation process can depend on the order in which the various GLM equations are chained together. More important, coefficient estimates suffer significantly when the number of missing observations is large, especially for categorical variables (Murray and Reiter, 2014).

12.5.3 Copula Methods

Conditional approaches like MICE do not necessarily produce a valid joint distribution. This cannot guarantee the proper behavior of confidence intervals and overall inference. One solution is to specify the joint distribution directly, as with the multivariate normal EM. This is increasingly complicated as the number of covariates increase. As a result, it is helpful to decouple the specification of the marginal distribution of each variable from the function that describes the joint behavior of all. *Copulas* are a way to decompose a multivariate distribution such that the dependence across variables can be considered separately from the marginal distribution of each variable. Once the new distribution is created, it is a simple matter to sample from it when values are needed, as in the case of missing value imputation.

The copula function brings together two (or more) univariate marginal distributions of known form to produce a new joint distribution.[1] Consider two random variables X and Y with associated univariate distribution functions $F_X(\cdot)$ and $F_Y(\cdot)$. Sklar's 1959 theorem establishes that there exists a copula $C(\ \cdot,\ \cdot\ ;\theta)$ such that a bivariate joint distribution is defined for all x and y in the extended real line as

$$F_{XY}(x,y) = \Pr(X < x \cap Y < y) = C\left(F_X(x), F_Y(y); \theta\right), \qquad (12.1)$$

where the association parameter, θ, represents the degree of dependence between X and Y. This result demonstrates a new bivariate distribution based on univariate marginal distributions.

This is widely studied for Gaussian copulas, where the multivariate dependence the function, C, produces a multivariate normal distribution having a standardized (co)variance, often denoted R. Of particular interest is the setting where no parametric form is specified for the marginal distributions. Even without making assumptions about the marginal distributions, the theoretical guarantees for the parameters of the copula model still hold, permitting the imputation of the missing data (Hoff et al., 2014).

---

[1] Discussion here draws on Chiba et al. (2015).

In case you were wondering ... 12.2 What is a copula?

We can characterize the density function and the conditional distribution functions using a copula:

$$f_{XY}(x,y) = \Pr(X = x \cap Y = y) = \frac{\partial C\left(F_X(x), F_Y(y); \theta\right)}{\partial x \, \partial y} \quad (12.2)$$

$$= \frac{\partial C\left(F_X(x), F_Y(y); \theta\right)}{\partial F_X(x) \, \partial F_Y(y)} \cdot f_X(x) \cdot f_Y(y)$$

$$f_{X|Y}(x,y) = \Pr(X = x | Y = y) = \frac{\Pr(X = x \cap Y = y)}{\Pr(Y = y)}$$

$$= \frac{f_{XY}(x,y)}{f_Y(y)}$$

$$F_{X|Y}(x,y) = \Pr(X < x | Y = y) = \int_{-\infty}^{x} f_{X|Y}(x,y),$$

where $f_X(\cdot)$ and $f_Y(\cdot)$ are the univariate density functions for X and Y.

The last step is to choose a particular copula function for $C(, ; \theta)$ to characterize functions in Equations (12.1) and (12.2). The Gaussian copula can can accommodate both positive and negative dependency:

$$C(u, v; \theta) = \int_{-\infty}^{\Phi^{-1}(u)} \int_{-\infty}^{\Phi^{-1}(v)} \frac{1}{2\pi(1 - \theta^2)^{1/2}}$$

$$\exp\left[\frac{-(s^2 - 2\theta st + t^2)}{2(1 - \theta^2)}\right] ds \, dt,$$

where $\Phi^{-1}()$ is the Gaussian quantile function, $-1 < \theta < 1$ is the association parameter, and $u = F_x(x)$ and $v = F_y(y)$ for random variables x and y. With the Gaussian copula, the density and the conditional functions have the following forms:

$$f_{XY}(x,y) = (1 - \theta^2)^{-\frac{1}{2}}$$

$$\exp\left[-\frac{1}{2}(1 - \theta^2)^{-1}(a^2 + b^2 - 2\theta ab)\right]$$

$$\exp\left[\frac{1}{2}(a^2 + b^2)\right] \cdot f_X(x) \cdot f_Y(y) \quad (12.3)$$

$$F_{X|Y}(x,y) = \int_{-\infty}^{a} f_{XY}(x,y) = \Phi\left(\frac{a + \theta b}{\sqrt{1 - \theta^2}}\right),$$

where $a = \Phi^{-1}(F_X(x))$, $b = \Phi^{-1}(F_Y(y))$, and $\Phi(\cdot)$ is the standard normal distribution function.

The Gaussian copula is useful for a number of reasons. It permits for independence as a special case ($\theta = 0$), meaning that this independence can be empirically tested. The Gaussian copula is *comprehensive* in that as θ approaches the lower (upper) bound of its permissible range, the copula approaches the theoretical lower (upper) bound. When data are missing at random, Gaussian copula imputation produces a full posterior for the missing data.

12.5.4 Combining Results Across Imputations

All multiple imputation techniques produce several "complete" data sets with missing values filled in. Traditional analysis, using a GLM, for example, then proceeds on each of these imputed data sets separately. How do we account for the *imputation uncertainty*?

Early work assumed that analysts wanted to report BUTONs, i.e., quantities like regression coefficients and standard errors. Rubin (1976, 1987, 1996, 2004) derived the rules for combining results across imputations. Suppose we have q imputed data sets. Our parameter of interest is the vector $\boldsymbol{\beta}$. We will denote the estimates of our parameter of interest for variable k from our analysis on one of d imputed data sets as $\tilde{\beta}_k^d$; let $\tilde{\sigma}_k^d$ be the corresponding standard error.

Point estimates of regression coefficients are simple averages across the coefficients, obtained as

$$\hat{\beta}_{k,MI} \equiv \frac{1}{q} \sum_{d=1}^{q} \tilde{\beta}_k^d.$$

Standard errors around these estimates are a combination of our within- and across-imputation uncertainty:

$$V_k^{within} = \frac{1}{q} \sum_{d=1}^{q} (\tilde{\sigma}_k^d)^2,$$

$$V_k^{between} = \frac{1}{q-1} \sum_{d=1}^{q} (\tilde{\beta}_k^d - \hat{\beta}_{k,MI})^2,$$

$$\hat{\sigma}_{k,MI} = \sqrt{V_k^{within} + \frac{q+1}{q} V_k^{between}}.$$

But there are other ways to incorporate imputation uncertainty in our analysis and interpretation. For example, we have often relied on simulation draws from the limiting distribution for the parameters to interpret and evaluate models. It is straightforward to modify this process, described in Section 3.4.5, to incorporate multiple imputation. We simply generate a series of draws from the models fit to each imputation and then pool the results:

1. Generate q complete data sets by multiple imputation.
2. For each imputed data set, estimate the proposed model by maximizing the likelihood function, storing the coefficient point estimates and the variance-covariance matrix. Let the former be denoted $\tilde{\boldsymbol{\beta}}^d$ and the latter $\text{cov}(\tilde{\boldsymbol{\beta}}^d)$.
3. Create $\mathbf{x}_\alpha$, a vector of values for the independent variables representing a scenario of analytic or substantive interest. If setting some values to a central tendency or particular sample quantile, be sure to calculate that value across all the imputed data sets.
4. For each imputed data set, draw many vectors of parameter values from $\mathcal{N}\left(\tilde{\boldsymbol{\beta}}^d, \text{cov}(\tilde{\boldsymbol{\beta}}^d)\right)$. Let $\tilde{\boldsymbol{\beta}}^{d_j}$ be the jth draw from the model fit to imputation d.
5. Produce the appropriate expected or predicted values based on $g^{-1}\left(\mathbf{x}_\alpha \tilde{\boldsymbol{\beta}}^{d_j}\right)$. Pool these estimates.
6. Produce a table or graphical display of these pooled estimates, fully reflecting our uncertainty.

Miles (2016) shows this process of pooling estimated quantities across imputations and then generating predictions gives virtually identical results to one in which we generate imputation-specific predictions (and standard errors) and then combine them using Rubin's rules. In MCMC estimation processes, the imputation step can be called at each iteration, embedding it directly in the model fitting algorithm and not requiring any additional post-processing. Copula methods are particularly well suited to this task.

12.6 BUILDING AN IMPUTATION MODEL

Imputation is not about substance or interpretation. Imputation is about predicting the missing data with minimum variance. As a result, we want to take advantage of all the information we have at hand in building the imputation model. This means including all the variables that are feasible to manage; it makes no difference whether or on which side of a subsequent analysis model a variable will appear. Moreover, the more information brought to bear on the imputation exercise, the more credible the MAR assumption.

Most of the EM and copula multiple imputation models, including Amelia, build on a multivariate normal model. While these models have been shown to work reasonably well with non-Gaussian data, problems sometimes arise. When they do, transformations to approximate normality can improve imputation performance, as can the specification of prior distributions that impose bounds or other restrictions on particular variables. Similarly, standardizing variables can also improve imputation speed and performance. Even without full standardization, ensuring variables are within about an order of magnitude of one another helps avoid computational problems.

12.7 EVALUATING IMPUTATION MODELS

Missing data are just that, so evaluating the quality of an imputation model requires using a variety of heuristic approaches to decide whether imputed values are plausible. Broadly, we are interested in evaluating the extent to which the distribution of imputed values for a particular variable are sufficiently different from observed values; these cases we should investigate further. Abayomi et al. (2008) advocate for a preliminary application of the Kolmogorov–Smirnov (KS) test to the distributions of observed and imputed values for a variable, flagging potentially problematic variables. We can also plot the distributions of observed and imputed variables to look for implausible relationships. Both these approaches have limitations, however. The KS test is low powered and unlikely to provide much insight if there is a relatively small number of imputed values. Visual tools are suggestive. Moreover, just because the distributions of observed and imputed data differ does not mean that the imputation model has failed. The possibility that the distribution of the missing values might differ systematically from the observed data is part of the rationale for imputation in the first place.

Overimputation is another useful tool. With overimputation, we randomly select some observed data and set them to missing before imputation. We can then impute the "missing" data and compare the imputed values to the known truth. Imputation models that are wildly incorrect should clearly be treated with caution and revised.

12.7.1 Empirical Replications: Sorens and Ruger

Although imputation methods are still underused, there is some visible progress. Sorens and Ruger (2012) published a recent study that explores the linkages between foreign investment and human rights. Employing a pooled OLS framework on data from 163 countries between 1975 and 2003, the authors find strong evidence that foreign investment does not affect repression, thereby contradicting previous studies suggesting that the political gains from repression outweigh economic costs for governments. Sorens and Ruger employed the EM approach implemented in `Amelia II` to produce five complete data sets with missing values imputed.[2]

Here we use the Sorens and Ruger (2012) data set to compare the various imputation techniques: Gaussian copula, `Amelia II`, and `MICE`. To evaluate their the performance, we use overimputation to create additional missingness via random draws from binomial distributions, where we set the $\Pr(m_{ij} = 1) = 0.1$. We then use the true values of the deleted observations to calculate errors and assess performance. Table 12.1 displays the level of initial missingness (first row) and additional missingness induced for overimputation (second row).

---

[2] This section is adapted from Hollenbach et al. (2008).

TABLE 12.1 *Missingness in Sorens and Ruger data. Variable names taken from original study.*

	avgrep	physint	fdiinflow2	fdiinward2	rgdpch	openk	grgdpch
Initial Missingness	257	993	191	226	17	27	17
Added Missingness	419	330	412	385	440	450	434

Additional Variables							
	internet	fle	resources	kaopen	fpi	fpistock	polity2
Initial Missingness	610	168	852	311	170	173	39
Added Missingness	351	406	332	363	411	402	399

Performance Across Imputation Techniques

Here are the procedures followed for imputing missing observations. For the Gaussian copula, the sbgcop.mcmc() function produced 2,000 complete data draws, from which every other imputation was saved. In addition, the first 250 imputations are discarded as burn-in, which leaves us with 750 imputations via Gaussian copula. The procedure for Amelia II follows Sorens and Ruger (2012) and produces five complete data sets. This model included country effects and a first-order polynomial to account for time trends. Last, MICE imputations are conducted using group and time effects. We set the number of imputations to 20 and left the number of maximum iterations at its default: 5.

Table 12.2 shows the root mean squared error (RMSE) for the imputations of the additionally created missing observations estimated via Gaussian copula, Amelia II, and MICE. The rows containing shaded cells report the ratio of RMSEs for easier comparison. Shaded cells highlight the variables where the copula performs better than the alternatives based on the RMSE. Copula imputation performs slightly better on the majority of variables in the Sorens and Ruger (2012) data set.

Similar to what we found in our analysis using the simulated data, the copula approach is also much faster than both Amelia II and MICE.[3] Unlike the case of simulated Gaussian data, in this real-world data set with a large number of missing observations, the EM algorithm that is the basis of the Amelia II imputation is very slow to converge. The MCMC algorithm of the Gaussian copula model is still quite fast, even though we increased the size of the data set by almost a factor of five by adding the lagged variables.

Figure 12.5 illustrates the similarity of the distribution of the Polity data with and without values imputed by the Gaussian copula, as shown in the code example. Although the distributions are quite similiar, imputation provides Polity scores on 29 additional countries (not actually in the Polity database).

---

[3] Generating five data sets through Amelia II took 124 minutes, MICE took 55 minutes to create 20 imputed data sets, and sbgcop.mcmc ran 2,000 imputations in 11 minutes. Each of the imputation algorithms was run on a single core.

TABLE 12.2 *Root mean square error on imputations of Sorens and Ruger (2012) data. Variable names taken from original study.*

	avgrep	physint	fdiinflow2	fdiinward2	rgdpch	openk	grgdpch
1) Amelia II	0.81	1.78	49.44	439.05	6635.17	34.47	10.96
2) Mice	0.82	1.81	52.99	770.89	7325.73	54.07	11.07
3) Copula	0.70	1.75	49.82	614.12	3631.11	22.18	9.63
Copula/Amelia II	0.87	0.98	1.01	1.40	0.55	0.64	0.88
Copula/Mice	0.86	0.96	0.94	0.80	0.50	0.41	0.87

Additional Variables

	internet	fle	resources	kaopen	fpi	fpistock	polity2
1) Amelia II	86.44	6.13	16.11	1.18	0.07	15.65	5.35
2) Mice	85.14	11.53	23.91	1.60	0.05	15.05	7.50
3) Copula	92.54	3.79	13.68	0.76	0.11	30.42	7.61
Copula/Amelia II	1.07	0.62	0.85	0.64	1.57	1.94	1.42
Copula/Mice	1.09	0.33	0.57	0.47	2.08	2.02	1.01

R Code Example 12.1 *Example of using sbgcop to impute data.*

```
rm( list = ls())
library(sbgcop)
# deleted code to gather a data frame, md.df:
# md.df is a data frame with 195 rows (countries)
# run sbgcop.mcmc with defaults
new.df<-sbgcop.mcmc(md.df)
colnames(new.df$Y.pmean)<-c("area.mi","gdp.mi","democ.mi","autoc.mi","polity.
    mi")
raw.df.mi<-cbind(raw.df,new.df$Y.pmean)
plot(las=1,density(raw.df.mi$polity,na.rm=T),xlim=c(-20,20),bty="n",xlab="
    Polity Score",main="",lwd=3)
lines(density(raw.df.mi$polity.mi),col="red",lwd=3)
```

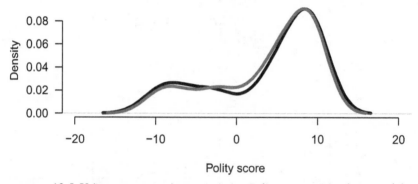

FIGURE 12.5 Using sbgcop to impute missing Polity scores. Distribution of the variable for only the cases with data (shown in black) compared to the distribution for the variable with missing values imputed (shown in gray/red).

12.8 CONCLUSION

Ultimately, the analyst has to make a case as to which is worse: analyzing complete cases or imputing the missing values. In general, imputation is much preferred to throwing away data and thereby making poor inferences. Fortunately, there are modern methods that facilitate the imputation of missing data that preserve the uncertainty that comes from imputing values. Like modern dentistry, early detection of missingness and use of these approaches can prevent a lot of subsequent pain. A general strategy is outlined as:

• Analyze missingness as if it were your dependent variable. Know what is missing and try to learn how that data disappeared.

• Imputation is not about substantive interpretation; it's about prediction. We want to include variables that will help predict missingness well. It doesn't matter if these variables are endogenous, lags, or leads. Including the dependent variable of your subsequent analysis is not a problem. Including variables not used in your subsequent analysis is not a problem.

- Include as much information in the imputation model as possible. The MAR assumption is key to the validity of standard imputation algorithms; including more data in the imputation model makes the MAR assumption more believable.
- Transform variables to approximate normality when possible.
- Standardizing variables to a mean of 0 and a standard deviation of 1 can help, especially where there are convergence issues.
- Ultimately the imputed data should resemble the real data you plan to analyze. Integer counts should all be integer counts; imputed values of categorical variables should look like the non-imputed values of the variable.

12.9 FURTHER READING

Applications

We searched the 22 quantitative empirical articles in the July 2017 issue of the *American Journal of Political Science* and the August 2017 issues of the *American Political Science Review* for the terms "attrition," "drop," "omit," "missing," "impute," "imputation," "nonresponse," and, "non-response." Only seven mention anything at all about the handling of missing data. Two undertake some form of imputation.

Wright and Frantz (2017) use multiple imputation to replicate an existing paper linking hydrocarbon income to autocratic survival and show that the original results fail to hold. Klasnja (2017) imputes missing data in the ANES.

Past Work

Schafer (1999) provides an early primer on multiple imputation for applied researchers. King et al. (2001) introduced the initial version of Amelia. Horton and Kleinman (2007) outline a variety of imputation approaches, ranging from EM through chained equations to MCMC. Ross (2006) is a famous application in political science, highlighting how poorer and more-authoritarian countries are less likely to report data.

Advanced Study

Two major texts on multiple imputation are Little and Rubin (2002) and Van Buuren (2012).

On the theory of copulas, see Nelsen (1970) and Trivedi and Zimmer (2005). On Gaussian copulas, see Chen et al. (2006); Klaassen et al. (1997); and Pitt et al. (2006). Hoff (2007) uses copulas in the context of rank likelihoods (Pettitt, 1982).

Software Notes

The `Amelia` library contains several useful features for diagnosing missing data, including `missmap`. The `VIM` package (Kowarik and Templ, 2016) contains many others.

The machine-learning revolution has focused a lot of attention on ways to impute missing data. As a result, $\mathcal{R}$ contains many packages with imputation tools. Kowarik and Templ (2016) present one recent overview, surveying a variety of *single-imputation* algorithms, including `yaImpute` (Crookston and Finley, 2007), `missMDA` (Josse and Husson, 2016), `AmeliaII` (Honaker and King, 2010), `mix` (Schafer, 2017), `missForest` (Stekhoven and Buehlmann, 2012), and others. The `VIM` package includes a variety of approaches for mixed, scaled variables in large databases with outliers. This packages also supports the multiple imputation methods that use the EM approach. The `MICE` library (Van Buuren and Groothuis-Oudshoorn, 2011) implements MICE, while the `mi` (Su et al., 2011) library also implements a conditional modeling approach. `mitools` (Lumley, 2014) and `Zelig` contain a variety of tools for managing and combining the results from multiple imputations. Van Buuren maintains an updated list of imputation-related software, including $\mathcal{R}$ packages, at http:// www.stefvanbuuren.nl/mi/Software.html.

PART V

A LOOK AHEAD

13

Epilogue

We have reached the end of our introduction to maximum likelihood methods for the social sciences. Along the way we have presented several models that have seen wide application. We illustrated refinements and extensions that enhance the flexibility of a likelihood perspective. But we don't see the likelihood approach as a be-all and end-all. Indeed, it stands at the core of Bayesian and frequentist approaches to statistical inference. As a result, the malleability of this approach makes it a gateway for further statistical training. In closing, we make a few observations about future directions.

For the sake of discussion, additional training can take two forms: further application and refinement of tools within the likelihood framework and branching out into newer fields that build upon or generalize ideas introduced herein. In reality, of course, all these things overlap considerably.

Most of the models we have examined here rely on the (conditional) i.i.d. assumption in deriving a likelihood function. As alluded to in Chapter 11, however, social scientists frequently encounter data where strong dependencies do exist. Time series analysis is a large branch of applied statistics and econometrics dealing with modeling temporal dependence. Complications here can extend to panels and time-series cross-section (TSCS) data, both of which are characterized by repeated measurements on several units. The likelihood perspective permeates much of this literature, and the potential complications are many. One of the most interesting areas of recent work is found in Brandt et al. (2014). Similarly, social scientists are often interested in outcomes for units distributed in space, where there might be spillovers or dependencies as a function of distance.

Interest in measuring and modeling linkages and dependencies between units has now generalized beyond space and time to the study of networks. Models of spatial dependence and network structure are particularly closely related.

Good examples of this abound in the network literature, especially Hoff (2009, 2015).

Mixture models – as we introduced in the context of zero-inflation and split-population models – relax the assumption that all our observed data are being generated by the same process, i.e., they relax the "identical" part of i.i.d. The strategy and estimation of mixture models, however, is much broader and can be considerably more complex than the examples we have provided. Some recent uses include unsupervised classification models (Ahlquist and Breunig, 2012). The application of the Dirichlet Process model has allowed for the construction of mixture models, where the number of components emerges as part of the estimation procedure itself. This set of tools is seeing wide application in machine learning, especially as applied to text corpora (Grimmer, 2010; Lucas et al., 2015; Spirling and Quinn, 2010). Future applications will likely extend to computer recognition of image and video data.

13.1 THE BROADER LANDSCAPE

Classical statistical analysis generally presupposes the existence of a "true" quantity of interest about which we are trying to make inference using observed data. Bayesian analysis jettisons this idea, instead introducing the concepts of subjective beliefs and learning. In a Bayesian framework, we begin with a set of prior beliefs about our quantity of interest, θ. These beliefs are represented by a probability distribution, $\Pr(\theta)$. We then gather new data, y, and update our beliefs using Bayes's Rule: $\Pr(\theta|y) = \Pr(y|\theta)\Pr(\theta)/\Pr(y)$. Note that the first term in the numerator, $\Pr(y|\theta)$, is the joint probability of the data, given the parameter of interest, also known as the likelihood. In this way the likelihood framework, along with the probability distributions we studied in this volume, form a core piece of the Bayesian machinery. The output of a Bayesian analysis, the posterior distribution, is a full probability distribution for the quantities of interest. As a result, the computational sampling and simulation logic we have emphasized throughout are integral to the estimation and interpretation of fully Bayesian models.

The likelihood framework is the jumping off point (and a special case of) several other estimation strategies designed to address shortcomings or challenges of MLE but without going in a Bayesian direction.

- The Generalized Method of Moments (GMM) is an estimation strategy that relies on specifying a certain number of "moment conditions," typically for the mean, rather than a full probability distribution, as in the likelihood framework. MLE can be expressed as a specific type of GMM estimator.

- M-estimators and other forms of "robust regression" attempt to anneal our estimates to possible problems that likelihood (and other) estimators may encounter in small samples or with high-leverage or other types of observations.

- Generalized Estimating Equations (GEE) provide a framework for modeling dependencies across observations in the GLM context, again without specifying a full probability distribution for outcomes. Rather, the analyst specifies a model for the mean and a "working" variance structure.

Political science is in the middle of a revolution in the amount, frequency, and types of data available to scholars. Much of this data is coming in the form of un- or weakly structured text. For example, in international relations, near-real-time data on conflict events is emerging from ongoing scraping of news and social media reports. In comparative and American politics, scholars are analyzing the recorded statements of politicians and their campaigns both in the legislature and in speeches, websites, and social media posts. The volume of information is simply too large to manage with teams of human coders. New tools, whereby computational algorithms extract information and classify texts, are a rapidly growing area of methodological research. In addition to specific models based on likelihoods, machine-learning tools have a particular goal of correctly identifying and classifying new observations as they arise. The predictive evaluation tools we described in this volume are key to the development and evaluation of machine-learning methods. Moreover, with the development of continuous, near-real-time data streams, we are now in a position to develop forecasting models for a variety of political and social events that might be of interest, including conflict.

The future of data analysis in the social sciences is exciting. More things are possible than ever before. As far as we can see forward, the maximum likelihood principle introduced by the most unlikely of characters, Sir R. A. Fisher (Stigler, 2007), will be at the core of many of these innovations and therefore remain a necessary component of modern applied statistical analysis.

Bibliography

Abayomi, Kobi, Gelman, Andrew, and Levy, Marc. 2008. Diagnostics for Multivariate Imputations. *Journal of the Royal Statistical Society Series C*, 57(3), 273–291.

Agresti, Alan. 2002. *Categorical Data Analysis*. 2nd edn. New York: John Wiley & Sons, Ltd.

Ahlquist, John S. 2010a. Building Strategic Capacity: The Political Underpinnings of Coordinated Wage Bargaining. *American Political Science Review*, 104(1), 171–188.

Ahlquist, John S. 2010b. Policy by Contract: Electoral Cycles, Parties, and Social Pacts, 1974–2000. *Journal of Politics*, 72(2), 572–587.

Ahlquist, John S., and Breunig, Christian. 2012. Model-Based Clustering and Typologies in the Social Sciences. *Political Analysis*, 20(1), 92–112.

Ahlquist, John S., and Wibbels, Erik. 2012. Riding the Wave: World Trade and Factor-Based Models of Democratization. *American Journal of Political Science*, 56(2), 447–464.

Ai, Chunrong, and Norton, Edward C. 2003. Interaction Terms in Logit and Probit Models. *Economics Letters*, 80(1), 123–129.

Akaike, Hirotugu. 1976. A New Look at the Statistical Model Identification. *IEEE Transactions on Automatic Control*, 19(6), 716–723.

Aldrich, John. 1997. R. A. Fisher and the making of maximum likelihood 1912–1922. *Statistical Science*, 12(3), 162–176.

Alfons, Andreas. 2012. *cvTools: Cross-Validation Tools for Regression Models*. R package version 0.3.2.

Alvarez, R. Michael. 1998. *Information and Elections*. Ann Arbor, MI: University of Michigan Press.

Alvarez, R. Michael, and Brehm, John. 1995. American Ambivalence towards Abortion Policy: Development of a Heteroskedastic Probit Model of Competing Values. *American Journal of Political Science*, 39(4), 1055–1082.

Alvarez, R. Michael, and Brehm, John. 2002. *Hard Choices, Easy Answers: Values, Information, and American Public Opinion*. Princeton, NJ: Princeton University Press.

Alvarez, R. Michael, and Nagler, Johathan. 1998. When Politics and Models Collide: Estimating Models of Multiparty Elections. *American Journal of Political Science*, 42(1), 55–96.

Andersen, Per Kragh, and Gill, Richard D. 1982. Cox's Regression Model for Counting Processes: A Large Sample Study. *Annals of Statistics*, 4, 1100–1120.

Angrist, Joshua D., and Pischke, Jorn-Steffen. 2009. *Mostly Harmless Econometrics*. Princeton, NJ: Princeton University Press.

Arel-Bundock, Vincent. 2013. *WDI: World Development Indicators (World Bank)*. R package version 2.4.

Arlot, Sylvain, and Celisse, Alain. 2010. A Survey of Cross-Validation Procedures for Model Selection. *Statistics Surveys*, 4, 40–79.

Aronow, Peter M. 2016. A Note on 'How Robust Standard Errors Expose Methodological Problems They Do Not Fix, and What to Do about It.' *arXiv:1609.01774*.

Aronow, Peter M., and Samii, Cyrus. 2012. ri: *R Package for Performing Randomization-Based Inference for Experiments*. R package version 0.9.

Bagozzi, Benjamin E. 2016. The Baseline-Inflated Multinomial Logit Model for International Relations Research. *Conflict Management and Peace Science*, 33(2), 174–197.

Bagozzi, Benjamin E., Koren, Ore, and Mukherjee, Bumba. 2017. Droughts, Land Appropriation, and Rebel Violence in the Developing World. *Journal of Politics*, 79(3), 1057–1072.

Bailey, Delia, and Katz, Jonathan N. 2011. Implementing Panel-Corrected Standard Errors in R: The pcse Package. *Journal of Statistical Software, Code Snippets*, 42(1), 1–11.

Barrilleaux, Charles, and Rainey, Carlisle. 2014. The Politics of Need: Examining Governors' Decisions to Oppose the "Obamacare" Medicaid Expansion. *State Politics and Policy Quarterly*, 14(4), 437–460.

Bartels, Larry M. 1997. Specification, Uncertainty, and Model Averaging. *American Journal of Political Science*, 41(2), 641–674.

Baturo, Alexander. 2017. Democracy, Development, and Career Trajectories of Former Political Leaders. *Comparative Political Studies*, 50(8), 1023–1054.

Beck, Nathaniel. 1991. The Illusion of Cycles in International Relations. *International Studies Quarterly*, 35(4), 455–476.

Beck, Nathaniel, and Katz, Jonathan N. 1995. What to Do (and Not to Do) with Pooled Time-Series Cross-Section Data. *American Political Science Review*, 89(3), 634–647.

Beck, Nathaniel, and Katz, Jonathan N. 2011. Modeling Dynamics in Time-Series Cross-Section Political Economy Data. *Annual Review of Political Science*, 14(1), 331–352.

Beck, Nathaniel, Katz, Jonathan N., and Tucker, Richard. 1998. Taking Time Seriously: Time-Series-Cross-Section Analysis with a Binary Dependent Variable. *American Journal of Political Science*, 42(2), 1260–1288.

Beck, Nathaniel, Gleditsch, Kristian Skrede, and Beardsley, Kyle. 2006. Space Is More Than Geography: Using Spatial Econometrics in the Study of Political Economy. *International Studies Quarterly*, 50(1), 27–44.

Beger, Andreas, Hill, Jr., Daniel W., Metternich, Nils W., Minhas, Shahryar, and Ward, Michael D. 2017. Splitting It Up: The spduration Split-Population Duration Regression Package. *arXiv*. The R Journal, 9(2):474-486.

Belia, Sarah, Fidler, Fiona, Williams, Jennifer, and Cumming, Geoff. 2005. Researchers Misunderstand Confidence Intervals and Standard Error Bars. *Psychological Methods*, **10**(4), 389–396.

Belkin, Aaron, and Schofer, Evan. 2003. Toward a Structural Understanding of Coup Risk. *Journal of Conflict Resolution*, **47**(5), 594–620.

Bell, Mark S., and Miller, Nicholas L. 2015. Questioning the Effect of Nuclear Weapons on Conflict. *Journal of Conflict Resolution*, **59**(1), 74–92.

Benoit, Kenneth, Conway, Drew, Lauderdale, Benjamin E., Laver, Michael, and Mikhaylov, Slava. 2016. Crowd-Sourced Text Analysis: Reproducible and Agile Production of Political Data. *American Political Science Review*, **110**(2), 278–295.

Bercovitch, Jacob, and Schneider, Gerald. 2000. Who Mediates? The Political Economy of International Conflict Management. *Journal of Peace Research*, **37**(2), 145–165.

Berkson, Joseph. 1944. Application of the Logistic Function to Bio-Assay. *Journal of the American Statistical Association*, **39**(227), 357–365.

Berkson, Joseph. 1946. Approximation of Chi-Square by 'Probits' and by 'Logits'. *Journal of the American Statistical Association*, **41**(233), 70–74.

Berkson, Joseph. 1953. A Statistically Precise and Relatively Simple Method of Estimating the Bioassay with Quantal Response, Based on the Logistic Function. *Journal of the American Statistical Association*, **48**(263), 565–599.

Berkson, Joseph. 1955. Maximum Likelihood and Minimum χ^2 Estimates of the Logistic Function. *Journal of the American Statistical Association*, **50**(269), 130–162.

Berry, William D., DeMeritt, Jacqueline H. R., and Esarey, Justin. 2010. Testing for Interaction in Binary Logit and Probit Models: Is a Product Term Essential? *American Journal of Political Science*, **54**(1), 248–266.

Berry, William, Golder, Matt, and Milton, Daniel. 2012. Improving Tests of Theories Positing Interaction. *Journal of Politics*, **74**(3), 653–671.

Bhat, Chandra R. 1996. A Heterocedastic Extreme Value Model of Intercity Travel Mode Choice. *Transportation Research B*, **29**(6), 471–483.

Bliss, Chester Ittner. 1935. The Calculation of the Dosage Mortality Curve. *Annals of Applied Biology*, **22**, 134–167.

Bolker, Ben, and R Development Core Team. 2016. *bbmle: Tools for General Maximum Likelihood Estimation*. R package version 1.0.18.

Bortkiewicz, Ladislaus von. 1898. *Das gesetz der kleinen Zahlen*. Leipzig: B. G. Teubner.

Box-Steffensmeier, Janet M., and DeBoef, Suzanna. 2006. Repeated Events Survival Models: The Conditional Frailty Model. *Statistics in Medicine*, **25**, 1260–1288.

Box-Steffensmeier, Janet. M., Freeman, John R., Hitt, Matthew, and Pevehouse, Jon C. W. (eds). 2015. *Time Series Analysis for the Social Scientist*. New York: Cambidge University Press.

Box-Steffensmeier, Janet M., and Jones, Bradford S. 2004. *Event History Modeling: A Guide for Social Scientists*. New York: Cambridge University Press.

Box-Steffensmeier, Janet M., Reiter, Dan, and Zorn, Christopher. 2003. Nonproportional Hazards and Event History Analysis in International Relations. *Journal of Conflict Resolution*, **47**(1), 33–53.

Box-Steffensmeier, Janet M., and Zorn, Christopher J. W. 2001. Duration Models and Proportional Hazards in Political Science. *American Journal of Political Science*, **45**(4), 972–988.

Box-Steffensmeier, Janet M., and Zorn, Christopher. 2002. Duration Models for Repeated Events. *The Journal of Politics*, **64**(4), 1069–1094.

Brambor, Thomas, Clark, William Roberts, and Golder, Matt. 2006. Understanding Interaction Models: Improving Empirical Analyses. *Political Analysis*, **14**(1), 63–82.

Brandt, Patrick T., Freeman, John R., and Schrodt, Philip A. 2014. Evaluating Forecasts of Political Conflict Dynamics. *International Journal of Forecasting*, **30**(4), 944–962.

Brandt, Patrick T., and Williams, John T. 2007. *Multiple Time Series Models*. Thousand Oaks, CA: Sage Publications.

Braumoeller, Bear F. 2004. Hypothesis Testing and Multiplicative Interaction Terms. *International Organization*, **58**(4), 807–820.

Brier, Glenn W. 1950. Verification of Forecasts Expressed in Terms of Probability. *Monthly Weather Review*, **78**(1), 1–3.

Broockman, David, Kalla, Joshua, and Aronow, Peter. 2015. *Irregularities in LaCour (2014)*.

Broström, Göran. 2012. *Event History Analysis with R*. Boca Raton, FL: Chapman & Hall/CRC Press.

Broström, Göran. 2017. *eha: Event History Analysis*. R package version 2.4-5.

Bueno de Mesquita, Bruce, Gleditsch, Nils Petter, James, Patrick, King, Gary, Metelits, Claire, Ray, James Lee, Russett, Bruce, Strand, Håvard, and Valeriano, Brandon. 2003. Symposium on Replication in International Studies Research. *International Studies Perspectives*, **4**(1), 72–107.

Cai, Chao, Zou, Yubo, Peng, Yingwei, and Zhang, Jiajia. 2012. smcure: An *R* Package for Estimating Semiparametric Mixture Cure Models. *Computer Methods and Programs in Biomedicine*, **108**(3), 1255–1260.

Cameron, A. Colin, Gelbach, Jonah B., and Miller, Douglas L. 2008. Bootstrap-Based Improvements for Inference with Clustered Errors. *Review of Economics and Statistics*, **90**(3), 414–427.

Cameron, A. Colin, and Miller, Douglas L. 2015. A Practitioner's Guide to Cluster-Robust Inference. *Journal of Human Resources*, **50**(2), 317–373.

Cameron, A. Colin, and Trivedi, Pravin K. 1990. Regression-Based Tests for Overdispersion in the Poisson Model. *Journal of Econometrics*, **46**, 347–364.

Cameron, A. Colin, and Trivedi, Pravin K. 2013. *Regression Analysis of Count Data*. Second edn. New York: Cambidge University Press.

Canty, Angelo, and Ripley, Brian. 2016. *boot: Bootstrap R (S-Plus) Functions*. R package version 1.3-18.

Carroll, Nathan. 2017. *oglmx: Estimation of Ordered Generalized Linear Models*. R package version 2.0.0.3.

Carrubba, Clifford J., and Clark, Tom S. 2012. Rule Creation in a Political Hierarchy. *American Political Science Review*, **106**(3), 622–643.

Carter, David B., and Signorino, Curtis S. 2010. Back to the Future: Modeling Time Dependence in Binary Data. *Political Analysis*, **18**(3), 271–292.

Chalmers, Adam William. 2017. When Banks Lobby: The Effects of Organizational Characteristics and Banking Regulations on International Bank Lobbying. *Business and Politics*, **19**(1), 107–134.

Chen, Xiaohong, Fan, Yanqin, and Tsyrennikov, Viktor. 2006. Efficient Estimation of Semiparametric Multivariate Copula Models. *Journal of the American Statistical Association*, **101**(475), 1228–1240.

Cheng, Simon, and Long, J. Scott. 2007. Testing for IIA in the Multinomial Logit Model. *Sociological Methods & Research*, **35**(4), 583–600.

Chiba, Daina, Metternich, Nils W., and Ward, Michael D. 2015. Every Story Has a Beginning, Middle, and an End (But Not Always in That Order): Predicting Duration Dynamics in a Unified Framework. *Political Science Research and Methods*, 3(3), 515–541.

Choi, Leena. 2011. *ProfileLikelihood: Profile Likelihood for a Parameter in Commonly Used Statistical Models*. R package version 1.1.

Choirat, Christine, Imai, Koske, King, Gary, and Lau, Olivia. 2009. *Zelig: Everyone's Statistical Software*. Version 5.0-17. http://zeligproject.org/.

Christensen, Rune Haubo Bojesen. 2015. *ordinal: Regression Models for Ordinal Data*. R package version 2015.6-28. www.cran.r-project.org/package=ordinal/.

Clarke, Kevin A. 2006. A Simple Distribution-Free Test for Nonnested Model Selection. *Political Analysis*, 15(3), 347–363.

Cleveland, William S., and McGill, Robert. 1984. Graphical Perception: Theory, Experimentation, and Application to the Development of Graphical Methods. *Journal of the American Statistical Association*, 79(387), 531–554.

Conway, Richard W., and Maxwell, William L. 1962. A Queuing Model with State Dependent Service Rates. *Journal of Industrial Engineering*, 12(2), 132–136.

Cook, Scott J., and Savun, Burcu. 2016. New Democracies and the Risk of Civil Conflict: The Lasting Legacy of Military Rule. *Journal of Peace Research*, 53(6), 745–757.

Cox, David R. 1958. The Regression Analysis of Binary Sequences (with Discussion). *Journal of the Royal Statistical Society Series B*, 20(2), 215–242.

Cox, David R. 2006. *Principles of Statistical Inference*. New York: Cambidge University Press.

Cox, David R, and Barndorff-Nielsen, Ole E. 1994. *Inference and Asymptotics*. Boca Raton, FL: Chapman & Hall/CRC Press.

Croissant, Yves. 2013. `mlogit`: *Multinomial Logit Model*. R package version 0.2-4.

Croissant, Yves, and Millo, Giovanni. 2008. Panel Data Econometrics in R: The plm Package. *Journal of Statistical Software*, 27(2), 1–43.

Crookston, Nicholas L., and Finley, Andrew O. 2007. yaImpute: An $\mathcal{R}$ Package for kNN Imputation. *Journal of Statistical Software*, 23(10), 1–16.

Cumming, Geoff, Williams, Jennifer, and Fidler, Fiona. 2004. Replication and Researchers' Understanding of Confidence Intervals and Standard Error Bars. *Understanding Statistics*, 3(4), 299–311.

DA-RT. 2015. *The Journal Editors' Transparency Statement (JETS)*.

Davidson, Russell, and MacKinnon, James G. 1984. Convenient Specification Tests for Logit and Probit Models. *Journal of Econometrics*, 25(3), 241–262.

Davison, A. C., and Hinkley, D. V. 1997. *Bootstrap Methods and Their Applications*. New York: Cambridge University Press.

Dempster, Arthur P., Laird, Nan M., and Rubin, Donald B. 1977. Maximum Likelihood from Incomplete Data via the EM Algorithm. *Journal of the Royal Statistical Society Series B*, 39(1), 1–38.

Desmarais, Bruce A., and Harden, Jeffrey J. 2013. Testing for Zero Inflation in Count Models: Bias Correction for the Vuong Test. *Stata Journal*, 13(4), 810–835.

Edwards, Anthony W. F. 1992. *Likelihood*. Expanded edn. Baltimore, MD: Johns Hopkins University Press.

Edwards, Barry, Crespin, Michael, Williamson, Ryan D., and Palmer, Maxwell. 2017. Institutional Control of Redistricting and the Geography of Representation. *Journal of Politics*, 79(2), 722–726.

Efron, Bradley, and Tibshirani, Robert J. 1998. *An Introduction to the Bootstrap*. Boca Raton, FL: Chapman & Hall/CRC Press.

Eifert, Benn, Miguel, Edward, and Posner, Daniel N. 2010. Political Competition and Ethnic Identification in Africa. *American Journal of Political Science*, 54(2), 494–510.

Einstein, Katherine Levine, and Glick, David M. 2017. Does Race Affect Access to Government Services? An Experiment Exploring Street-Level Bureaucrats and Access to Public Housing. *American Journal of Political Science*, 61(1), 100–116.

Esarey, Justin. 2017. *clusterSEs: Calculate Cluster-Robust p-Values and Confidence Intervals*. R package version 2.3.3.

Faraway, Julian J. 2004. *Linear Models with R*. Boca Raton, FL: Chapman & Hall/CRC Press.

Fearon, James D., and Laitin, David D. 2003. Ethnicity, Insurgency, and Civil War. *American Political Science Review*, 97(1), 75–90.

Feliciano, Gloria D., Powers, Richard D., and Kearl, Bryant E. 1963. The Presentation of Statistical Information. *Audiovisual Communication Review*, 11(3), 32–39.

Firth, David. 1993. Bias Reduction of Maximum Likelihood Estimates. *Biometrika*, 80(1), 27–38.

Fox, John. 1997. *Applied Regression Analysis, Linear Models, and Related Methods*. Thousand Oaks, CA: SAGE Publications.

Fox, John, and Weisberg, Sanford. 2011. *An R Companion to Applied Regression*. 2nd edn. Thousand Oaks, CA: SAGE Publications.

Franzese, Robert, and Hayes, Jude C. 2007. Spatial Econometric Models of Cross-Sectional Interdependence in Political Science Panel and Time-Series-Cross-Section Data. *Political Analysis*, 15(2), 140–164.

Freedman, David A. 1983. A Note on Screening Regression Equations. *Journal of the American Statistical Association*, 37(2), 152–155.

Freedman, David A. 2006. On The So-Called "Huber Sandwich Estimator" and "Robust Standard Errors." *The American Statistician*, 60(4), 299–302.

Freedman, David A. 2008. Survival Analysis: A Primer. *American Statistician*, 62(2), 110–119.

Friendly, Michael. 2000. *Visualizing Categorical Data*. Cary, NC: SAS Institute.

Fullerton, Andrew S. 2009. A Conceptual Framework for Ordered Logistic Regression Models. *Sociological Methods & Research*, 38(2), 306–347.

Gelman, Andrew. 2008. Scaling Regression Inputs by Dividing by Two Standard Deviations. *Statistics in Medicine*, 27(15), 2865–2873.

Gelman, Andrew. 2011. Why Tables Are Really Much Better than Graphs. *Journal of Computational and Graphical Statistics*, 20(1), 3–7.

Gelman, Andrew, and Hill, Jennifer. 2007. *Data Analysis Using Regression and Multilevel/Hierarchical Models*. Analytical Methods for Social Research. Cambridge: Cambridge University Press.

Gelman, Andrew, Jakulin, Aleks, Pittau, Maria Grazia, and Sufi, Yu-Sung. 2008. A Weakly Informative Prior Distribution for Logistic and Other Regression Models. *Annals of Applied Statistics*, 2(4), 1360–1383.

Gelman, Andrew, Pasarica, Cristian, and Dodhia, Rahul. 2002. Let's Practice What We Preach: Turning Tables into Graphs. *American Statistician*, 56(2), 121–130.

Gelman, Andrew, and Su, Yu-Sung. 2016. *arm: Data Analysis Using Regression and Multilevel/Hierarchical Models*. R package version 1.9-3.

Gentleman, Robert, and Temple Lang, Duncan. 2007. Statistical Analyses and Reproducible Research. *Journal of Computational and Graphical Statistics*, 16(1), 1–23.

Gerber, Alan S., and Green, Donald P. 2012. *Field Experiments: Design, Analysis, and Interpretation*. New York: W. W. Norton.

Gerber, Alan S., Green, Donald P., and Nickerson, David. 2001. Testing for Publication Bias in Political Science. *Political Analysis*, 9(4), 385–392.

Gerber, Alan S., and Malhotra, Neil. 2008. Do Statistical Reporting Standards Affect What Is Published? Publication Bias in Two Leading Political Science Journals. *Quarterly Journal of Political Science*, 3, 313–326.

Gill, Jeff. 1999. The Insignificance of Null Hypothesis Significance Testing. *Political Research Quarterly*, 52(3), 647–674.

Glasgow, Garrett. 2001. Mixed Logit Models for Multiparty Elections. *Political Analysis*, 9(1), 116–136.

Glasgow, Garrett, and Alvarez, R. Michael. 2008. Discrete Choice Methods. In Box-Steffensmeier, Janet M., Brady, Henry E., and Collier, David (eds.), *The Oxford Handbook of Political Methodology*. New York: Oxford University Press, 513–529.

Gleditsch, Kristian Skrede, and Ward, Michael D. 2013. Forecasting Is Difficult, Especially the Future: Using Contentious Issues to Forecast Interstate Disputes. *Jounal of Peace Research*, 50(1), 17–31.

Gleditsch, Nils Petter, Metelits, Claire, and Strand, Havard. 2003. Posting Your Data: Will You Be Scooped or Will You Be Famous? *International Studies Perspectives*, 4(1), 89–97.

Goldstein, Judith, Rivers, Douglas, and Tomz, Michael. 2007. Institutions in International Relations: Understanding the Effects of the GATT and the WTO on World Trade. *International Organization*, 61(1), 37–67.

Graham, John W. 2009. Missing Data Analysis: Making It Work in the Real World. *Annual Review of Psychology*, 60(1), 549–576.

Greene, William H. 2008. Functional Forms for the Negative Binomial Model for Count Data. *Economic Letters*, 99(3), 585–590.

Greene, William H. 2011. Fixed Effects Vector Decomposition: A Magical Solution to the Problem of Time-Invariant Variables in Fixed Effects Models? *Political Analysis*, 19(2), 135–146.

Greenhill, Brian D., Ward, Michael D., and Sacks, Audrey. 2011. The Separation Plot: A New Visual Method for Evaluating the Fit of Binary Data. *American Journal of Political Science*, 55(4), 991–1002.

Greenhill, Brian D., Ward, Michael D., and Sacks, Audrey. 2015. separationplot: *Separation Plots*. R package version 1.1.

Grimmer, Justin. 2010. An Introduction to Bayesian Inference via Variational Approximations. *Political Analysis*, 19(1), 32–47.

Grimmer, Justin, and Stewart, Brandon M. 2013. Text as Data: The Promise and Pitfalls of Automatic Content Analysis Methods for Political Texts. *Political Analysis*, 21(3), 267–297.

Gurland, John. 1959. Some Applications of the Negative Binomial and Other Contagious Distributions. *American Journal of Public Health*, 49(10), 1388–1399.

Habel, Kai, Grasman, Raoul, Gramacy, Robert B., Stahel, Andreas, and Sterratt, David C. 2015. geometry: *Mesh Generation and Surface Tesselation*. R package version 0.3-6.

Hamilton, James D. 1994. *Time Series Analysis*. Princeton, NJ: Princeton University Press.

Hardin, James W., and Hilbe, Joseph M. 2012. *Generalized Estimating Equations*. 2nd edn. Chapman & Hall/CRC Press.

Harrell, Jr., Frank E. 2017. *rms: Regression Modeling Strategies*. R package version 5.1-0.

Hasan, Asad, Wang, Zhiyu, and Mahani, Alireza S. 2016. Fast Estimation of Multinomial Logit Models: R Package mnlogit. *Journal of Statistical Software*, 75(3), 1–24.

Hastie, Trevor, Tibshirani, Robert J., and Friedman, Jerome. 2008. *Elements of Statistical Learning*. New York: Springer-Verlag.

Hastie, Trevor, Tibshirani, Robert, and Friedman, Jerome. 2016. *The Elements of Statistical Learning: Data Mining, Inference, and Prediction*. Second edn. New York: Springer.

Hausman, Jerry A., and McFadden, Daniel. 1984. Specification Tests for the Multinomial Logit Model. *Econometrica*, 52(5), 1219–1240.

Heckman, James J., and Snyder, Jr., James M. 1997. Linear Probability Models of the Demand for Attributes with an Application to Estimating Preferences of Legislators. *RAND. Journal of Economics*, 28(Special Issue in Honor of Richard E. Quandt), 142–189.

Heinze, Georg and Ploner, Meinhard. 2016. *logistf: Firth's Bias-Reduced Logistic Regression*. R package version 1.22. https://CRAN.R-project.org/package=logistf.

Heinze, Georg, and Schemper, Michael 2002. A Solution to the Problem of Separation in Logistic Regression. *Statistics in Medicine*, 21(16), 2409–2419.

Henningsen, Arne, and Toomet, Ott. 2011. maxLik: A Package for Maximum Likelihood Estimation in *R*. *Computational Statistics*, 26(3), 443–458.

Herndon, Thomas, Ash, Michael, and Pollin, Robert. 2014. Does High Public Debt Consistently Stifle Economic Growth? A Critique of Reinhart and Rogoff. *Cambridge Journal of Economics*, 38(2), 257–279.

Hilbe, Joseph M. 2008. *Negative Binomial Regression*. New York: Cambidge University Press.

Hilbe, Joseph M. 2014. *Modeling Count Data*. New York: Cambidge University Press.

Hill, Daniel W., and Jones, Zachary M. 2014. An Empirical Evaluation of Explanations for State Repression. *American Political Science Review*, 108(03), 661–687.

Ho, Daniel E., and Imai, Kosuke. 2006. Randomization Inference with Natural Experiments: An Analysis of Ballot Effects in the 2003 California Recall Election. *Journal of the American Statistical Association*, 101(475), 888–900.

Hoaglin, David C. 1980. A Poisonness Plot. *American Statistician*, 34(3), 146–149.

Hoaglin, David C., and Tukey, John W. 1985. Checking the Shape of Discrete Distributions. In Hoaglin, David C., Mosteller, F., and Tukey, John W. (eds.), *Exploring Data Tables, Trends, and Shapes*. Hoboken, NJ: John Wiley & Sons, 345–416.

Hoekstra, Rink, Morey, Richard D., Rouder, Jeffrey N., and Wagenmakers, Eric-Jan. 2014. Robust Misinterpretation of Confidence Intervals. *Psychometric Bulletin and Review*, 21(5), 1157–1164.

Hoff, Peter. 2009. Multiplicative Latent Factor Models for Description and Prediction of Social Networks. *Computational and Mathematical Organization Theory*, 15(4), 261–272.

Hoff, Peter D. 2007. Extending the Rank Likelihood for Semiparametric Copula Estimation. *Annals of Applied Statistics*, 1(1), 265–283.

Hoff, Peter D. 2015. Multilinear Tensor Regression for Longitudinal Relational Data. *Annals of Applied Statistics*, 9(3), 1169–1193.

Hoff, Peter D., Niu, Xiaoyue, Wellner, Jon A. 2014. Information Bounds for Gaussian Copulas. *Bernoulli*, 20(2), 604–622.

Hollenbach, Florian M., Metternich, Nils W., Minhas, Shahryar, and Ward, Michael D. 2014. Fast & Easy Imputation of Missing Social Science Data. *arXiv preprint arXiv:1411.0647. Sociological Methods and Research*, in press.

Honaker, James, and King, Gary. 2010. What to Do about Missing Values in Time-Series Cross-Section Data. *American Journal of Political Science*, 54(2010), 561–581.

Honaker, James, King, Gary, and Blackwell, Matthew. 2011. Amelia II: A Program for Missing Data. *Journal of Statistical Software*, 45(7), 1–47.

Horrace, William C., and Oaxaca, Ronald L. 2006. Results on the Bias and Inconsistency of Ordinary Least Squares for the Linear Probability Model. *Economic Letters*, 90(3), 321–327.

Horton, Nicholas J., and Kleinman, Ken P. 2007. Much Ado about Nothing: A Comparison of Missing Data Methods and Software to Fit Incomplete Data Regression Models. *American Statistician*, 61(1), 79–90.

Huber, Peter J. 1967. The Behavior of Maximum Likelihood Estimates under Non-Standard Conditions. *Proceedings of the Fifth Berkeley Symposium on Mathematical Statistics and Probability*, 1, 221–233.

Imai, Kosuke, King, Gary, and Lau, Olivia. 2008. Toward a Common Framework for Statistical Analysis and Development. *Journal of Computational and Graphical Statistics*, 17(4), 892–913.

Imai, Kosuke, and Tingley, Dustin H. 2012. A Statistical Method for Empirical Testing of Competing Theories. *American Journal of Political Science*, 56(1), 218–236.

Imai, Kosuke, and van Dyk, David A. 2005. MNP: $\mathcal{R}$ Package for Fitting the Multinomial Probit Model. *Journal of Statistical Software*, 14(3), 1–32.

Ioannidis, John P.A. 2005. Why Most Published Research Findings Are False. *PLoS Medicine*, 2(8), E124.

Jackson, Christopher. 2016. flexsurv: A Platform for Parametric Survival Modeling in $\mathcal{R}$. *Journal of Statistical Software*, 70(8), 1–33.

Jones, Bradford, and Branton, Regina P. 2005. Beyond Logit and Probit: Cox Duration Models of Single, Repeating, and Competing Events for State Policy Adoption. *State Politics and Policy Quarterly*, 5(4), 420–443.

Josse, Julie, and Husson, François. 2016. missMDA: A Package for Handling Missing Values in Multivariate Data Analysis. *Journal of Statistical Software*, 70(1), 1–31.

Kalbfleisch, John D., and Prentice, Ross L. 2002. *The Statistical Analysis of Failure Time Data*. Hoboken, NJ: Wiley-Interscience.

Kam, Cindy D., and Franzese, Robert J. 2007. *Modeling and Interpreting Interactive Hypotheses in Regression Analysis*. Ann Arbor, MI: University of Michigan Press.

Kastellec, Jonathan P., and Leoni, Eduardo L. 2007. Using Graphs Instead of Tables in Political Science. *Perspectives on Politics*, 5(4), 755–771.

King, Gary. 1988. Statistical Models for Political Science Event Counts: Bias in Conventional Procedures and Evidence for the Exponential Poisson Regression model. *American Journal of Political Science*, 32(3), 838–863.

King, Gary. 1989a[1998]. *Unifying Political Methodology: The Likelihood Theory of Statistical Inference*. Ann Arbor, MI: University of Michigan Press.

King, Gary. 1989b. Variance Specification in Event Count Models: From Restrictive Assumptions to a Generalized Estimator. *American Journal of Political Science*, 33(3), 762–784.

King, Gary. 1995. Replication, Replication. *PS: Political Science & Politics*, 28(3), 444–452.

King, Gary, Alt, James, Burns, Nancy, and Laver, Michael. 1990. A Unified Model of Cabinet Dissolution in Parliamentary Democracies. *American Journal of Political Science*, 34(3), 846–871.

King, Gary, Honaker, James, Joseph, Anne, and Scheve, Kenneth. 2001. Analyzing Incomplete Political Science Data: An Alternative Algorithm for Multiple Imputation. *American Political Science Review*, 95(1), 49–69.

King, Gary, and Roberts, Margaret E. 2014. How Robust Standard Errors Expose Methodological Problems They Do Not Fix, and What to Do about It. *Political Analysis*, 23(2), 159–179.

King, Gary, and Signorino, Curtis S. 1996. The Generalization in the Generalized Event Count Model. *Political Analysis*, 6, 225–252.

King, Gary, Tomz, Michael, and Wittenberg, Jason. 2000. Making the Most of Statistical Analyses: Improving Interpretation and Presentation. *American Journal of Political Science*, 44(2), 341–355.

King, Gary, and Zeng, Langche. 2001. Logistic Regression in Rare Events Data. *Political Analysis*, 9(2), 137–163.

King, Gary, and Zeng, Langche. 2006. The Dangers of Extreme Counterfactuals. *Political Analysis*, 14(2), 131–159.

King, Gary, and Zeng, Langche. 2007. When Can History be Our Guide? The Pitfalls of Counterfactual Inference. *International Studies Quarterly*, 51(1), 183–210.

Klaassen, Chris A. J., Wellner, Jon A. 1997. Efficient Estimation in the Bivariate Normal Copula Model: Normal Margins Are Least Favourable. *Bernoulli*, 3(1), 55–77.

Klasnja, Marko. 2017. Uninformed Voters and Corrupt Politicians. *American Politics Research*, 45(2), 256–279.

Kleiber, Christian, and Zeileis, Achim. 2016. Visualizing Count Data Regressions Using Rootograms. *American Statistician*, 70(3), 296–303.

Knuth, Donald Ervin. 1984. Literate Programming. *Computer Journal*, 27(2), 97–111.

Kordas, Gregory. 2006. Smoothed Binary Regression Quantiles. *Journal of Applied Econometrics*, 21(3), 387–407.

Kosmidis, Ioannis. 2017. brglm: *Bias Reduction in Binary-Response Generalized Linear Models*. R package version 0.6.1.

Kowarik, Alexander, and Templ, Matthias. 2016. Imputation with the $\mathcal{R}$ Package VIM. *Journal of Statistical Software*, 74(7), 1–16.

Krain, Matthew. 2005. International Intervention and the Severity of Genocides and Politicides. *International Studies Quarterly*, 49(3), 363–388.

Kriner, Douglas L., and Shen, Francis X. 2016. Conscription, Inequality, and Partisan Support for War. *Journal of Conflict Resolution*, 60(8), 1419–1445.

Kropko, Jonathan, Goodrich, Ben, Gelman, Andrew, and Hill, Jennifer. 2014. Multiple Imputation for Continuous and Categorical Data: Comparing Joint Multivariate Normal and Conditional Approaches. *Political Analysis*, 22(4), 497–519.

Kuhn, Max. 2016. *A Short Introduction to the* caret *Package*. R package version 1.6.8.

Laitin, David D., and Reich, Rob. 2017. Trust, Transparency, and Replication in Political Science. *PS: Political Science & Politics*, 50(1), 172–175.

Lall, Ranjit. 2016. How Multiple Imputation Makes a Difference. *Political Analysis*, 24(4), 414–443.

Land, Kenneth C., McCall, Patricia L., and Nagin, Daniel S. 1996. A Comparison of Poisson, Negative Binomial, and Semiparametric Mixed Poisson Regression Models with Empirical Applications to Criminal Careers Data. *Sociological Methods & Research*, 24(4), 387–442.

Lander, Jared P. 2016. *coefplot: Plots Coefficients from Fitted Models*. R package version 1.2.4.

LeCam, Lucian. 1990. Maximum Likelihood: An introduction. *International Statistical Review*, 58(2), 153–171.

Li, Jialiang, and Fine, Jason P. 2008. ROC Analysis with Multiple Classes and Multiple Tests: Methodology and Its Application in Microarray Studies. *Biostatistics*, 9(3), 566–576.

Little, Roderick J. A., and Rubin, Donald B. 2002. *Statistical Analysis with Missing Data*. Hoboken, NJ: Wiley.

Lo, Adeline, Chernoff, Herman, Zheng, Tian, and Lo, Shaw-Hwa. 2015. Why Significant Variables Aren't Automatically Good Predictors. *Proceedings of the National Academy of Sciences of the United States of America*, 112(45), 13892–13897.

Long, J. Scott. 1997. *Regression Models for Categorical and Limited Dependent Variables*. Thousand Oaks, CA: SAGE Publications.

Lucas, Christopher, Nielsen, Richard A., Roberts, Margaret E., Stewart, Brandon M., Storer, Alex, and Tingley, Dustin. 2015. Computer-Assisted Text Analysis for Comparative Politics. *Political Analysis*, 23(2), 254–277.

Lumley, Thomas. 2014. *mitools: Tools for Multiple Imputation of Missing Data*. R package version 2.3.

MacFarlane, John. 2014. *Pandoc: A Universal Document Converter*. New York: Wiley.

Mares, Isabela. 2015. *From Open Secrets to Secret Voting: Democratic Electoral Reforms and Voter Autonomy*. New York: Cambidge University Press.

Markatou, Marianthi, Tian, Hong, Biswas, Shameek, and Hripcsak, George. 2005. Analysis of Variance of Cross-Validation Estimators of the Generalization Error. *Journal of Machine Learning Research*, 6(Jul), 1127–1168.

Marshall, Monty G., Gurr, Ted Robert, and Jaggers, Keith. 2016. *Polity IV Project: Political Regime Characteristics and Transitions, 1800–2015, Dataset Users' Manual*. College Park, MD: Center for Systemic Peace.

Martin, Lanny, and Stevenson, Randolph T. 2010. The Conditional Impact of Incumbency on Government Formation. *American Politial Science Review*, 104(3), 503–518.

Mayo, Deborah G. 2014. On the Birnbaum Argument for the Strong Likelihood Principle (with Discussion & Rejoinder). *Statistical Science*, 29(2), 227–266.

McCullagh, Peter, and Nelder, John A. 1989. *Generalized Linear Model*. London: Chapman & Hall.

McFadden, Daniel L. 1974. Conditional Logit Analysis of Qualitative Choice Behavior. In Zarembka, Paul (ed), *Frontiers in Econometrics*. New York: Academic Press, 105–142.

McKelvey, Richard D., and Zaviona, William. 1975. A Statistical Model for the Analysis of Ordinal Level Dependent Variables. *Journal of Mathematical Sociology*, 4(1), 103–120.

Mebane, Walter R., and Sekhon, Jasjeet S. 1998. Genetic Optimization Using Derivatives: Theory and Application to Nonlinear Models. *Political Analysis*, 7, 189–210.

Mebane, Walter R., and Sekhon, Jasjeet S. 2002. Coordinates and Policy Moderation at Midterm. *American Political Science Review*, **96**(1), 141–157.

Mebane, Walter R., and Sekhon, Jasjeet S. 2004. Robust Estimation and Outlier Detection for Overdispersed Multinomial Models of Count Data. *American Journal of Political Science*, **48**(2), 392–411.

Mebane, Walter R., and Sekhon, Jasjeet S. 2011. Genetic Optimization Using Derivatives: The rgenoud Package for $\mathcal{R}$. *Journal of Statistical Software*, **42**(11), 1–26.

Merkle, Edgar C., and Steyvers, Mark. 2013. Choosing a Strictly Proper Scoring Rule. *Decision Analysis*, **10**(4), 292–304.

Meyer, David, Zeileis, Achim, and Hornik, Kurt. 2016. *vcd: Visualizing Categorical Data*. R package version 1.4-3.

Miguel, Edward, Camerer, Colin, Casey, Katherine, Cohen, Joshua, Esterling, Kevin M., Gerber, Alan, Glennerster, Rachel, Green, Don P., Humphreys, Macartan, Imbens, Guido, et al. 2014. Promoting Transparency in Social Science Research. *Science*, **343**(6166), 30–31.

Miles, Andrew. 2016. Obtaining Predictions from Models Fit to Multiply Imputed Data. *Sociological Methods and Research*, **45**(1), 175–185.

Molenberghs, Geert, Fitzmaurice, Garrett, Kenward, Michael G., Tsiatis, Anastasios, and Verbeke, Geert. 2014. *Handbook of Missing Data Methodology*. Boca Raton, FL: Chapman & Hall/CRC Press.

Monogan, III, James E.. 2015. *Political Analysis Using $\mathcal{R}$*. New York: Springer.

Montgomery, Jacob M., Hollenbach, Florian M., and Ward, Michael D. 2012a. Ensemble Predictions of the 2012 US Presidential Election. *PS: Political Science & Politics*, **45**(4), 651–654.

Montgomery, Jacob M., Hollenbach, Florian M., and Ward, Michael D. 2012b. Improving Predictions Using Ensemble Bayesian Model Averaging. *Political Analysis*, **20**(3), 271–291.

Mroz, Thomas A. 1987. The Sensitivity of an Empirical Model of Married Women's Hours of Work to Economic and Statistical Assumptions. *Econometrica*, **55**(4), 765–799.

Murray, Jared S., and Reiter, Jerome P. 2014. Multiple Imputation of Missing Categorical and Continuous Values via Bayesian Mixture Models with Local Dependence. *arXiv*.

Mutz, Diana C., and Reeves, Byron. 2005. The New Videomalaise: Effects of Televised Incivility on Political Trust. *American Politial Science Review*, **99**(1), 1–15.

Nagler, Jonathan. 1994. Scobit: An Alternative Estimator to Logit and Probit. *American Journal of Political Science*, **38**(1), 230–255.

Nanes, Matthew J. 2017. Political Violence Cycles: Electoral Incentives and the Provision of Counterterrorism. *Comparative Political Studies*, **50**(2), 171–199.

NCAR - Research Applications Laboratory. 2015. *verification: Weather Forecast Verification Utilities*. R package version 1.42.

Nelder, John A., and Wedderburn, Robert W. M. 1972. Generalized Linear Models. *Journal of the Royal Statistical Society Series A*, **135**(3), 370–384.

Nelsen, Roger B. 1970. *An Introduction to Copulas*. 2nd edn. Berlin: Springer Verlag.

Nyhan, Brendan, and Montgomery, Jacob. 2010. Bayesian Model Averaging: Theoretical Developments and Practical Applications. *Political Analysis*, **18**(2), 245–270.

Open Science Collaboration. 2015. Estimating the Reproducibility of Psychological Science. *Science*, **349**(6215), aac4716-1 – aac4716-8.

Park, Jong Hee. 2012. A Unified Method for Dynamic and Cross-Sectional Heterogeneity: Introducing Hidden Markov Panel Models. *American Journal of Political Science*, **56**(4), 1040–1054.

Park, Sunhee, and Hendry, David J. 2015. Reassessing Schoenfeld Residual Tests of Proportional Hazards in Political Science Event History Analyses. *American Journal of Political Science*, **59**(4), 1072–1087.

Pawitan, Yudi. 2013. *In All Likelihood: Statistical Modeling and Inference Using Likelihood*. 1st edn. Oxford: Oxford University Press.

Peterson, Bercedis, and Harrell, Jr., Frank E. 1990. Partial Proportional Odds Models for Ordinal Response Variables. *Applied Statistics*, **39**(2), 205–217.

Pettitt, Anthony N. 1982. Inference for the Linear Model Using a likelihood Based on Ranks. *Journal of the Royal Statistical Society Series B (Methodological)*, **44**(2), 234–243.

Pitt, Michael, Chan, David, and Kohn, Robert. 2006. Efficient Bayesian Inference for Gaussian Copula Regression Models. *Biometrika*, **93**(3), 537–554.

Poisson, Siméon Denis. 1837. *Recherches sur la probabilité des jugements en matière criminelle et en matiére civile: Précédées des régles générales du calcul des probabilités*. Paris: Bachelier.

Prado, Raquel, Ferreira, Marco A. R., and West, Mike. 2017. *Time Series: Modelling, Computation & Inference*. 2nd (forthcoming) edn. Boca Raton, FL: Chapman & Hall/CRC Press.

Raftery, Adrian E. 1995. Bayesian Model Selection in Social Research. *Sociological Methodology*, **25**, 111–163.

Rainey, Carlisle. 2016. Dealing with Separation in Logistic Regression Models. *Political Analysis*, **24**(3), 339–355.

Rauchhaus, R. 2009. Evaluating the Nuclear Peace Hypothesis: A Quantitative Approach. *Journal of Conflict Resolution*, **53**(2), 258–277.

Resnick, Sidney I. 2014. *A Probability Path*. Ithaca, NY: Cornell University Press.

Ripley, Brian, and Venables, William. 2016. *Package nnet*. R package version 7.3-12.

Rose, Andrew K. 2004. Do We Really Know That the WTO Increases Trade? *American Economic Review*, **94**(1), 98–114.

Ross, Michael L. 2006. Is Democracy Good for the Poor? *American Journal of Political Science*, **50**(4), 860–874.

Rozeboom, William W. 1960. The Fallacy of the Null Huypothesis Significance Test. *Psychological Bulletin*, **57**, 416–428.

Rubin, Donald B. 1976. Inference and Missing Data. *Biometrika*, **63**(3), 581–592.

Rubin, Donald B. 1987. *Statistical Analysis with Missing Data*. Hoboken, NJ: John Wiley & Sons.

Rubin, Donald B. 1996. Multiple Imputation after 18+ Years. *Journal of the American Statistical Association*, **91**(434), 473–489.

Rubin, Donald B. 2004. *Multiple Imputation for Nonresponse in Surveys*. New York: John Wiley & Sons.

Saket, Bahador, Scheidegger, Carlos, Kobourov, Stephen G., and Börner, Katy. 2015. Map-Based Visualizations Increase Recall Accuracy of Data. *Computer Graphics Forum*, **34**(3), 441–450.

Schafer, Joseph L. 1999. Multiple Imputation: A Primer. *Statistical Methods in Medical Research*, **8**(1), 3–15.

Schafer, Joseph L. 2017. mix: *Estimation/Multiple Imputation for Mixed Categorical and Continuous Data*. R package version 1.0-10.

Sellers, Kimberly F., Borle, Sharad, and Shmueli, Galit. 2012. The COM-Poisson Model for Count Data: A Survey of Methods and Applications. *Applied Stochastic Models in Business and Industry*, 28(2), 104–116.

Shao, Jun. 1993. Linear Model Selection by Cross-Validation. *Journal of the American Statistical Association*, 88(422), 486–94.

Shao, Jun. 1997. An Asymtotic Theory for Linear Model Selection. *Statistica Sinica*, 7, 221–264.

Shih, Victor, Adolph, Christopher, and Liu, Mingxing. 2012. Getting Ahead in the Communist Party: Explaining the Advancement of Central Committee Members in China. *American Political Science Review*, 106(1), 166–187.

Signorino, Curtis S. 1999. Strategic Interaction and the Statistical Analysis of International Conflict. *American Political Science Review*, 92(2), 279–298.

Signorino, Curtis S. 2002. Strategy and Selection in International Relations. *International Interactions*, 28(1), 93–115.

Singal, Jesse. 2015. The Case of the Amazing Gay-Marriage Data: How a Graduate Student Reluctantly Uncovered a Huge Scientific Fraud. *The Cut*, www.thecut.com/2015/05/how-a-grad-student-uncovered-a-huge-fraud.html.

Sklar, Abe. 1959. *Fonctions de répartition à n dimensions et leurs marges*. PhD diss. Université Paris.

Sorens, Jason, and Ruger, William. 2012. Does Foreign Investment Really Reduce Repression? *International Studies Quarterly*, 56(2), 427–436.

Spirling, Arthur, and Quinn, Kevin M. 2010. Identifying Intra-Party Voting Blocs in the UK House of Commons. *Journal of the American Statistical Association*, 105(490), 447–457.

Stekhoven, Daniel J., and Buehlmann, P. 2012. missForest: Non-Parametric Missing Value Imputation for Mixed-Type Data. *Bioinformatics*, 28(1), 112–118.

Stigler, Stephen M. 2007. The Epic Story of Maximum Likelihood. *Statistical Science*, 22(4), 598–620.

Stoll, Heather, King, Gary, and Zeng, Langche. 2014. *WhatIf: Software for Evaluating Counterfactuals*. R package version 1.5-6.

Stone, Mervyn. 1977. An Asymptotic Equivalence of Choice of Model by Cross-Validation and Akaike's Criterion. *Journal of the Royal Statistical Society, Series B*, 39(1), 44–47.

Su, Yu-Sung, Gelman, Andrew, Hill, Jennifer, and Yajima, Masanao. 2011. Multiple Imputation with Diagnostics (mi) in $\mathcal{R}$: Opening Windows into the Black Box. *Journal of Statistical Software*, 45(1), 1–31.

Subramanian, Arvind, and Wei, Shang-Jin. 2007. The WTO Promotes Trade, Strongly but Unevenly. *Journal of International Economics*, 72(1), 151–175.

Therneau, Terry M., and Grambsch, Patricia M. 2000. *Modeling Survival Data*. New York: Springer.

Thrower, Sharece. 2017. To Revoke or Not Revoke? The Political Determinants of Executive Order Longevity. *American Journal of Political Science*, 61(3), 642–656.

Tibshirani, Rob, and Leisch, Friedrich. 2017. *bootstrap: Functions for the Book "An Introduction to the Bootstrap."* R package version 2017.2.

Titiunik, Rocío, and Feher, Andrew. 2017. Legislative Behaviour Absent Re-Election Incentives: Findings from a Natural Experiment in the Arkansas Senate. *Journal of the Royal Statistical Society Series A*, 180(pt. 3), 1–28.

Tomz, Michael, Goldstein, Judith, and Rivers, Douglas. 2007. Do We Really Know That the WTO Increases Trade? *American Economic Review*, 97(5), 2005–2018.

Tomz, Michael, Wittenberg, Jason, and King, Gary. 2001. *CLARIFY: Software for Interpreting and Presenting Statistical Results*. Version 2.0. Harvard University, Cambridge, MA.

Train, Kenneth E. 2009. *Discrete Choice Methods with Simulation*. 2nd edn. New York: Cambidge University Press.

Treier, Shawn, and Jackman, Simon. 2008. Democracy as a Latent Variable. *American Journal of Political Science*, 52(1), 201–217.

Trivedi, Pravin K., and Zimmer, David M. 2005. *Copula Modeling: An Introduction for Practitioners*. Boston: Now Publishers, Inc.

Tufte, Edward R. 1992. *The Visual Display of Quantitative Information*. Cheshire, CT: Graphics Press.

Tukey, John W. 1977. *Exploratory Data Analysis*. Reading, MA: Addison-Wesley.

Uscinski, Joseph E., and Klofstad, Casey A. 2010. Who Likes Political Science? Determants of Senators' Votes on the Coburn Amendment. *PS: Political Science & Politics*, 43(4), 701–706.

Van Buuren, Stef. 2012. *Flexible Imputation of Missing Data*. Boca Raton, FL: Chapman & Hall/CRC Press.

Van Buuren, Stef, and Groothuis-Oudshoorn, Karin. 2011. MICE: Multivariate Imputation by Chained Equations in $\mathcal{R}$. *Journal of Statistical Software*, 45(3), 1–67.

van den Boogaart, K. Gerald, and Tolosana-Delgado, Raimon. 2013. *Analyzing Compositional Data with R*. Berlin: Springer-Verlag.

van den Boogaart, K. Gerald, Tolosana, Raimon, and Bren, Matevz. 2014. *compositions: Compositional Data Analysis*. R package version 1.40-1 edn.

Venables, William N., and Ripley, Brian D. 2002. *Modern Applied Statistics with S*. fourth edn. New York: Springer.

Ver Hoef, Jay M., and Boveng, Peter L. 2007. Quasi-Poisson vs. Negative Binomial Regression: How Should We Model Overdispersed Count Data? *Ecology*, 88(11), 2766–2772.

von Hippel, Paul. 2009. How to Impute Squares, Interactions, and Other Transformed Variables. *Sociological Methods and Research*, 39(1), 265–291.

Walter, Stefanie. 2017. Globalization and the Demand-Side of Politics: How Globalization Shapes Labor Market Risk Perceptions and Policy Preferences. *Political Science Research and Methods*, 5(1), 55–80.

Wang, Xia, and Dey, Dipak K. 2010. Generalized Extreme Value Regression for Binary Response Data: An Application to B2B Electronic Payments System Adoption. *Annals of Applied Statistics*, 4(4), 2000–2023.

Ward, Michael D., and Gleditsch, Kristian Skrede. 2018. *Spatial Regression Models*. Thousand Oaks, CA: SAGE Publications.

Ward, Michael D., Greenhill, Brian D., and Bakke, Kristin M. 2010. The Perils of Policy by p-Value: Predicting Civil Conflicts. *Journal of Peace Research*, 47(4), 363–375.

Ward, Michael D., Metternich, Nils W., Dorff, Cassy L., Gallop, Max, Hollenbach, Florian M., Schultz, Anna, and Weschle, Simon. 2013. Learning from the Past and Stepping into the Future: Toward a New Generation of Conflict Prediction. *International Studies Review*, **16**(4), 473–490.

Wedderburn, Robert W. M. 1974. Quasi-Likelihood Functions, Generalized Linear Models, and the Gauss-Newton Method. *Biometrika*, **61**(3), 439–447.

White, Halbert L. 1980. A Heteroskedasticity-Consistent Covariance Matrix Estimator and a Direct Test for Heteroskedasticity. *Econometrica*, **48**, 817–838.

Williams, Richard. 2016. Understanding and Interpreting Generalized Ordered Logit Models. *Journal of Mathematical Sociology*, **40**(1), 7–20.

Wilson, Paul. 2015. The Misuse of the Vuong Test for Non-Nested Models to Test for Zero-Inflation. *Economics Letters*, **127**, 51–53.

Winkelmann, Rainer. 1995. Duration Dependence and Dispersion in Count-Data Models. *Journal of Business & Economic Statistics*, **13**(4), 467–474.

Wolford, Scott. 2017. The Problem of Shared Victory: War-Winning Coalitions and Postwar Peace. *Journal of Politics*, **79**(2), 702–716.

Wooldridge, Jeffrey M. 2010. *Econometric Analysis of Cross Section and Panel Data*. 2nd edn. Cambridge, MA: MIT Press.

Wright, Joseph, and Frantz, Erica. 2017. How Oil Income and Missing Hydrocarbon Rents Data Influence Autocratic Survival: A Response to Lucas and Richter (2016). *Research & Politics*, **4**(3).

Xie, Yihui. 2015. *Dynamic Documents with R and knitr*. 2nd edn. New York: CRC Press.

Yee, Thomas W. 2010. The VGAM Package for Categorical Data Analysis. *Journal of Statistical Software*, **32**(10), 1–34.

Zeileis, Achim. 2004. Econometric Computing with HC and HAC Covariance Matrix Estimators. *Journal of Statistical Software*, **11**(10), 1–17.

Zeileis, Achim, and Kleiber, Christian. 2017. *countreg: Count Data Regression*. R package version 0.2-0.

Zeileis, Achim, Kleiber, Christian, and Jackman, Simon. 2008. Regression Models for Count Data in R. *Journal of Statistical Software*, **27**(8), 1–25.

Zeileis, Achim, Koenker, Roger, and Doebler, Philipp. 2015. *glmx: Generalized Linear Models Extended*. R package version 0.1-1.

Ziegler, Andreas. 2011. *Generalized Estimating Equations*. New York: Springer.

Zorn, Christopher. 2005. A Solution to Separation in Binary Response Models. *Political Analysis*, **13**(2), 157–170.

Zorn, Christopher. 1998. An Analytic and Empirical Examination of Zero-Inflated and Hurdle Poisson Specifications. *Sociological Methods and Research*, **26**(3), 368–400.

Zorn, Christopher J. W. 2000. Generalized Estimating Equation Models for Correlated Data: A Review with Applications. *American Journal of Political Science*, **45**(2), 470–490.

Index